T0334517

"The second edition of *Understanding Employee Engagement* is a gem. It is timely, up to date, and packed with research and practical examples. This book is an urgent guide for scholars and practitioners alike."

> – **Daniel H. Pink**, #1 New York Times *best-selling*
> *author of* When, Drive, *and* To Sell Is Human

"In too many workplaces, employee engagement isn't much more than a buzzword. As a leading expert on the science and practice of engagement, Zinta Byrne is here to change that. Her book includes the latest research on measuring and increasing engagement, rejuvenating it coming out of a pandemic, and managing it across cultures."

> – **Adam Grant, Ph.D.**, *Wharton organizational psychologist,*
> #1 New York Times *best-selling author of* Think Again,
> *and host of the TED podcast WorkLife*

"*Understanding Employee Engagement* second edition is an absolute must-read. A masterful translation of the science into rich and meaningful evidence-based practice. It is timely, up-to-date, and incredibly complete. A game-changer for those in the work or employee engagement arena."

> – **Steven G. Rogelberg, Ph.D.**, *President, Society for Industrial*
> *and Organizational Psychology (2021); Chancellor's Professor,*
> *University of North Carolina at Charlotte*

"Zinta Byrne provides a comprehensive and thorough review of the science and practice of employee engagement. She combines and integrates employee engagement research with real-world examples from employees and organizations. The result is a perfect blend of employee engagement research and practice that will be a valuable resource for academics, practitioners, and students."

> – **Alan M. Saks, Ph.D.**, *Professor of Organizational Behaviour*
> *and HR Management, University of Toronto Scarborough*

"This book is an absolute pleasure to read. Dr. Byrne does a masterful job of synthesizing theory, research, and practice in ways that make clear the importance and practicality of the concept of engagement at work. She makes a compelling argument for taking engagement seriously, as a cornerstone of organizational behavior. Dr. Byrne ought to be proud of this book: it does justice to the complexity and importance of engagement theory."

> – **William A. Kahn, Ph.D.**, *Professor of Organizational Behavior,*
> *Boston University*

"Professor Byrne's updated edition provides vital current and timely information on employee engagement. The breadth of topics included in this second edition, such as aging workforces and new studies on cross-cultural applications of engagement, is well-chosen and demonstrates the scientific and practitioner importance of employee engagement. The material is timely as leaders grapple with reconstituting their workforces after the pandemic, while also increasing inclusivity. Leaders, HR professionals, managers, and organizational scientists need to know and implement the updated content in this volume, and they have Professor Byrne to thank for making the material available and accessible in one volume."

– **Theodore L. Hayes, Ph.D.**, *Personnel Psychologist,*
U.S. Department of Defense
(All opinions in this review are solely the author's and
do not imply or constitute endorsement of any product,
service, or enterprise by DoD.)

UNDERSTANDING EMPLOYEE ENGAGEMENT

Understanding Employee Engagement is a comprehensive source for the science and practice of employee engagement. This book provides a rigorous and objective review of scholarship and empirical research on engagement from around the world.

Grounded in theory and empirical research, this book debates the definitions of engagement, provides a thorough evaluation of empirical findings in the engagement field including a focus on international findings, and offers practice implications for organizations. The book is broad, with references and research across disciplines and countries, as well as new sections addressing current challenges, such as virtual engagement, engaging the aging workforce, and perspectives on diversity and inclusion. Employers can learn how to foster an engaged organization; practitioners can learn how to measure, identify, and implement evidence-based solutions to disengagement; and researchers can master the existing engagement literature and begin to study the many propositions and new models the author proposes throughout the book.

This book is an essential read for scholars, researchers, practitioners, and business leaders alike for understanding how to measure, identify, and implement evidence-based solutions to foster employee engagement.

Zinta S. Byrne is Professor of Industrial/Organizational Psychology at Colorado State University. She is a SIOP Fellow, APS Fellow, and former Senior Consultant for PDI.

Series in Applied Psychology

Jeanette N. Cleveland
Colorado State University

Donald Truxillo
Portland State University

Edwin A. Fleishman
Founding Series Editor (1987–2010)

Kevin R. Murphy
Emeritus Series Editor (2010–2018)

Bridging both academic and applied interests, the Applied Psychology Series offers publications that emphasize state-of-the-art research and its application to important issues of human behavior in a variety of societal settings. To date, more than 50 books in various fields of applied psychology have been published in this series.

Diversity Resistance in Organizations 2e
Kecia M. Thomas

Positive Psychological Science 2e
Stewart I. Donaldson, Mihaly Csikszentmihalyi and Jeanne Nakamura

Historical Perspectives in Industrial and Organizational Psychology 2e
Edited by Laura Koppes Bryan

How Groups Encourage Misbehavior
Kevin R. Murphy

Understanding Employee Engagement
Theory, Research, and Practice 2e
Zinta S. Byrne

For more information about this series, please visit: www.routledge.com/Applied-Psychology-Series/book-series/SAP

UNDERSTANDING EMPLOYEE ENGAGEMENT

Theory, Research, and Practice

Second Edition

Zinta S. Byrne

Routledge
Taylor & Francis Group

NEW YORK AND LONDON

Second edition published 2022
by Routledge
605 Third Avenue, New York, NY 10158

and by Routledge
2 Park Square, Milton Park, Abingdon, Oxon, OX14 4RN

Routledge is an imprint of the Taylor & Francis Group, an informa business

© 2022 Zinta S. Byrne

The right of Zinta S. Byrne to be identified as author of this work has
been asserted in accordance with sections 77 and 78 of the Copyright,
Designs and Patents Act 1988.

All rights reserved. No part of this book may be reprinted or reproduced or utilised in any form or by any electronic, mechanical, or other
means, now known or hereafter invented, including photocopying and
recording, or in any information storage or retrieval system, without
permission in writing from the publishers.

Trademark notice: Product or corporate names may be trademarks
or registered trademarks, and are used only for identification and
explanation without intent to infringe.

First edition published by Routledge 2014

Library of Congress Cataloging-in-Publication Data
A catalog record for this book has been requested

ISBN: 978-0-367-77388-5 (hbk)
ISBN: 978-0-367-77387-8 (pbk)
ISBN: 978-1-003-17113-3 (ebk)

DOI: 10.4324/9781003171133

Typeset in Bembo
by Apex CoVantage, LLC

To Jon Byrne

CONTENTS

SERIES FOREWORD

Innovative approaches are needed to address the complexity of human relationships in today's world. These approaches are more likely to succeed when they are based on sound theory and research. The Applied Psychology Series provides such a basis: it offers publications that describe state-of-the-art research and its application to behavioral issues across a variety of social settings.

Over recent decades, employee engagement has been recognized as a key variable in understanding attitudes and behavior in work organizations. It is for this reason that engagement is of such keen interest to policy-makers, employers, practitioners, employees, and organizational researchers. In the current volume, Zinta S. Byrne skillfully describes the latest science regarding employee engagement as well as the current best practices for supporting engagement in organizations. Professor Byrne bases her work on an impressively thorough review of the scientific literature, using language that is accessible to organizational decision-makers. The result is a book that is both scientifically rigorous and highly readable, making it a go-to reference for practitioners and researchers alike. As she notes in the preface, Professor Byrne has provided numerous updates to this second edition, including the integration of the most recent research, a description of organizational interventions to increase engagement, and sections on inclusion in organizations and the engagement of older workers.

This second edition of *Understanding Employee Engagement: Theory, Research, and Practice* is organized into four parts. Part I covers the various definitions of engagement, including what engagement is and what it is not. It also discusses how engagement relates to, and is distinct from, other employee attitudes and behaviors. Part II describes possible interventions to enhance employee engagement. New material in this section focuses on addressing the engagement of older workers and managing employee engagement during the COVID-19 pandemic. Professor Byrne also describes the factors that may enhance or inhibit the development of employee engagement, drawing from an extensive body of empirical research (including her own) as well as qualitative and quantitative reviews of the literature. Professor Byrne concludes Part II with an in-depth, practical discussion of the different ways to measure engagement. This includes the psychometric properties and theoretical bases of the available measures of engagement as well as how to select a measure to address a specific organizational context or research question.

In Part III, Professor Byrne discusses traditional human resource practices as ways to support engagement and provide competitive advantage to organizations. This includes how to select engaged workers and ensure that engagement spreads and takes hold in an organization. New material in this section includes a discussion of how socialization practices can help develop inclusive organizations and how to enhance team-level engagement, including engagement among virtual teams. Recognizing that employee engagement is associated with positive work experiences, Byrne persuasively argues that employee engagement provides an important ingredient for developing a healthy organization.

Part IV of the text explores employee engagement across organizations internationally. Byrne notes that engagement may manifest itself in different ways depending upon cultural norms, which is an important consideration for multinational organizations. Byrne also describes the negative outcomes of engagement if it is carried too far, such as workaholism and rigidity – the "dark side" of employee engagement.

In short, Professor Byrne's second edition of *Understanding Employee Engagement: Theory, Research, and Practice* provides a cutting-edge review of employee engagement from both scientific and practical perspectives, and I am delighted to welcome it to the Applied Psychology Series.

Donald M. Truxillo
University of Limerick

ACKNOWLEDGMENTS

The first edition would not have happened without key support from Jeanette Cleveland, Kevin Murphy, Anne Duffy, Lynn Shore, Maria Kuznetsova, Kurt Kraiger, Dirk Steiner, Jackie Coyle-Shapiro, James Weston, Amos Engelbrecht, Kathryn Rickard, and Janet Peters. I thank Elaine LeMay for leading me into the field by asking me, "What do you know about employee engagement?" Special thanks to Jennifer Anderson, Gaynel Tanner, and Rachel Lee, all of whom supported my first research and consulting efforts in engagement. Inspiring the second edition are Paul Levy, Steven Rogelberg, Bryan Dik, Joel Philo's editorial review in *Personnel Psychology*, and Sonia Johnson's Amazon. com customer review. Thank you all so much!

PREFACE

Understanding Employee Engagement: Theory, Research, and Practice has been comprehensively updated for this second edition. The second edition remains intended for employers, practitioners, researchers, and students who want a comprehensive evaluation of empirical findings in the field of engagement and the implications of those findings for science and practice in organizations. The second edition includes:

- Update on research on engagement (over 1,500 articles!) since the first edition, up through 2021
- Updated research on success of interventions to improve/increase engagement
- New section reviewing latest research on re-establishing "normal" workplaces after the COVID-19 pandemic
- Updated costs associated with engagement/disengagement
- New section reviewing latest research on older workers' engagement
- Expanded section on the measurement of engagement, including the latest research evaluating existing measures
- Expanded sections on workaholism, passion, and inclusion
- Significantly updated and expanded chapter on international studies
- Existing examples updated to increase clarity
- Tables and figures updated to include most recent developments in the literature
- New examples added throughout every chapter to increase clarity and capitalize on latest research findings

- All chapters have more clearly marked headings for easier use of the book and to facilitate ease in finding sections.

This second edition incorporates new material on selection, personality, aging, diversity/inclusion/equity, virtual engagement, impact of the COVID-19 pandemic, and interventions not previously reviewed. Research often crosses multiple boundaries; therefore, you may find some studies reviewed in more than one chapter of the book.

1

THE STORY OF ENGAGEMENT

> I don't know how to describe it – I just feel alive. I feel energized, excited, stimulated, almost on edge, and yet I can focus as if nothing else exists. When I'm engaged, I feel connected and feel like I'm doing something that matters; I'm making a difference, even if in a small way. It's a choice, really, to be that "into" my job – I wasn't always this way and I'm not always 100% in this mode.
>
> *– Interview 45*

Employee engagement, also referred to as job or work engagement, is a widely discussed topic in both practice and academe. Engagement is frequently described as a motivational state associated with several positive and desirable consequences for organizations, such as high levels of job performance and positive attitudes like job satisfaction. Employee engagement is about investing oneself at work, being authentic in the job, and delivering one's work performance with passion, persistence, enthusiasm, and energy. As I will review in Chapter 2, there are several different definitions for engagement at work; one of them, however, is not student engagement. Student engagement refers to a pattern of behaviors and emotions associated with students, in particular (Fredricks, Blumenfeld, & Paris, 2004). For example, students' participation in class, affective reactions to their instructors and peers, level of effort in learning, and feeling of connection with peers and school are all part of the student engagement construct. In this book, when I refer to engagement, I am talking about employee engagement at work.

Make no mistake: employee engagement is a challenging concept to describe and study because there are many approaches to explaining what engagement at work is (see Chapter 2). Engagement seems to manifest itself in many ways

DOI: 10.4324/9781003171133-1

across industries, defying initial attempts to box it into a single and simple definition. Thus, despite the recent explosion in research articles and books offering definitions of engagement, many authors still refer to engagement in terms of what it looks like (e.g., high performance) as opposed to what it is.

Most of the reasons shared in practice about why you should care about engagement continue to revolve around *disengagement*. In the early 2000s, the Gallup Organization (2002, 2013a, 2013b) reported upward of $355 billion lost annual revenue in the United States, all due to unengaged workers. In their 2017 report on the American workplace, Gallup (2017a) revised the loss to between $483 billion and $605 billion annually. Also in the 2000s, they reported that 87% of employees across 142 countries were disengaged. In 2017, using data they collected across 155 countries between 2014 and 2016, Gallup (2017b) revised their previous report and stated that 85% of employees were disengaged, of which about 18% were *actively* disengaged (described as resentful and undermining work efforts; p. 23). The costs of disengaged employees are not unique to the United States. Disengaged workers reportedly cost the British economy between £37.2 billion and £38.9 billion per year (roughly $58.8 to $61.5 billion; Flade, 2003). Kenexa Research Institute reported in 2009 that an analysis of 64 organizations revealed engaged employees were responsible for *twice* the annual net income of their unengaged contemporaries. On one of SHRM's (Society for Human Resource Management's) web pages, they note that Molson Coors reported unengaged employees suffered more safety and lost-time incidents than did engaged employees in just 1 year, adding up to about $1.7 million for the company that year (see SHRM, n.d.). According to these combined reports (and many others I did not cite here), having disengaged employees results in enormous financial losses, which is the key reason why you should care about engagement.[1] There are exceptions to the disengagement reason for caring about engagement. For instance, the Dale Carnegie Organization (2007) suggested managers should care about engagement because engaged employees are productive, and high-engagement workplaces attract people who want to work hard for the organization. Glassdoor says they care about engagement because engaged employees drive business success (Clark, 2018).

If you look for a reason beyond disengagement to propel you into caring about employee engagement, you might consider peer pressure: everyone seems to be focusing on engagement; therefore, it must be important, right? Simple searches on the Internet, online bookstores, and electronic research databases reveal thousands of hits on employee/job/work engagement. Of the engagement books available on the market today, nearly all are targeted at the practitioner, human resource (HR) manager, and/or business leader explaining how to get engagement and the presumed consequence of high job performance. Even though few,

---

1 These reports provide few, if any, details on how the studies were conducted, including essential information about the samples and how engagement versus disengagement was operationalized.

if any, of these books incorporate research evidence to support their claims,[2] the sheer number of books suggests organizational leaders, consultants, and HR managers are running full steam ahead pursuing the *idea* of employee engagement.

Reasons other than fear of disengagement or recent fads to get you focused on employee engagement include the results of research catching up with practice. Some scholars have suggested researchers are attempting to legitimize engagement, an "intuitive construct" (Newman & Harrison, 2008), which requires significant theory, debate, and empirical studies for clarifying its uniqueness and validity in causing the effects heavily marketed by human resources and consulting firms (Macey & Schneider, 2008). This explanation may be true, but regardless of the reasons for the explosive scholarly interest in the topic, findings across many studies examining the relationship between engagement and performance, job satisfaction, and commitment, for example, indicate engagement uniquely contributes to explaining and predicting important organizational behavior (e.g., performance, innovation).

Another key reason to care about employee engagement is its relationship to employee health: engaged employees report positive physical and mental health outcomes and well-being, and the scientific literature strongly supports these relationships. A substantial number of studies report negative relationships between engagement and burnout, stress, and psychosomatic illness (Halbesleben, 2010). The negative relationship means that as employees report higher levels of engagement, they report lower levels of burnout, stress, and/or psychosomatic illness. Since health care spending accounts for nearly 20% of the U.S. gross domestic product (see the U.S. Centers for Medicare and Medicaid Services website), focusing on increasing engagement could translate into fewer dollars spent on employee health programs or lost days of work (e.g., sick leave).

Business reasons less tied to financial gains or losses for caring about engagement include framing engagement as a component of corporate social responsibility, which refers to the idea that companies integrate social and environmental concerns, making these concerns a joint corporate priority. For example, corporate social responsibility efforts include re-establishing the trust of the public in the ethical practices and intentions of the organization. By connecting corporate social responsibility to the well-being and general welfare of employees (through fostering their engagement levels at work), organizations may be able to send the message they care about profits and, importantly, not at the expense of their employees' health (physical and psychological).

While many reasons exist to care about employees' engagement levels, scholars remain challenged in defining the construct and agreeing on a single definition. Engagement seems to manifest itself in many different ways across

---

2 For an exception among the many books offering fast tips for boosting engagement scores, see John P. Meyer and Benjamin Schneider's edited book, *A Research Agenda for Employee Engagement in a Changing World of Work*, in which authors provide research-informed perspectives on engagement.

people, jobs, and industries, calling into question whether a single definition can suffice. The following are a few illustrative excerpts taken from actual interviews targeted toward understanding what employee engagement is and what it looks/feels like to employees. I changed names and personal information of the interviewees to protect their confidentiality.

DeWayne is a 40-year-old associate professor in the social sciences at a mid-sized university on the East Coast of the United States. His answers to questions about how he felt about work initially indicated he was feeling burned out. One of the dominant approaches to employee engagement started with the assumption engagement is the opposite of burnout – if you feel burned out, you cannot also be engaged. However, DeWayne tells a different story:

> Well, a few years ago, I would say I was getting burned out at work. I hated going to staff meetings and when there, I would just crawl into a corner and focus on my own thoughts and notes. I avoided people by working from home as much as I could – just so I didn't have to be in that environment. So much backstabbing and so little accountability [*he looks disgusted*]. They expect a ton of you and never recognize how much you do. I felt so different, so energized when I could work at home for a couple of days in a row. Just being away from my coworkers – don't get me wrong, I'm sure they are good at what they do. I just don't really like them all that much. They do nothing to make me feel supported [*paused for a while as if collecting thoughts*]. I really like what I do – I feel so intellectually stimulated, writing, and problem-solving in my research. It's a challenge to me to figure out how to convey our field in simple terms to the students, so that they can see how exciting the material is and . . . well, I like to find ways to make it come alive [*paused for a moment*]. My wife complains that I work too much – I get lost in what I'm doing, ya' know, lose track of time and then I'm late for dinner, finding excuses for why I couldn't tear myself away from my research. I just really like what I do – it invigorates me.

Becky's story conveys how important the people at work are to her and the value of relationships in promoting her engagement at work. Becky is a 55-year-old mental health care worker at a nonprofit organization in the midwestern United States.

> When I started, the organization was a tiny version of its current self, and so in those days people were much less specialized and did a lot of different things; had a lot of different roles. We had more variety [*she paused for a few moments*]. Things have gotten much more bureaucratic. There were fewer levels to go through for decisions, we had easier access up the ladder, power used to be delegated downward more, we had more say in decision-making. It doesn't feel like the camaraderie is happening [*she*

started crying]. Relationships are different now and it used to be easier to talk through things – now it's all e-mail; so distant between people, even with people sitting a desk away.

[I ask her] *So why are you still here, what keeps you going?*

I love my job. I love the clients. What I do matters in their lives – I've known some of them for years and when they come in, it's like seeing a good friend. Having a long-term perspective helps me. I don't always feel like everything is engaging for me, but I like the big picture and it helps me know that it's valuable in the long run. I like what we do, I like our vision and I like what we provide. I think we do a really good job for our clients. There's a lot of wonderful people here.

Petrus is a 46-year-old consultant in South Africa. He used to work for a large corporation, but when the government instituted new policies for selection and promotion in efforts to rectify many years of apartheid oppression, he left and started his own consulting firm. I asked him about his consulting work because he specializes in helping organizations with promoting engagement:

I really liked my work at [*organization*] – I was there for at least 20 years before I decided to leave. I don't begrudge the organization for what it was doing – they had to follow the law. I do a number of different things now, which makes my work so interesting. I work with a variety of organizations all around South Africa – none are the same. I develop leadership training programs – I focus a lot on communication, conveying clear vision, and basic management principles. There's such a large pay discrepancy here between the lowest level worker and the managers, a problem that I can't solve. So we focus on developing employee appreciation programs, finding ways to match employees' skills to the right jobs, and teaching them how to work together in teams. I use both surveys and focus groups to measure engagement – I wouldn't say everything we do works every time, but for the most part, we make a difference.

Lastly, Valerray is a 30-year-old businessperson in Russia who responded to my questions about engagement in the following way (we conversed through translators):

I'm not sure I understand your question. Happiness? You want to know about happiness? Look at us, we're very happy. We love to have fun [*we discuss how happiness is not the same as engagement*]. Involvement, engagement? [*the translator offered that she thinks they are all the same word*] I don't know. The older workers are struggling with what it means to be independent – they grew up in a government where they knew their place at work and felt pride about doing something the government needed and wanted. The younger workers don't know that system, so we experience work differently. We are challenged and excited about making our way in this new world. We are happy; we work hard; I work hard. We do as much as we can and feel good. We are passionate about what we do and find ways to make it good for the people – I have nice offices for my employees, give them time off when they need, have work they like to do, and we talk a lot about work. I send my employees to training programs; they like to learn and then they do better on the job.

Road Map for This Book

By Chapters

The first form of engagement proposed (i.e., Kahn, 1990) says employee engagement is about investing oneself, being authentic in the job, and delivering one's work performance with passion, attention, persistence, and energy (Chapter 2 provides details on this definition). Engagement is generally characterized as a motivational state, positively associated with performance, which is different from organizational attitudes frequently mentioned, such as job satisfaction and commitment (Chapter 3 reviews differences and similarities between engagement and various similar constructs). Most organizational leaders believe they can promote employees' engagement, not only by providing the right environment and good leadership (Chapter 4), but also by removing inhibitors (Chapter 5). Of course, fostering engagement also means being able to assess (measure) how often employees report being engaged and by how much (Chapter 6 reviews measures of engagement).

Given the benefits associated with employee engagement (I review many in the first few chapters), organizations seek to use engagement for competitive advantage (Chapter 7 discusses how to do so). Although one of the benefits associated with engagement is improved health for the employee, I introduce in Chapter 8 the possibility that engagement can improve the health of the organization through a concept called *engagement contagion*. Most of the benefits associated with engaged employees have been studied and demonstrated in a number of countries. However, a gap exists in that only a few have examined engagement across cultures – that is, comparing one culture to another (Chapter 9 reviews engagement in the international landscape). In addition to this gap, another exists in that engagement has primarily been considered a positive and very desirable state for employees; more seems to be better. However, researchers and practitioners suggest there may be a dark side to engagement – an unexplored paradox refuting the notion that more is necessarily better (Chapter 10 reviews studies on the dark side of engagement). For this second edition, I updated all the chapters to draw on the latest research studies and new insight gained from case studies shared on the Internet in non-research and non-academic-oriented outlets, and to infuse new understandings and questions derived from my own research conducted since the publication of the first edition. This book, therefore, offers a comprehensive review and a discussion of employee engagement as we know it today!

By Parts

I grounded this book in theory and empirical research, yet it also includes, when appropriate, references and reviews of efforts in the practice realm of employee engagement. The first few chapters in Part I are devoted to setting the stage for where we are in the literature today. I start with a review of the many definitions of engagement, since progress in identifying predictors and consequences of engagement requires recognizing and understanding from which perspective one takes. Critics challenge whether engagement is different from existing constructs that are already staples in the organizational behavior literature. Therefore, I provide a review of the empirical findings demonstrating the uniqueness and similarity of engagement to existing constructs such as job involvement, flow, satisfaction, and commitment.

Part II of this book focuses on the applied side of understanding employee engagement, in the sense of how one gets employees engaged, what prevents employees from being engaged, and how you know if they are engaged. Thus, these chapters focus on application, with a strong foundation in theory and research. What empirical evidence do we have or are we missing to feel confident that recommended solutions work in organizations? Much of the attention in organizational sciences is on how we use theory and research to make a difference in organizations – not only to advance the sciences but also, importantly, how to apply what is learned. I wrote the chapters in Part II with these objectives in mind: advancing science and furthering its application. Parts I and II bring you up to speed on what is currently known about engagement. I updated these sections to incorporate new research and practice introduced since the first edition.

Part III focuses on how engagement serves as a competitive advantage and not just because of high-performing employees. Instead, I focus on building an organizational culture to improve competitive advantage, and on how employees themselves grow the organization's engagement capacity.

Part IV is about what is still not known at this time about employee engagement and why it should be known – what the new frontiers are in engagement. In this part of the book, I shine a light on the gap in knowledge about engagement across cultures. Although researchers are conducting studies in many countries around the globe – more so since the first edition of this book – there remain very few studies with a cross-cultural focus (i.e., comparing samples collected in different cultures). Furthermore, one cannot simply compare studies conducted in different countries to each other and assume the researchers were studying the same construct (i.e., employee engagement). Some words simply do not translate from one culture to another. I was raised bilingual and in a non-U.S. country and culture; therefore, I was already exposed to the subtleties in translating colloquial speech before I visited Russia in 2012 and 2013. Made especially clear to me in my interactions in Russia was that translation of scientific ideas is even more complicated than colloquial speech because the exact word choice is critical to advancing science. I share some of these challenges in Chapter 9. However, I only scratch the surface of the gap in international studies in Chapter 9. I hope this "scratch" will lead to rigorous efforts to promote the study of engagement cross-culturally (and not just engagement in a different country, for which there are many new studies since the first edition of this book). Additionally, in Part IV of this book, I turn several ideas on their heads to expose other perspectives of engagement. By reviewing theories and literature that may be brought to the study of the topic, these chapters have immediate utility as opposed to just being a presentation of possible ideas for future research.

Although many researchers and practitioners might not agree on a single definition or approach to employee engagement, perhaps the one thing we can agree on is that engagement is not a simple concept. Transporting engagement from practice to science is not easy. Yet, the concept of employee engagement holds promise for generating much conversation, even more than it has already, about employees in organizations. I hope you find this revised and updated second edition of the book even more helpful and inspiring than the first.

PART I

Engagement Under the Microscope

2

WHAT IS EMPLOYEE ENGAGEMENT?

Employee engagement has been fiercely growing in popularity among practitioners, organizational leaders, and researchers in the organizational sciences over the last two decades. *And why not?* According to an article in *Business Week* magazine,

> companies with engaged employees boosted operating income by 19% compared with companies with the lowest percentage of engaged employees, which saw operating income fall 33%. What does that mean in real dollars? For S&P 500 companies, Watson Wyatt reports that a significant improvement in employee engagement increases revenue by $95 million.
>
> *(Irvine, 2009)*

Although astounding financial gains and losses are attributed to engaged and unengaged workers, consensus is still elusive on what exactly engagement is, and whether it is a new topic or one comprising a number of existing topics (Newman & Harrison, 2008). Furthermore, a review of websites, books, and trade magazines, as well as academic journals, reveals a reasonably large disparity between research and practice concerning the definition and use of the phrase *employee engagement* or *work engagement*. For example, practitioner writings (e.g., white papers, consulting firm websites, blogs, books) refer to engagement as an umbrella or overarching term that subsumes many different concepts (e.g., attitudes, behaviors, dispositions) relevant to the performance of individuals in groups or the organization as a whole (see Mone & London, 2010). In contrast, researchers seek parsimony, specificity, and uniqueness in their definitions of the concept, distinguishing attitudes from behaviors and

DOI: 10.4324/9781003171133-3

dispositions (i.e., personality), with a tendency toward focusing on an individual. To confuse matters more, the word *engagement* is sometimes used as a verb signifying behavior and performance (e.g., to be engaged or involved in an activity; Miles, 2001; Miller, Greene, Montalvo, Ravindran, & Nichols, 1996); as an adjective, whereby engagement describes a person in a particular state of being or energy level (e.g., *self-engagement* as a form of personal responsibility: Britt, 1999); or as a noun representing a certification (e.g., *Community Engagement, Curricular Engagement*: classifications of the Carnegie Foundation for the Advancement of Teaching, 2009). So what is employee or work engagement?

Defining Engagement as Investing in One's Work Role

Just over 30 years ago, Kahn (1990) proposed the first definition of *employee engagement* used in research literature. He introduced personal engagement as "the harnessing of organization members' selves into their work roles; in engagement, people employ and express themselves physically, cognitively, and emotionally during role performances" (1990, p. 694). He clarified his definition of engagement by also defining disengagement as the opposite point on an engagement continuum, where disengagement or "unemployment of the self" (Kahn, 1990, p. 701) is akin to detachment and self-defense (see Chapter 5 for more on Kahn's disengagement). Kahn grounded his work in Goffman's (1961) studies of symbiotic relationships and suggested that the more people draw themselves into their various work roles (i.e., engagement), the better their performance and the more happiness they experience. Drawing on oneself means *self-employment* (effort, involvement, flow, mindfulness, intrinsic motivation, and psychological presence) and *self-expression* (creativity, personal voice, emotional expression, authenticity, non-defensive communication, playfulness, and ethical behavior). Kahn developed his definition based on two studies: one involved observations, document analysis, and interviews of camp counselors at an athletic summer camp for adolescents, and the other involved interviews with employees of an architectural firm. Kahn's focus on engagement was primarily as a moment-to-moment concept (he did not specify how long a moment is; W. A. Kahn, personal communication, May 6, 2012; Kahn, 1990), although some have applied his idea of engagement as a general stable state (e.g., May, Gilson, & Harter, 2004). Researchers using Kahn's definition of engagement generally refer to it as *employee* engagement and retain the foundational characteristic of harnessing the self into the work role (e.g., Cooper-Thomas, Xu, & Saks, 2018).

Defining Engagement as the Opposite of Burnout

Another definition of engagement in the research literature was proposed by Maslach and colleagues (e.g., Maslach & Leiter, 1997; Maslach, Schaufeli, & Leiter, 2001) and later refined by Schaufeli, Salanova, González-Romá, and

Bakker (2002). Maslach and Leiter (1997) originally defined engagement as a concept composed of three elements – energy, involvement, and efficacy – each being the direct opposite of one of three burnout dimensions: emotional exhaustion, depersonalization, and lack of efficacy, respectively. Burnout has been traditionally defined as a three-component construct comprising *emotional exhaustion* (emotionally drained), *depersonalization* (detached and often cynical), and *reduced personal accomplishment* or *lack of efficacy* (experienced as an overwhelming internal feeling of failure; Maslach, 1982). Maslach and Leiter (1997) proposed the use of the Maslach Burnout Inventory (MBI) to assess engagement, with low exhaustion and cynicism scores and high efficacy scores reflecting high levels of engagement. Their perspective was that engagement was a positive state – the opposite of burnout. Reflecting on their years of scholarship in studying burnout, they determined that when people were not feeling burned out, they were often in a positive state of energy, involvement, and efficacy.

Schaufeli, Salanova, and colleagues (2002) modified Maslach and Leiter's definition, referring to engagement as indicating "a positive, fulfilling, work-related state of mind characterized by vigor, dedication, and absorption" (p. 74). They further clarified that "rather than a momentary and specific state, engagement refers to a more persistent and pervasive affective-cognitive state" (p. 74). *Vigor* refers to high levels of energy while working and persistence when confronted with challenges. *Dedication* refers to experiencing enthusiasm, pride, inspiration, challenge, and significance. *Absorption* refers to "being fully concentrated and deeply engrossed in one's work, whereby time passes quickly, and one has difficulty detaching oneself from work" (Schaufeli, Martínez, Marques Pinto, Salanova, & Bakker, 2002, p. 75). Most researchers using the "opposite of burnout" perspective of engagement employ Schaufeli et al.'s simplified definition from page 74, but they call it *work* engagement instead of *employee* engagement (for just a few examples, see Albrecht, Breidahl, & Marty, 2018; Alfes, Veld, & Fürstenberg, 2020; Costantini, Ceschi, Viragos, De Paola, & Sartori, 2019; Hakanen, Peeters, & Schaufeli, 2018; Kim & Beehr, 2020; Rofcanin, Bakker, Berber, Gölgeci, & Las Heras, 2019). From here on, I use *employee engagement* and *work engagement* interchangeably.

Schaufeli et al.'s (2002) definition has morphed over time. For instance, the definition has been modified to suggest engagement is a *transient* state characterized by vigor, dedication, and absorption, which *fluctuates within individuals over short time frames* (Sonnentag, Dormann, & Demerouti, 2010).

Other Definitions

Other, less cited definitions of engagement exist. For example, engagement has been defined as a combination of commitment and organizational citizenship behaviors (i.e., extra-role or discretionary performance behaviors that facilitate organizational productivity and teamwork; CIPD, 2009; Matthews, 2010). It has been described as a form of happiness or satisfaction (Edwards, 2009); a positive attitude (Robinson, Perryman, & Hayday, 2004); psychological presence comprising attention and absorption (Rothbard, 2001); discretionary effort (Hay Group, 2010); a connection with the company, accompanied by a willingness to demonstrate extra-role behaviors (Towers Perrin, as cited in Gebauer, Lowman, & Gordon, 2008); an emotional and intellectual connection that triggers citizenship behavior (Gibbons, 2006); actively using personal resources at work (Liu, Chen, & Li, 2021); and a three-dimensional construct comprising alignment, affect, and action-orientation (Shrotryia & Dhanda, 2020). Although these and many other definitions have been proposed, a search of the Web of Science citation database (a database of citations of scientific and conference publications offered by Thomson Reuters) reveals few, if any, have been used by anyone other than the authors proposing the definition.

In contrast to other approaches in describing engagement, Macey and Schneider (2008) proposed a framework to encompass the "variety of meanings the engagement construct subsumes" (p. 4). The framework suggests (a) employees have a predisposition to view life and work with enthusiasm, called *trait* engagement, which (b) determines their *state* engagement (feelings of energy and absorption) and subsequently leads to (c) their discretionary extra-role effort, called *behavioral* engagement. Initial research supports the linear relationship between trait and state engagement (Sonnentag, 2003). Macey and Schneider proposed that, overall, when organizations implement practices to promote the right conditions for fostering state engagement in employees who possess trait engagement, the organization will be rewarded with behavioral engagement that sets the organization apart from all others (i.e., competitive advantage). Recent empirical work has leveraged Macey and Schneider's framework (see Christian, Garza, & Slaughter, 2011), and consultants (besides Macey and Schneider themselves) have applied the model in organizational interventions (Mone & London, 2010).

Attempts at a Unifying Definition

A key similarity between the two most prominent academic definitions of engagement (i.e., Kahn, 1990; Schaufeli et al., 2002) is engagement described as a positive, motivation-like construct comprising three components: affective or dedication, cognitive or absorption, and behavioral or vigor. The distinguishing features of Kahn's (1990) definition include the focus on *employee* engagement as a moment-to-moment experience that includes presence and authenticity, and the grounding of engagement in a social interaction/self-presentation perspective. The distinguishing characteristics of Schaufeli et al.'s (2002) definition is its basis in the stress literature, such that *work* engagement serves as a form of well-being, and that engagement is considered a "persistent and pervasive affective-cognitive state" (p. 74). Compared to other academic and non-academic definitions, both Kahn's and Schaufeli et al.'s are multifaceted, representing the complexity of the construct, thus avoiding the deficiencies observed by narrowing the definition to achieve simplicity.

One reason understanding engagement remains challenging is that too many different definitions exist in the literature, creating confusion and divisiveness among camps of researchers. Another reason is that academic definitions fail to recognize key aspects of engagement as referred to by practitioners and organizational leaders alike; namely, performance directed toward achieving organizational goals (e.g., Macey & Schneider, 2008; Mone & London, 2010).

In the first edition of this book, I suggested we can make more progress in understanding engagement by creating a unifying definition that (a) combines and leverages similarities across definitions, (b) captures the key components that make engagement unique from other similar existing constructs, (c) integrates key perspectives from both science and practice, and (d) separates antecedent and consequence constructs from the definition itself. Several authors, including myself, have attempted to offer a unifying definition, with none gaining much traction. For example, Shuck et al. (2017) offered that engagement is "a positive, active, work-related psychological state operationalized by the maintenance, intensity, and direction of cognitive, emotional, and behavioural energy" (p. 269). Fleck and Inceoglu (2010) proposed engagement as a two-dimensional, higher-order construct representing the focus of engagement: one's job or one's organization. Within each dimension, engagement is a cognitive and affective state. Job engagement's cognitive state is referred to as *absorption*, and the affective state is referred to as *energy* (what employees draw from their work). Organization engagement's cognitive state is referred to as *alignment* (employee and organization are aligned in direction), and the affective state is referred to as *identification*.

I propose the following unifying definition of employee engagement:

> a moment-to-moment state of motivation, wherein one is psychologically present (i.e., in the moment) and psychophysiologically aroused, is focused on and aligned with the goals of the job and organization, and channels one's emotional and cognitive self to transform work into meaningful and purposeful accomplishment.

Moment-to-Moment State of Motivation

Many references and explanations of engagement, or descriptions of how engagement manifests in the workplace, reflect employee engagement as a *state of motivation*. We cannot directly observe motivation (Kanfer, 1990); rather, we infer its existence by observing the direction of one's attention and energy, the intensity with which one persists on a task, and the effort one exerts in working toward accomplishing a task (J. Campbell, Dunnette, Lawler, & Weick, 1970; Kanfer, 1990; Ployhart, 2008). Like motivation, engagement varies over time and across activities (Reina-Tamayo, Bakker, & Derks, 2017). Engagement, however, is more than just motivation, because one can be motivated in a direction that fails to support the organization's goals, have directed effort with manipulative or purely instrumental intent, or be motivated without skill, which can be counterproductive. Consistent with engagement as understood within the practice and consulting literature, engaged employees focus on meeting organizational goals. I challenge you to find an organization that refers to employees who spend their time working against organizational goals as engaged. Several existing approaches to engagement refer to it as a motivational state or use the language of motivation to describe engagement and/or engaged employees (e.g., Bakker, Schaufeli, Leiter, & Taris, 2008; Halbesleben, Harvey, & Bolino, 2009; Kahn, 1990; Maslach et al., 2001; Schaufeli et al., 2002). For instance, Schaufeli et al. (2002) refer to vigor as persistence and invested effort, which are aspects of motivation (Kanfer, 1990).

I agree with others (see Kahn, 1992; Macey & Schneider, 2008; Maslach et al., 2001) who have said that one cannot be engaged at all times. Thus, I retain the moment-to-moment aspect of Kahn's (1990) definition because engagement, like motivation, is not a steady, continuous state, lasting for hours on end and day in and day out. The extent to which engagement fluctuates or remains stable, and over what measure of time, are empirical questions (see Chapter 11). Thus, scholars and practitioners, alike, will need to operationalize what they mean by a "moment."

Psychologically Present

Kahn (1992) defined *psychological presence* as a state wherein one is fully attentive to the present moment, connected, integrated, and focused. He suggested presence enables engagement. One can achieve psychological presence through mindfulness (K. Brown & Ryan, 2003; Dane, 2011; Herndon, 2008), which refers to an awareness resulting from focusing on the present moment (Coo & Salanova, 2018). Interventions wherein participants engaged in mindfulness training showed significant increases in work engagement (e.g., Coo & Salanova, 2018; Klatt, Steinberg, & Duchemin, 2015). When psychologically present, one is *in the moment* rather than thinking about other events or people, either in the past or in the future (K. Brown & Ryan, 2003). Given the definition of psychological presence, it makes sense that psychological availability is necessary for presence, which enables engagement (Kahn, 1990). Daydreaming or mind-wandering on the job is a sign of a lack of psychological presence; hence, focusing on the current task and being psychologically present can also mean losing track of time similar to flow (Csikszentmihalyi, 1996). Csikszentmihalyi and Rathunde (1993) described flow as "the subjective state that people report when they are completely involved in something to the point of forgetting time, fatigue, and everything else but the activity itself" (p. 59). Psychological presence subsumes Schaufeli et al.'s (2002) absorption.

Psychophysiological Arousal

My unifying definition of engagement refers to *psychophysiological arousal*, rather than physical energy, because many jobs do not require people express themselves physically, yet they can report high levels of engagement. One can be physiologically aroused without demonstrating physical movement and action (Duffy, 1957; Lacey, Bateman, & VanLehn, 1953; Shipman, Heath, & Oken, 1970). Research in psychophysiology (i.e., physiological bases underlying psychological processes) has determined that people respond with physical arousal (e.g., increased heart rate and/or electrodermal activity) to psychological experiences (e.g., enjoyment of music, chess, gambling) without necessarily demonstrating overt physical movement and action (e.g., running, jumping; Alpers, Adolph, & Pauli, 2011; Studer & Clark, 2011). That is, people can be involved in a non-physically demanding task, such as playing chess, but can place "metabolic demands on their bodies that begin to approach those of athletes during the peak of a competitive event" (Sapolsky, 2004, p. 5). Recent research has shown both direct and indirect associations between non-physically manipulated engagement and sympathetic arousal at work and increases in brain activity (Baethge, Junker, & Rigotti, 2020; Kokubun, Ogata, Koike, & Yamakawa, 2020; Reis, Arndt, Lischetzke, & Hoppe, 2016), supporting my inclusion of psychophysiological arousal in defining engagement.

Kahn's (1990) illustrations of the physical component of his conceptualization of engagement are all observably physical activities like "darting about checking gear" (p. 700) and "flying around the room" (p. 701). His examples may suggest that observable physical activity, even if just minor, is required for engagement. In contrast to Kahn, Schaufeli et al.'s (2002) concept of vigor might be similar to what I refer to here, in that vigor is the *feeling* of energy rather than the expression of physical activity. Heightened arousal levels are characteristic of the state of engagement, and I propose the derivation of energy from goal progress and achievement accounts for this heightened and sustained arousal.

Psychophysiological arousal incorporates physiological arousal; therefore, my definition also applies to physically demanding jobs. Physiological arousal refers to the excitation or activation of biological functions such as cardio activity, as indicated by blood pressure or heart rate, brain activity, concentration of blood sugar or lactic acid, or body temperature. One cannot have physical activity without physiological arousal.

Focus and Alignment With Organizational Goals

Focus is a concept incorporated in many definitions of engagement and, therefore, in my unifying definition. I specifically include an alignment of employees' focus with the organization's goals, because including focus with no target leaves this component of engagement vague and fails to incorporate an important aspect of what practitioners note is critical for engagement (i.e., goal alignment). When discussing engagement with other consultants, corporate and office leaders and managers, and human resource representatives, they all refer to engaged employees as those focused on achieving organizational goals (see also Robinson et al., 2004). Consistently, organizational representatives referred to employees whose engagement seems focused elsewhere as "challenging" employees, also known as "problem" employees. These employees expend great energy toward a goal that is not in the organization's current vision and not where the organization wants employees to expend their efforts or enthusiasm. Such an employee, in the worst case, may be misusing organizational resources and creating performance problems. For example, in one of my consulting projects, a few employees who the organization considered unengaged were actually, by all other definitions, engaged; they were just not focused on the tasks of the job – they had found a side project of great interest to which they were completely absorbed. Engagement outside of work may be wonderful for the employee, but organizational leaders are not invested in promoting employees' personal pet side projects unless those projects support the organization. The inclusion of focus on organizational goals within my unifying definition is consistent with Fleck and Inceoglu's (2010) organizational engagement cognitive state.

Channeling Emotional and Cognitive Self for Meaningful Accomplishment

My definition of engagement is similar to existing definitions in its inclusion of *affect and cognition*. Not every job requires the same amount of emotional or cognitive energy, nor does it require employees invest themselves affectively or cognitively to the same level at all times. Therefore, when employees are in a state of engagement, they employ and combine varying levels of their emotional and cognitive selves as they transform their work tasks and specific activities into meaningful accomplishment. In the edited book *Purpose and Meaning in the Workplace* (Dik, Byrne, & Steger, 2013), Ashforth and Kreiner (2013) wrote a chapter about finding meaning in dirty work. Dirty work, they suggest, refers to occupations that society views as socially unclean or physically ugly, such as funeral services or trash and maintenance services. They proposed that workers in dirty occupations create a cognitive shift in what work means, enabling them to derive new meaning, and essentially transforming their job/tasks into work that is meaningful and purposeful for them. The authors emphasize how meaningfulness of work is not what others deem meaningful, but what oneself considers meaningful.

Not only do different jobs or occupations require different investments of one's cognitive and/or emotional self; people are also different in how they approach their work and interpret the world around them. Specifically, some people tend to be more logically oriented, opting for a cognitive explanation for sense-making and decision-making. Others are more driven to decisions and understanding through their emotions. This distinction between thinking versus feeling is often ascribed to the Myers-Briggs Type Indicator (Myers & McCauley, 1985) and has been long debated, discussed, and supported in scholarly literature (see Ochsner, 2007; Zajonc, 2008). Basically, some individuals prefer to view and respond to their job tasks from an emotional base, where they allow their emotions to lead their decisions and they invest their affective selves through emotional expression in their work. Others prefer to view and respond to their job tasks from a thinking base, where they think through what the work means to them and base decisions on their thoughts. People's preferences may vary by the task and are not exclusive of one another; some people balance their affective and cognitive investments relatively equally, as can best be determined by how they express themselves in their work.

My incorporation of the emotional and cognitive self into a definition of engagement is consistent with the foundation of engagement. For example, Schaufeli et al.'s (2002) definition incorporates enthusiasm and absorption. Similarly, Kahn (1990) refers to engagement as an investment of the self into the work role, an investment that includes drawing on one's self-employment (effort, involvement, flow, mindfulness, intrinsic motivation, and psychological presence) and self-expression (creativity, personal voice, emotional expression, authenticity, non-defensive communication, playfulness, and ethical behavior; see Kahn, 1990, p. 700). The distinction between self-employment and self-expression mirrors that between cognitive and affective investment, respectively. Self-employment is drawn from our thinking selves, whereas self-expression is drawn from our affective selves. Rather than attempt to include all the possible ways of describing affective and cognitive responses, I simplify the definition by merely stating engagement has both a cognitive and affective component.

Lastly, the synergistic mix of these aspects of oneself is directed toward a *transformation* of tasks or activity into accomplishment that is meaningful or has significance to the individual. Classical motivation theorists proposed individuals have innate needs for work that is meaningful. For example, Alderfer (1972), Maslow (1968), and Rogers (1961) all developed theoretical models describing the inherent need of individuals to seek higher-order values that translate into meaningfulness and purpose. In contrast, diminished accomplishment, or lack of successful achievement at work, is considered a component of job burnout (e.g., Maslach & Jackson, 1981). Thus, employees enter a state of engagement to fulfill their need for purposeful accomplishment, which they do by transforming the meaning of their work through the full expression of themselves. Engagement without striving for meaningful or purposeful accomplishment may be more akin to flow or meditation. Note that achieving meaningfulness or purpose is not part of the definition: engagement might result in these outcomes, as it did for those working dirty jobs in Ashforth and Kreiner's (2013) chapter.

Excluding Antecedents and Consequences From the Definition

Kahn (1990) and Schaufeli et al. (2002) both incorporated antecedents (e.g., significance, challenge) and consequences (e.g., involvement, pride) into their definitions of engagement. However, Rich, LePine, and Crawford (2010) constructed a measure of Kahn's engagement that excluded antecedents and outcomes, whereas Schaufeli et al.'s measure retains antecedent and consequence constructs. Like Fleck and Inceoglu (2010), I wanted a unifying definition of engagement *only*, such that if you ask a respondent about their engagement levels, they can answer without also having to determine whether the incorporated antecedent or outcome fits their situation. Therefore, I did not include the antecedents or the consequences of engagement into the unifying definition. As such, researchers can examine various antecedents and outcomes of engagement independently of the construct, using measures specifically designed for accurately and adequately assessing those constructs.

Is Engagement the Same for Every Organization?

It appears no one yet has explored whether the existing conceptualizations of engagement hold across organizations. My guess for why that was is because no one asked the question, "What does engagement mean and look like *here?*" I explored these ideas in a couple of consulting projects that offered me the opportunity to conduct research in parallel with the consulting effort, otherwise known as action research (Lewin, 1946, 1947). Although my exploration is limited, my results provide some initial insight into whether engagement is unique to each organization or potentially similar across organizations.

In one of my consulting/action-research projects conducted in 2010, my team and I interviewed employees (32 one-on-one interviews and six focus groups of eight people each) from across a variety of jobs, departments, and locations of a medium-sized not-for-profit community health care system ($N = 4,985$ employees). The focus of the project was to understand what engagement is and what drives engagement for these employees. We analyzed the content of the interviews and extracted several themes for how people described their own engagement and for what drove their engagement. In their own words, employees said being engaged meant experiencing work as invigorating and energizing. They reported feeling time moved faster and they got lost in time, feeling a self-imposed need to accomplish their tasks – to push themselves harder and faster, take the initiative, switch into a drive mode, and thrive. They also said they chose to be engaged rather than be told to be engaged. In a follow-up survey of a representative sample of the same organization ($n = 517$, using proportionate sampling techniques), I confirmed this was indeed what engagement meant across the entire organization.

In another consulting/action-research project conducted in 2012, also aimed toward identifying what engagement means to employees and what drives their engagement, my team and I again interviewed employees (46 one-on-one interviews and four focus groups of eight people each) from across a variety of locations, jobs, and departments of a small not-for-profit community mental health care provider ($N = 437$ employees). I additionally interviewed representatives of three partner organizations that each provided mental health services in conjunction with the focal organization. One partner organization made referrals to this organization, another handled the medical and insurance claims, and the third offered a supporting medical service. My research team and I transcribed all the interviews and conducted content analysis, resulting in the extraction of several themes. Themes for what engagement meant included focusing on the work, getting a job done, caring about how what a person did helped the organization, energy, and curiosity. Managers added that engagement is the feeling of accomplishment from removing roadblocks and giving that big-picture perspective, providing context and meaning to work. Again, we validated these qualitative findings with quantitative results.

The qualitative and quantitative data from just the two organizations noted suggest engagement may be a similar construct across organizations, answering the question, "Does engagement look the same in every organization?" The conclusion is limited, as both organizations were health care based. Furthermore, in the second organization, employees used a broader scope to define *job* than did those in the first, which affects how one defines and refers to what employee engagement is. Specifically, they defined *job* as "what my organization needs me to do," "what my team needs me to do," and "what I am hired to do." Not everyone in the organization defined *job* as incorporating all three emphases when referring to engagement. Thus, to some, engagement referred to being focused on and energized about just the tasks they were hired to perform, but not also toward what the team needs and/or what the organization needs. In contrast, for others, engagement to them included it all; they described engagement as being fully committed to this all-encompassing expenditure of self toward all three aspects: tasks, team, and organizational needs. Thus, how *job* is defined may influence what engagement means across organizations.

The multiple conceptualizations of what it means to do one's job are similar to some degree to Saks's (2006) *job engagement* and *organization engagement*. Saks proposed employees reciprocate (following the tenets of social exchange theory; Blau, 1964) benefits and resources from the organization with job and organizational engagement. Saks maintained that employees occupy two roles: a work or job role and an organizational role or the role of a member of the organization. Therefore, employees can be engaged in more than one work role, resulting in two forms of engagement. Saks's delineation of engagement is akin to supervisory and organizational commitment (e.g., Cheng, Jiang, & Riley, 2003) or to perceived supervisory and organizational support (e.g., Eisenberger et al., 2002; Kottke & Sharafinski, 1988), where the construct can be expressed across two foci or beneficiaries of the exchange. I did not find the two-foci definition of engagement in the second organization described earlier; however, what is somewhat similar between my findings and Saks's idea of multiple expressions of engagement is there could exist an overall concept of having multiple work expectations that can be incorporated within an umbrella of the focus of one's engagement. Thus, one's investment of self, one's transformation of work, and one's energy can be toward whatever *job* is defined to be, and how this is manifested apparently varies by organization.

Based on these consulting/research projects, in addition to others, I concluded that although both Kahn's (1990) and Schaufeli et al.'s (2002) definitions of engagement each contained many of the key components shared in these interviews and seemed to make up engagement (as did a few other, not so popular definitions; Dvir, Eden, Avolio, & Shamir, 2002; Macgowan, 2000; Seijts & Crim, 2006; Vansteenkiste et al., 2007), neither alone was enough to provide a definitive conceptualization. Furthermore, both were missing the ideas of alignment with organizational goals, transformation of work, and accomplishment, all of which have been described, to some degree, in the practice literature and were revealed in my own qualitative work.

Although the essence of what employees experienced when engaged seemed similar across the two organizations studied here, they differed significantly in what fostered or promoted engagement, a topic I discuss in Chapter 4.

What Does Employee Engagement Look Like in Organizations?

Most descriptions of employee engagement capture how it manifests itself – what it looks like when/if seen by others. In organizations, employee engagement looks like high-quality/high-quantity job performance, discretionary effort, high energy, enthusiasm, commitment to the organizational mission, and expressions of passion, initiative, and collaboration. Engagement in organizations looks like employees loving their jobs. These employees are so into what they are doing they forget to take their breaks and ignore the clock on the wall that says it is time to go home. They block everything out so they can focus on the task at hand. They ask what else they can do to help the situation improve or to relieve someone who is overwhelmed. They look for what is missing or out of place and fix it without being asked and without expecting to be rewarded or recognized in return. Descriptions of engaged employees include the following: they deliver improved business performance (CIPD, 2009); they are aware of business issues, improve performance, go the extra mile, believe in the organization, and respect others (Robinson et al., 2004); and they have higher productivity, innovation, stay longer, have higher-quality discretionary efforts, are energetic, enthusiastic, and solve more problems than disengaged employees (Scarlett, 2009).

Engaged employees transform nonmeaningful work into something mean-ingful. For example, the nurses we interviewed talked about performing "grunt work" (e.g., "wiping poopie butts") as being required regularly – the job is not all glamorous. Instead of describing it as the hassles of the job, they referred to their job as promoting mental and physical health in all aspects of each patient's life. They transformed the negative aspects of the job (e.g., paperwork, sometimes cleaning up after a patient who lacks bowel control) into important parts of the mental and physical health–recovery chain. Likewise, some of the caseworkers in the mental health organization talked about how important they were to providing the clients with stability; they felt their job was to be the stable relationship in their client's life, rather than adding to the requirements, stressors, and constant changes that some mental health patients endure when trying to deal with their illness. Thus, they did not refer to work as the job of providing therapy, prescribing medicine, or tracking their patients; instead, they transformed their work from providing mental health care to offering the stability and support of a long-term relationship.

In organizations, employee engagement does look like a combination of constructs some researchers have spent considerable effort delineating from engagement (e.g., Demerouti, Bakker, de Jonge, Janssen, & Schaufeli, 2001; Hakanen, Bakker, & Schaufeli, 2006; Hallberg & Schaufeli, 2006; Rich et al., 2010; Richardsen, Burke, & Martinussen, 2006; Saks, 2006; Schaufeli, Taris, & Bakker, 2006). For example, a strong work ethic can masquerade as high engagement. However, although engagement may result in outcomes that appear similar, such as citizenship behavior, commitment, job involvement, and job satisfaction, what engagement is, what triggers it, and how it is defined are different. I review those differences in the next chapter.

Conclusion

Since the first edition of this book was published, numerous research stud-ies on employee or work engagement have been published; yet looking across all those studies, many of the same concerns identified then still exist today. Therefore, it seems fitting to re-emphasize what engagement is and is *not* and shine a spotlight on the progress made since the first edition. Chapter 3 focuses on what engagement is not, providing evidence for how it is different from other constructs associated with engagement.

WALK-AWAY POINTS

- Employee engagement refers to a state of motivation, wherein one is psychologically present (i.e., in the moment) and psychophysiologically aroused, is focused on and aligned with the goals of the job and organization, and channels one's emotional and cognitive self to transform work into meaningful and purposeful accomplishment.
- Employee engagement appears to be quite similar across organizations; however, how it manifests itself and how it is fostered varies.
- You cannot see engagement per se, but you can infer engagement levels from people's emotional expressions, how they talk about their work, and their behavior on the job.

3

WHAT MAKES ENGAGEMENT DIFFERENT FROM OTHER CONCEPTS?

Some researchers have referred to engagement as an attitude (e.g., Dalal, Baysinger, Brummel, & LeBreton, 2012; S. Fine, Horowitz, Weigler, & Basis, 2010; Newman & Harrison, 2008). An attitude is a tendency to evaluate a psychological object's attributes, typically resulting in value-laden labels such as pleasant/unpleasant, good/bad, or likable/dislikable (Ajzen, 2001; Eagly & Chaiken, 1998, 2007). A specific attitude is generally part of an associative network, wherein beliefs, feelings, and thoughts are connected within and between attitudes; the activation of one attitude can spark an associated attitude (Eagly & Chaiken, 2007). Attitudes do not exist until an individual perceives an object, after which an initial evaluation occurs and leaves mental residue to be reactivated on a second encounter. The attitude is separate from its behavioral expression (Eagly & Chaiken, 2007). In contrast, engagement is a multidimensional construct comprising moment-to-moment psychophysiological arousal, absorption, focus, mindfulness or psychological presence, self-expression, self-employment, and intrinsic motivation (Kahn, 1990; Schaufeli, Salanova, González-Romá, & Bakker, 2002). When employees become engaged, they generate positive emotions about their work experience (Kahn, 1990), and they may form attitudes about work.

Distinguishing whether engagement is or is not an attitude is both a theoretical and an empirical question. To understand a construct, it often helps to be clear on what the construct is and is not, and to what it is related or not related; in other words, it helps to map out the construct's nomological network (Cronbach & Meehl, 1955). A nomological network is the pattern of relationships between the focal construct and other constructs, and information about how those constructs are or are not related to one another; this information can be in the form of theories or statistical data, such as correlations (Cronbach & Meehl, 1955).

DOI: 10.4324/9781003171133-4

As a sequel to Chapter 2, which explains what engagement is, this chapter focuses on what engagement is *not*, with the intent of distinguishing engagement from other potentially similar concepts (see also Schohat & Vigoda-Gadot, 2010, for another type of comparison to commitment, job involvement, and citizenship behavior). Constructs considered like employee engagement include job performance and organizational citizenship behavior, job involvement, job satisfaction, and organizational commitment (Newman & Harrison, 2008). Although similar, evidence suggests engagement is distinct from these concepts (see Hallberg & Schaufeli, 2006; Rich, LePine, & Crawford, 2010; Saks, 2006). I also include how engagement is similar to but different from intrinsic motivation, flow, and happiness.

What Engagement Is Not

Job Performance Behaviors

The study of job performance has a long history and large research domain; thus, I focus the review here explicitly on what makes job performance similar to or different from employee engagement, as opposed to a review of the entire job performance literature.

Job performance is what people do on the job toward completing tasks assigned by the organization or tasks that contribute to achieving organizational goals; job performance is what an employee is actually hired to do (J. Campbell, McHenry, & Wise, 1990). Job performance may be considered most closely tied to people's behavior that contributes value to the organization (i.e., Motowidlo, 2003), their readiness to do the job (e.g., military personnel, police, or firefighters), or the result of on-the-job behavior (e.g., when the job is primarily cognitive, such as analyst or strategist; Murphy, 1989). Another view is to consider job performance as a process or outcome, whereby *process* refers to the actions or behaviors taken to complete work tasks and *outcome* refers to the product or result of actions taken (Roe, 1999).

The job performance construct has been delineated into several dimensions or factors, with some common to most, if not all jobs, and other dimensions specifically aimed at certain types of jobs. For example, J. Campbell's (1990) model of job performance comprises eight dimensions and was derived from a study of U.S. Army personnel. In contrast, Murphy's (1994) model of job performance comprises four dimensions and was derived from a study of U.S. Navy personnel. Although both are based on military personnel, the models are quite different. For example, Campbell's model has eight different dimensions, whereas Murphy's model has only four. The eight levels of Campbell's model were intended to describe the top of the hierarchy of all jobs listed in the *Dictionary of Occupational Titles* (1991) and focus primarily on positive or productive job performance. In contrast, Murphy's model covers a large and diverse set of jobs, is meant to be both broad and general, and includes inconvenient job performance-reducing behaviors as well as destructive, counterproductive performance behaviors. Dimensions of the models include types of specific tasks employees perform or the technical aspects of the job (e.g., welding, typing, driving, surgery, communication); employees' management of themselves on the job (e.g., whether acting within safety guidelines or carelessly, emotion regulation); and how employees interact with others (e.g., interpersonally, through others).

Another classification system for the performance domain includes *task* versus *contextual* performance (Borman & Motowidlo, 1997). Task performance refers to behaviors considered part of the selection and performance management system, which transform raw materials into finished products of value to the organization (e.g., actual production, selling, teaching, banking). Contextual performance includes activities ignored within the selection system, but facilitate the production of organizational goods, yet do not in and of themselves result in the final goods (e.g., planning, coordinating, social support). Contextual performance describes performance in terms of the support the expressed behaviors provide toward the functioning of the organization, more so than in terms of the type or the quality of behavior displayed (e.g., whether it is discretionary).

A similar classification to the task versus contextual performance is one that divides job performance into *in-role* performance and *extra-role* performance, and considered within the organizational citizenship behavior domain (e.g., Bateman & Organ, 1983; Katz, 1964; Motowidlo & van Scotter, 1994; O'Reilly & Chatman, 1986; Organ, 1988; Williams & Anderson, 1991). In-role job performance refers to prescribed behaviors, such as completing assigned tasks and attending required events or meetings, as outlined in a formal job description (when that exists; not all jobs or organizations provide job descriptions). In-role job performance is the work expected of an employee within a given work role. In contrast, extra-role behavior is described as contributing to the effective functioning of the organization and may or may not be formally expected of employees or recognized within the reward system. Organizational citizenship behavior's definition has morphed over time, from being "individual behavior that is discretionary, not directly or explicitly recognized by the formal reward system, and that in the aggregate promotes the effective functioning of the organization" (Organ, 1988, p. 4) to being synonymous with contextual performance (Organ, 1997). Many still use the in-role versus extra-role categorization (e.g., Salanova, Lorente, Chambel, & Martínez, 2011; Sosik, Juzbasich, & Chun, 2011; Tremblay, Cloutier, Simard, Chênevert, & Vandenberghe, 2010; Walumbwa, Morrison, & Christensen, 2012).

The most defining characteristic of job and/or task performance and citizenship behaviors that distinguishes performance from employee engagement is that performance is about behaviors or the results of behaviors, whereas engagement is about how one feels about or experiences the job (Kahn, 1990; Saks, 2006; Schaufeli, Salanova et al., 2002). Employee engagement is not a behavior per se, but rather a state of mind manifested in behavior. In direct contrast to this supposition regarding engagement as a state and separate from performance is Macey and Schneider's (2008) proposal. Recall from Chapter 2 that I noted these authors suggested engagement is a process whereby *state engagement* leads to *behavioral engagement*, which they define as the combination of extra-role performance and organizational citizenship behavior. However, empirical evidence along with criticism about behavioral engagement being sometimes considered engagement and sometimes not (depending on the situation and tasks), and giving a new label to an old concept (see Griffin, Parker, & Neal, 2008; Newman & Harrison, 2008), has led the current engagement scholarly conversation away from engagement incorporating or equating with performance.

Job Performance's Relationship to Engagement

Empirical studies provide evidence of the distinctiveness of engagement from job performance. For example, Rich et al. (2010) showed that job engagement, as assessed using their scale (Job Engagement Scale [JES]) designed to measure Kahn's (1990) conceptualization of engagement, is distinct from task performance (supervisory rated using Williams & Anderson's [1991] measure) and organizational citizenship behaviors (as assessed using K. Lee & Allen's [2002] scale). Distinctiveness was demonstrated using confirmatory factor analysis, which, put simply, is a statistical technique for verifying that scale items are interpreted as grouping together consistent with the construct's predetermined conceptualization. Thus, taking Kahn's three-dimensional conceptualization of engagement, the confirmatory factor analysis uses participants' responses on the JES and determines/shows using inter-item correlations whether the items group together as proposed for measuring those three factors. In Rich et al.'s study, the authors included responses to items measuring task performance and citizenship behaviors to show the items from those measures would correlate most strongly with each other as opposed to with the JES items. Rich et al.'s results confirmed the items all measured their respective constructs, and that job engagement correlated with performance and with citizenship behavior at .35 each. In my own research (Byrne, Peters, & Weston, 2016), I also found confirmatory factor analysis support for the uniqueness of employee engagement. I used the JES and Schaufeli, Martínez, Marques Pinto, Salanova, and Bakker's (2002) Utrecht Work Engagement Scale (UWES, which assesses Schaufeli et al.'s definition) long form (17 items versus the short 3- or 9-item versions) to measure engagement, and Van Scotter, Motowidlo, and Cross's (2000) measure to assess contextual performance. The correlation between the UWES-17 and performance was .59, and .47 between the JES and performance.

In studies not reporting confirmatory factor analyses results, correlations between engagement and job performance are consistent with those that do. For example, in their meta-analysis, Christian, Garza, and Slaughter (2011) demonstrated the uniqueness of engagement from task performance and contextual performance, with correlations of .36 and .38, respectively. Dalal and colleagues (2012) examined the relative weights contribution of various job attitudes including job satisfaction, job involvement, and organizational commitment, and engagement for explaining the variance in task performance. Relative weights analysis, or relative importance analysis, evaluates the proportional contribution of each predictor (taking correlations into consideration) to the overall variance explained by the regression model, thus providing a relative ordering of the importance of each predictor in predicting the outcome or focal construct, in this case performance (Azen & Budescu, 2003; J. Johnson & LeBreton, 2004; LeBreton et al., 2007). Dalal et al. (2012) found that satisfaction, involvement, and engagement contributed relatively equal amounts of explained variance in performance. Stated another way, respondents' variability in performance ratings can be equally determined by their levels of job satisfaction, job involvement, and engagement. Job satisfaction explained 16%, engagement 15%, job involvement 11%, and organizational commitment 4% of the variance in task performance. Dalal et al.'s results suggest these constructs are not redundant with task performance, indicating some distinctiveness. These authors further reported a correlation of .23 between task performance and employee engagement. Halbesleben, Wheeler, and Shanine (2013) found engagement, as assessed using Schaufeli et al.'s (2002) UWES-9, was correlated with Williams and Anderson's (1991) in-role performance measure between .21 and .26, and with citizenship behaviors directed at the organization and individuals between .23 and .42, across three samples and both self- and other-rated performance behaviors.

Unrelated to demonstrating its uniqueness from job performance, researchers have shown the performance–engagement relationship appears consistent across rater sources, such that engagement is similarly related to self-rated performance (r^1 = .28), coworker-rated performance (r = .27), and supervisor-rated job performance (r = .32), as assessed using Williams and Anderson's (1991) task performance measure (Halbesleben & Wheeler, 2008). Thus, regardless of who provides the performance rating within a study, the correlation between job performance and engagement tends to be relatively low (the two constructs may not be proximally related) and about the same.

---

1 r is the statistical symbol for the correlation coefficient of a sample.

In summary, researchers have demonstrated engagement's distinctiveness from job performance in its various forms, including task and contextual or citizenship performance, and provided evidence engagement and performance are positively related. Correlations between engagement and the various forms of performance behaviors tend to be low to moderate (see Table 3.1 for a few studies reporting relationships between various forms of performance and engagement). The overall implication of all these study findings is that engagement is a different concept from performance and is positively correlated with performance. For practitioners, this may not be surprising news; many consulting firms report highly engaged workers are high performers. We cannot say, however, whether performance leads to high engagement or vice versa.

TABLE 3.1 Relationship Between Job Performance and Engagement

Study (Alphabetical Order)	Construct	Correlation With Engagement
Byrne et al. (2016)	Self-rated contextual performance	.59 (UWES)
		.47 (JES)
Christian et al. (2011) (corrected in Christian et al., 2014)	Task performance	.39
	Contextual performance	.43
Dalal et al. (2012)	Self-rated task performance	.23 (engagement measured using a composite based on a few different measures of engagement)
Halbesleben and Wheeler (2008)	Self-rated in-role job performance	.28
	Coworker-rated in-role job performance	.27
	Supervisor-rated in-role job performance	.32
Halbesleben et al. (2013)	In-role job performance	.21 to .26
	Citizenship behavior	.23 to .42
Jiang and Shen (2020)	Self-rated contextual performance	.56
Mackay, Allen, and Landis (2017)	Contextual performance	.32
Parke, Weinhardt, Brodsky, Tangirala, and DeVoe (2018)	Self-rated in-role performance	.58
Rich et al. (2010)	Job performance	.35
	Citizenship behavior	.35
Yuan, Ye, and Zhong (2021)	Supervisor-rated task performance	.22

Job Involvement

In practice, engagement and job involvement have sometimes been considered the same. However, they are distinct constructs. Job involvement refers to a stable cognitive judgment about how central work is to one's life and identity (Lawler & Hall, 1970). Originally defined as the "internalization of values about the goodness of work or the importance of work in the worth of the person" (Lodahl & Kejner, 1965, p. 24), job involvement refers to the centrality of work in a person's life, the importance of work, and the connection of work to one's core self-image. Job involvement is the "degree to which one is cognitively preoccupied with, engaged in, and concerned with one's present job" (Paullay, Alliger, & Stone-Romero, 1994, p. 225) or "a cognitive or belief state of psychological identification" (Kanungo, 1982, p. 342). Furthermore, this cognitive identification depends on individuals' personal needs and the potential of the job to meet those needs (Kanungo, 1982). Job involvement is essentially about how one sees oneself with regard to the job and is a cognitive judgment of whether the job can satisfy one's needs (Kanungo, 1982). According to a meta-analysis by S. B. Brown (1996), this conceptualization of job involvement appears to be the most used and the clearest. Rabinowitz and Hall (1977) suggested job involvement, although relatively stable, increases with success on the job; hence, greater achievement leads to more job involvement. Lastly, employees with high intrinsic motivation report high levels of job involvement (C. Chen & Chiu, 2009; Lambert, 1991). Hackman and Lawler (1971) similarly suggested job involvement leads to internal motivation.

Job Involvement's Relationship to Engagement

Employees must be motivated to experience job involvement. Indeed, motivation and job involvement are correlated with one another ($r = .55$; Brown & Leigh, 1996), but Brown suggested "motivation is likely both an antecedent and consequence of job involvement" (p. 238). Hallberg and Schaufeli (2006), and Rich and colleagues (2010), demonstrated using confirmatory factor analyses that job involvement and employee engagement are distinct constructs. These authors reported correlations of .35 and .47 between job involvement and engagement, respectively. Other researchers have reported similar correlations. For example, using Schaufeli et al.'s (2002) UWES, Kühnel, Sonnentag, and Westman (2009) found correlations of .32 and .30 with job involvement, and Steele et al. (2012) reported a correlation of .54 using the same scale for engagement. Likewise, using a composite of Schaufeli et al.'s work engagement scale and May, Gilson, and Harter's (2004) engagement measure, Dalal et al. (2012) reported correlations of .57 between engagement and job involvement. Additionally, as previously noted, Dalal and colleagues conducted a relative weights analysis to determine the relative importance of several job attitudes on task performance. They reported that employee engagement explained more variance in task performance than did job involvement (15% vs. 11%, respectively), and even more in citizenship behaviors than did task performance (25% engagement vs. 6% job involvement).

In sum, correlations between engagement and job involvement, regardless of measure used, tend to be moderate (see Table 3.2). The overall implication of research findings is that engagement and job involvement are similar but different concepts. One can experience both engagement and job involvement, and the experience will be qualitatively different. Engagement includes emotional and physical arousal components, whereas job involvement is primarily a cognitive judgment about work.

Job Satisfaction

Like job performance, job satisfaction has a long and rich history in the organizational sciences; therefore, I focus this review only on literature that sheds light on how job satisfaction is related to and different from employee engagement. Engaged employees are satisfied with their jobs, partly because they derive meaning and accomplishment from the work (Fairhurst & May, 2006; Fairlie, 2011; Guion & Landy, 1972; May et al., 2004), which leads to a positive evaluation of work. Although early views of job satisfaction were primarily focused on understanding performance (Hoppock, 1935; Organ, 1977; Roethlisberger & Dickson, 1939), the definition of job satisfaction evolved into an overall positive emotional evaluation resulting from the appraisal of one's job (Brooke, Russell, & Price, 1988; Locke, 1976; Mowday, Steers, &

TABLE 3.2 Relationship Between Job Involvement and Engagement

Study (Alphabetical Order)	*Correlation of Job Involvement With Engagement*
Dalal et al. (2012)	.57
Eldor, Harpaz, and Westman (2020)	.37
Hallberg and Schaufeli (2006)	.35
Kühnel et al. (2009)	.30 and .32
Mackay et al. (2017)	.60
Rich et al. (2010)	.47
Scrima, Lorito, Parry, and Falgares (2014)	.42 (vigor) .29 (dedication) .41 (absorption)
Shuck, Osam, Zigarmi, and Nimon (2017)	.53 (UWES-9) .46 (JES)
Steele et al. (2012)	.54

Porter, 1979). Job satisfaction has been described as comprising multiple facets or dimensions, such as satisfaction with pay, coworkers, supervisor, and the work itself (Dunham, Smith, & Blackburn, 1977; Locke, Smith, Kendall, Hulin, & Miller, 1964). Another characterization of job satisfaction is as a multidimensional response to the job that includes cognitive, affective, and behavioral components (Hulin & Judge, 2003), giving it a conceptual link to employee engagement (Kahn, 1990). Considered an evaluation held by a single individual, as opposed to an attitude experienced or determined by a group (Locke, 1976), job satisfaction is distinguishable from performance and citizenship behaviors, although the constructs are related with correlations between .20 and .40 (Bateman & Organ, 1983; Dalal et al., 2012; Judge, Thoresen, Bono, & Patton, 2001; LePine, Erez, & Johnson, 2002; Organ & Ryan, 1995; Schleicher, Watt, & Greguras, 2004).

Job Satisfaction's Relationship to Engagement

Several engagement studies include job satisfaction among the assessed job attitudes. For example, Saks (2006) examined job satisfaction, organizational commitment, and intention to quit as outcomes of engagement. Saks proposed employees direct their engagement toward their jobs and/or the organization in exchange for job characteristics or global organizational resources. Using his own measures of engagement to represent this targeted exchange, Saks reported a positive moderate correlation of .52 between job satisfaction and job engagement, and .57 between job satisfaction and organization engagement. Using the UWES, Mauno, Kinnunen, Mäkikangas, and Nätti (2005) reported a positive moderate correlation of .50 between job satisfaction and engagement. Likewise, Vecina, Chacón, Sueiro, and Barrón (2012) reported a correlation of .60 between the UWES and task satisfaction.

Using several different measures of engagement (e.g., UWES, JES, job and organization engagement, May et al.'s, 2004 scale; see Chapter 6 for details) in their meta-analysis, Christian et al. (2011) reported a moderate correlation between engagement and job satisfaction of .53. Similarly, Dalal et al. (2012) created a composite measure of engagement drawing from several existing measures (e.g., UWES, job engagement, May et al.'s, 2004 scale) and reported a correlation between job satisfaction and engagement at .69.

Other studies reporting similar correlations include Alarcon and Lyons (2011), with a reported correlation of .56 to .73. Alarcon and Lyons made an additional contribution to the study of engagement and job satisfaction; they compared a factor model wherein engagement subsumed job satisfaction to a model in which engagement covaried with satisfaction (not subsumed under engagement). The authors found the model with engagement and satisfaction as separate parallel factors (i.e., covaried) fit the data best. Their findings provide direct evidence for engagement's distinctiveness from job satisfaction. Lastly, in one of my own field studies (Byrne, Peters, Rechlin, Smith, & Kedharnath, 2013), confirmatory factor analysis corroborated the distinctiveness of engagement (assessed using Rich et al.'s [2010] measure) from job satisfaction assessed using Warr, Cook, and Wall's (1979) multidimensional measure; the correlation between the two measures was .52.

Thus, the correlations between job and task satisfaction, and engagement tend to be moderate to high (see Table 3.3 for a sampling of studies examining engagement and job satisfaction). The implication of the cumulative findings noted is that engagement is a different concept from job satisfaction, though there is some overlap. In particular, job satisfaction is an emotionally laden concept, and engagement also includes an affective component. Thus, both constructs provide a sense of positive evaluation or experience of work.

Organizational Commitment

Several consulting websites refer to engagement as a form of commitment to the organization. Organizational commitment is an affective attachment to, an identification with, and an involvement in a particular organization (Mowday et al., 1979). Often referred to as *affective commitment* or simply *commitment*, it is typically characterized by an employee's internalization of the organization's goals and values. Employees demonstrate a strong desire to remain a member of the organization, which results in a willingness to exert extensive energy on behalf of the organization. D. Harrison, Newman, and Roth (2006) suggested organizational commitment is an attitude (an evaluation or appraisal) with a specific target (e.g., supervisor, organization) but not tied to a specific action. Researchers have also defined commitment as an attitudinal reaction to the work environment and leadership (Ashforth & Mael, 1989). People can commit

TABLE 3.3 Relationship Between Job Satisfaction and Engagement

Study (Alphabetical Order)	Construct	Correlation With Engagement
Alarcon and Lyons (2011)	Job satisfaction	.56 to .73
Byrne et al. (2013)	Job satisfaction	.52
Christian et al. (2011)	Job satisfaction	.53
Dalal et al. (2012)	Job satisfaction	.69
Eldor et al. (2020)	Job satisfaction	.55
Mackay et al. (2017)	Job satisfaction	.44
Mauno et al. (2005)	Job satisfaction	.50
Saks (2006)	Job satisfaction	.52 (job engagement)
		.57 (organization engagement)
Shuck et al. (2017)	Job satisfaction	.75 (UWES)
		.69 (JES)
Vecina et al. (2012)	Task satisfaction	.60

or attach to different foci (T. Becker, 1992), such as their team, supervisor, organization, career (e.g., Okurame, 2012), or work in general, and various studies show the foci of commitment matter (e.g., Chan, Snape, & Redman, 2011; Morin et al., 2011; Tsoumbris & Xenikou, 2010; Vandenberghe, Bentein, & Stinglhamber, 2004; Veurink & Fischer, 2011).

Other scholars, however, have suggested commitment is more than just an attitude, that it is a psychological state with behavioral linkages (Meyer & Allen, 1991). Scholars endorsing this perspective further suggest commitment has three components: affective, continuance, and normative (N. Allen & Meyer, 1990; Meyer & Allen, 1991). *Affective commitment* refers to an attachment to a particular focus (usually the organization), where the emphasis is on feeling a sense of membership and desire to remain a member. This is the form of commitment most researchers use in their studies and when referring to organizational commitment or just commitment in general. Organizational affective commitment is sometimes confused with organizational identification, possibly due to the overlap in definitions and the constructs' moderate to high correlation with each other (r = .55 to .78 in Harris & Cameron, 2005; r = .67 in Van Knippenberg & Sleebos, 2006). Organizational identification refers to a cognitive categorization process whereby employees develop a sense of self-concept or oneness with the organization. Identification relies on social identity theory (Tajfel, 1978; Tajfel & Turner, 1979), which states people categorize themselves into social groups based on their similarity to the group and often define themselves by the characteristics of the group. Perhaps the most definitive explanation of how commitment and identification differ is that commitment is an affective reaction exchanged as part of the work contract, whereas identification is about one's self-concept and depends on the saliency of the leader and one's interactions (N. Allen & Meyer, 1990; van Knippenberg & Sleebos, 2006). Although conceptually and empirically closely related, the two have been supported as distinct constructs (e.g., Mael & Tetrick, 1992). Commitment has also been likened to job satisfaction, but researchers have similarly shown these two constructs to be distinct (Brooke et al., 1988; Mowday et al., 1979). I list several studies reporting correlations between engagement and affective commitment in Table 3.4.

Continuance commitment is about staying with the organization out of a recognition the cost of leaving is not in one's favor. Thus, the perceived cost of staying versus leaving (i.e., cost–benefit ratio) drives one's desire to remain a member of the organization. This formative calculation is attributed to Becker's (1960) side-bets theory, which says a person makes a series of judgments that ultimately determine a final decision, which is either consistent with or contradictory to other decisions and actions this person takes. A brief scenario from Becker makes the theory clearer. A few months after Rodriguez accepts a job offer that he believes advances his career, he is offered another that is truly far superior to the one he just accepted. Although very tempted to take the new offer, he realizes that, on the side, he bet his reputation for trustworthiness and integrity on not moving again for a respectable amount of time, and therefore, he is compelled to turn down the superior job. In Rodriguez's case, the side bet is implied: general norms of society are that when you take a job, you stay with it for a preliminary period. Likewise, some organizations have similar norms about accepting various positions (e.g., when you take an overseas assignment, you are expected to stay in that role for a few years to recoup the hiring costs, such as shipping you overseas, job and culture ramp-up). Similarly, the "golden handcuff" rule is that by staying with the organization for X number of years, you become eligible for a lucrative financial (hence, the word *golden*) leave package (e.g., stock, bonuses based on tenure, money paid into retirement accounts) that grows each year you remain beyond the eligibility date. However, if you leave the organization before X number of years are up, you lose the amazing package; thus, these golden handcuffs keep you in place because they are too good to let go of, and the side bet is that if you leave, you release your golden handcuffs. Thus, the side bet or trade-off might be made for you by the norms of the situation. Side bets are not necessarily financial; they can include other valuable intangibles such as seniority (along with its associated power), social networks (all your friends and power within the network), comfort with familiarity, or other intangible benefits (e.g., status). Clearly, the example using Rodriguez's job situation draws on norms that may no longer exist or are fitting only for a few industries and not others. Important in Becker's theory is the recognition of the cost of discontinuing the path one has already pursued, because the theory is really about consistency of actions. Without this recognition, Becker suggests there is no commitment. After an extensive search through various online databases, I found only two studies incorporating both engagement and continuance commitment. Cesário and Chambel (2017) used "a questionnaire based on the . . . UWES" (p. 154) and reported a correlation of −.11 *ns* with continuance commitment. Meyer, Stanley, and Parfyonova (2012) used the UWES and found a correlation of .07 *ns*.

Normative commitment is the third component of organizational commitment identified by Meyer and Allen (1991). This form of commitment, based on personal norms, refers to a sense of obligation to remain a member of the organization. Applied to the preceding example, Rodriguez might refuse the superior job offer because he feels it is morally wrong to take a job and then immediately leave it for another one. Normative commitment may be more evident in religiously oriented organizations or nonprofit organizations, for example, in which people join and stay because they feel obligated to those whom the organization serves (e.g., a mental health facility or food bank), or they were helped by the organization at one time and they feel a need to reciprocate. Normative commitment is more about personal norms, values, and sense of obligation than about emotional connection (e.g., with affective commitment) or societal or external ties (e.g., with continuance commitment;

Meyer & Allen, 1991). Across all my searches of articles, I found only four studies reporting correlations between engagement and normative commitment. These included Cesário and Chambel (2017) reporting a correlation of .43 with engagement assessed using the UWES. Also using the UWES, Lee, Wang, and Liu (2017) reported their correlation at .60, and Meyer et al. (2012) reported a correlation of .50. In contrast, Gillet et al. (2020) used the JES and reported a correlation of .24.

Meyer, Gagné, and Parfyonova (2010) proposed that engagement and the three-component model of commitment (affective, normative, continuance) can be integrated using self-determination theory (Deci & Ryan, 1985). They created a continuum from disengagement (uncommitted, amotivation – absence of goal-directed activity), to contingent engagement (continuance and/or normative commitment, extrinsic motivation), to full engagement (affective and/or normative commitment, intrinsic motivation). Meyer et al. described how the disengaged, contingent, or fully engaged worker appears/behaves in terms of varying commitment levels. For example, they suggested a fully engaged worker would likely have strong affective commitment and be intrinsically motivated. In a field study, Meyer et al. (2012) examined the commitment/engagement continuum, creating six profiles/groups of individuals based on varying combination levels of the three forms of commitment. For example, the *uncommitted* group comprised respondents with the lowest average scores on all three forms of commitment. In contrast, the *fully committed* group comprised respondents with the highest average scores on all three forms of commitment. The *continuance commitment dominant* group had the highest average scores on continuance commitment and the second lowest average scores on affective and normative commitment. The authors' results specific to engagement indicated significant differences in engagement ratings between the groups. For instance, individuals in the continuance commitment dominant group reported significantly lower mean engagement scores ($M = 3.40$) than those in the fully committed group ($M = 5.00$). The integrated framework provides a unique approach to understanding how employees' levels and types of commitment combine to affect their subsequent attitudes and behaviors.

Commitment's Relationship to Engagement

Most of the research examining the relationship between engagement and organizational commitment hypothesizes engagement as a predictor of commitment (i.e., Demerouti, Bakker, de Jonge, Janssen, & Schaufeli, 2001; Hallberg & Schaufeli, 2006; Hakanen, Schaufeli, & Ahola, 2008; Richardsen, Burke, & Martinussen, 2006; Saks, 2006). Additionally, researchers rarely indicate which form of organizational commitment they study (unless more than one form is studied); however, it is usually affective commitment. When other forms of commitment are studied, they are usually explicitly called out (i.e., normative).

A number of studies using the UWES support an association between organizational commitment; however, some researchers only assessed vigor ($r = .42$) and dedication ($r = .47$; Hakanen, Bakker, & Schaufeli, 2006), leaving out absorption. Also using the vigor and dedication scales only of the UWES, Hakanen, Perhoniemi, and Toppinen-Tanner (2008) found engagement at Time 1 was related to commitment measured 3 years later ($\beta^2 = .23$). Richardsen et al. (2006) found organizational commitment was positively correlated with engagement ($r = .55$). Similarly, Hallberg and Schaufeli (2006) reported a correlation of .46, where they assessed engagement using all three dimensions of the UWES. Likewise, a number of other studies incorporating the full UWES show correlations of .62, .61, .57, and .66, respectively (Brunetto et al., 2012; De Beer, Rothmann, & Pienaar, 2012; Kanste, 2011; Vecina et al., 2012). Using vigor, dedication, and absorption as separate scales (i.e., not combined to form a single engagement score), Demerouti and colleagues (2001) reported correlations of .49, .59, and .45, respectively. Scrima et al. (2014) used an Italian version of the three scales of the UWES and reported somewhat lower correlations with affective commitment than all other studies using the UWES (see Table 3.4). In contrast, Aboramadan and Dahleez (2020), also using Italian translations of the UWES and commitment, reported a correlation of .79 between engagement and commitment. I specifically point out these studies using the UWES because researchers have criticized the overlap of items on the UWES with commitment, in particular the dedication scale (see Newman & Harrison, 2008). While there is overlap, only one of the studies reported here included a correlation that by T. Brown's (2006) or Kline's (2005) standards would be a little too high for comfort (i.e., Aboramadan & Dahleez, 2020).

Using his own conceptualizations of engagement, Saks (2006) found correlations of .53 and .69 between organizational commitment and job engagement and organization engagement, respectively. Using a composite measure for engagement as noted previously, Dalal et al. (2012) reported similar results, with engagement and organizational commitment correlating at .60. Christian et al. (2011) reported a moderate correlation between engagement and organizational commitment ($r = .59$) in their meta-analysis.

In summary, for the most part, correlations between engagement and commitment range from moderate to high (see Table 3.4). The implications of all these study findings is that although engagement and affective commitment have quite a bit of overlap, they are distinct constructs. The experience of affective commitment is mostly an emotional one, whereas engagement includes additional components of cognition and physiological arousal/energy.

---

2 The Greek letter beta, when capitalized as it appears here, represents a standardized regression coefficient.

TABLE 3.4 Relationship Between Organizational Commitment and Engagement

Study (Alphabetical Order)	Correlation of Organizational Commitment* With Engagement
Brunetto, Teo, Shacklock, and Farr-Wharton (2012)	.62
Byrne, Peters, and Drake (2014), Sample 2	.51 (JES) .66 (UWES-17) .40 (Saks's [2006] org engagement scale) .75 (Saks's [2006] job engagement scale)
Byrne et al. (2014), Sample 3	.37 (JES) .40 (UWES-17) .42 (Saks's [2006] org engagement scale) .30 (Saks's [2006] job engagement scale)
Cesário and Chambel (2017)	.70 (affective commitment) .43 (normative commitment) −.11 *ns* (continuance commitment)
Christian et al. (2011)	.59
Dalal et al. (2012)	.60
De Beer et al. (2012)	.61
Demerouti, Bakker, de Jonge, Janssen, and Schaufeli (2001)	.49 (vigor) .59 (dedication) .45 (absorption)
Gillet, Morin, Jeoffrion, and Fouquereau (2020) [using JES to measure engagement]	.42 (affective commitment) .24 (normative commitment)
Hakanen et al. (2006)	.42 (vigor) .47 (dedication)
Hakanen et al. (2008)	.23 (vigor and dedication)
Hallberg and Schaufeli (2006)	.46
Kanste (2011)	.57
Lee et al. (2017)	.60 (normative commitment)
Mackay et al. (2017)	.54
Meyer et al. (2012)	.56 (affective commitment) .50 (normative commitment) .07 *ns* (continuance commitment)
Richardsen et al. (2006)	.55
Saks (2006)	.53 (job engagement) .69 (organizational engagement)
Scrima et al. (2014)	.26 (vigor) .53 (dedication) .34 (absorption)
Shuck et al. (2017)	.72 (UWES-9) .62 (JES)
Vecina et al. (2012)	.66

Note: ns = not significant.

* Affective commitment, unless specified otherwise.

Intrinsic Motivation

Intrinsic motivation refers to a drive or push instigated and propelled by interest and spontaneous enjoyment with and from an activity (Porter & Lawler, 1968). It is self-fulfilling in that the interest and satisfaction with the activity is internally rewarding, encouraging more of the same activity. Intrinsic motivation is considered a biological need for moderate arousal (Berlyne, 1966), an innate need to demonstrate mastery and competence (e.g., White, 1959), a need for personal control and self-determination (e.g., Deci, 1975), or a state wherein one does an activity for its own sake (Rheinberg, 2008). Intrinsic motivation has also been characterized as a drive that has no specific goal, achieves optimal arousal and competence, and is enjoyable (see Thierry, 1990). Very simply, intrinsic motivation refers to motivation derived from internal rewards or satisfaction, and is typically contrasted with extrinsic motivation, derived from an external reward or reinforcement (Thierry, 1990). A contrast between intrinsic versus extrinsic motivation was recently demonstrated using functional magnetic resonance imaging. W. Lee, Reeve, Xue, and Xiong (2012) showed a portion of the brain (the insular cortex) related to feelings or emotions, in particular the satisfaction of needs, determines intrinsically motivated actions. By comparison, extrinsically motivated or incentive-based actions caused excitation in the right posterior cingulate cortex, which is associated with value assessment and processing learned reinforcements. The implication of Lee and colleagues' findings is that intrinsic motivation has a neurological basis. Thus, intrinsic motivation is not learned or tied to external incentives, which has implications for engagement, as researchers suggest engagement may subsume intrinsic motivation.

Unlike intrinsic motivation, engagement is not a drive to continue doing something/anything purely out of enjoyment and the reinforced enjoyment to continue. Employee engagement is about being driven across multiple platforms of the self toward goal achievement that just happens to be intrinsically rewarded. Engagement refers to employees making "choices about how much of their real selves they would bring into and use to inform their role performances" (Kahn & Fellows, 2013, p. 105).

Intrinsic Motivation's Relationship to Engagement

Rich et al.'s (2010) confirmatory factor analyses and structural equation modeling results show intrinsic motivation and engagement (assessed using the JES) are only low to moderately correlated ($r = .35$), and modeled as parallel constructs (as opposed to one predicting the other). When considered predictors of task performance, only engagement significantly related to task performance and organizational citizenship behavior; intrinsic motivation was not related to either. Tziner, Shkoler, and Bat Zur (2019) reported a higher correlation of

.59 when using the UWES to assess engagement. Of note, Tziner et al. found engagement and extrinsic motivation highly correlated at .74. Also using the UWES, Ilies, Liu, Liu, and Zheng (2017), and Ghosh, Sekiguchi, and Fujimoto (2020) reported correlations of .52 and .46, respectively, with intrinsic motivation. Lastly, Putra, Cho, and Liu (2017) found correlations of .61, .73, and .47 between intrinsic motivation and vigor, dedication, and absorption, respectively. They also reported correlations of .29, .39, and .29 with extrinsic motivation and vigor, dedication, and absorption, respectively.

Overall, correlations between engagement and intrinsic motivation tend to be high, and higher when using the UWES than the JES. Given that engagement has consistently been defined and explained as a form of motivation, it is not surprising to see high correlations between the constructs.

Flow

Csikszentmihalyi and Rathunde (1993) described flow as "the subjective state that people report when they are completely involved in something to the point of forgetting time, fatigue, and everything else but the activity itself" (p. 59). When one experiences flow, all attention is directed to the activity such that distractions or other random thoughts are ignored (Csikszentmihalyi & Kleiber, 1991). Flow propels action for the sake of enjoyment and the reward of the action, involves little or no conscious effort, includes an element of loss of self-consciousness, and can occur with any activity (Csikszentmihalyi, 1997; Csikszentmihalyi & Rathunde, 1993). However, it rarely occurs in everyday life (Csikszentmihalyi & Rathunde, 1993). Thus, like engagement, flow subsumes intrinsic motivation but is bigger than just intrinsic motivation alone.

Although employee engagement shares some conceptual space with flow, it is not the same as flow. The state of optimal cognitive processing, which is characteristic of engagement, resembles flow (Csikszentmihalyi, 1996); however, engagement is different from flow in that employees may be in an engaged state and perceive the activity as worth doing because it creates meaning and moves them closer to goal attainment, as opposed to doing the job or task for its own sake as with flow (Nakamura & Csikszentmihalyi, 2002). Also, unlike flow, there is no precondition of possessing a skill to become engaged. Flow requires "a balance between perceived challenges and perceived skills" (Csikszentmihalyi, Abuhamdeh, & Nakamura, 2005, p. 601). People who are learning but have not yet acquired a new skill can enter a state of engagement.

Flow's Relationship to Engagement

Burke (2010) reported a positive relationship between measures of engagement and flow, however, the article provides no data; thus, no statistical information can be confirmed or relayed here. Weintraub, Cassell, and DePatie (2021) recently examined the relationship between flow and engagement (measured using the JES) as part of a goal-setting intervention study. They conducted a 5-day experience sampling study to see if their goal-setting intervention affected participants' reported levels of flow, and whether flow subsequently affected employees' engagement levels. They found a strong relationship ($r = .72$) between flow and engagement. Using the UWES, Mesurado, Richaud, and Mateo (2016) reported correlations for their Argentinean participants of .55, .51, and .45 with vigor, dedication, and absorption, respectively, and .65, .59, and .54, respectively, for their Filipino participants.

Happiness

During my visit to Saratov, Russia (on the Volga River, not far from the Kazakhstan and Ukraine borders) in 2012 and 2013, I asked what employee engagement is. My hosts had never heard of the concept. After I described a bit about it, in the spirit of trying to be helpful, they suggested that perhaps it was the same as happiness. Engaged employees may display happiness at various times during work; however, engagement and happiness are different constructs. First, happiness is considered an affective construct without a cognitive component (A. Campbell, 1976). That is, happiness is experienced without first going through an intellectual process of evaluating the current state to either the past or an ideal state, like one does in forming a job attitude (e.g., job satisfaction; A. Campbell, 1976). Happiness is defined as a brief and intense emotional reaction to a specific event (Clore, Schwarz, & Conway, 1994; Ekman, 1992; Russell, 1991) – a response to a trigger such as, for example, success (Fredrickson, 2001; Isen, 2000). Discrete emotions (emotions are distinct and specific) like happiness can affect one's judgment, behavior, or experience (e.g., Frijda, 1987; Lench, Flores, & Bench, 2011; Lerner & Keltner, 2000). In this way, happiness may be part of the experience of becoming engaged but is not itself the state of employee engagement. Unique to engagement is the alignment with corporate objectives and the simultaneous emotional, cognitive, and physical investment of oneself into the work role.

Happiness's Relationship to Engagement

In their examination of Zimbabwean bus drivers, Buitendach, Bobat, Muzvidziwa, and Kanengoni (2016) reported a correlation of .55 between engagement (assessed using the UWES) and happiness. Also using the UWES, Singh, David, and Mikkilineni (2018) found work engagement and happiness of Indian knowledge workers correlated at .31. Bakker and Oerlemans (2016) reported a correlation of .46 between engagement assessed with the UWES and happiness. Kim (2019) reported a correlation of .38 between engagement (assessed using Saks's [2006] job engagement scale) and happiness. Combining Saks's (2006) job and organization engagement scales into a single engagement measure, Santhanam and Srinivas (2020) reported a correlation of .60 with happiness for their sample of shop-floor workers across several Indian manufacturing facilities. Overall, correlations between engagement (all assessed using the UWES) and happiness range from .31 to .60.

So What Does Engagement Give Us Beyond Existing Constructs?

The preceding review can be summarized in the following way: job performance is about our behaviors directed toward fulfilling or completing a specific job task. Job involvement is about how central those behaviors are to our identity at work. Job satisfaction is the positive emotional evaluation we make about our job, and organizational commitment is the emotional attachment we have with our employer. None of these concepts embraces or conveys the coupling of ourselves to our work role or how we channel our emotional, cognitive, or physical energies into our jobs – all of which, at some level, represent engagement.

Most existing definitions of engagement are insufficient at capturing both what academicians call the *construct* and what employers and/or consultants come to understand and refer to as *engagement*. The currently published definitions offered by Schaufeli et al. (2002), Kahn (1990), Saks (2006), and Macey and Schneider (2008), to name a few, fail to incorporate the *zest* of engagement that has excited industry leaders. For the engaged employees, work is something entirely different from being just a set of tasks, job description, or a series of projects.

EMPLOYEES' REFLECTIONS

In a recent engagement consulting project, I interviewed employees to understand what they think of their work, what excites or bores them, and in general, why they come to work. The intent was to extract from their qualitative response what engagement is to them. One interview in particular stands out, though it was not the only one in which the following type of answer was shared. I interviewed a hospital janitor, who was likely one of the lowest paid employees in the hospital. Here is how he described what he does.

> My job is to maintain a clean and sterile environment, free of any source of bacteria or smell, so that everyone there can work in a healthy and infectious-free environment. It's critical that I do my job well because infection is a big problem at hospitals – it's well known – people come into a hospital to get better but the longer they stay, the greater their chance of getting some other illness. I take care of ensuring a healthy disease-free work environment by taking away the stuff that breeds bacteria and just

> *makes the place look un-kept. I make it look clean and that makes people feel better.*
>
> He went on to say more, but what this response conveyed to me is instead of just telling me, "I take out the trash," the employee described a mental transformation of his work into something purposeful, goal-directed, and meaningful than the simple task of trash removal. I interviewed other employees in the same unit and a few described their work in this manner. Many simply gave me their task list, with a few moments of engagement sprinkled in here and there.

Can we achieve the kind of transformation described by the janitor described in the Employees' Reflections box with job involvement, job satisfaction, commitment, or job performance? It seems highly unlikely, given the conceptual definition of each construct and the empirical evidence supporting their nomological networks.

For some, *job crafting* (Wrzesniewski & Dutton, 2001) may come to mind after reading this example of employees' transforming work tasks into meaningful accomplishment. Job crafting refers to a process by which employees design or craft their jobs by shaping the tasks and social interactions comprising their work. Wrzesniewski and Dutton defined job crafting as an action wherein "the physical and cognitive changes individuals make in the task or relational boundaries of their work" (2001, p. 179) alters employees' work identities and meanings (i.e., understanding of the purpose of work). Through job crafting, employees can change the meaningfulness or perceived significance of work (Berg, Dutton, & Wrzesniewski, 2013; Wrzesniewski, Berg, & Dutton, 2010). The essential action of job crafting is changing one's frame or perspective of the purpose of work and/or how one interacts with others to do the work. Job crafting is complementary to job redesign: it offers a way in which employees themselves can create work that is more satisfying and fulfills their needs for positive self-image and connection with others (Wrzesniewski & Dutton, 2001). Recently, some scholars have reframed job crafting to a process by which employees modify their job resources (e.g., increase social support by interacting more with coworkers socially, restructure job tasks to increase autonomy, variety, and opportunities for development). Research using the job demands–resources version of job crafting report higher ratings of engagement assessed using the UWES (e.g., Tims, Bakker, & Derks, 2013). Bakker (2010) proposes job crafting is an action engaged employees may take to sustain their engagement. I talk more about job crafting in Chapters 4, 7, and 11.

WHAT DOES ENGAGEMENT LOOK LIKE THAT MAKES IT UNIQUE?

Johan has been in his job for a while; thus, he knows it really well. Johan lives in the small community where the organization he works for is the biggest game in town. His family has worked there, and most of his friends currently work there. Thus, you could say that work is central to Johan's life. For the most part, Johan is very satisfied with his job; his pay is OK, especially compared to his cousin's. He has decent benefits that provide for his family, and he knew when getting into the job what was expected of him. When you see Johan, he is usually happy. He has fun at work, laughing with his friends and cousins. He does, at times, become frustrated with some of the problems that pop up in his job, but he does not worry for long because he tells management about them so they can be fixed. Johan is considered a good performer because he knows the job well and he is conscientious. Johan tends to work at a steady pace, and though you would say he is not tired, he is not bouncing with energy. He goes out of his way to help others, but only if he thinks it will not take much time. Johan is very committed to his job. He cannot imagine where else he would work because there are few options available in his small town. He also feels a sense of obligation to the organization; after all, his entire family has worked there, and it is a big part of the community and part of his life now.

What Johan is missing is a sense of meaningfulness and purpose in his work. If you ask Johan whether he gets absorbed in his work, lost in time, or feels a sense of passion about what he is doing and how it makes a contribution to the organization, Johan would not know what you are talking about. Johan's job is what it is, and he does not see that it could be anything else. He does not think to go beyond the actual tasks of the job, not so much in helping others but in terms of improving the quality, making the work more efficient, or combining his job with another job that makes logical sense and would save the organization money. Johan does not see that as his role, and he does not think about it in terms of making it his role. Would you say that Johan is a good worker? Yes, but you could also say that Johan is easily distracted by the antics of his friends, that his mind tends to wander a bit while is working on his tasks, and that he does not seem very excited about the work he is doing. Johan is not engaged.

In contrast, Johan's cousin Bob has the same fun that Johan has, but when he is at work he really focuses on his job. He seems enthusiastic about what he is doing, and he asks questions about how to improve the quality of the product. He has sometimes made suggestions about how the company can combine jobs to make the work more efficient and increase sales. When Bob runs into a problem at work, he sticks with it and tries to solve it on his own before asking for help. Bob offers to help others to make sure that the job gets done, even if it means he has to rethink how he is going to get his own work done. At times it seems almost as though Bob is slowing work production because he is focused so much on solving a process problem, but the end result is that the new process saves time in the long run. So management is generally pretty flexible about letting Bob work out some of the problems on his own. In general, Bob is described as energetic, bouncing from project to project, and ready to go when the next task is thrust on the team. Both Bob and Johan are good performers for the organization. The biggest difference between the two is that Bob demonstrates the characteristics of engagement. He really enjoys the role he has in the organization, and he expands the role on his own so that he can express his enthusiasm, his creative problem-solving skills, and his focus on the job. His energy creates excitement around him, and he seems to get excited by his own energy.

Conclusion

Although hard to articulate in simple terms what employee engagement is, engagement contributes to organizational behavior beyond current job attitudes and job performance and seems more than just a static concept. Perhaps Macey and Schneider (2008) are on to something when they refer to engagement as a process as opposed to just a single trait, state, or outcome. Researchers may not agree on what exactly goes into the process (see Dalal, Brummel, Wee, & Thomas, 2008; Griffin et al., 2008; Hirschfeld & Thomas, 2008), but engagement represents some kind of transformation, production of energy, and synergistic force that creates motion in a particular direction that is aligned with the organization's goals, and this is different from current constructs studied in organizational sciences.

This chapter provided a review of the existing literature on how engagement is related to yet different from existing constructs in the behavioral and organizational sciences. So how do we effectively use this information? First, it helps to know in what way and by how much engagement is related to constructs that are, for the most part, currently understood. Second, by taking a broad, higher-level perspective to understand what all this information tells us about engagement, we might conclude that engagement is "more than the sum of its parts." That is, engagement seems to include within in it some part or form of existing job constructs, such as intrinsic motivation and flow, but is more than just the sum of these two constructs. Clearly, engagement shares conceptual space with some existing job attitudes and is related to existing job behaviors. This may explain why both Kahn (1990) and Schaufeli et al. (2002)

used so many descriptors to convey each dimension of engagement and that dimensions embracing emotions, cognition, and physiology were all necessary. Third, what this review also suggests, however, is that there is space within the engagement domain that is *not* shared by existing job attitudes and behaviors; there are still parts of engagement that have yet to be identified and that potentially explain why and how engagement is different from other concepts studied thus far. For example, engagement includes a dynamic component (a moving part), some construct yet to be named, that captures the mental processing/transformation aspect of engagement.

WALK-AWAY POINTS

- Employee engagement is a different construct than job performance and citizenship behaviors, happiness in the job, intrinsic motivation, job involvement, job satisfaction, organizational commitment, and flow. It not only shares conceptual space but also has unique space not shared with existing constructs.
- Employee engagement contributes significant added variance above and beyond a number of these different constructs in predicting outcomes such as job performance, job satisfaction, or customer service satisfaction.
- Engagement incorporates the idea of employees transforming their work into something meaningful and purposeful.

PART II

Securing an Engaged Workforce

4

HOW DO WE GET EMPLOYEE ENGAGEMENT?

In the previous chapters, I explored what employee engagement is and is not, and what makes it unique from other valuable organizational and job constructs (e.g., performance, job satisfaction). The next logical question is, how do we foster or promote employees' engagement?

There is no standard, off-the-shelf approach, because organizations are not all the same, industries vary, and people vary. That said, research and theory provide some guidance, as do some interventions applied in practice. I draw special attention on how employees regain engagement after experiencing the COVID-19 pandemic.

Theory- and Research-Supported Approaches to Getting Engagement

Leadership as a Means for Getting Employee Engagement

Popular press and consulting websites assert leaders are responsible for employee engagement. Most likely, this assignment of responsibility is because leaders oversee aspects of work that directly affect employees. These aspects include job resources, job demands, job characteristics, and rewards or recognition. Thus, scholars suggest leadership is a key component in fostering a work environment for encouraging employees to experience psychological meaningfulness, psychological availability, and psychological safety. Several leadership styles in particular have been hypothesized or studied as antecedents of engagement.

DOI: 10.4324/9781003171133-6

Full Range Leadership

Research has identified transformational leadership, in particular, as a potential focus of career and leadership development programs for fostering engagement. Using Burns's (1978) original classification of transactional versus transformational leadership, Bass (1985) advanced development on the constructs by specifying in greater detail the behaviors and focus of each leadership style. Both transactional leaders and transformational leaders recognize the needs of their followers alongside their own needs, and convey to followers what they need to do to meet both sets of needs. Transactional leaders do so by using contingent rewards and management by exception. Transformational leaders, in contrast, recognize both sets of needs, but instead of telling followers what to do, they arouse higher needs, activating the followers to achieve more on their own.

Extending Bass's work, Avolio (1999) introduced the full range model of leadership, which represents both transformational and transactional styles but also non-transactional leadership. According to Avolio, transactions form the foundation upon which transformational leadership adds. To appreciate the full range model, one must take into consideration both the individual and the situation, thus building on earlier contingency (i.e., leadership style depends on what the situation requires) and charismatic leadership theories. The full range model, therefore, considers all forms of leadership, providing a framework of leadership skills. Furthermore, Avolio specified four principles core to full range leadership, incorporated within the Full Range Leadership Development program: (a) good leaders balance their vulnerabilities by embracing and confronting them, as opposed to avoiding or denying them; (b) relationships between leaders and followers are based on commitment and not compliance; (c) leaders with whom followers can identify and see as vulnerable are those who followers will trust the most; and (d) good leaders have a clear vision of all perspectives or sides of the issue and manage those perspectives and the situation effectively.

There is no empirical evidence, yet, that the full range model of leadership positively relates to employee engagement. Studies that examine how a leader shifts their style between various leadership forms, over time and across situations, would be necessary for providing adequate evidence for the full range leadership approach in promoting engagement.

Transformational Leadership

Transformational leaders provide an inspiring vision, aligning their followers' goals with those of the organization. They transform the workplace norms and motivate employees to achieve high levels of performance to fulfill the inspiring vision. To achieve these higher motivational levels in followers, transformational leaders must possess or display four different competencies or factors:

charismatic leadership (later called individualized influence), inspirational motivation, individualized consideration, and intellectual stimulation (Burns, 1978). Individualized influence refers to the leader being a role model through displaying strong ethical principles and supporting group benefits over individual gains. Inspirational motivation refers to the leader's ability to articulate effectively and clearly with an excitement that inspires employees to achieve. Individualized consideration refers to the leader treating each employee as an individual, appreciating them, and recognizing their unique needs. Lastly, transformational leaders provide intellectual stimulation to encourage employees to be creative and challenge their own thinking.

Researchers have shown a positive relationship between transformational leadership and engagement. Although none of the research demonstrates a causal relationship – meaning you cannot conclude that transformational leadership leads to engagement – the results are still informative. For example, research has shown transformational leadership relates directly to engagement (β = .36; Aryee, Walumbwa, Zhou, & Hartnell, 2012; r = .47; Hawkes, Biggs, & Hegerty, 2017), and also indirectly through employees' perceptions of psychological meaningfulness (indirect β = .19) and psychological responsibility (indirect β = .14; Aryee et al., 2012). Psychological responsibility is a component of the job characteristics theory (Hackman & Oldham, 1976), a theory often used to explain how the work environment influences employees' perceptions of psychological meaningfulness and ultimately engagement (see Fostering Motivation in this chapter). The value of Aryee et al.'s results are that if one assumes leadership plays some role in fostering engagement, one can conclude from their results that transformational leadership is directly involved in promoting engagement and in creating a positive work environment to which employees react with engagement.

Other scholars have reported positive relationships like Aryee et al.'s (2012). For instance, Gerards, de Grip, and Baudewijns (2018) found transformational leadership related to engagement at .45, similar to Li's (2019) correlation of .42 and Faupel and Süß's (2019) correlation of .44. Also reporting a direct relationship between transformational leadership and engagement is Vincent-Höper, Muser, and Janneck (2012), who found a correlation of .46. Although the authors applied a gender lens to their study, they did not find a significant difference between men and women in their ratings of leadership and engagement. Combined, these studies suggest that regardless of sample, a moderate relationship exists between transformational leadership and engagement, and the relationship is the same for men and women.

Comparing the effects of transformational leadership to leader–member exchange (a leadership style grounded in social exchange theory; Blau, 1964), Burch and Guarana (2014) reported correlations of .77 and .49 for leader–member exchange and transformational leadership with engagement, respectively. When considered in the same structural model, the relationship between transformational leadership and engagement became non-significant, whereas that between leader–member exchange and engagement remained significant, indicating employees' engagement might be encouraged more by a leader focused on a social exchange relationship than one aimed to inspire and intellectually stimulate their followers. Social exchange theory says that through a series of obligations and reciprocation fulfillments, employees form trusting relationships with their organization. Thus, as the organization or its representatives provide support, leadership, or fairness, for example, employees reciprocate with some complementary commodity such as performance, commitment, or in this case, engagement.

Researchers acknowledge transformational leaders might vary in how much or how often they demonstrate certain leadership skills. Therefore, several researchers have examined the relationship between daily/weekly transformational leadership and daily/weekly engagement levels. In Breevaart and Bakker's (2018) study, every day for 10 days, Dutch elementary school teachers rated their principal's transformational leadership and reported their own engagement level. Transformational leadership correlated with employee engagement at .09. Breevaart and colleagues (2014) tested the simultaneous effects of transactional and transformational leadership using a sample of Norwegian naval cadets on a 40-day sailing trip. Cadets completed daily questionnaires about the team leaders and levels of engagement. Cadets took on different leadership positions at different rotations, which means ratings were not about a single person in a leadership role for the entire 40 days. The authors found a correlation of .19 between transformational leadership and engagement. Lastly, again using the same study methodology, Breevaart, Bakker, Demerouti, and Derks (2016) examined the relationship between weekly transformational leadership and engagement, over 5 weeks, using leader–employee dyads. The authors reported a correlation of .41 between leadership and engagement. The collective findings from Breevaart and colleagues' studies indicate the relationship between daily variability in leadership and daily engagement is low, but when examined on a weekly basis, the relationship goes up to a moderate strength – similar to one-time sampling studies of engagement and transformational leadership, such as Gerards et al. (2018), Li (2019), Faupel and Süß (2019), and Vincent-Höper et al. (2012). One might conclude, therefore, on any given day, leadership has little effect on engagement, but when considering cumulative effects over time, leadership plays a bigger role.

In contrast to the moderate correlation between transformational leadership and engagement, the correlation between transactional leadership and engagement appears low. For instance, Li (2019) reported a correlation between transactional leadership and engagement of .25, and Breevaart et al. (2014) found a correlation of .15.

None of the results reviewed thus far are causal. Therefore, we cannot say if leadership increases engagement, vice versa, or even whether either construct *increases* the other; the constructs may simply covary because of some other unmeasured construct. However, if you assume leaders increase engagement in workers, then increasing transformational or transactional leadership behaviors is the logical intervention approach to securing an engaged workforce.

In an effort to determine to what degree an organization can increase transformational leader characteristics, W. Brown and May (2012) studied 660 employees in a leadership training program at a manufacturing unit in a large international technology firm. Their study included two parts: (1) initial baseline assessment designed to evaluate relationships between leadership behaviors (specifically transformational and transactional) and productivity and organizational outcomes, and (2) a yearlong leadership development program designed to increase transformational leadership levels among supervisors and management. After training was complete, researchers conducted their assessments to determine success of the training, in the form of improved productivity and organizational outcomes. The intervention itself involved several steps. First, management, including the top management levels, shared the results of their initial baseline assessments regarding their management style (scores on the Multifactor Leadership Questionnaire [MLQ; Bass & Avolio, 1990] and on outcomes such as follower job satisfaction and supervisor satisfaction). The purpose of sharing survey results was to increase managers' vulnerability, encourage transparency, have them make a formal and public commitment to change in their own style and in the culture, and take immediate personal ownership for changes by starting with the self (demonstrating commitment and accountability). Second, managers who were not on board with the changes or willing to participate in personal leadership improvement were offered opportunities to make a "dignified lateral transfer" (Bass & Avolio, 1990, p. 528) or take a nonmanagerial position without penalty. The third step involved 2 days of training designed according to Avolio and Bass (1994) and Bass (1998). Goal-setting strategies were employed, and public commitment to practicing the new skills was encouraged. The fourth step lasted for 1 year, in which consultants hired to facilitate the overall program sent reminders to managers regarding their personal action plans, scheduled management meetings to discuss behavioral changes and progress to date, and conducted follow-up interviews with the managers. Results of evaluation surveys 11.5 months later showed significant changes in organizational productivity and in managers meeting organizational outcomes. The authors concluded that training for contingent reward and transformational leadership behaviors is doable and that it can result in positive changes within the organization. One possible limitation with the sample, however, is that those not wanting to participate in personal leadership improvement were encouraged out of the program, thus leaving only motivated participants in the study. It is unclear whether the same changes in leadership behavior would be achieved with reluctant or unmotivated participants.

Although W. Brown and May's study was not about engagement per se, it provided empirical evidence that leadership development programs designed to increase transformational (and contingent reward) leadership behaviors work. Other research supports this assertion. For example, Parry and Sinha (2005) examined the effectiveness of the Full Range Leadership Development program (see Avolio, 2011; Sosik & Jung, 2010). Parry and Sinha conducted pre-intervention 360-degree assessments and post-intervention (3 months later) 360-degree assessments of the frequency with which participants (i.e., leaders) displayed transformational leadership behaviors. The authors found all transformational leadership behaviors were displayed more frequently after training than before. They also found the training program was equally effective in public and private organizations, indicating there is nothing specific about the program that benefits only one sector of industry and not another. Lastly, they examined whether coaching could increase the effectiveness of the training program – no significant effects were found. Thus, coaching did not accelerate or enhance the effectiveness of the training program.

Overall, the implications of the preceding research findings are that, in general, transformational leadership behaviors support a work environment that makes employees feel able to engage, or develop a sense of meaningfulness, which encourages their engagement. The evidence suggests this influence is not strong, indicating transformational leadership is only one component in creating the right work climate for engagement. Furthermore, other forms of leadership (e.g., leader–member exchange) seem to encourage engagement, whereas others (e.g., transactional leadership) appear less influential in fostering engagement.

Empowering Leadership

Like transformational leadership, empowering leadership (i.e., leadership aimed at encouraging employees to lead and manage themselves; Conger & Kanungo, 1988) has been empirically related to engagement (positive correlations) and may be considered another avenue for leadership development to enhance engagement in the workplace (Tuckey, Bakker, & Dollard, 2012). Tuckey et al. (2012) speculated empowering leaders "directly inspired work engagement in followers" (p. 22); however, like nearly all other leadership studies, theirs was a correlational study (a single-instance survey; $r = .38$), and thus, no causal inferences can be made about the direction of influence. Similarly, Tian and Zhang (2020) examined the direct relationship between empowering leadership and engagement within a single survey and reported a correlation of .32.

Other scholars, like Kim and Beehr (2020), suggested empowering leadership encourages employees to take responsibility for themselves by taking independent (or autonomous) action, recognize their own success, and develop collaborative team relationships. Such actions satisfy basic needs proposed within self-determination theory (Ryan & Deci, 2000), namely autonomy, competence, and relatedness, respectively. When those needs are satisfied, employees are more likely to become engaged at work. In partial support, Kim and Beehr reported moderate-sized path coefficients of $\beta = .69$ between empowering leadership and the basic needs of self-determination theory, and $\beta = .50$ between needs satisfaction and engagement. They also found a direct path between empowerment and engagement $\beta = .49$) when needs satisfaction and empowerment were considered simultaneously. Thus, the results support both a direct and indirect relationship between empowering leadership and engagement.

Empowering leaders do more than simply encourage employees to self-manage. They encourage employees to lead one another on teams, involve them in decision-making, and help them believe they can achieve high performance (Ahearne, Mathieu, & Rapp, 2005). Consequently, Park, Kim, Yoon, and Joo (2017) hypothesized empowering leaders increase their employees' belief in their own capabilities (optimism), their self-confidence (self-efficacy), their perseverance to achieve (hope), and their ability to bounce back from setbacks (resiliency). Optimism, self-efficacy, hope, and resiliency form the basis of psychological capital, or *PsyCap* (Luthans, Avolio, Avey, & Norman, 2007). Park et al. (2017) further proposed that empowering leadership fosters engagement via PsyCap, because PsyCap relates to organizational behavior, such as happiness and commitment (Youssef & Luthans, 2007), which are considered similar constructs to engagement. Park et al.'s results showed empowering leadership both directly related to engagement ($\beta = .23$) and indirectly related via PsyCap ($\beta = .59$ leader to PsyCap, $\beta = .65$ PsyCap to engagement).

In sum, initial evidence suggests empowering leadership relates to engagement at moderate levels, comparable to the levels demonstrated with transformational leadership. Although no causal or directional studies exist showing increases in empowering leadership style resulting in increases in engagement levels, if you assume leaders' influence flows to employees rather than the other way around, you might conclude that leaders can stimulate an engaged workforce by demonstrating empowering leadership behaviors.

Leaders' and Employees' Emotional Intelligence

Another strategy to increasing levels of engagement in employees may be to increase leader awareness of their effects on followers through raising leaders' emotional intelligence. Research supports a positive relationship between leaders with high emotional intelligence and followers' work engagement (e.g., Ravichandran, Arasu, & Kumar, 2011; Van Oosten, McBride-Walker, & Taylor, 2019). Emotional intelligence refers to a set of interrelated skills associated with interpersonal relationships and emotional regulation. Specifically, it refers to accurate perception, appraisal, and expression of emotion, whereby one accesses and generates feelings that facilitate thought, emotional understanding, and knowledge of emotional regulation and expression (Caruso, Mayer, & Salovey, 2002; Mayer & Salovey, 1995; Salovey & Mayer, 1989). Mayer, Caruso, and Salovey (2000) developed a measure to assess the four areas of abilities (perception, facilitation, understanding, and management of emotions) that characterize emotional intelligence. In an intervention study, Van Oosten and colleagues (2019) trained 85 senior leaders and provided executive coaching, with the aim of increasing their emotional intelligence. The results were positive. Leaders' emotional intelligence increased, as did their levels of engagement and overall job performance.

Raising the emotional intelligence in employees themselves may be another avenue for increasing engagement. Although not designed to test this causal proposition, using a sample of 193 police offers in Australia, Brunetto, Teo, Shacklock, and Farr-Wharton (2012) found a positive relationship ($r = .43$) between police officers' emotional intelligence and their engagement levels. Likewise, using samples of nurses in China, Y. Zhu et al. (2015) reported a correlation of .60 between emotional intelligence and work engagement, Yan et al. (2018) a correlation of .49, and Gong et al. (2020) a correlation of .44. J. Liu and Cho (2018) found a regression beta weight of $\beta = .20$ between emotional intelligence and engagement after controlling for emotional labor display rules ($\beta = .14$). Display rules are the rules or standards an organization has for what emotions employees must show or display on the job (e.g., customer service workers must smile when working with customers).

When considering the relative effects of emotional intelligence on engagement as compared to the effects of stable personality traits, Akhtar et al. (2015) found that emotional intelligence predicted engagement, even after considering participant age, gender, Big Five personality traits (openness, conscientiousness, extraversion, agreeableness, neuroticism), and Hogan personality scales (adjustment, ambition, sociability, interpersonal sensitivity, learning approach, prudence, inquisitive). Although the additional variance in engagement explained by emotional intelligence was small (1%), the significance of these results is important because emotional intelligence remained significant after considering so many other constructs and, importantly, it can be trained, unlike the other constructs assessed.

We can infer from the cumulative research findings that increasing emotional intelligence should lead to an increase in engagement, regardless of personality, age, or gender. Beyond the results for emotional intelligence, another important takeaway from Akhtar et al.'s study, in particular, is that stable personality traits (e.g., openness, agreeableness, extraversion) predict engagement, which is currently considered a moment-to-moment state (i.e., not as stable as personality; more on the stability of engagement in Chapter 11). It may be that certain personality traits predispose employees toward engagement.

Supportive and Interpersonal Leadership

In my own research, my students and I have studied the relationship between supportive and interpersonal leadership and employee engagement. In one study (Byrne, Peters et al., 2013), following the lead of other researchers, we defined supportive leadership as supervisory support combined with interpersonal and informational justice. Perceived supervisory support entails providing flexible work schedules, conveying value and importance, demonstrating appreciation and concern, and being available when employees need help (see Eisenberger, Huntington, Hutchison, & Sowa, 1986). Interpersonal fairness refers to being treated with respect and consideration, and informational justice refers to being given honest and adequate explanations for decisions (Bies & Moag, 1986). We created this multidimensional construct to represent the positive interpersonal relationships with leaders that researchers note are related to engagement, different from leader-member exchange (e.g., Aryee et al., 2012; Groysberg & Slind, 2012; Tuckey et al., 2012; Xu & Thomas, 2011; Yang et al., 2018; Zhu, Avolio, & Walumbwa, 2009). In a different study (Hansen, Byrne, & Kiersch, 2014), we combined transformational leadership characteristics (e.g., vision, inspirational communication, supportive leadership, intellectual stimulation, personal recognition; Rafferty & Griffin, 2004) with informational and interpersonal justice to create the concept of interpersonal leadership characteristics. Both studies leveraged prior works suggesting employees focus on their leaders' interpersonal characteristics, such as communication, support, and interpersonal fairness when responding with engagement (Aryee et al., 2012; Tuckey et al., 2012; Xu & Thomas, 2011). In both studies, we used field samples with data collected at two time points, and we employed several of Podsakoff, MacKenzie, Lee, and Podsakoff's (2003) suggestions for minimizing common method bias (variance in scores are attributed to the methodology as opposed to actual differences). We analyzed both data sets using structural equation modeling to simultaneously test hypotheses about relationships with engagement and rule out competing hypotheses. In both studies, we used measures with adequate reliability (greater than .90) and confirmatory factor validity evidence to support our measures and latent constructs. Our findings showed interpersonal leadership positively related to employee engagement. In the one study, we showed employees respond with engagement to leaders who promote identification and connection with the organization. In the other, we showed leadership and job characteristics both related to engagement through experienced psychological meaningfulness and safety (see Figure 4.1).

Like most of the other studies reviewed in this chapter, our studies were not causal, and therefore we can draw no firm conclusions about directionality of influence. The practical implications of the research, however, are that the supportive and interpersonal characteristics of leaders may play a role in fostering work climates in which engagement flourishes. Busse and Regenberg (2019)

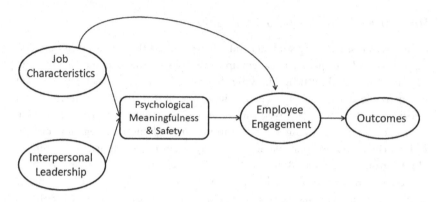

FIGURE 4.1 Adapted From Byrne, Peters, Rechlin, Smith, and Kedharnath (2013)

examined inclusive leadership, which arguably is comparable to or related to interpersonal leadership. Inclusive leadership focuses on how leaders interact with employees to promote, value, and recognize their unique contributions. The authors found positive correlations between leadership inclusiveness, psychological meaningfulness, and engagement.

The qualitative data we captured as part of our studies confirmed it is the interpersonal fairness and support characteristics of leaders that positively affects employees' engagement levels.

EMPLOYEES' REFLECTIONS

Some of the employees in our studies shared the following:

- "That's what keeps me engaged . . . it's that appreciation and affirmation."
- "My input is valued. In this job, I like the autonomy and also the appreciation. That what I do is important – that they trust me to make important decisions and to know when to involve others versus when I can do it myself."
- "[T]here's a lot about fairness, I mean, there's a big thing about what's fair and what's not and the executive team is pretty much in agreement that it's important to be fair – it's one of those things where ultimately people have to be engaged. Fairness is important."
- "I get tons of support from my boss."
- "I really liked what he [CEO] had to say about employee engagement, how much he values employees, and how much he tries to balance work and life, not only for himself but his employees."

> • "Upper management is so approachable – you can start a conversation any time . . . they take time to visit with you, talk to you and ask how your day is goin', and if there's anything they can do for me and that kind of thing. I feel really appreciated."

Fostering Motivation

Job Characteristics

Interventions, such as job (re)design, focus on changing the work environment (i.e., with the job itself or with the reporting structure) to affect employee motivation, job satisfaction, and other work outcomes. Considerable research evidence supports job redesign (e.g., Holman et al., 2010). An important first step in job redesign is to conduct a job diagnosis, perhaps using the Job Diagnostic Survey (JDS; Hackman & Oldham, 1975), to determine what part of the job needs modification to address potential motivation issues. The JDS has questions about employees' perceptions of their job and their reactions to the job itself. Specifically, the JDS includes questions about working with others, autonomy, task variety, whether the job involves completing only a small part of a larger project or completing the entire project, the importance of the job, feedback on the job, level of challenge in the job, satisfaction with the job, sense of ownership and responsibility on the job, availability of opportunity for growth or recognition, and preferences for one job over another (when the two comparative jobs presented on the survey differ on a variety of factors such as commute time, pay, level of responsibility, challenge, variety, and other job characteristics; see Hackman & Oldham, 1975, for details). The JDS is specifically designed to assess the components of job characteristics theory (see Figure 4.2), a theory that explains how job factors lead to motivation and other work outcomes. Job characteristics theory states that core job dimensions (skill variety, task identity, task significance, autonomy, and feedback) trigger critical psychological states (experienced meaningfulness, felt responsibility, and knowledge of results), which lead to employees' having internal motivation and various job attitudes. The results of the JDS provide information as to what in one's job, if changed, would most positively affect motivation. As mentioned, the JDS was specifically designed with the job characteristics theory in mind; therefore, those using it should be aware of its purpose and limitations.

Research supports a positive relationship between job redesign and engagement. For instance, Hernaus, Vujčić, and Aleksić (2017) conducted a four-wave longitudinal diary study looking at the effects of a managerial job redesign intervention on employees' engagement. The redesign focused on modifying aspects of the job that touched on all components of the job characteristics

CORE JOB DIMENSIONS   CRITICAL PSYCHOLOGICAL STATES

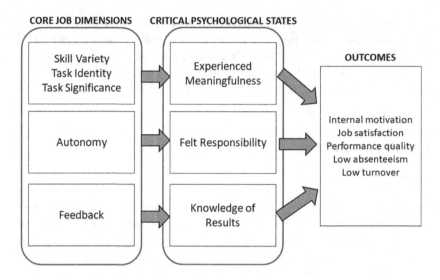

FIGURE 4.2 Job Characteristics Model

Source: Adapted from Hackman & Oldham (1976).

model. Overall, the authors found the changes in job characteristics that employees perceived, specifically those affecting task significance, resulted in subsequent changes in work engagement.

The job characteristics theory has received general empirical support, especially relating job characteristics to psychological states that then lead to motivation (see a study by Behson, Eddy, & Lorenzet, 2000). For example, research shows job characteristics (e.g., task significance, autonomy) are positively correlated with psychological meaningfulness (Becherer, Morgan, & Richard, 1982; Champoux, 1991), one of Kahn's (1990) key psychological conditions preceding engagement. Some preliminary support for job characteristics explaining variance in engagement also exists (e.g., Christian, Garza, & Slaughter, 2011), indicating the job characteristics theory holds promise for serving as input into interventions designed to promote employee engagement.

Job Rotation or Enrichment

Job characteristics theory is not the only job redesign solution. Job redesign includes many approaches or strategies that change certain job characteristics, affecting employees' experience of the meaningfulness of their jobs, which should lead to engagement (Kahn, 1990). For instance, one could implement job rotation, which involves periodically rotating employees into different jobs on the same job level. Thus, employees have a chance to use job skills they possess but do not get to use in their current role, as well as learn new skills. Job enrichment, another job redesign approach, involves increasing the scope of one's immediate job by adding tasks directly relevant to the job itself, thereby increasing skill variety and overall interest (Walker, 1950).

Guest (1964) shares an illustrative story of job enrichment or enlargement, wherein a chairman of the board asks an employee what she would do with the job if she were the boss. The answer was, "with very little extra training she could learn not only how to operate the machine but to set up her own machine (a task which the setup men performed), keep track of the inventory of different types of parts (a task of the stock men), and do her own inspection of the parts, (a job which the inspectors were doing)" (Guest, 1964, p. 3). Unfortunately, no empirical studies testing the relationship between these types of job redesign strategies and employee engagement could be found, but the answer given to the chairman of the board is illustrative of how, theoretically, an employee could be engaged by modifying the job.

Job redesign is not a panacea; it is not always effective (e.g., Frank & Hackman, 1975; Lawler, Hackman, & Kaufman, 1973). It requires attention to whether those in the job are ready for the change and whether the change is best for those in the job. Hence, job design is appropriate some of the time but not all the time. Hackman and Lawler (1971) demonstrated an employee's need for growth (called *growth need strength*) factors into the relationship between job dimensions and job satisfaction.

Job Crafting

Not all jobs can be designed to offer autonomy, challenge, or skill variety; thus other approaches to redesign, such as job crafting (Wrzesniewski & Dutton, 2001), may be used to achieve the same overall conceptual contribution that social support or specific job resources carry. Employees can be trained in job crafting, an approach to job redesign that incorporates physical and cognitive changes employees themselves make in how they envision the task or with the relational boundaries in their work. Job crafting may or may not involve structural changes to the job; rather, it tends to emphasize how employees see what is and is not (and what can be) in the various roles they have at work. Job crafting emphasizes the ownership of the employee in designing or changing their work toward creating more meaningful work, reinforcing the concept of empowerment, and giving employees more control over their job boundaries. Job crafting can be done across three different domains: (a) task, (b) relational, and (c) cognitive. Task job crafting involves changing the actual tasks of the job by increasing or reducing the number of tasks, changing how the tasks are completed, or reprioritizing tasks. Note, task job crafting is not about changing jobs; thus, the tasks required for completing the job remain the same. Relational job crafting involves changing how and when relationships and interactions are sought and invoked (or avoided), and with whom. New relationships may be formed, whereas others may be broken or minimized to reduce interactions. Cognitive job crafting involves changing how work is perceived, framed, or understood in terms of one's identity. Employees can use one or more of these techniques to shape the meaningfulness of their jobs. Berg, Dutton, and Wrzesniewski (2013) provided a rich description of job crafting along with several proven suggestions for application in the field (including references and resources). An original intent behind job crafting was to improve the meaningfulness of one's work. One of my students examined the relationship between the three types of job crafting and meaningfulness and found only cognitive crafting significantly related to meaningfulness (β = .45; Holcombe, 2015). Meng, Wang, and Tian (2021) may be one of the only studies published thus far (it was the only one I could find) to examine the relationship between job crafting and psychological meaningfulness, and ultimately engagement. The authors also included psychological safety and availability – Kahn's (1990) key antecedents to engagement. Using a sample of 194 employees from 16 different social work organizations in China, Meng et al. found positive relationships between job crafting and psychological meaningfulness (as well as availability), which subsequently positively related to job engagement. Although their study, like so many others in the engagement literature, was not causal, they relied on Kahn's (1990) and Wrzesniewski and Dutton's (2001) theoretical frameworks to hypothesize directionality.

Studies exist for the application of job crafting (e.g., Berg, Grant, & Johnson, 2010; Wrzesniewski, Dutton, & Debebe, 2003) demonstrating its success in triggering higher motivation levels, including engagement. In these studies, job crafting was specifically measured using scales designed to assess cognitive, task, and relational crafting. For example, Yang, Ming, Ma, and Huo (2017) examined how servant leaders encouraged employee job crafting, which was positively related to engagement. They showed that the empowering component of servant leadership was related to task crafting, whereas the emotional healing aspect of servant leadership was related to relational crafting. Leadership and job crafting were directly related to engagement; thus, job crafting only partially mediated the leadership to engagement relationship. Slemp, Zhao, Hou, and Vallerand (2020) showed how job crafting and leader autonomy support positively related to both harmonious and obsessive passion for work, which were positively related to engagement. They demonstrated the same relationships using two different samples: one from Australia and the other from China. Using a randomized controlled trial with an intervention group and a control group over 6 months, Sakuraya, Shimazu, Imamura, and Kawakami (2020) took a novel approach to testing role-based job crafting in Japan. They used a job crafting intervention specifically designed based on Wrzesniewski and Dutton's (2001) three types of crafting, tested and evaluated in a previous project. Contrary to expectations and previous studies, their results were not significant for the total intervention group: the job crafting intervention showed no significant effect on work engagement as compared to the control group. The authors provided a few potential reasons for the lack of significant findings, which provide value in terms of figuring out how to implement job crafting interventions.

Wrzesniewski and Dutton's (2001) model is considered role based, focusing on how employees expand and contract tasks and relational boundaries to improve their role with the objective of increasing the meaningfulness of work. Bakker, Tims, and Derks (2012) reconceptualized job crafting as a resource-based approach based on the Job Demands–Resources (JD-R) model. Specifically, the authors proposed that job crafting is about employees making changes to their jobs to increase job resources and reduce job demands (Tims & Bakker, 2010). The majority of studies using job crafting as an intervention to foster engagement apply the reconceptualized version grounded in the JD-R model. As expected, based on the success of the JD-R model correlating positively with work engagement, all studies using Bakker et al.'s (2012) version of job crafting report positive significant results for boosting engagement (e.g., Bakker & Oerlemans, 2019; Bakker, Rodríguez-Muñoz, & Vergel, 2016; Dubbelt, Demerouti, & Rispens, 2019; Gordon et al., 2018; Hakanen, Seppälä, & Peeters, 2017; Hulshof, Demerouti, & Le Blanc, 2020; Kuijpers, Kooij, & van Woerkom, 2020; Mäkikangas, 2018; Petrou, Bakker, & van den Heuvel, 2017; Petrou, Demerouti, & Schaufeli, 2018; Philip, 2021; van Wingerden, Bakker, & Derks, 2017; Vogt et al., 2016). Although the activity used to increase resources and/or challenge demands differs by study, as does the inclusion of different mediators or moderators, meta-analytic studies confirm positive results for these job crafting efforts with engagement as the outcome (Frederick & VanderWeele, 2020; Lichtenthaler & Fischbach, 2019; Oprea et al., 2019). One study provides an interesting exception to using engagement as an outcome. Zeijen, Peeters, and Hakanen (2018) proposed that instead of being an outcome of crafting, engagement serves as an antecedent. Their results show that engagement at Time 1 relates to job crafting (e.g., self-management, self-goal setting) at Time 2, 3 months later.

Most of the resource-based job crafting studies report having only the JD-R as the underlying theoretical framework. However, some scholars also include the conservation of resources theory to explain the beneficial impact of resources. For example, Harju, Hakanen, and Schaufeli (2016) examined the resource spiral gain/loss mechanism of the conservation of resources theory using a 3-year cross-lagged panel study design. They focused on highly educated workers who have the potential for job boredom, proposing that employees job craft (i.e., seek resources) to prevent future anticipated boredom. Using the cross-lagged study design, they tested the opposite direction of influence; engaged employees seek to gain even more resources, which leads them to job craft. Their results were consistent with their hypotheses. Job crafting was associated with higher work engagement and reduced job boredom, and work engagement (but not boredom) increased the potential for future job crafting. Kuijpers et al. (2020) focused on a different challenge for employees: high workload. The authors proposed that job crafting (gaining resources) would boost engagement specifically for those with high workloads (losing resources), because resources are most beneficial during cycles of resource loss. Their results supported their supposition.

Intrinsic and Extrinsic Motivation

According to cognitive evaluation theory (Deci, 1975; Deci & Ryan, 1980), the precursor to self-determination theory (Deci & Ryan, 1985; Ryan & Deci, 2000), feelings of competence and autonomy underlie intrinsic motivation, which is motivation propelled by internal interest and spontaneous satisfaction from an activity. In contrast, motivation driven by an external reward or payment from an external source is called extrinsic motivation (Porter & Lawler, 1968). Research shows that challenging tasks are intrinsically motivating (e.g., Danner & Lonky, 1981), and positive feedback on tasks promotes a sense of competence (Fisher, 1978; Ryan, 1982) that fosters intrinsic motivation (Deci, Koestner, & Ryan, 1999).

Self-determination theory extends cognitive evaluation theory by describing internal and external motivation in more detail (Deci & Ryan, 1985; Ryan & Deci, 2000). The theory suggests people are often motivated even when the task is not intrinsically interesting, either because they understand and strongly value the benefit their behavior ultimately provides or because their behavior is fully integrated into their identity, such that it is self-determined. Self-determination theory builds on the fundamental belief that humans have innate tendencies toward intrinsic motivation by identifying three needs (competence, autonomy, and relatedness) important for triggering and enhancing intrinsic motivation (Ryan & Deci, 2000). As long as people interpret their work environment as supporting their feelings of competence (i.e., they believe they have the ability and resources necessary) and giving them self-control (i.e., autonomy), and one that is characterized by a sense of relatedness (i.e., valued and appreciated by others), they will believe their actions or behaviors are self-determined (i.e., consistent with core values and freely chosen). Consequently, they will be intrinsically motivated (Ryan & Deci, 2000). Thus, we can hypothesize using self-determination theory that employees become engaged because it makes them feel self-determined; that they are competent, in control, and intrinsically rewarded by the work they do (Meyer & Gagné, 2008). In support, across two studies, Gillet, Huart, Colombat, and Fouquereau (2013), using self-determination theory as the theoretical framework, demonstrated self-determined motivation mediated the relationship between supervisory and organizational support and employee engagement. Similarly, Rahmadani, Schaufeli, Ivanova, and Osin (2019) showed using two samples, one from Indonesia and the other from Russia, that basic needs satisfaction mediated the relationship between engaging leadership (i.e., inspiring, strengthening, empowering, connecting) and work engagement.

An outgrowth of self-determination theory, the self-concordance model of motivation (Sheldon & Elliot, 1999) suggests people naturally pursue self-generated or self-integrated goals, that when attained, produce high levels of satisfaction and well-being, promoting ongoing goal-striving and achievement. Self-concordant goals are intrinsic or *identified motivation*, which Sheldon and Elliot (1998) argue makes them self-integrated; that is, they are generated from within and thus are deeply valued. Identified motivation is described as acting out of personal conviction, pursing goals consistent with one's internal compass. They stress "valued" is not synonymous with "pleasant"; instead, the goals have personal meaning and individuals feel a sense of ownership of the goal. Sheldon and Elliot (1998, 1999) proposed that people are driven to achieve self-concordant goals, and attainment of a goal results in performance and psychological well-being. Hence, by applying the self-concordance model to employee engagement, we can hypothesize people inherently pursue self-concordant goals, and the process of achieving such goals provides a positive feeling of accomplishment and ultimately more goal-striving behavior, expressed as the motivated state of employee engagement. To date, it does not appear anyone has tested the self-concordance model of motivation and engagement, except in student engagement literature (Vasalampi, Salmela-Aro, & Nurmi, 2009).

Employees with high core self-evaluations (i.e., locus of control, self-esteem, generalized self-efficacy, and emotional stability) tend to report high self-concordant work goals; they pursue internally driven goals with which they identify and find intrinsically rewarding (Judge, Bono, Erez, & Locke, 2005). As a result, they tend to demonstrate and report high levels of goal attainment and satisfaction. One can conclude from this research that employees with high core self-evaluations may also be more likely to become engaged because of their high goal attainment. A few studies support a positive relationship between core self-evaluations and engagement (e.g., Karatepe, Keshavarz, & Nejati, 2012; Yan & Su, 2013).

In summary, applying self-determination theory and self-concordance model of motivation, we can surmise that changing the work environment to facilitate employees' ability to feel competent, in control (some autonomy), with needs for relatedness met, and pursue a self-generated goal will lead to high levels of employee engagement. Changes to the environment can include appropriate redesign of task or job characteristics (i.e., job autonomy, feedback from the job, feedback from supervisor) to promote feelings of empowerment and intrinsic motivation (Gagné, Senécal, & Koestner, 1997), and structuring a reward and recognition system that includes feedback in addition to tangible rewards that are not contingent on task performance (Deci et al., 1999).

Stress Reduction

Cognitive Activation

Although stress reduction is just that – a focus on reducing stress – by doing so we might also enjoy higher levels of engagement. Cognitive activation theory suggests those who expect positive coping demonstrate a fast cognitive activation for problem-solving, whereas those with a negative expectancy for coping demonstrate a slow cognitive activation of coping responses (hence, their stress levels rise). Andreassen, Ursin, and Eriksen (2007) used the cognitive activation theory of stress (Ursin & Eriksen, 2004) to explain how enjoyment of work is positively related to work engagement for those who expect it to be positive, and internal motivation and inner compulsion for work are related to job stress and burnout, but only for those who expect work to be negative. The implied intervention solution here is toward changing expectancies for coping within stressful situations. If the expectation can be positive and toward constructive employment, the response should be engagement. No empirical study has tested this specific hypothesis as of yet. Additionally, the premise of cognitive activation theory is a response to stressful situations; thus, this model is most appropriate if considering engagement from the stress literature perspective (i.e., Schaufeli, Martínez, Marques Pinto, Salanova, & Bakker, 2002).

Job Resources

Consistent with the JD-R model (Bakker & Demerouti, 2008), researchers suggest organizations should increase job resources, such as social support, performance feedback, job characteristics (e.g., autonomy, skill variety, challenging work) and learning opportunities (Bakker, 2009), to increase their employees' engagement. Within the JD-R model, job resources are key to enabling engagement, and the presence of job demands make resources much more salient. The JD-R model combines the demand–control model (Karasek, 1979) and the effort–reward imbalance model (Siegrist, 1996) to suggest there are two groups of job components affecting employees' stress levels: job demands and job resources. Both resources and demands include physical, psychological, social, and organizational components of the job. These components are considered demands when they cost the employee, either physically or psychologically. They are considered resources when they are associated with reductions in job demands (i.e., they help achieve work goals or reduce physical or psychological costs) and/or when they stimulate growth. Job demands lead to strain, whereas job resources lead to motivation. Although the various presentations of the JD-R model are a bit vague as to how exactly the model works or what exactly constitute job resources or demands, it seems, in general, that the JD-R model suggests when perceived demands exceed resources, employees experience burnout; when resources exceed demands, employees engage because resources reduce the costs associated with ongoing demands. Numerous studies using the JD-R as a framework have shown support for a positive relationship between job resources and work engagement (e.g., Albrecht & Marty, 2020; Hawkes et al., 2017; Kallioniemi et al., 2018; Ning & Alikaj, 2019; Patience, De Braine, & Dhanpat, 2020; Seppälä et al., 2018).

Recent advances to the use of the JD-R framework include coupling self-determination theory (Ryan & Deci, 2000) to explain how job resources trigger motivation, which the JD-R suggests results in engagement. Specifically, researchers (Albrecht, 2015; Van den Broeck et al., 2008) hypothesize job resources might fulfill the basic psychological needs of self-determination theory, which include competence, autonomy, and relatedness. It is through the satisfaction of these needs that motivation is triggered, resulting in engagement. Another advancement to the JD-R model is the delineation of job demands into hindrance and challenge demands (Crawford, LePine, & Rich, 2010). It turns out people appraise demands differently, considering some stressful and others motivating (Cavanaugh et al., 2000). Using meta-analyses, Crawford et al. (2010) demonstrated support for hindrance versus challenge demands relating more strongly to burnout versus engagement, respectively. In particular, challenge demands related to engagement ($\beta = .21$) more strongly than with burnout ($\beta = .10$), whereas hindrance demands related to burnout ($\beta = .25$) more strongly than with engagement ($\beta = -.19$). On the job resource front, researchers have begun making explicit what constitutes a job resource, including concepts such as job autonomy, development opportunities, job feedback, skill utilization, and social support (e.g., Albrecht & Marty, 2020; Malinowska & Tokarz, 2020).

Also a stress theory, the conservation of resources theory (Hobfoll, 1989) has been used in the stress/employee engagement research. Using this framework, researchers hypothesize that because resources buffer the negative effects of various work settings or stressors on work engagement, individuals hoard resources and conserve them to the best of their ability (e.g., Bakker et al., 2007; Baethge, Junker, & Rigotti, 2020; Hakanen, Perhoniemi, & Toppinen-Tanner, 2008; Kim, Cho, & Park, 2021; Rothmann & Joubert, 2007). Specifically, the conservation of resources theory says "people strive to retain, protect, and build resources and that what is threatening to them is the potential or actual loss of these valued resources" (Hobfoll, 1989, p. 516). Hobfoll (1989) defined resources as objects (e.g., home, assets), personal characteristics (e.g., stress resistant personality, strong social support system), and situations or conditions (e.g., tenure, seniority, good partnership) that are valuable to the individual. For example, skill mastery, self-esteem, financial security, employability or employment, and learning potential are considered resources that enable people to build, retain, and protect their resources.

In a cross-lagged longitudinal study, Hakanen, Perhoniemi et al. (2008) found support for the general hypotheses of the conservation of resources theory; those with resources conserved and accumulated more, whereas those prone to using resources continued to do so over time. Similarly, using conservation of resources as their theoretical foundation, Luria and Torjman (2009) conducted a quasi-field experiment examining the effects of various resources on coping with perceived stress (induced by a 2-day selection process). The resources included personality in the form of core self-evaluations (e.g., locus of control, self-esteem, generalized self-efficacy, and emotional stability), physical fitness, cognition such as problem-solving ability and time management, and peer acceptance. Their results showed that participants reporting high levels of core self-evaluation perceived much lower stress levels across the study compared with those reporting low scores on the core self-evaluation measure. The tasks were quite physical, and so as expected, high physical fitness contributed positively to stress coping. Cognitive ability had no effect on coping; neither did peer acceptance in this study. Peer rejection, in contrast, did increase perceived stress levels. The implication of this study is that positive core self-evaluations appear to play a positive role in coping with stress and, therefore, could potentially act as a resource for promoting offsetting negative conditions that take away from one's ability to become engaged. Other intervention-based studies show similar support for the fundamental hypothesis of the JD-R model and conservation of resources theory – that increasing job resources promotes engagement (e.g., Bakker & van Wingerden, 2021; Dubbelt, Demerouti, & Rispens, 2019; Seppälä et al., 2018).

Not all researchers have found support for job resources uniformly increasing engagement. For example, Dikkers, Jansen, de Lange, Vinkenburg, and Kooij (2010) found job resources in the form of support (e.g., help from supervisor) and job control and job demands (e.g., enough time to get the job done, working hard) were not related to engagement over time. Their findings suggest engagement might be relatively stable regardless of perceived resources and job demands. However, the authors explained the lack of influence of resources on engagement, suggesting that examining engagement over 18 months may not be the right period. Instead, they suggested engagement should be assessed more frequently, such on a daily or hourly basis. Dikkers et al. framed their study using Schaufeli et al.'s definition of engagement and measure; hence, their explanation contradicts Schaufeli et al.'s (2002) original assertion that engagement is a persistent and stable state. However, as noted in Chapter 2, Schaufeli et al.'s original definition has changed over time to suggest engagement is a transient state that fluctuates within individuals over short time frames (Sonnentag et al., 2010). Ning and Alikaj (2019) found that age factored into the extent to which specific job resources related to engagement. In particular, they found older adults' engagement was more affected by maintenance-oriented resources (e.g., autonomy, job security, work-family-life balance policies), whereas younger or more junior employees' engagement was more affected by development-oriented job resources (e.g., feedback, development opportunities, skill variety, promotions). Halinski and Harrison (2020) found that supervisor support had a stronger effect on engagement for regional office employees than on head office employees. Head office employees responded with higher engagement when given organizational support versus supervisor support. These studies combined demonstrate that not all job resources are created equal in terms of their potential influence on engagement. Clearly, what employees consider to be a job resource matters and may not uniformly increase engagement.

Overall, research supports a positive relationship between job resources and work engagement (even among dairy farmers; see Kallioniemi et al., 2018 [job resources included working with cattle and animal health]). The cumulative findings also suggest that job demands are stressful, and when stressed, people report lower engagement than otherwise.

Re-establishing "Normal" Workplaces After COVID-19

The COVID-19 pandemic, first identified in late 2019, continues to disrupt the workplace, causing prolonged distress and fear, to say the least. Because of how the pandemic has impacted the work environment and people's ability to focus, a few researchers have quickly launched studies examining its effects on engagement and how to re-engage employees as workplaces return to some level of normalcy. For example, applying a job reattachment framework to reactivate employee engagement, Yuan, Ye, and Zhong (2021) examined workers' engagement, withdrawal, and perceptions of leader safety commitment in Wuhan, China, the epicenter of the pandemic. Their results showed the positive relationship between job reattachment (e.g., thoughts about preparing for work, positive expectations about work) and engagement (assessed using the JES) was moderated by leader safety commitment, such that high leader safety commitment strengthened the reattachment to engagement relationship. Leader safety commitment was evidenced by how much the leader proactively encouraged, if not enforced, safety behaviors (e.g., mask wearing, temperature monitoring). Engagement was negatively related to work withdrawal and positively related to the use of personal protective equipment and task performance. The implications of Yuan et al.'s findings are that organizations can encourage employees to think about and prepare for returning to work before actually returning, to re-activate their attachment to work. Additionally, supervisors can demonstrate high commitment to a safe workplace, thus facilitating employees' planning and preparedness for returning to work.

In their first study, Liu, Chen, and Li (2021) examined frontline health care workers (i.e., nurses) at a major hospital in Chengdu, China, which is about

720 miles (1,159 kilometers) west of Wuhan. They studied the degree to which perceived COVID-19 crisis strength (i.e., novelty, disruption, and criticality of crisis) affected the engagement levels for nurses who provided care to COVID-19 patients in and outside of the intensive care unit (ICU). Additionally, they examined whether nurses' perceived work meaningfulness would moderate the effects of the COVID-19 disruption on engagement. The authors found a significant negative effect of COVID-19 crisis strength on engagement ($\gamma^1 = -.31$; data were nested in teams) and a positive moderating effect of meaningfulness on work engagement ($\gamma = .41$). Digging deeper, they found that as meaningfulness increased, the negative relationship between COVID-19 crisis strength and engagement became non-significant. To follow-up on their findings from Study 1, Liu et al. (2021) launched a second pre–post intervention (control group) study with medical professionals (i.e., nurses, doctors, support staff) in the ICU at the same hospital, this time initiating an intervention to see if they could promote increase engagement by reducing perceived COVID-19 crisis strength and/or increasing work meaningfulness. Those in the COVID-19 crisis strength intervention, who also received the meaningfulness intervention, reported the largest increase in work engagement. Participants in the same crisis strength intervention who did not get the meaningfulness intervention experienced no significant change in engagement compared to pre-intervention levels. The implications of their work are that the pandemic negatively affects engagement levels, but organizations can do something about it by implementing interventions to reduce crisis strength and increase meaningfulness. The authors provided their measures and intervention materials in the appendices of the manuscript.

Framing their study using terror management theory, Hu, He, and Zhou (2020) examined to what extent pandemic-triggered mortality salience instigates anxiety, which acts as a psychological mechanism through which mortality salience reduces job engagement. They additionally studied whether servant leadership could moderate (i.e., reduce or mitigate) the negative effects of anxiety on engagement. Using samples from Eastern China and MTurk (authors did not indicate the geographical location of workers, though as noted in the abstract of the article, they were located in the United States; MTurk is a crowdsourcing platform), the authors found support for their supposition that pandemic-triggered mortality salience negatively affects job engagement by triggering workers' anxiety about their own death. Servant leadership mitigated that effect. The implication of Hu et al.'s findings is that leadership can play a key role during the pandemic in preventing employees' engagement levels from substantially dropping, even though employees will experience general and death-specific anxiety. By providing attention to employees' emotional

---

1 The Greek letter gamma represents an overall regression coefficient obtained using multilevel modeling, as would be the case with nested data (such as teams within an organizational unit).

suffering and acknowledging the stress of the situation, servant leaders can help employees feel "normal" in experiencing anxiety and recognize their contributions to work still matter during these challenging times.

Some scholars speculate the pandemic will have long-term effects on what workplaces look like, including adopting hybrid models of in-person and remote work, or fully remote locations. Others will return to fully in-person work environments but may increase work flexibility to be more accommodating to workers' personal needs (Rudolph et al., 2021). These scholars and others (e.g., Rabenu & Tziner, 2021) suggest returning to normalcy, whatever that looks like, might first tax employees' already overextended health and psychological capabilities to the point of burnout. They recommend attending to these concerns by determining organizational and individual capability for remote versus in-person work to ensure a successful shift to a new normal routine. If organizational leaders leverage scholarly writings such as these to reconsider how work is accomplished (i.e., re-envisioning what "normal" work is), we might see higher levels of engagement resulting from more personalized/customized work environments that fit employees' needs.

Are Older Workers Engaged?

Older workers are consistently underestimated and considered less capable than their younger colleagues. For example, Allen, van Someren, and Gutierrez (2020) reviewed literature suggesting younger workers are more adaptable, resilient, creative, and innovative than older workers. However, contrary to the literature, their actual study results showed that older workers (age 40 and older) have higher potential on creativity and innovation than do younger workers (under age 40). Similarly, older workers are assumed to be less engaged than younger workers, but it turns out the reverse is true, particularly on the dedication and absorption dimensions of the UWES (e.g., Douglas & Roberts, 2020). Furthermore, employees nearing retirement age do not necessarily fall into a "mental" retirement gap wherein their engagement levels plummet. Instead, researchers have shown employees may experience constant low engagement nearing retirement, which could be offset by interventions aimed at boosting motivation (e.g., de Wind et al., 2017), but they are still engaged.

When researchers have focused on human resource management flexibility, such as flexible work schedules, options for time off, phasing into retirement, leave without pay, and breaks (e.g., sabbaticals), these flexibility practices positively relate to the engagement levels of younger employees (i.e., about age 30) but not older employees (i.e., about age 55; Bal & De Lange, 2015). Thus, one might make more flexible human resource management practices available to employees, especially if the average age of the organization's employees is relatively low (see Piszczek & Pimputkar [2020] for an exception regarding flexible schedules), and implement programs to boost motivation, especially where employees' average age is relatively high. Programs to boost motivation might include job crafting, which I reviewed earlier. Focusing specifically on older workers, Kooij et al. (2020) showed that increasing work pressure (e.g., having a lot of work tasks) and autonomy stimulated older workers to job craft to make their jobs interesting, and in doing so increased their daily engagement levels.

Because older workers (about age 49 or older) are more engaged than younger workers (about age 27 and younger) when working on interdependent tasks, but younger workers are more engaged when interacting with those outside the organization (e.g., stakeholders; Fazi et al., 2019), organizations could benefit by uniquely challenging age-diverse employees along this interdependent versus external orientation bifurcation. However, younger workers experience more job satisfaction and engagement than older workers when their jobs incorporate a lot of task variety (e.g., Zaniboni et al., 2014). Therefore, organizational leaders need to avoid narrowing the variety of younger workers tasks to just interactions with external stakeholders; more variety is better for them.

Creating Meaningful Work[2]

Classical theories of motivation and humanistic psychology propose that people need work that is meaningful and purposeful (Alderfer, 1972; Herzberg, Mausner, & Snyderman, 1959; Maslow, 1943, 1968; Rogers, 1959, 1961). Scholars studying meaning have proposed that a search for meaning in work exists because of the weakening of religious and spiritual systems and with erosion in connected communities. As such, work has become a place for belongingness from which employees find or create meaning in life (Frankl, 1967, 1978; Hall, 1996; Heil, Bennis, & Stephens, 2000; Maslow, 1998; Morin, 1995; Viljoen, 1989). This search for meaning may be stronger as a result of the long work closures and social distancing efforts employed to reduce the spread of the COVID-19 virus. Researchers note individuals seek meaning through personal accomplishments (Frankl, 1984), by associating their existence with something bigger or something perceived as more significant than the self (Allport, 1961) and by fulfilling purpose, value, efficacy, and self-worth (Baumeister, 1991).

There is no clear consensus on what meaningful work is (Bailey et al., 2019). Researchers often use the terms meaningfulness and meaningful work interchangeable. Some scholars refer to meaningful work but describe and measure perceptions of Kahn's (1990) meaningfulness (e.g., Landells & Albrecht, 2019). Kahn's explicit definition of psychological meaningfulness is "a feeling that one is receiving a return on investments of one's self in a currency of physical, cognitive, or emotional energy. People experienced such meaningfulness when they felt worthwhile, useful, and valuable" (pp. 703–704). Other scholars use

---

2 See Dik, Byrne, and Steger (2013). This book contains several chapters from notable experts about how to create meaning and purpose at work.

Steger, Dik, and Duffy's (2012) conceptualization and measurement instrument, which combines meaningful work with meaningfulness and motivation (e.g., Demirtas et al., 2017; Johnson & Jiang, 2017). Specifically, Steger et al. suggest meaningful work constitutes the subjective experience of personal significance of work, the extent to which life is more meaningful because of doing meaningful work, and meaningful work creates motivation to support the greater good. Other researchers rely on spiritual definitions of meaningfulness (Ashmos & Duchon, 2000; Duchon & Plowman, 2005). Lastly, some scholars like Ashforth and Kreiner (2013) refer explicitly to meaningful work.

A qualitative study of earthquake survivors in China provides empirical support for a relationship between meaningful work and engagement (X. Wang et al., 2011). Survivors reported their efforts in providing post-quake relief and reconstruction was meaningful and gave them energy (they explicitly reported not being exhausted by this effort), making them feel engaged in the work. The authors' findings are supportive of the subjective definitions of meaning, where deriving meaning from one's work is about having purpose or direction (see Park, 2010) that may result from seeing one's actions contribute to goal achievement (King et al., 2006; McGregor & Little, 1998). An implication of this research is that creating a higher-order goal or purpose to which employees' work contributes might help employees find meaning or value in their work.

Scholars seem to agree that approaches to creating meaningful work (i.e., work employees consider significant and valuable; Pratt & Ashforth, 2003) include job redesign focusing on the aspects of the job important to employees, such as challenging work and task significance. People ask if what they do matters in the big picture of the organization (i.e., task significance) and whether it provides connection. Becherer et al. (1982) examined the relationship between task significance with experienced meaningfulness and found a correlation of .20. Autonomy and feedback were also positively correlated with meaningfulness ($r = .10$ and $r = .25$, respectively). Their study suggests possible approaches to job redesign that rely on components of the job characteristics theory might play a role in creating opportunities for finding meaning at work. Important within the constantly changing workplace, employees' perceptions of job fit (i.e., how work was, how work will be) mediate the relationship between Kahn's (1990) antecedent states and engagement (Hernandez & Guarana, 2018). One can surmise from these findings that organizations should maintain a long-view perspective of how employees experience their workplace (i.e., fit), as opposed to a short-term snapshot view, to maximize their psychological meaningfulness, safety, and availability.

Other aspects of work, such as role clarity and expected outcomes, potentially facilitate creating meaningfulness. Meaningfulness and role clarity are positively correlated ($r = .49$; Nielsen et al., 2008). According to Vroom's (1964) expectancy theory of motivation, people want something valuable in exchange for their work (called *valence*). If the outcome of their effort is clearly of little value to them, they will not be motivated to direct their efforts to achieve that outcome. Tests of Vroom's theory suggest the theory is most predictive of individuals' intended behavior when faced with several choices, as opposed to when faced with just one choice (Van Eerde & Thierry, 1996). Role clarity may offer information on what one can expect of the job, thereby connecting role clarity to expectancy theory.

Overall, regardless of how researchers describe or measure meaningfulness, their findings support a positive relationship between psychological meaningfulness and engagement (e.g., Busse & Regenberg, 2019; Fletcher, 2019; Landells & Albrecht, 2019). Byrne, Peters, and Weston (2016) show this relationship as more than just a correlation; they stated, "in light of our results, it may be that engagement is more accurately defined as incorporating meaningfulness rather than being fostered by meaningfulness" (p. 1218).

Meaningful Organizations

In one of my consulting projects, I worked with a nonprofit health care provider with a very clear mission (i.e., a formal statement of the unique purpose of the organization that defines its identity within its market; Pearce, 1982); in fact, though not prompted, nearly every employee interviewed mentioned the organization's mission. The first part of the consulting project was to understand how the organization defined employee engagement, to identify what supports engagement, and to determine potential roadblocks to helping employees become more engaged. Some employee comments from the project are provided in the Employees' Reflections box.

EMPLOYEES' REFLECTIONS

When asked what gets them out of bed and into work, interviewees produced statements such as the following:

- "[B]eing connected to the mission of the organization."
- "I really like work for this organization; it has a good mission; a mission I believe in. I get why . . . why we need to be the way we are. The mission itself is really important to me."
- "Being able to support the mission is important to me. Not only that it exists and I agree with it, but being able to actively promote the mission by making sure our financials are clean, we get clean audits, we're in good financial standing, and that, at least in a financial way, we are well respected for our practice is important to me."

- "I really do have a lot of connection to the work that we do here, and the mission of this organization. It is meaningful."
- "[T]he mission does seem to really drive conversation and decision-making such as I've witnessed so far. And again that unity, I don't know, in my experience, derives from clarity in leadership, a clear vision from leadership, so clearly that's being conveyed here. So, I think it's quite impressive actually."
- "[I]t's just in the way we talk about our work and identify with this mission of the organization. It gives me a lot of information about where are we as an organization because it's all going to come back to engagement and the feeling of being engaged or not."
- "I've read things about leadership and being a part of a mission-oriented organization and some of it is just what I believe and what I come to with myself which is knowing why you're working where you're working. I feel it's important to have a purpose behind my work I feel like it's important to be aligned in your purpose."

Suh, Houston, Barney, and Kwon (2011) examined organization mission fulfillment (OMF) and employee mission engagement (EME) in a large non-profit health care organization. They defined OMF as the degree to which the actions and messages of an organization are congruent with its stated mission, and operationalized it (i.e., measured) as mission strength – meaning the respondent agrees the organizational decisions are consistent with the mission statement and the culture sustains the mission. EME was defined as "a psychological state in which an employee desires to exert effort and devote careful attention to ensure the fulfillment of a mission that he or she perceives as significant or meaningful" (Suh et al., 2011, p. 78). EME was operationalized as working hard to ensure the mission is carried out and the extent to which one is motivated by the mission. Unfortunately, the authors' three-item measure of EME did not quite capture their definition, and it is not a measure of employee engagement; therefore, we can draw no conclusions from the study about employee engagement. However, the results of the study are nonetheless informative because (a) this appears to be one of the only studies focused on organizational mission and (b) the results indicate OMF and EME are positively correlated. Because transformational leadership incorporates the idea that the leader provides an inspiring vision, perhaps future research could tie transformational leadership to Suh et al.'s OMF and EME and examine their relationship to engaging employees.

People seek work that is meaningful out of a desire to have a good working life (Brown et al., 2001; Csikszentmihalyi, 1990). Meaningful work is valued, provides connection to others, and allows one to feel a part of something bigger than the self (Baumeister, 1991; Baumeister & Vohs, 2002). Thus, organizations that can provide a superordinate goal to which employees can connect and feel joined with others in achieving may encourage employees finding meaning at work and ultimately engagement (Chalofsky & Krishna, 2009; Kahn, 1990; Rosso, Dekas, & Wrzesniewski, 2010). A meaningful organization with a strong mission to which an employee can relate, can offer organizational and leadership purpose, as well as the opportunity for personal purpose through goal and value alignment. Lastly, it may be that a strong and clear mission ties into concepts relevant in expectancy theory, in that what employees are working for is clearly defined in the mission.

Table 4.1 provides a comprehensive list of possible interventions or solutions for engagement, their theoretical foundation, and what kind of supportive evidence they have for their use in promoting engagement.

TABLE 4.1 Interventions for Promoting Employee Engagement

Suggested Intervention	Theoretical Foundation	Examples of Empirical and/or Practical Support
Change expectancy for coping and self-efficacy for coping	Cognitive activation theory (Ursin & Eriksen, 2004)	None for engagement; see Meurs and Perrewé (2011) for use in occupational stress and potential application with the JD-R
Conserve or obtain resources to buffer stress; build resource capability	Conservation of resources theory (Hobfoll, 1989)	Two-wave, 3-year longitudinal: Hakanen, Perhoniemi et al. (2008); Bakker and van Wingerden (2021)
Empowering leaders	Empowering leadership (Conger & Kanungo, 1988)	Correlational support: Tuckey et al. (2012); Kim and Beehr (2020)
Full Range Leadership Development, transformational leadership training	Full range theory of leadership (Avolio & Bass, 2002) Transformational leadership theory (Bass, 1985)	Experimental design: Howell and Frost (1989) and Kirkpatrick and Locke (1996) both looked at charismatic leadership Quasi-experimental support: Barling, Weber, and Kelloway (1996); W. Brown and May (2012); Dvir et al. (2002); Parry and Sinha (2005) Practice support by Avolio and Bass (1994)
Increase emotional intelligence	Mayer and Salovey (1995)	Correlational support: Ravichandran et al. (2011) Longitudinal experiment: Cherniss, Grimm, and Liautaud (2010) Intervention support: Van Oosten et al. (2019)

Increase job resources	Job demands–resources model (Bakker & Demerouti, 2008) Reconceptualized job crafting (Bakker et al. (2012)	Correlational support: see preceding text; there are too many to list here. Intervention support: Gordon et al. (2018); Kuijpers et al. (2020); van Wingerden et al. (2017)
Increase work-related intrinsic motivation	Self-determination theory (Deci & Ryan, 1985)	Correlational support for related concepts, not engagement per se: Gagné et al. (1997); combined with JD-R (see job resources)
Job redesign	Job characteristics theory (Hackman & Oldham, 1976) Job crafting (Wrzesniewski & Dutton, 2001)	Meta-analytic support for the job characteristics theory: Behson et al. (2000) Not with engagement per se: Berg et al. (2010)
Meaningful organization and/or meaningfulness	Meaningfulness (Baumeister, 1991) Psychological meaningfulness (Kahn, 1990)	Paper on how to develop a mission statement: Cochran, David, and Gibson (2008) Chapter on creating meaningful work: Pratt, Pradies, and Lepisto (2013) Empirical studies: Busse and Regenberg (2019); Landells and Albrecht (2019)

What Might Research-Based Interventions Look Like for Engaging an Employee?

Lena has been working for a few years at a job that pays minimum wage. She works for a supermarket chain where her job varies between stacking the shelves, greeting customers at the door, servicing the cash register, and moving inventory around the store. Her organization has recently been promoting the idea of employee engagement, a concept that she understands means she needs to be more involved at work and come across as more enthusiastic or excited about the work. She's not sure if that's what they mean by engagement, but that's what it seems to her.

In Lena's last performance evaluation, her boss talked about what the organization expects of her now that she has been there for a while. He talked about her taking charge of deciding when she performs her various duties, such as when she should be greeting at the door versus when she should be moving or stocking inventory. He provided her access to the overall scheduling system so that she could determine when she is most needed at which position. Lena told him she was not sure if she could handle the stress of figuring out where she should be and when. He told her that she has actually already been managing her schedule when she has come to him and suggested that she switch positions because she noted that people needed help and when she has offered to work extra hours because a larger than expected shipment arrived. They talked about it a little bit, and Lena realized that indeed she has been managing her own stress levels by asking for help when she needs it or by identifying when she needs time off because she has been working extra hours. It just never occurred to her that that was what she was doing. Her boss also asked her what she thinks her work really means to the organization and to herself. He asked her to create an individual mission statement that would reflect what she thinks is important in the work that she does for the store. Finally, her boss asked for feedback on whether he has been providing appropriate direction, conveying excitement about the store's overall goals, and what he can do to help her develop her work skills so that she can move to the next levels in the organization.

What Lena experienced in her performance appraisal was her boss developing her self-efficacy for coping and managing her own stress. Her boss also used aspects of job characteristics theory to give Lena more autonomy and the opportunity to feel more task identity by understanding how she can fit in and contribute to the bigger picture of managing the store by allowing her to rearrange her schedule of tasks. Lastly, her boss made efforts to work on developing his own transformational leadership style by helping her to determine how to create more meaningful work for herself and by asking for feedback on whether he is displaying characteristics of transformational leadership, such as inspirational motivation and individualized consideration.

Practice-Based Approaches to Getting More Engagement

When considering practice-driven solutions, most indirectly incorporate the essential components of Kahn's (1990) model, relying heavily on the principles of the job characteristics theory (Hackman & Oldham, 1976). For example, a publication on the SHRM website reports the results of a survey (no date for the survey provided) that rates employees' responses as to which corporate practices (i.e., appear to be mostly benefits and/or compensation) were effective in keeping them engaged (not defined). Most were about job characteristics such as challenge, autonomy, and skill variety, along with growth opportunity (e.g., promotions, training) and feedback (e.g., performance reviews), and Kahn's psychological conditions of meaningfulness and safety (e.g., encouraged to share ideas; see SHRM, n.d.).

Zappos, rated in the top 25 of *Fortune* magazine's "100 Best Companies to Work For," is an online shoe and clothing store recently acquired by Amazon. com, another online store that sells a much broader variety of products. Zappos uses a number of strategies for hiring and promoting an engaged workforce, as reported by Perschel (2010). Though no empirical support for the strategies is provided, they appear consistent with the principles of the job characteristics theory and seeking person–organization fit. Specifically, their strategies include (a) hiring people whose values match those of the organization (this may be considered similar to hiring based on person–organization fit); (b) training new hires on the culture and core values, clarifying expectations for engagement; (c) challenging and growing employees' skills (similar to challenging work and skill variety core job dimensions of job characteristics theory); (d) empowering employees and giving them autonomy to implement their best judgment (similar to autonomy of job characteristics theory); (e) creating a culture for free expression (this may be considered creating a culture for Kahn's [1990] state of psychological safety); and (g) providing feedback in the form of rewards for behaviors consistent with the organization's goals and values (similar to feedback in job characteristics theory).

Using an internal survey, PricewaterhouseCoopers (PwC) CEO Bob Moritz (2014) determined that millennials have a different spin on the workplace than their older colleagues, though the underlying topics are the same. Namely, while work–life balance is important to older workers, millennials expect the organization to promote and ensure their ability to have a life outside of work, and if not forthcoming, they quit and find a company that does. Importantly, work is not that central to the millennials at PwC, though that does not mean they do not work hard or value their work. Rather they want and value interesting work that is aligned with the company mission, one that is more than simply making money and gives back to the community. Put another way, they want their work to be meaningful. We can infer from Moritz's findings that meaningfulness is central to work for newer generations, potentially more so than prior generations that focused more on reward systems and career growth. Similarly, organizational leaders often think career development and reward progression is most important to employees. However, it turns out that organizations with strong volunteer programs (i.e., pay employees to volunteer in the community) improve the attractiveness of an organization because job seekers who like to volunteer or care about the community anticipate pride in their affiliation with the organization, envision an organization with similar values, and assume an organization that pays its employees to volunteer treats its employees well. Volunteering increases well-being and sense of purpose, resulting in higher perceived meaningfulness and ultimately, higher engagement. Rodell (2021) noted on her work with United Way and the Junior League that volunteers felt a greater sense of meaningfulness because they were able to help others. Thus, rather than focusing inward, on internal reward mechanisms, organizations might consider looking externally (i.e., volunteering) to what employees find rewarding.

In an application of job redesign, Microsoft Corporation implemented a career model framework with an accompanying leadership development program to create the focused workforce necessary for a strategic product change (Olesen, White, & Lemmer, 2007). The first step was an assessment of the current state of the organization's managers and company culture. The second step was to develop clearly defined materials outlining management levels, job descriptions, training plans, and career paths for each level. The third step involved testing the materials and developing an online system to facilitate the career path planning that took place at annual performance evaluations. The materials, or what they called the career model, specified standards for identifying, assessing, managing, and developing employees along a particular career path. Employees identify a career path that it is achievable, given their competencies or capabilities, performance, and experience. Furthermore, they had to ensure the career path included development aligned with organizational goals and with the value propositions for the company. Full details of the model and its development can be found in Olesen et al. (2007). Progress over a 3-year time frame was tracked, with specific measures in place for assessing progress and change. Although the study authors did not provide empirical evidence for the success of the model in changing engagement levels, they concluded the model did address employee engagement as part of career development and talent management. They further noted that employees recognized the organization's commitment to them and their development, which could translate into perceptions of increased support and value and feelings of significance. According to the job characteristics theory (Hackman & Oldham, 1976), efforts that develop greater significance and overall perceived value will translate into higher levels of motivation.

Originally aimed at addressing issues of turnover, strategies to improve job fit may have the side benefit of facilitating engagement. Specifically, Moreland (2013) recommended one approach similar to Perschel (2010), namely, hiring people whose skills and education match the position requirements, and then continuing their education to maintain the match as job requirements change. Although she did not call it job analysis, Moreland recommended assessments to determine specific competencies necessary for success on the job and then make those requirements for knowledge, skills, and abilities clear during recruitment and selection. Ongoing assessments of employees are recommended throughout their tenure to re-evaluate fit as job requirements change and as employees develop. Again, no empirical evidence is provided in support of these recommendations. However, if we assume that job fit, like person–organization fit, represents a match between the employee's knowledge, skills, abilities, and values with those of the organization, and such a match promotes experienced psychological meaningfulness, employees experiencing fit will be engaged.

Some empirical support for job fit positively relating to engagement exists (e.g., Bui, Zeng, & Higgs, 2017; Cai, Cai, Sun, & Ma, 2018; de Beer, Rothmann, & Mostert, 2016; Ybema, Koopman, & Peeters, 2020); thus, we can conclude there may be merit to interventions designed around increasing job fit.

Other practitioners suggest the way to foster employee engagement is by focusing on career development and career planning (e.g., Wozniak, 2013), because "engagement is a byproduct" (Wozniak, 2013, p. 44). Wozniak (2013) defined engagement as emotional involvement and commitment to the organization. By understanding how employees have an impact on the overall organization (one could interpret this as task significance from job characteristics theory), Wozniak suggests that employees will become emotionally involved and committed.

Stevens (2013) proposed that if you match employees' wants for a worthwhile and inspiring job (one could interpret this as meaningfulness and challenge) with organizations' wants for high-performing employees, you get the "basis for employee engagement" (p. 91). Stevens defined engagement as a combination of a psychological contract, satisfaction, and motivation. Stevens suggested the way to promote engagement is to create a supportive and nurturing work environment by having learning opportunities, an open-door management policy (i.e., employees can meet with the manager at any time), shared ownership in projects and the organization overall, task significance, and an "inspiring leader" (Stevens, 2013, p. 92). Furthermore, she suggested organizations can build engagement by recruiting those who most likely fit the culture (i.e., one could interpret this as person–organization fit); having a socialization process, opportunities for career development, reward and recognition programs; conveying value via surveys (i.e., assessing pay and benefit satisfaction, opportunity for input); having flexible work schedules; and building trust. Although none of these suggestions is harmful, there is no evidence any are related to employee engagement.

In a similar fashion, Lavigna (2013) advocated for improving employee engagement, defined as "a heightened employee connection to work, the organization, the mission or coworkers" (p. 11). Specifically, Lavigna's approaches included publicly advocating for government and public service, providing strong and stable leadership, supporting employee development, articulating goals and values of the organization, emphasizing the organization's vision, involving employees in decision-making, encouraging risk-taking, encouraging higher levels of education, accommodating unique employee needs, weeding out "bad fits" (p. 12), setting clear performance expectations, and treating employees fairly. Again, although the recommendations may not be harmful to the organization or its employees, there is no evidence (except for fairness) to support these suggestions foster (or are even related to) employee engagement. However, it may be possible that one or more of these various approaches indirectly affects employees' engagement levels.

A. Harrison (2012) provided no definition of engagement but outlined five tips for improving engagement, which she reports is lacking in more than 70% of U.S. workers (she refers to results from a Kenexa Research Institute [2009] study). Harrison recommended the organization must (a) evaluate team members and resources to ensure you have "the right people on your team and the right resources in your artillery" (p. 10); (b) make sure organizational values are clearly communicated to employees so they can "live them" (p. 10); (c) be open to feedback from employees; (d) "live the brand" (p. 10), which means employees must be "brand ambassadors" (p. 10); and (e) make sure communication messages within the organization are clear and say what you want (i.e., do not focus so much on how it is said, but what is said). The language of the article is exciting (e.g., artillery, ambassador, live the brand) but lacks substance (i.e., what exactly is engagement, and what does it mean to live the brand or be a brand ambassador?) and evidence the suggestions have anything to do with employee engagement – assuming you know what Harrison means by engagement.

Many practice-based approaches to fostering engagement seem to touch on one or more of the principles of job characteristics theory; however, not all do. There is one practice approach that takes a personal, reflective perspective for fostering "resolution, passion, and energy," resulting in being more "proactive and self-assured," leading to faster and clearer thinking, which together allows you to "express your personal intentions, identity, ideals, values, and driving force" – all implied as the definition of engagement (Rampersad, 2006, p. 18). Employee engagement is not formally defined. The intention of the article is to convey how to create the right social and contextual environment that can foster one's engagement. Specifically, Rampersad introduces the "personal balanced scorecard" (2006, p. 18), which comprises four dimensions assessed using seven questions. The dimensions include internal (physical and mental health), external (relations with others), knowledge and learning (knowledge, skills, and abilities), and financial stability. The seven questions include (1) Who am I? (2) Where am I going? (3) What type of relationship would I like to have with others? (4) Which factors make me unique? (5) Which results do I want to achieve? (6) How can I measure my personal results? and (7) How do I want to achieve the results? (see Rampersad, 2006, for details). The answers create an awareness of the self in the form of a personal balanced scorecard, from which an action plan can be written and tracked. Rampersad suggests permanent and long-term changes can be achieved by following his plan, with the implications being that positive engagement follows.

The list of publications similar to these reviewed earlier is long and continues. Although most recommendations are provided by people with years of experience in human resources or in-depth experiences within a particular organization, none provides evidence the recommendations are related to engagement, and most fail to provide a definition of engagement. Nearly all include at least one component of job characteristics theory (e.g., task signifi-cance, challenging work, autonomy), refer to resources of some kind, or men-tion meaningful work.

In my capacity as a trusted advisor and technical expert in psychometrics for a medium-sized organization (about 12,000 employees) in the United States, I was asked to review a number of vendor solutions for assessing and develop-ing employee engagement. Keeping the names of the vendors confidential, I can share the following observations: instead of measuring employee engage-ment, the vendors' solutions assessed organizational affective commitment, satisfaction, organizational citizenship behaviors, and climate factors associ-ated with employee engagement. For example, their surveys measured super-visory support, coworker relations, and general resources, not unlike those resources noted as examples in the Job Demands–Resources and conservation of resources models (e.g., flextime, benefits, training). During their presenta-tions, when I asked about whether they assess engagement itself versus what is considered a driver of engagement (e.g., climate factors that are thought to relate to engagement), the vendors each acknowledged their instruments do not actually measure employee engagement but rather measure aspects of work they believe predict or drive engagement. None defined engagement using definitions proposed in the academic literature, such as Kahn's (1990) and Schaufeli et al.'s (2002), nor did they use any other published definition or model for that matter (e.g., Saks, 2006). None (at that time) offered validity evidence for their solutions in changing scores on "engagement." An important limitation of my anecdotal evidence is that I was only asked to review a small number of solutions; there are hundreds available (at least according to searches on the Internet), and it is possible that some have roots in the research literature and/or provide substantial validity evidence.

In summary, there are many practice-based approaches to fostering employee engagement, yet none to date is accompanied by solid, publicly available valid-ity evidence supporting their assertions that they foster or increase employee engagement.

Reflections From Byrne's Qualitative Work

The approaches to fostering engagement reviewed in this chapter are based in either theory or practice, yet none is based on what employees themselves have said might foster their engagement. In 2010, I worked with a health care orga-nization that asked me to identify what engagement is in the organization and what prevents engagement for their employees. Using a qualitative methodol-ogy, my team and I interviewed 32 individual employees. The research team facilitated an additional four focus groups of four to eight people each, across the four branch locations. We used interview scripts with items such as, "What about your job do you like least?" "What prevents you from getting into your job?" and "What would it take for you to work to your fullest capacity – to give all of yourself (mind, soul, and body) into this job?" In 2011, I conducted another similar project, working with another health care organization that asked me to identify for them what engagement is and what prevents engagement for their employees. Again using a qualitative methodology, my team and I interviewed 48 individuals and conducted an additional four focus groups ranging from four to eight participants each, held at the organization's different locations. The questions were scripted so all interviews and focus groups were asked the same questions. Example questions included, "Can you tell me about a situation at work (within the last month) in which you would say you felt unengaged?" "What does being unengaged at work mean?" "What does it look and feel like?" and "What made you feel that you couldn't become engaged?"

Table 4.2 shows the themes extracted from both studies that reflect potential drivers or factors that encourage engagement. Although these drivers have not been confirmed in a larger sample that might provide generalizability information, they came from employees themselves (and a reasonably large number for qualitative work).

TABLE 4.2 Qualitative Findings on Drivers of Engagement

Theme	Examples
Meaningfulness	Meaning of work itself
	Meaning of the mission or vision of the organization
	Fulfilling work
	Making a difference
Alignment	Head and heart alignment
	Goal alignment within organization
	Value and skill match between self and the organization (P–O fit)
Relationships	Great colleagues and coworkers
	Mentors and being able to mentor others
	Supervisory support
	Organizational support
	Mutual respect
	Trust
Communication	Clarity of goals and vision for the organization
	Clear job and role expectations
	Small power distance
Job itself	Challenging work
	Opportunity to participate in work-related activities that are not directly tied to the job (e.g., volunteer within the organization)
	Fun or can have fun while doing it
	Involvement in innovation, creativity, and developing new things or solutions
	Skill and task variety

Personal (i.e., valuable)	Developmental opportunities
	Learning environment
	Voice; being asked for input and using the input
	Being asked to speak up when you see ways to improve the organization
	Regular and timely feedback that provides validation of the self and how to become validated (when the feedback is constructive toward improvement)
	Benefits that allow for downtime when it's needed
Good leadership	Skilled, effective, and authentic

What to Do About Engagement?

In a recent meta-analysis, Vîrgă, Maricuțoiu, and Iancu (2019) focused on assessing the efficacy of controlled interventions at improving employee engagement. Although interventions overall were effective, the average effect size was small. However, the most interesting result from their study was their moderator analyses. They determined the effectiveness of the intervention declined steeply within 3 months after the intervention, suggesting most interventions (at least those they reviewed) only worked for about 3 months. They further determined short interventions, up to 2 weeks, were the most effective, providing support for engagement as a momentary construct versus a stable-persistent construct. The implications of their findings are that interventions to boost engagement are likely more effective if they are short and occur frequently.

Given most approaches reviewed previously have only correlational support, at best, for relating to employee engagement, what should an organization and researchers do about employee engagement? First, additional evaluation studies are sorely needed. If organizations and academic researchers can collaborate to evaluate implemented solutions in the workplace, these findings will go a long way toward offering insight into whether and how one can foster engagement. Experiments within organizations can be hard to coordinate, but quasi-experiments and longitudinal studies are feasible with enough cooperation between both parties.

Second, if researchers expand the scope of their investigations into engagement beyond the primary and overwhelmingly dominant goal of advancing theory, these studies could make a broader contribution that reciprocally influences theoretical thinking about engagement. That is, after reading several peer-reviewed journals, one could argue a majority of the research in the academic realm is so focused on theory that the practice of the field seems a very distant cousin at best. Because of business trade-offs, pure practice-based papers often leave out the scientific rigor necessary for drawing causal conclusions (e.g., experimentation, controls for common method variance, reliable and public domain measures), making them impossible to use in meta-analyses (because they tend not to report full correlation tables, effect sizes, and complete measurement information) or for researchers evaluating the full merits of the study. Thus, meeting in the middle is necessary.

There are enough studies on engagement that Table 4.1 of suggested interventions is still useful in guiding researchers and practitioners as to what to do about engagement. Contributions to understanding what drives engagement can be made by conducting experimental studies to accurately assess the antecedents of engagement. For example, although correlational studies show a relationship between engagement and leadership, job characteristics, and job resources, and most suggest via theory that these are predictors of engagement, few, if any, causal studies support this assumed direction of relationships. If engagement is a state of motivation, we can assume employees become engaged on their own given the right conditions and work factors. Thus, climate factors such as norms, expectations, company policies, and organizational culture in general will likely influence the probability of employees finding the right conditions to become engaged (e.g., Byrne, Palmer, Smith, & Weidert, 2011).

Individual differences may influence engagement levels (e.g., Akhtar et al., 2015; Philip, 2021); hence, researchers should consider a person–situation interactionism framework. For example, some have suggested that a proactive personality (i.e., a stable tendency to, under one's own initiative, change one's work environment for meaningful improvements; Bateman & Crant, 1993) may be an individual difference construct worth studying with engagement (e.g., Bakker et al., 2012). Preliminary findings show a positive relationship between engagement and proactive personality (Cai et al., 2018; Dikkers et al., 2010). Others have initiated studies examining the personality factors of the Big Five (conscientiousness, neuroticism, extraversion, agreeableness, openness to experience) and engagement (see H. Chen et al., 2020; Inceoglu & Warr, 2011; Liao, Yang, Wang, Drown, & Shi, 2013).

Practitioners may consider a number of these strategies, knowing that even though correlation does not mean causation, it does mean covary; thus, as one construct goes up, so does the other, and most likely the relationships are actually reciprocal. For example, it is quite possible engaged employees attract leaders who feel comfortable with a transformational or authentic leadership style, because those types of leaders are at their best leading engaged employees. Similarly, it is possible employees who are engaged are able to find and obtain resources that enable them to be even more engaged, allowing them to attract and effectively use more of their resources.

Conclusion

We need more research to understand what drives engagement, and what truly results from it and not from tangential increases or changes in mood, ability, skill, or general attitude toward work and leadership. Collaboration between the research and practice community is needed to more fully realize the gains from both research and practice. Lastly, it may be that a perfect set of interventions eludes us because "there are no guarantees about when individual workers will fully engage. There are some workers who may never become engaged, and others who will do so easily and often" (Kahn & Fellows, 2013, p. 111).

WALK-AWAY POINTS

- Several approaches for promoting employee engagement exist, some with theoretical backing and others without. Leadership as a driver for engagement is popular; however, surprisingly few studies demonstrate that leadership is related to engagement, and none shows that it increases engagement.
- Meaningful work and meaningful organizations show promise in fostering engagement.
- Very few, if any, research- and practice-related suggestions for how to increase levels of engagement in employees have empirical, causal support indicating that applying the techniques or changes suggested will actually result in changes in engagement.
- When employees are asked what promotes their engagement, they respond with a variety of drivers that may be grouped into seven categories, including alignment, communication, and personal factors.

5

WHAT PREVENTS EMPLOYEE ENGAGEMENT?

Many consulting or practice documents refer to engagement by describing the costs of disengaged employees to industry. However, none of these popular writings describes or defines what disengagement is or what unengaged workers look like or do. Their focus is on engagement as an outcome (Wefald & Downey, 2009), which they define as the opposite of disengagement.

What Is Disengagement?

Kahn (1990) defined personal disengagement as the "uncoupling of selves from work roles; in disengagement, people withdraw and defend themselves physically, cognitively, or emotionally during role performances" (p. 694). He noted when people disengage, they withdraw, becoming passive in their roles. He likened disengagement to robotic or automatic behaviors, such as displaying effortless and disinterested performance. He further suggested people who are disengaged hide their identity, thoughts, and feelings while at work. These people perform their roles in a thoughtless script, as opposed to interpreting their role in becoming involved or connected with what they are to accomplish. When disengaged, their goal is to protect their inner self, to tamp down emotions, or just let go of caring. Some scholars have summarized disengagement as being on autopilot, simply going through the motions. They may push their tasks onto others or, when in a managerial role, may excessively delegate to their employees in an effort to withdraw cognitively from their role. Ideas are kept to the self and creativity is diminished. Similarly, Fineman (1983), in his exploration of the meaning of work through examining individuals recently unemployed, also defined disengagement a psychological distancing and withdrawal from work. Disengagement was marked by the passage of time

DOI: 10.4324/9781003171133-7

with little thought to the job tasks, but being sufficiently present to do the job. Disengagement goes beyond the absence of engagement; it is a *deliberate or intentional action* taken by employees to actively protect their preferred selves by distancing themselves cognitively, emotionally, and physically (Wollard, 2011).

Is Job Burnout the Same as Disengagement?

The descriptions of disengagement offered by Kahn (1990) and Fineman (1983) may seem similar to those of job burnout. Job burnout refers to "the response to chronic emotional and interpersonal stressors on the job and is defined here by the three dimensions of exhaustion, cynicism, and sense of inefficacy" (Maslach, 2003, p. 189). Thus, burnout is a response to an overwhelming or chronic stressor. Exhaustion leads employees to distance themselves emotionally and cognitively from their work. Cynicism is characterized by a negative and callous response to coworkers and to the job itself, and is highly correlated with exhaustion. Feelings of inefficacy are feelings of ineffectiveness and inability to accomplish one's goals or job tasks. Inefficacy develops because of exhaustion and cynicism, but also in parallel with these two dimensions of burnout (Maslach, 2003).

Maslach (2003) emphasized that burnout is a social construct: the interpersonal framework in which burnout develops is a key component of understanding burnout. Burnout is not just an individual's response to stress; it is also a reaction to the interchange between the individual and others in the workplace, and to the general work situation itself. Although some research has demonstrated a connection between burnout and a few demographic variables (e.g., single vs. married, younger vs. older; Maslach, Schaufeli, & Leiter, 2001), most findings lean toward situational context rather than demographic or dispositional factors. For example, excessively or chronically challenging jobs, imbalance of resources versus demands, and constant personal and role conflict consistently show up in the situations most likely to elicit burnout (Schaufeli & Enzmann, 1998). Maslach (2003) suggested burnout represents a misfit between the person and their work environment: the job exceeds the individual's capacity in some form.

Although research is needed to examine the potential similarities and differences between disengagement and burnout, conceptually there appear to be a few key differences. First, job burnout is a stress response – a personal reaction to the work environment and its dynamics. Disengagement is referred to as a purposeful decoupling of the self from the job, of which burnout may be a behavioral display of disengagement, but not necessarily instigated by stress. Disengagement might predict burnout. Second, burnout refers to a complete exhaustion level at which one cannot perform the job task and at which one becomes negative and cynical toward others and the job. In contrast, disengagement does not necessarily include physical exhaustion;

disengaged individuals can complete their work, but do so with an emotional detachment that removes their sense of identity with the work and the organization. After developing a measure for assessing disengagement, Manning (2015) reported correlations of .59 between burnout and disengagement, −.71 between engagement and disengagement, and .61 with work withdrawal. Manning's confirmatory factor analyses verified the distinctiveness of his measure relative to the UWES and JES. Additional validity evidence is necessary to support Manning's measure as assessing a construct distinct from low engagement; however, his preliminary evidence is solid and suggests disengagement is unique from low engagement, withdrawal, and burnout. To date, no other measure of disengagement exists. Perhaps a valuable delineation between burnout and disengagement can be found within several qualitative studies my students and I have conducted (some reviewed in Chapter 4 and in what follows).

Byrne's Qualitative Field Research on What Is Disengagement

As noted in Chapter 4, I worked with a health care organization that asked me to identify what engagement looks like in the organization and what prevents engagement for the employees. As part of the project, interviewees identified what disengagement felt like and looked like, and what prevented them from becoming engaged. Similarly, and described in more detail in Chapter 4, I worked with another health organization, also to identify what engagement looks like and what prevents engagement for employees.

Table 5.1 lists themes extracted from the responses from both studies of what disengagement is.

Some of the examples within these themes are similar to those noted by Kahn (1990), such as distancing oneself and disconnecting from the organization or others. Likewise, some are similar to those used for describing burnout (Maslach, 2003). Some interviewees suggested feeling emotionally exhausted led to their becoming disengaged. Specifically, employees talked about how emotionally draining the work itself could be, even though they loved what they did, and they referred to how having to collaborate and gain consensus on every single decision (even small) became emotionally exhausting. Additionally, though they were exhausted, they did not describe cynicism or inefficacy, nor did they completely withdraw from the work; rather, they conscientiously reduced their contribution. A number of examples we extracted that were different from burnout and from Kahn's work include doing sloppy work and complaining, which we categorized as counterproductive.

An interview we had with another individual outside the scope of these two studies gave us some insight into potentially key differences between burnout and engagement.

TABLE 5.1 Themes Extracted From Qualitative Work: What Is Disengagement

Theme	Examples
Hiding	Flying under the radar
	Psychological, emotional, and cognitive distancing of oneself from others at work
	Escape from the work stuff that is draining, such as the politics and personal conflicts
Counterproductive	Resisting change but not being able to say why
	Complaining and becoming argumentative
	Doing sloppy work; not feeling motivated to try to make the work of good quality (do what it takes to just get by, but nothing more)
Negative emotions	Feeling disconnected from the organization
	Feeling disconnected from the system and from others in the system
	Feeling a lack of control over the work, the work environment, and things you should be able to control to do your job well
	Feeling a lack of curiosity when you used to have a lot of curiosity that drove your energy
	Feeling trapped, like you can't get out of the bad situation and it's not the work that's pushing you away; you want to do the work but can't
	Feeling rejected, like a failure, unable to achieve success after constant trial and error
	Lack of feeling of ownership
	Feeling helpless to change what isn't working around me; learned helplessness
	Low morale
	Not meeting one's own bar for success; disappointment in the self that continues on and can't seem to find a way or get the help needed to jump over one's own bar
Withdrawal	Dislike the job itself; not interested in the work or the objective
	Not wanting to do the work anymore even though it's what you say and intuitively know you enjoy
	Making excuses for not performing responsibilities
	Refusing to partake in organizational initiatives
	Passivity
Time factor	Not an overnight thing; seemed to happen after a succession of ongoing events, issues, lack of support, etc.

EMPLOYEES' REFLECTIONS

When I think about whether I'm truly disengaged, I think that perhaps I'm burned out – but not actually disengaged. I don't think I'm disengaged because I have a ton of work opportunities that I'm excited about, lots of work to do that I typically enjoy, am excited about moving my personal success forward, I've started some new projects that I can control and work on independently, and I have focus – though I do get tired and distracted. I feel emotionally excited about what I do and I seem to have enough energy to do it when I get into it. I wake up and go to work, though I tire easily from the excessive interaction and stupid things that people around me say and do. If I could just be in my own space and do my own thing, I think I would be seen as very engaged. I feel burned out because I'm wanting to be away from these people – I am cynical about their ability to change and all of a sudden become good leaders, and I am more tired than I used to be. I feel like having to deal with that outside noise takes me away from doing what I really want to do, which is engage in my work.

What Inhibits or Prevents Engagement?

My research suggests a variety of organizational and individual factors inhibit or prevent employees from becoming engaged. Tables 5.2 and 5.3 list themes of what inhibits engagement, extracted from both studies.

The results from my qualitative research suggest both individual and organizational factors get in the way of employees becoming engaged. Specifically, organizational factors refer to those over which the organization seems to have the most influence or control, such as the amount of work individuals do on a daily or weekly basis, the amount of management they receive (or the lack thereof), whether individuals' behavior or decisions are appropriately scrutinized or people are held accountable for their decisions, and the establishment and reinforcement of norms that might suggest speaking up in the interest of helping your organization (i.e., voice) is considered resistance to organizational policies or change (Van Dyne & LePine, 1998). Individual factors were those that individuals could control or interpret on their own, based on their own personal situations. For example, whether family problems (e.g., sick family members) result in an inability to focus at work is an individualized response (Lazarus, 1991; Lazarus & Folkman, 1984). Some people compartmentalize their home and work lives such that when they are at work, they do not focus attention on what is happening at home because they feel they have taken care of the home needs so they can go to work (e.g., J. Howard, Rechnitzer, & Cunningham, 1975). Others are unable to take a compartmentalized approach, and so they maintain passive or constant thinking about worries at home. Lack of progress toward goal achievement could be either an individual or an organizational factor, depending on what is preventing the progress. However, how one interprets lack of progress and the response to it is really individualized (Linnenbrink & Pintrich, 2010). Some people may feel the lack of progress is

TABLE 5.2 Qualitative Findings on Organizational Inhibitors to Engagement

Theme	Examples
Resources	Lack of support
	Resource constraints, such as people, time, and equipment
	Technology that inhibits one's ability to do the job effectively
	Lack of work–life balance
Interpersonal	Overly chatty coworkers, subordinates, bosses, or other work colleagues who mean well but you can't deter them because the norm prevents you from stopping excessive time-wasting like this (i.e., a lack of ability to control your work environment)
	Hostile or emotionally abusive work environment (secretive, manipulative, emotionally punishing)
	Lack of demonstration of caring about individual development, growth in the job and/or to be able to do other jobs; demonstration of lack of commitment to employees
	Lack of professionalism among coworkers and/or supervisor, and little ability to fix
	Feeling lack of trust from others that you can do the job
Leadership	Being micromanaged
	Poor and ineffective management and leadership
	Negative organizational politics
	Lack of accountability
	Inequity
	High or excessive workload; prevents goal achievement
	Lack of voice or ability to provide input to positively change the system or job so that it is more efficient; demonstrates a lack of trust
	Too much focus on the bottom line, not enough on process
	A norm that suggests or implies speaking up about concerns implies lack of support for the organization; thus, suggestions meant for improving the work environment are seen as resistance to change or disagreement with management
	Constant change that creates transition confusion and lack of clarity over roles and objectives
	Poor communication, non-direct communication (e.g., beating around the bush and not addressing the "real" issues); miscommunication and lack of communication (information vacuum)
Other	Mundane work

solely attributed to the organization and just a part of working: they focus on what they can achieve. For others, the lack of progress on one task inhibits their ability to feel engaged in their work in general (Ouweneel, Schaufeli, & Le Blanc, 2013). They feel stuck, and they cannot focus on other tasks because the one task is not getting done.

Emotional exhaustion, as defined in the responses from our interviewees, was not a general or a global emotional exhaustion or burnout to which the

TABLE 5.3 Qualitative Findings on Individual Inhibitors to Engagement

Theme	Examples
Significance	Feeling undervalued, not recognized
	Feeling taken advantage of, taken for granted
Fit	Work that is not a match for one's skills, knowledge, and ability (lack of fit)
	Lack of agreement or alignment between the head and the heart (what makes sense intellectually, versus what feels right)
	Lack of necessary skills for self or others
Non-work related	Family problems, such as sick family members
	Inability to focus on work due to non-work interferences
	Non-work-related factors that require attention but take time and thus compete with work (e.g., life maintenance, home care, pet care, needy family members)
Communication	Relational issues (conflicts, personality clashes); very long learning curve or when feedback on performance has a long delay cycle
	Emotional exhaustion from the work itself and by having to excessively cooperate with others to gain consensus or agreement on every decision
Stress	Physical constraints, such as injury or chronic pain
	Lack of progress toward goal achievement; inability to complete job or accomplish work goals, or inability to do the job with high quality because of excessive workload or deadlines

term generally refers. That is, individuals referred to how emotionally taxing the work was itself, in particular within the health care institution.

The job itself required a lot of them emotionally, and because they loved the work and believed what they were doing was important, they were unable to invest of themselves in a balanced or managed fashion. Thus, every day and every case (i.e., client/patient) was emotionally draining. Interviewees explained that when you do this day in and day out, the emotional drain regarding that work, in particular, takes its toll. Additionally, excessive need for cooperation or gaining consensus or agreement on every decision, though perhaps originally intended to keep everyone involved as part of creating a positive work environment became negative, preventing people from goal accomplishment. Individuals had to use a lot of emotional energy to negotiate, communicate, and understand the perspective of many others within the organization before any action or decision could be made. This energy expenditure was perceived as negative, especially when it was about very small decisions that could easily have been made by one person without detrimental effects to others. It was clear from these interviews the exhaustion was targeted at the specifics of the job; people did not talk about being exhausted about all aspects of the job or all the time, they did not seek to distance themselves from others, nor did they talk about becoming cynical. Thus, they did not describe being burned out, just emotionally spent at various times.

Following up on the second qualitative study I conducted, I asked participants questions about injustice, job demands, and supervisor or coworker incivility. The injustice questions were those developed to specifically ask about
injustice (i.e., violation of social, moral, and fairness norms; Bies, 1987; M. Fine,
1983), as opposed to low levels of justice (e.g., fairness perceptions at work). Job
demands included pressure to complete tasks; pressure to get a lot done; role
ambiguity; poor physical working conditions, such as poor lighting, noisy or
distracting sounds, or uncomfortable or cramped office design; and resource
inadequacies. Participants rated how often their job included or required the
items/actions. Lastly, incivility items (see Cortina, Magley, Williams, & Langhout, 2001) focused on how often participants had been put into a situation by
their supervisor or coworker and included "put you down," "make demeaning
remarks about you and/or to you," and "made unwanted attempts to draw you
into a discussion of personal matters." Results of the analysis showed supervisor
incivility and injustice were both negatively related to employee engagement.
Thus, the more incivility or injustice an employee perceived, the lower their
reported engagement levels. Research has shown that responses to incivility or
injustice at work include detachment, and avoidance and withdrawal behaviors (Cortina & Magley, 2009; L. Howard & Cordes, 2010), and such reactions
appear to be associated with disengagement as noted in our qualitative studies.
Researchers who reverse-score engagement as way of assessing disengagement
(e.g., Azeem, Bajwa, Shahzad, & Aslam, 2020) have found injustice positively
relates to disengagement (Aslam, Muqadas, Imran, & Rahman, 2018), and both
psychological contract violation and job dissatisfaction positively relate to disengagement (Azeem et al., 2020).

In summary, the themes extracted from the qualitative studies on inhibitors
to engagement cumulatively suggest aspects of the organization and within the
individual's life play a role in preventing or inhibiting engagement. Notable
in the qualitative data is that themes for engagement inhibitors did not mirror drivers of engagement; thus, job characteristics, a frequently noted driver
of engagement, was not mentioned in the negative (i.e., a lack of job characteristics creates disengagement). Some of the themes were job demand and
job resource related, suggesting the job demands–resources model (Bakker &
Demerouti, 2008) might serve to help predict what inhibits engagement. Thus
far, this model's primary value is in predicting engagement, but perhaps its
greater utility is in examining when employees are or will become disengaged
(i.e., once demands exceed resources).

Theoretically Derived Inhibitors/Roadblocks

Very little research to date has examined what disengagement is and what
inhibits or prevents employees from becoming engaged. An examination of
the research and theory leads us to the following possible theoretically derived
inhibitors or roadblocks to engagement, shown in Table 5.4.

TABLE 5.4 Theoretically Based Inhibitors to Engagement

Inhibitor	Foundational Theory or References
Control, lack of autonomy, feedback suggests incompetence regardless of competence level, and inability to relate to others	Self-determination theory (Deci & Ryan, 1985)
	Job characteristics theory (Hackman & Oldham, 1976)
Distrust	Theory of collective distrust; Kramer (1994)
Inequity	Organizational justice (Bies & Moag, 1986; Deutsch, 1985)
Lack of clear mission or vision provides meaningful goals and purpose to the work	Meaningful work; Baumeister (1991)
Lack of job or organizational fit; work value congruence	Person–job or person–organization fit; Adkins, Russell, and Werbel (1994); Bretz, Ash, and Dreher (1989); Chatman (1991); Meglino, Ravlin, and Adkins (1989)
	Attraction-selection-attrition (ASA) model; Schneider (1987)
Negative organizational politics	Ferris, Frink, Beehr, and Gilmore (1995); Ferris, Russ, and Fandt (1989)
Organizational change	Interdependence theory (Kelley, 1984); Michela and Vena (2012)
Reduction and loss of job resources	Job demands–resources model (Bakker & Demerouti, 2008); Conservation of resources theory (Hobfoll, 1989)
Threats to psychological availability (e.g., distraction from non-work-related concerns, illness)	Kahn's (1990) engagement model
Threats to psychological meaningfulness (e.g., inability to determine purpose of work, lack of fit with organizational vision, job does not relate to goal of the team)	Kahn's (1990) engagement model
Threats to psychological safety (e.g., untrustworthy supervisor, workplace gossip, work concerns taken out of context and used against oneself)	Kahn's (1990) engagement model

According to Kahn

Kahn's (1990) work leads us to the following possible inhibitors of engagement. First, the three psychological states – psychological safety, psychological availability, and psychological meaningfulness – lead to employee engagement. Thus, anything that takes away from individuals' ability to feel psychologically safe and available or to get a sense of psychological meaningfulness from the job should inhibit their ability to become engaged.

Threats to Psychological Safety

Working in an environment that lacks trust in employees, fosters criticism, and promotes discrimination against individuals who may approach work uniquely will produce a work environment that threatens psychological safety. Environments that inhibit or exclude individuals from lesbian, gay, bisexual, transgender, or queer (LGBTQ) communities; individuals with alternative religious or spiritual beliefs; individuals of color; individuals with disabilities; or individuals belonging to other marginalized groups will create perceived lack of psychological safety. Employees who convey an unpopular opinion, but one offered in the spirit of improving the work environment (e.g., voice behaviors; Van Dyne & LePine, 1998), will feel psychologically unsafe in an organization that stifles or fails to encourage such positive and constructive criticisms. The presence of excessive negative organizational politics will also inhibit psychological safety because organizational politics are intentional actions that promote and protect some individuals at the expense of others or the organization (R. Allen, Madison, Porter, Renwick, & Mayes, 1979; Ferris & Kacmar, 1992). Additionally, organizational policies that appear to discriminate against individuals of multicultural races or differing personal relationship preferences may inhibit perceptions of psychological safety.

Supervisors who are untrained in positive coaching can also contribute to a negative psychological safety climate by giving inappropriate or poorly communicated feedback. For example, when employees make mistakes or behave in ways the organization does not sanction, supervisors who are unskilled may fail to understand why employees make mistakes or how these mistakes may be avoided in the future, and unable to give the necessary feedback that preserves employee self-esteem while fostering improvement. Additionally, employees who are treated inappropriately are unlikely to ask for help when they need it or may even retaliate against supervisors who are perceived as punishing (Hershcovis et al., 2007; Treviño & Brown, 2005). Arnetz et al.'s (2018) findings suggest workplace bullying is a threat to psychological safety, which we expect would contribute to disengagement. Likewise, when employees feel their supervisors and coworkers treat them with incivility (e.g., demeaning remarks, cut off in conversation, no credit for work), they report low psychological safety and psychological availability (Reio & Sanders-Reio, 2011).

Threats to Psychological Availability

For employees to feel psychologically available, they must be able to focus in the moment at work. This includes employees feeling capable of caring for their family, addressing financial stresses appropriately, and feeling physically able to perform on the job. To facilitate employees' psychological availability, workplaces need to consider implementing family-friendly policies and employee assistance programs. For example, policies such as flextime (e.g., being able to come to and leave work between a range of hours as opposed to a specific single time, such as arriving between 7 and 10 a.m. and leaving between 4 and 7 p.m.) might support employees in multiple ways. Namely, employees who need more time in the morning to get to work (e.g., individuals with family responsibilities or who live far from work and deal with horrible commutes) and those have non-work obligations in the early afternoon or evening (e.g., picking up kids from day care, caring for elder parents) will be able to meet these needs without taking time off. Feelings of job insecurity will also inhibit psychological availability. That is, if employees are constantly worried about their job security, they will not feel able to focus on the job because they are worried about messing up or doing something that puts the job at risk.

Another way to inhibit psychological availability is constantly asking employees about outside non-work-related issues as opposed to giving employees freedom to discuss when desired. For example, although they have good intentions, co-workers or managers who constantly ask about a chronically ill family member or a recent financial disaster will create an environment that prevents psychological availability for the employee who is truly trying to focus on work while at work. Additionally, constantly receiving phone calls or e-mails from non-work-related entities will also reduce psychological availability. One could claim the use of social media sites such as Facebook or Twitter reduces psychological availability; however, if frequent visits to these sites relieves anxiety about how a family member or close friend is doing, one could argue contrarily that social media facilitates their feelings of availability.

Threats to Psychological Meaningfulness

Psychological meaningfulness is achieved when an employee feels their investment in the job role is rewarded by the positive feelings and energy the job creates, and the sense of personal value from doing the job. Psychological meaningfulness is not necessarily something a leader must give to an employee; employees do not always need outside recognition to feel their work is meaningful or to be assigned a job society considers "meaningful" (e.g., health care worker or firefighter; see Ashforth & Kreiner [2013] on finding meaning in dirty work). Employees who feel the work itself makes a meaningful contribution to society, to something bigger than themselves, or inherently pays them back emotionally, physically, and cognitively will feel psychological meaningfulness (Kahn, 1990). For example, the employees of the second health organization I studied felt the work they did, regardless of whether it was recognized by the organization, was meaningful because it made a difference in the lives of those patients who needed help. Taking away employees' ability to complete the job, restricting their use of skills to complete a variety of tasks on the job, or taking away their ability to make their work feel like a meaningful contribution will inhibit their ability to perceive psychological meaningfulness in their work role and thereby will inhibit engagement. Recently, scholars proposed the COVID-19 pandemic transformed some previously considered meaningful occupations into dirty work (Glerum, 2021). Specifically, Glerum described how frontline health care workers in contact with infected patients were called heroes yet ostracized within their organizations for being in contact with COVID-19 patients. These workers lost their identity, autonomy, and psychological safety because of restrictions applied due to their exposure (Glerum, 2021) – all a result of their occupation *becoming* dirty work. They struggle to find meaning because they are both valued and rejected.

With the forced increased reliance on computer-mediated-communications (e.g., email, audio and video conferencing) resulting from the COVID-19 pandemic, threats to psychological meaningfulness may become more challenging to avoid. A recent study about the use of technology illustrates how little it takes to destroy meaningfulness. Roberts and David (2017) found that boss phubbing (supervisors who are distracted by their smartphone while meeting with an employee) was negatively related to employees perceived psychological meaningfulness, which affected employee engagement. The authors concluded that by focusing on the phone instead of the employee, the boss/supervisor was essentially saying to the employee that they and their work were not valued, resulting in lowering employees' feelings of value and meaningfulness.

Psychological Withdrawal

Kahn (1990) suggested disengagement occurs when an employee withdraws from the work role, detaching from identification with the organization and fulfilling tasks in an automated or robotic manner. Although Kahn did not specify what leads to disengagement, we can hypothesize from the literature on withdrawal and identity creation within organizations as to what might lead to disengagement. Research on psychological withdrawal suggests employees' distance themselves when their relationships within the organization are threatened (e.g., Arnetz et al., 2018; Michela & Vena, 2012). For example, during organizational change when employees are unclear on how the change affects them, they will enter in a self-protective function that involves psychological distancing. Psychological distancing is achieved through devaluing the organization and reducing organizational identification. Uncertainty from change or mergers triggers distancing in the form of loss of affective commitment and satisfaction (Michela & Vena, 2012). Lack of perceived insider status, associated with workplace incivility, also relates to low organizational identification and low engagement (Guo, Qiu, & Gan, 2020), and ultimately turnover

(Tricahyadinata et al., 2020). Perceptions of inequity in relationships, such as exclusion or low insider status, can also result in withdrawal (Taris, van Horn, Schaufeli, & Schreurs, 2004). Researchers have further noted various forms of withdrawal exist, such as psychological withdrawal, lateness, absenteeism, and turnover (Beehr & Gupta, 1978). Thus, psychological withdrawal is not the only kind of withdrawal employees' experience that might result in this disengagement. In the sociology literature, alienation or powerlessness within the specific organizational setting results in social isolation (Shepard, 1972), which might also contribute to disengagement as it may affect employees' psychological availability (Kahn, 1990).

It appears the findings from my qualitative studies provide initial support for using Kahn's (1990) model to explain inhibitors to engagement. Many of the examples from the interviews could be construed as threats to psychological availability, meaningfulness, and safety, and those threats were what employees said caused or directly related to their disengagement and/or reduced engagement at work.

According to the Job Demands–Resources Model

Maslach and Leiter (1997), and Maslach, Schaufeli, and Leiter (2001) suggested disengagement occurs when one's energy turns into exhaustion, involvement becomes cynicism, and efficacy becomes ineffectiveness – essentially the three dimensions of burnout. Thus, according to Maslach and colleagues, disengagement is the same as burnout. This definition became the foundation of Schaufeli, Salanova, González-Romá, and Bakker's (2002) engagement definition, which is most often used with the JD-R model (Bakker & Demerouti, 2008).

Threats to Job Resources

If we use the JD-R model to hypothesize potential antecedents to disengagement, we would likely propose that a lack of resources and excessive demands should result in disengagement. Thus, if an organization withdraws support or does not provide organizational support, does not have policies and procedures that provide for family care, has management that provides no feedback, or fails to provide learning or developmental experiences for employees, employees should perceive a resources vacuum. The model implies job demands must be in excess of job resources to experience a lack of engagement, but it is not clear quite how job resources and job demands work together. For example, what is the tipping point for employees at which they feel their resources are too low? Do employees constantly calculate the demands-versus-resources ratio, or do they just feel supported versus not supported at varying times? We can hypothesize if there are not enough resources to offset demands, demands at some point become too overwhelming, making it hard for employees to become engaged (Bakker & Demerouti, 2008).

A similar framework to the JD-R model, the conservation of resources theory (Hobfoll, 1989), suggests people seek to obtain, foster, and conserve resources (e.g., personal, social, material) that are of core value to themselves, and the aggressive loss of these resources ends in burnout and other stress-related outcomes. Thus, threats to one's ability to foster and retain core resources will result in burnout or disengagement (Schaufeli, Martínez, Marques Pinto, Salanova, & Bakker, 2002). For example, traumatic stress or conditions of rapid loss of resources challenge one's ability to retain and foster resources, whereas job-related demands result in slow resource loss (Hobfoll & Shirom, 2001), which might not lead to burnout if individuals have enough reservoirs of other resources to cope with this slow drain. An additional aspect of the conservation of resources theory not present in the JD-R is the desire and need to conserve (almost hoard) resources. Thus, threats to one's ability to conserve and continuously replenish resources even when no excessive job demands are present, might lead to initial levels of disengagement.

Threats of High Demands

As noted earlier, the JD-R suggests the presence of excessive job demands without job resources to offset those demands will result in burnout. For example, if the organization creates work assignments that have high emotional, mental, or physical pressures and demands, and in general pushes employees to their limit, according to the JD-R model, disengagement will follow. High demands that tax employees' ability to cope and recover either physically or emotionally will drain their reserves. The JD-R model is simple in that it proposes employees experiencing job burnout will be or become disengaged. Another aspect of the model is personal resources, such as personality characteristics or traits that lend themselves to resiliency, and recovery and coping from stressful situations (Xanthopoulou, Bakker, Demerouti, & Schaufeli, 2007). Thus, we might hypothesize some employees with specific personalities not robust to stress, such as neuroticism, might be more prone to disengagement (Burtaverde & Iliescu, 2019).

Other Models of Engagement

Saks's Model of Engagement

Saks (2006) proposed employee engagement (i.e., "the degree to which an individual is attentive and absorbed in the performance of their roles," p. 602) depends on one's role (Rothbard, 2001); as such, employees develop both job and organizational engagement. Relying on social exchange theory (Blau, 1964), Saks claimed employees choose to become engaged in response to developing an exchange relationship with their organization. Although social exchange relationships are exclusive of economical exchanges (see Blau, 1964), Saks proposed that in return for the economic and socioemotional resources given to them by the organization, employees give varying levels of job and organizational engagement (Saks, 2006). Saks's correlational study showed that job characteristics (e.g., autonomy, task identity, skill variety, task significance, feedback from others, and feedback from the job) were predictors of job engagement and that organizational support was a predictor of both job and organizational engagement (although a stronger predictor or organizational than job engagement). Support from the supervisor, rewards and recognition, and fairness were not significant predictors of either form of engagement. Job and organizational engagement were measured using scale items developed by Saks. Moderate to high correlations were reported between the two forms of engagement and between job and organizational engagement with attitudes such as organizational commitment and job satisfaction (e.g., correlations ranged from .52 to .69).

Saks's (2006) study offers potential suggestions for inhibitors to engagement, namely, the lack of job characteristics may hinder an employee's ability to become engaged. Likewise, a lack of support from the organization in particular may inhibit engagement. Lack of support from the immediate supervisor, according to Saks's results, should not matter because supervisory support was not significantly related to either form of engagement. Another possible hypothesis from Saks's model may be that anything threatening the social exchange relationship with the organization should result in disengagement. That is, issues with trust, lack of reciprocity, or psychological contract breaches may result in a weakening of the social exchange relationship, resulting in at least a reduction of engagement, if not actual disengagement (e.g., Agarwal & Bhargava, 2013; Azeem et al., 2020).

Trust issues and lack of support from the organization were noted in the qualitative results shared previously, suggesting there could be merit to using Saks's (2006) model to hypothesize when disengagement may occur. None of the interviewees, however, noted that issues might be more clearly indicative of a breach in a social exchange relationship, indicating my findings are not as supportive of the use of Saks's model as they are of the other models for proposing inhibitors and causes of disengagement.

Macey and Schneider's Model of Engagement

Macey and Schneider (2008) suggest there are three forms of engagement: trait, state, and behavioral. Trait engagement cannot be changed by the organization or person as it is a dispositional characteristic. Thus, engaged employees are proactive, positive, conscientious, or autotelic, and those without such personality traits are not likely to demonstrate trait engagement, which leads to state engagement. Scoring high in these personality traits, however, leads to feelings of energy and absorption, which Macey and Schneider say compose state engagement. Thus, when engaged, employees are satisfied, involved, and committed to their workplace. As a consequence of their feelings of energy and positive attitudes, they demonstrate behavioral engagement in the form of extra-role behaviors, personal initiative, and they adapt to the job. According to this model, we could hypothesize inhibitors to engagement include personality characteristics that tend to reflect negative affectivity or mental disorders that prevent an otherwise positive disposition from emerging (e.g., clinical depression). State engagement may be inhibited by excessive demands that drain energy or reduce positive feelings at work, such as excessive conflict or by having to juggle too many competing tasks that inhibit involvement in any single project or task. Additionally, Macey and Schneider proposed that job characteristics or work attributes moderate the relationship between trait and state engagement. Therefore, work environments that inhibit employees' autonomy and are monotonous or overly simple may inhibit even the personalities predisposed to engagement from becoming engaged (perhaps just experiencing very low engagement). Macey and Schneider also hypothesized transformational leadership as a moderator to the state engagement–behavioral engagement pathway. Thus, poor leadership that fails to empower employees may stifle the normally positive employee. Lastly, if employees are placed in work conditions or in organizations with norms that fail to allow them to exhibit extra-role behaviors or personal initiative, their level of behavioral engagement will be inhibited or reduced.

Some examples and themes extracted from my qualitative studies appear to provide initial support for using Macey and Schneider's (2008) model to hypothesize disengagement. For example, excessive demands, conflicts, poor leadership, excessively controlling work environments, and monotonous work were reported as inhibitors in the qualitative studies, and they appear here as possible inhibitors.

Other Inhibitors From Related Research

Inability to Balance Work and Life Demands

My qualitative studies revealed a number of inhibitors to engagement for which some research support exists. For example, consequences of micromanagement include inhibited performance, stifled innovation, and strained communication between employees and supervisors (e.g., Francaro, 2007). The inability to achieve perceived work–life balance can have negative consequences on employees' ability to invest themselves in work (Hobson, Delunas, & Kesic, 2001). However, employees do not always work because their job is a career or fulfills them; they work as a means to supporting their non-work-related activities, where they fulfill their goals and life ambitions (S. Friedman, Christensen, &

DeGroot, 1998). Ways to encourage disengagement for these individuals is to fail to recognize the value and importance of their life outside of work. It may be that achieving a balanced integration of work and life requires taking advantage of the gains one gets from non-work-related activity (see S. Friedman et al. [1998] for good examples of how balance is achieved). Work can be fulfilling or meaningful for those who see it as a means to an end, such as where the end might be a better non-work-related life. Thus, recognizing different value systems and appreciating that meaning and engagement may be in the eye of the beholder have merit.

Threats to Competence, Autonomy, and Relatedness

Self-determination theory (Deci & Ryan, 1985; Ryan & Deci, 2000) proposes employees' intrinsic motivation is triggered to fulfill feelings of competence and autonomy. Self-determination theory suggests people are motivated, even when tasks are not intrinsically interesting, because they know their behavior will provide or meet their needs for competence, autonomy, and relatedness. Thus, anything that inhibits employees' efforts to feel competent on the job or to enjoy autonomy or control will constrain their engagement. For example, a work environment that seems overly controlling or rigid, exclusionary (e.g., ostracism; Haldorai, Kim, Phetvaroon, & Li, 2020), or that seems to stifle employees' needs to relate to others will create a negative work climate for engagement.

Poor Leadership

Leadership has frequently been promoted as a means for fostering engagement. Researchers have shown leadership is positively related to engagement (e.g., Aryee, Walumbwa, Zhou, & Hartnell, 2012; Tuckey, Bakker, & Dollard, 2012). The results from my qualitative work suggest leaders also play a key role in inhibiting engagement. For example, though their measure of disengagement is actually an assessment of withdrawal (i.e., quitting, changing departments, taking time off) due to bullying, Arnetz et al. (2018) found nurses who were bullied at work reported higher withdrawal than those reporting no bullying experiences. No surprise there! The more informative aspect of their study, however, is the negative relationship between psychological safety and bullying because threats to psychological safety are likely to result in disengagement.

Leaders who demonstrate high levels of emotional intelligence have been associated with employees' reporting high engagement (e.g., Ravichandran, Arasu, & Kumar, 2011); thus, leaders without this social intelligence are likely to inhibit engagement in their followers. Lastly, in my own research, interpersonal and supportive leadership has been positively associated with high levels of engagement; therefore, leaders who fail to provide the caring, relationship-oriented, and work-related supportive behaviors of interpersonal and supportive leaders may inhibit employees' ability to perceive the psychological conditions or identification that is necessary for becoming engaged.

Lack of Organizational Purpose

Research on meaningful organizations suggests employees who work for organizations that do not consider their need for meaning in their work will inhibit their employees' ability to become engaged (A. Brown et al., 2001; Chalofsky & Krishna, 2009; Kahn, 1990). Thus, failing to provide a clear superordinate goal, a clear mission, or a vision, or failing to create clear order and purpose to the goals of the organization may result in employees struggling to become engaged; their need to understand what makes their work meaningful will be inhibited by their lack of clear purpose.

Distrust

A lack of trust within organizations inhibits becoming engaged. Specifically, trust within organizations allows employees to be vulnerable to the actions of the organization (Kramer, 1994). Employees who trust the organizational leaders believe they will make decisions in their best interest (Kramer, 1999). Distrust – the lack of confidence in others and their actions or intentions – can be triggered by situational cues that hint of hidden agendas or unfaithful intentions (G. Fine & Holyfield, 1996). Cues can be as simple as being considered a part of one group, such that those in other groups are automatically viewed as different, untrustworthy, and in some way less than those in one's own group (see social categorization; Sherif, 1963; Tajfel, 1978; Tajfel, Billig, Bundy, & Flament, 1971). Based on a review of the literature, Kramer (1999) hypothesized that unmet expectations, healthy suspicion of organizations, computer monitoring and surveillance, unintended consequences of regulations meant to be positive (e.g., a trucker's log book was to promote compliance with driving hours laws but resulted in either truckers driving while too tired or having two log books – one for inspection and one for actual hours driven), and psychological contract breach can all result in distrust.

Stifled Innovation and Broken Promises

Organizational climates that stifle innovation and creativity, and jobs where tasks become monotonous and predictable, lead to disengagement (Fineman, 1983). Employees feel trapped by their work as opposed to energized by it, leading them to psychologically, if not physically, withdraw. Broken promises, unmet expectations, and failure to see a productive end to one's job effort (e.g., working hard on a project only to have it cancelled and dismantled) all lead to disengagement (S. Fineman, 1983). Empowering leaders promote both innovative behaviors and engagement (Tian & Zhang, 2020), which suggests leaders who focus mostly on controlling, authoritative behaviors may stifle both innovation and engagement.

Does Workaholism Equal Too Much Engagement?

I cover the idea of too much engagement and workaholism in Chapter 10 in more detail, but it warrants some mention here regarding disengagement. Some researchers suggest too much engagement leads to disengagement (Macey, Schneider, Barbera, & Young, 2009). Macey and colleagues (2009) based their assertion on the idea that engagement is like other constructs; when too much is present, it results in an overload of the psychological system. Although no empirical work has yet explored whether there is such a thing as too much engagement, the literature on passion and workaholism may shed light on what Macey et al. (2009) were suggesting. Andreassen, Ursin, and Eriksen (2007) examined two components of workaholism – drive and enjoyment of work – and found positive relationships between one aspect of engagement (i.e., absorption) and enjoyment of work. Enjoyment of work was characterized as being motivated to work for sheer enjoyment and satisfaction. Thus, this research suggests high absorption at work is related to workaholism. In contrast, when examining passion as a two-dimensional construct comprising obsessive (e.g., inability to control one's need to work) and harmonic passion (e.g., appreciate work more when learning new things), consistent with Vallerand and Houlfort (2003), and engagement, Forest, Mageau, Sarrazin, and Morin (2011) determined that harmonious passion was consistent with positive well-being, autotelic experience, and concentration at work. Obsessive passion was associated with low levels of well-being. Obsessive passion was not associated with flow or affective commitment, both of which are often sometimes aspects of engagement (Saks, 2006; Schaufeli et al., 2002). Workaholism refers to self-imposed demands that are compulsive and neglectful of other areas of life (Burke, 2009), similar to Vallerand and Houlfort's (2003) definition of obsessive passion. However, working compulsively is positively associated with engagement ($r = .27$; Schaufeli, Taris, & Bakker, 2006). In summary, the research is inconclusive about whether too much engagement results in disengagement. See Chapter 10 for more on workaholism and passion versus engagement.

Lack of Person–Organization Fit

Job fit is positively related to engagement (e.g., Bui, Zeng, & Higgs, 2017; Cai, Cai, Sun, & Ma, 2018; de Beer, Rothmann, & Mostert, 2016; Ybema, Koopman, & Peeters, 2020). Thus, we can assume a lack of fit might inhibit engagement or even contribute directly to disengagement. This assumption is consistent with Maslach's (2003) supposition about disengagement. Based on the comments from my interviews, I suspect lack of fit leaves employees struggling to connect with others in the organization. This lack of connection most likely contributes to a mismatch with support or aligned purpose. Negative consequences, such as low commitment and low job satisfaction, occur when employees lack congruence between their values and those of their supervisor or organization (Bretz et al., 1989; Cable & Judge, 1996; Gregory, Albritton, & Osmonbekov, 2010). Employees perceiving a mismatch or lack of fit or congruence between their personalities and organizational attributes are less likely than those perceiving a match to feel they belong in that organization (Cable & Judge, 1996; Chatman, 1989; Meglino et al., 1989). Substantial research in recruitment and selection demonstrates fit matters in terms of prospective employees' choices for places to work and initial attitudes once on the job (e.g., McCulloch & Turban, 2007; Nikolaou, 2003; Pfieffelmann, Wagner, & Libkuman, 2010; Resick, Baltes, & Shantz, 2007; Saks & Ashforth, 2002). Therefore, additional studies of person–organization fit are warranted to determine to what degree a lack of fit inhibits feelings of belongingness that ultimately ties into feelings of disengagement.

Virtual or Remote Work

Virtual work is not a new concept, though the COVID-19 pandemic forced many workers to work remotely from home for the first time. For some, this work at home increased their psychological availability because they could reduce workplace distractions. However, for others, working from home included homeschooling young children and/or managing other home distractions (e.g., pets), which created less psychological availability than pre-pandemic conditions (e.g., Chawla, 2021). A recent research study of mine supported this bifurcation of experiences of psychological availability. I used a mixed-methods approach with faculty in several engineering departments at different universities to understand their perceptions of organizational culture. As part of the study efforts, I included several questions in the survey and interviews to learn more about their engagement levels during the forced-virtual work conditions during the pandemic. My findings showed those who commented during interviews on having increased opportunity for focus and fewer distractions reported feeling more engaged at work and more productive. In contrast, those who talked about homeschooling their children or sharing small quarters with others who were also forced to work at home reported feeling less psychologically available and less engaged. Aggregated responses to my surveys were consistent with the interview data. These preliminary findings suggest Kahn's (1990) component of psychological availability is key to engagement in remote work situations. In addition to the home distractions, suddenly working remotely full-time presents technology and communication challenges for both employees and their employers (Bilotta et al., 2021). These challenges, including information overload, communication disruptions and misunderstandings, and technology complexity (Bilotta et al., 2021), are all threats to psychological availability.

For those who are not new to virtual work, such as those needing to bridge across distributed work environments, engagement plays a potentially beneficial role with regard to performance. Specifically, Halgin et al. (2015) examined the engagement of employees in distributed teams within a large multinational corporation. They found that employees with well-developed personal and professional networks tended to be more highly engaged than those without strong network ties. They concluded that engaged workers were more successful at networking and taking advantage of the distributed work environment than less engaged workers. The study was not causal; therefore, it is unclear whether employees who were good at networking became engaged as they developed connections with others across the distributed landscape, as opposed to the other way around. The implications of the study results are that regardless of when, why, or how workers are placed in virtual work settings, being skilled at networking across the virtual landscape relates to engagement levels.

WHAT DOES INHIBITED ENGAGEMENT LOOK LIKE?

Maxim has been an assistant professor for about 4 years. Recently, he has been contemplating whether he should find another job. He still likes the job, but he thinks it may be a bad fit, that this is not the right career for him or maybe not the right university. On one hand, he feels that the work he is doing is very valuable, that he is making a difference for his students, especially when their parents tell him at graduation how he changed their kids' lives. On the other hand, he struggles to find his work meaningful beyond that; after all, how many people actually read and not just cite his articles?

Maxim feels under constant scrutiny as to whether he is producing enough publications, getting good enough teacher ratings, and involved in the same level of service as his colleagues around him. He feels that he cannot ask for help from the faculty in his department; he is afraid that if he shares his struggles with any of them, they will hold it against him when he comes up for tenure and promotion. In his mid-tenure review, he was told he is doing OK but that he needs to produce more and get better teacher ratings; this feedback made him feel like a failure, and besides, it did not tell him how to produce more or teach better. He also heard some of the professors who he thought liked him brought up concerns he felt were unsupported and unfair. It seems as though there is definitely a club at work to which he does not belong. He has very little seniority, and he is constantly reminded of that when decisions are made. He has interjected his suggestions into discussions, but his opinions are often ignored; he feels as though he is invisible at times. As a result, he has started avoiding the faculty in his department by scheduling office hours during the regular faculty meeting. He likes his colleagues, but he feels they exclude him from decision-making and from hallway conversations, so he avoids them. He figures that if he detaches from work a bit and distances himself from his colleagues, he will not feel so hurt by their actions. Sadly, his department head has done nothing to reach out to him or hold the faculty accountable for his success. After all, they hired him, and at that time they believed he would be successful; should they not be helping him, making him feel valuable and that he belongs?

Maxim has little connection with the university, mainly because no one has reached out to him to offer guidance or support. No one has offered to show him the best way to get materials from the library, which local restaurant has the best food, or where the quietest coffee shop is on campus; when he is at work, he feels alone most of the time. Unfortunately, Maxim also feels alone at home: he works all the time including weekends. He has two small children, but he does not feel that he actually sees them much because he is always tucked away in his home office, working.

Conclusion

There is little definitive information about disengagement; much that is stated comes from low ratings of engagement, reverse scored engagement measures, or anecdotes from practitioners (including myself). Thus, the preceding propositions are mostly theoretical with some related research suggesting they may be plausible. We can infer from research on engagement and on potential inhibitors of engagement what may lead to disengagement, assuming disengagement is the opposite of engagement, a supposition that needs empirical testing. Kahn (1990) proposed engagement is a moment-to-moment phenomenon; thus, it may be possible that people vacillate between engagement and disengagement (or maybe disengagement is just nonengagement) all day long, but when averaged over the course of a day, those people might report general high levels of engagement. Or, moments of disengagement simply may not register in their memories, since it could be disengagement is just not as salient to them as are moments of engagement. Of course, the opposite may also be true; disengagement may be so unpleasant that people remember their experiences with disengagement very well, and researchers need to do better to tap into these experiences. Empirical research is necessary to understand what disengagement is and what it is relative to engagement, withdrawal, and burnout.

WALK-AWAY POINTS

- Inhibitors to engagement in the workplace include factors within the organization's control and within the employees' control; some are situational, some are employee disposition, and some are interactions between situation and employee; fit matters.

- By focusing on what creates engagement, we may be able to avoid disengagement; however, even with all the support, the right situational characteristics, the ideal circumstances, and the best of leadership, some people still may not be engaged.

- Employees who are asked to become engaged or to be more engaged than they are now are essentially being asked to share their intensity, enthusiasm, persistence, and adaptability when they may not be willing or able to do so. Thus, knowing inhibitors does not translate into automatic success in achieving 100% engagement from all employees at all times.

- Research into disengagement can be advanced by combining theories into a mega-theory of disengagement.

6

HOW DO WE ASSESS EMPLOYEE ENGAGEMENT AND CHOOSE A GOOD MEASURE?

Several years ago, a client of mine invited me to a vendor selection meeting. In my role as the expert in psychometrics (i.e., field of psychological measurement), I was there to evaluate the quality of the measures and solutions offered by each vendor. Of the four consulting firms that presented, not one was able to provide answers to basic measurement questions about its engagement surveys and packaged solutions. The irony of the situation is that all the vendors were informed by the client that an expert in psychological measurement would be sitting in on the meeting to evaluate solutions and to help choose one for the client, yet none was prepared with the information the vendors should have known I would ask for. Not only were their definitions of engagement *not* about engagement, but they also had no evidence their measures assessed their chosen definition, nor how well. The client would have chosen one of these solutions thinking an engagement measure and a solution for fostering engagement in the culture was soon to be deployed, yet none of these measures and solutions would ultimately provide information about levels of employee engagement or how to change them.

The client's lack of detailed knowledge of psychological measurement or organizational design is not atypical, nor is it a criticism of this particular client or of clients in general. We cannot all be experts in everything at all times. Although I cannot share an entire process of organizational development and design aimed at engagement in one chapter, I can share how to ask a few of the basic and fundamental questions that guide the development of a solution and selection of a good measure of engagement. For example, two fundamental questions you should ask are (a) Does the measure consistently and accurately assess engagement every time it is used? and (b) Does it assess engagement as it claims it does? Without the answers to these questions, it is difficult to choose

DOI: 10.4324/9781003171133-8

the right engagement instrument. How can interventions be designed, conclusions be drawn about research or investigative results, or recommendations be provided about what to do with engagement without knowing if engagement was actually measured? Furthermore, with survey in hand, another basic question should be, how is this survey best used to affect culture change or help establish the desired culture? The answers to these questions can put the researcher or practitioner on a good path toward an engagement solution that actually gets at employee engagement.

Asking and answering the first two questions (e.g., consistently accurate, measure what is claimed) require some basic understanding of psychological measurement. This chapter will help. I first discuss how to evaluate a psychological measure of employee engagement and then discuss other approaches to assessing engagement, approaches that do not involve an already established instrument or survey. Following that, I review some basics about using surveys to effect culture change. Lastly, I review the available measures of engagement that can be reviewed without purchasing a proprietary instrument or violating company copyright agreements.

Although this chapter may seem fundamental to those trained in psychological measurement, this is not just a review of basic measurement terms. How that knowledge is used in practice is not always taught in graduate school programs, and if it is taught, science versus practice trade-offs typically are not. For those trained a while ago, sometimes a refresher on the basics is just what is needed; thus, this chapter should prove helpful. Why include a chapter about measurement in a book such as this? Because we so often leave information about psychological measurement to complex measurement books, which only those knowledgeable in the area know to read or buy, we create an artificial separation between understanding what engagement is and how it is measured. It is as if the measurement happens somewhere else, other than with the construct. Measuring engagement accurately is critical for successful interventions and advancement of the scientific and practice approaches – we must treat the topic in parallel with engagement, recognizing an artificial separation causes more harm than good.

Some Basics About Measurement

There are no doubt a large number of books and articles available that review psychometrics in great detail, but not everyone needs to understand measurement theory or technique to that extent. Armed with a basic understanding of a few fundamentals in psychological measurement can go a long way toward placing the researcher or practitioner in a more informed position when selecting a good engagement survey. The basics can be grouped into two large categories: (a) the validity of inferences, conclusions, or decisions made with the survey; and (b) the reliability of the survey scores.

Validity refers to the evidence available that supports the interpretation of the scores from the survey or measurement instrument, in this case, the interpretation of the scores from an engagement survey. Thus, the fundamental question validity answers is whether there is sufficient evidence to say the interpretation one wants to make from the engagement scores is an acceptable interpretation – we have evidence these scores can accurately be interpreted in this way. Validity is about how the scores will be used – what conclusions are made from the scores (American Education Research Association [AERA], American Psychological Association [APA], & National Council on Measurement in Education [NCME], 1999). There are various sources of validity evidence rather than different types (Binning & Barrett, 1989). Each source of evidence speaks to the overall validity evidence available for evaluating the quality of decisions or conclusions one can make about test scores (AERA et al., 1999). To evaluate the validity evidence for a measure, one has to start with a definition of employee engagement. I have reviewed a few definitions from the research community and have offered my own in Chapter 2. An organization can also develop its own definition, as one of my clients in health care did recently. Although a few aspects of existing definitions appealed to them, they wanted one that more closely reflects the nature of their work, particularly their focus on patient care, and they wanted a definition that incorporated the language of their organizational culture.

Face Validity: What the Items Look Like They Measure

When considering an existing measurement instrument to assess engagement, one should look at the items and evaluate the measure's face validity. Face validity refers to whether the measurement instrument, typically a survey in the case of engagement, *looks* like it assesses what it claims. Do the questions look like they ask about employee engagement? With definition in hand, looking at the items of a measure provides perspective on how members of the organization will view the items when responding and whether they will question the overall intent of the measure. For example, an item on the UWES (Schaufeli & Bakker, 2003) says, "At my work, I feel bursting with energy." Engagement is about feeling energetic on the job, and thus this question appears to fit the concept being measured. Another question, however, which asks about whether coworkers are dedicated to producing quality work (a question similar to one that appears on the Gallup Organization Q^{12}, which Gallup purports measures engagement; see Buckingham & Coffman, 1999; Gebauer, Lowman, & Gordon, 2008) seems off track from the construct of interest; respondents may naturally wonder how that question is directly about their own engagement level. When I am asked questions like this, I often answer with, "How would I know whether my coworkers are dedicated to quality or not? I can't read their minds!" In Gallup's defense, other people may see your dedication to quality by observing how you work or examining the product of your effort. In this case, I would respond that you could be dedicated to quality but lack the ability/capability to produce quality. It is best not to have questions on your measure that require the respondent to have special insight into how other people think.

Face validity is not sufficient for deciding if a measurement instrument is a good one because some items that are good at assessing the underlying meaning of a construct do not always look as though they are getting at the construct; for example, items simply do not say, "I am engaged." Valuable questions may assess levels of engagement by asking indirect questions, such as "I am energetic in my work tasks" (from the UWES; Schaufeli & Bakker, 2003; Schaufeli, Martínez, Marques Pinto, Salanova, & Bakker, 2002), or questions that assess underlying components of engagement, such as "At work, I concentrate on my job" (from the JES; Rich, LePine, and Crawford, 2010). Although not sufficient by itself, face validity provides information about how individuals may view the items and respond, which does affect how the scores should be interpreted. That is, if respondents look at the items and believe they are being asked about topics they consider personal but were told they would be surveyed about their engagement levels, they may be hesitant to complete the survey and respond inappropriately (e.g., choosing a neutral response or not responding at all) just to hide their personal thoughts from the test giver. Face validity is a subjective judgment about the items of the scale: it is a guess about how the respondents may view and complete the measure; it is not an evaluation of how well the items assess the construct.

Construct Validity: Evidence That the Measure Assesses Its Purported Construct

Construct validity, in general, refers to whether there is empirical evidence the measurement instrument assesses the construct it was intended to assess (AERA et al., 1999). Construct validity evidence says this measure assesses employees' engagement level and not commitment, involvement, job satisfaction, or any other construct that is not engagement. Validity is not an either/or quality and is not based on a single study. Validity evidence is constantly accumulating in support of a measurement instrument's ability to assess its purported construct or another construct it appears to be measuring instead (Guion & Gibson, 1988). Specific validity evidence that contributes to evaluating whether a measurement instrument is a good one to use includes internal structural, convergent, divergent, and criterion-related validity evidence (Cronbach & Meehl, 1955). The focus is on looking for cumulative evidence that suggests the measure is assessing what it claims and does this well (Cascio, 1998).

Internal Structural Construct Validity

Internal structural or factorial construct validity evidence refers to information that confirms the conceptual structure of the measurement instrument as proposed by theory. It provides evidence the relationships among test items fit the theoretical construct. Specifically, if the theory suggests engagement comprises three components – physical energy, emotional expression, and cognitive processing – the factorial construct validity evidence for the measurement instrument should confirm the assessment of three individual components or dimensions. Typically, this evidence comes in the form of confirmatory factor analysis. Confirmatory factor analysis is a statistical technique that provides information about how well items within a measure correlate with each other, or do not, as they are expected a priori (B. Thompson, 2004). Based on the theory, the researcher inputs into the statistical tool how items are supposed to relate to one another and not relate to one another. The confirmatory factor analysis then determines how closely the data represent the structure the researcher inputted (B. Thompson, 2004). Current dominant theoretical perspectives of employee engagement are that it comprises three components, though exactly what those three are varies by theory (see Kahn, 1990; Schaufeli, Salanova, González-Romá, & Bakker, 2002). Thus, each measurement instrument assessing employee engagement as defined by Kahn (1990) and by Schaufeli et al. (2002) should have within it items assessing these three components. The theoretical frameworks also suggest these three components may be correlated, but should not be identical. Items within the measurement instrument that assess energy level should be correlated with the items assessing the emotional aspect of employee engagement, but not be so highly correlated they are considered identical for assessing the same construct. Additionally, if the researcher inputs into the software package that items within each subscale of the measurement instrument should relate most strongly to one another (as opposed to relating more highly with other items within other subscales), the results of the confirmatory factor analysis should support this structure. Finally, confirmatory factor analysis is often used to provide not only factorial construct validity evidence but also convergent and divergent validity evidence (Cronbach & Meehl, 1955).

Convergent Validity Evidence

Convergent validity evidence is accumulated when one shows that assessments of constructs theoretically expected to relate to, or correlate with, the construct of interest actually do. For example, convergent validity evidence for a measure of commitment would be that measures of loyalty are positively and moderately correlated with commitment (e.g., $r = .30$ to $r = .50$; see J. Cohen, 1988). In the case of engagement, convergent validity evidence would be in the form of measures of high energy levels, enthusiasm for the job, motivation, and cognitive focus correlating moderately with the measure of engagement. If the correlations are too high (e.g., $r = .70$ or more), one should be concerned the measure of employee engagement is too similar to measures of other constructs that should be theoretically related, but not be identical, to engagement.

Divergent or Discriminant Validity Evidence

Divergent or discriminant validity evidence is shown when constructs that are theoretically expected to differ from or not relate to the construct of interest do not. For employee engagement, constructs such as intelligence or loyalty should show low or nonsignificant correlations with employee engagement. Divergent validity evidence is important in distinguishing whether employee engagement is different from other similar constructs in the workplace, such as intrinsic motivation. It is also important to know whether the measure one is using to assess employee engagement does not itself assess constructs expected to be different from employee engagement, such as loyalty. If validity evidence demonstrates the engagement measure assesses loyalty as well as employee engagement, the measure is not a clean assessment of engagement, or we say that it is confounded or contaminated by other constructs.

Combined, convergent and divergent validity evidence for a measure of employee engagement demonstrates the measure assesses employee engagement and not other similar constructs, or constructs it should not be measuring. Thus, when obtaining scores on a measure of employee engagement that has supportive convergent and divergent validity evidence, one can be confident the results inform the organization of levels of employee engagement and not something else.

Criterion-Related Validity Evidence

Criterion-related validity evidence provides information about what (i.e., attitudes or behaviors) employee engagement is expected to predict in the workplace. That is, what criteria or outcomes do scores on this measure of employee engagement relate to, and by how much? For example, employee engagement is expected to predict job performance in the workplace (Bakker & Demerouti, 2008; Britt, 1999; Kahn, 1990). Thus far, scores on the two most popular measures of employee engagement, the UWES and the JES, are both positively related to job performance in the form of contextual performance and self-reported performance behaviors. I could find no research reporting experimental data that would provide evidence confirming that engagement truly predicts job performance. Existing research suggests a strong positive correlation between employee engagement and job performance; however, the direction of influence is unknown without experimental data. Because motivation results in effort in a particular direction (Kanfer, 1990), which in the work-place generally means job performance, and theoretical models of engagement suggest engagement is a motivational state (e.g., Kahn, 1990), it follows that employee engagement should precede job performance and not the other way around. However, it is quite possible employees who perform well on the job are enthused by positive feedback they receive on their performance, building their self-efficacy (e.g., Karl, O'Leary-Kelly, & Martocchio, 1993) and their sense of meaningful contribution, thereby becoming even more engaged. Thus, most likely, the relationship between employee engagement and job performance is reciprocal, which is expected if engagement is indeed a motivational construct (e.g., see Skinner & Belmont's [1993] study of student engagement's recipro-cal relationship with performance in the classroom). Another example of a criterion with which employee engagement should relate is well-being. The job demands-resources (JD-R) model (Bakker & Demerouti, 2008) suggests engaged employees should report positive well-being, and research supports this assertion (e.g., Mostert & Rothmann, 2006).

Criterion-related validity requires attention to both the validity evidence for the measure of interest and the measures of the criteria variables (Cascio, 1998). One challenge with obtaining criterion-related validity is attributed to first having a measure of the construct of interest, in this case employee engage-ment, with substantial construct validity evidence in the form of convergent and divergent evidence. Second, the criterion must also be measured using an instrument with construct validity evidence of its own. To know the responses obtained with the measure of interest are truly related to the criterion of inter-est, one must know that the two measures assess unique and different con-structs. For example, if the criterion is job satisfaction, the measure of employee engagement must assess engagement and not job satisfaction; the measure of job satisfaction must assess satisfaction, not commitment. Another example from the engagement literature is that engagement is often referred to as the finan-cial loss resulting from unengaged workers. A measure of unengaged workers should exist, and a way of measuring financial loss must be available to make this claim. To date, there is no known measure of unengagement/disengagement, and assuming it is simply the opposite or low end of the engagement scale is using a measure that has no validity evidence.

Reliability: Does the Measure Assess the Same Construct Every Time?

Another important criterion for the measurement quality of the instrument is the reliability of the data obtained using that instrument (Nunnally & Ber-nstein, 1994). The reliability of data says that every time the measurement instrument is used under the same conditions using the same sample, the same results should be obtained (assuming some stability in the construct of interest).

Thus, if I ask participants or respondents to complete a measure of employee engagement today, when I ask them to complete the same measure 1 month from now, I should obtain the same responses. This assumes the construct of employee engagement is stable enough that levels of engagement will not dramatically change between now and then. If the construct varies considerably from day to day, perhaps the two times to offer the measure should not be 1 month apart but rather 1 hour apart. Reliability is a necessary condition for validity: it is difficult if not impossible to accumulate validity evidence if the scores obtained using the same measure are randomly changing within the same sample. Furthermore, poor reliability can attenuate relationships (Reinhardt, 1996) between engagement scores and its criteria, which one may interpret as indicating no relationship exists when one actually does.

The reliability of data obtained using a measure can be assessed using a variety of statistical techniques, such as test–retest, which is the method I have described here as giving the same measure twice to the same sample. Reliability is sample dependent (Pedhazur & Schmelkin, 1991); it can only be obtained from a set of test scores, not from the test itself (Gronlund & Linn, 1990; Vacha-Haase, 1998). Therefore, like validity evidence, reliability is not a property of a scale or measurement instrument itself.

A frequently used analogy for the reliability of data is the use of a ruler. When a ruler is used to measure a desk, every time that ruler is used to measure that desk, the same results should be obtained. If the desk is 3 meters long, every time the same desk is measured using that same ruler, the length assessed should be 3 meters. Of course, no one is perfect, and each time the ruler is used, the reported result may vary slightly from the previous instance. Instead of exactly 3 meters, the second reading may be 3.1 meters or 2.95 meters. This minor fluctuation in measurement – the inability to be perfect every time – is called *error of measurement*. The range of error of measurement should be very small (e.g., ± .05), and likewise for a measure of employee engagement. Because of the various forms of systematic error that enter into assessing psychological constructs, such as remembering the specific items on the measurement instrument from the first time it was taken to the second time (meaning that people just respond the same way the second time as the first because they remember their previous response), different approaches to estimating the reliability of data other than test–retest (administering the same instrument twice to the same group of people) are available to deal with the different kinds of error of measurement.

Because this is not a textbook on psychological measurement, I will not go into additional details here on all the different approaches for obtaining reliability estimates. There is, however, one other method besides test–retest worth mentioning because it is probably the most often reported method and not always the most appropriate. Specifically, that method is internal consistency, and it produces a reliability estimate called the coefficient alpha, also called the alpha coefficient (Cronbach, 1951). Unlike test–retest, deriving coefficient alpha requires only one test administration. Alpha coefficient is an estimate of the degree to which each item within the scale is correlated with every other item within the same scale for a particular sample. A high correlation coefficient suggests the items are all measuring the same thing because they are all highly related to one another. The alpha coefficient is influenced by the number of items in a scale (tends to increase reliability up to a point) and by their average correlations; a low alpha (< .50) may suggest the test is too short or the items are not similar enough to one another to capture the same construct (Nunnally & Bernstein, 1994). A low alpha may also suggest the measure is not unidimensional; it assesses more than one single construct. The assessment of internal consistency only makes sense for constructs with a single dimension or whose dimensions are highly related. Using the current definitions of employee engagement as comprising at least three dimensions (e.g., Britt, 1999; Kahn, 1990; Macey & Schneider, 2008; Schaufeli et al., 2002), engagement is a multidimensional construct and requires a scale that assesses its dimensions. Therefore, depending on how the items on your engagement scale are written to assess each dimension, a single alpha coefficient estimate may not be appropriate because items that assess one dimension of the construct may not be very highly correlated with items that assess another dimension.

Current measures of engagement tend to have dimensions with items that are similar enough to be related, yet distinct enough to capture the nuanced differences between dimensions. When dimensions are substantially different, like those of core self-evaluations (see Judge & Kammeyer-Mueller, 2012), each dimension or subscale should report a high alpha coefficient estimate because each dimension should be assessing a single subcomponent of the construct. With engagement measures assessing current definitions, because the dimensions are supposed to be related and reflect overlap with the other dimensions of the measure, the dimensions should demonstrate reasonably high correlations, suggesting that it is likely high alpha coefficients can be obtained. Indeed, researchers have reported high alpha coefficient estimates in their studies when using the JES, UWES, or Saks's job and/or organization engagement (e.g., Andreassen, Ursin, & Eriksen, 2007; Haldorai, Kim, Phetvaroon, & Li, 2020; Rich et al., 2010). There are no set standards for what a "good" reliability estimate of the data should be, but many have used above .7 for research and above .9 for decision-making, based on the works of Nunnally and Bernstein (1994). Reliability estimates lower than .8 are usually considered too fraught with measurement error. Think about it: if you're making decisions and/or taking actions based on the reported averages from respondents who have completed your engagement measure, you want to be sure that (1) you actually are looking at averages for their engagement levels, and (2) that these scores are reliable – they are not unusually high or low because of some random factor.

The Consequences of Using a Measure Without These Pieces of Evidence

Using a measurement instrument without evidence that it measures what it claims to assess, in this case employee engagement, can result in a few consequences with varying ramifications depending on why engagement was measured in the first place. Let me be clear here: those who move forward with surveys assessing employee engagement and have not been armed with some knowledge about psychological measurement may not know whether the instruments they are using assess engagement. The assumption is that when the vendor provides a given scale, it is a good one. Alternatively, in some cases, you may be forced to choose a measure without validity evidence for financial and practicality reasons. There simply are times and situations in which one must move ahead with what is in hand and, knowing the limitation of not having the necessary evidence, be ready to evaluate, explain, and make trade-offs.

Individuals in organizations assess engagement and then use the numerical results to make research decisions or financial decisions about where to invest and how much to improve engagement. Before learning about the value of validity evidence, some of my clients previously put money into award-and-benefit systems, held their leaders accountable for their employees' engagement scores by managing amount of pay raises or promotion opportunities based on those scores, threatening to let go of those with the lowest scores or who do not improve them after two measurement cycles, and attacking the usual sources of job satisfaction such as pay, benefits, and extras such as picnics and T-shirts – thinking these efforts will ensure higher engagement scores. Although some of these efforts may affect the intended audience, the effect is not always the desired one and not toward increasing engagement.

Organizations often issue the same measure every 6 months to 1 year, obtaining trending data on whether their organizational interventions are working. When organizations use measures of job satisfaction and commitment, rather than engagement, they implement interventions designed to affect these constructs as opposed to engagement. However, job satisfaction and commitment are affected by the economy (e.g., Green, 2010; Maguire, 1983; Pryce-Jones, 2011), among other factors such as pay (Locke, 1976), and therefore may or may not change much because of actions on the part of the organization. Gallup Organization's *State of the American Workplace* (2013a) report suggests that between 2008 and 2010, efforts by organizations to improve employee engagement were not working. Because Gallup's measure of engagement actually assesses satisfaction with the manager and not engagement as defined in the research literature (see the later discussion), these reports are actually about the efforts organizations have been making to change job satisfaction and commitment. Gallup's report may well be stating that organizations are not changing their employees' satisfaction levels, which is valuable when focusing on satisfaction. Additionally, one could take the report to suggest some of the same factors that influence job satisfaction and may potentially influence engagement as well are not improving. However, important here is employee engagement can change and remain high even when external factors associated with the economy are low (Kahn, 1990; Mauno, Kinnunen, & Ruokolainen, 2007; Schaufeli et al., 2002), factors that may independently affect job satisfaction but not engagement (see Chapter 3, in which I discuss how engagement is not the same as job satisfaction). The key point is that tracking the wrong indicator or basing staffing or leadership decisions on erroneous information may be misleading for researchers and practitioners alike, not to mention harmful for the employees themselves.

For the researcher, using a measure without validity information can be detrimental. The accuracy of the nomological network (Cronbach & Meehl, 1955) relies on knowing the relationships identified and connected in the network are backed by solid evidence – evidence that can be replicated and supported in other studies. Because science and practice are intertwined, each reciprocally affects the other; the paths taken in science and the conclusions drawn from the research find their way into practice and ultimately have financial and real-people consequences.

How to Use This Information for Selecting a Measure of Engagement

The preceding information may seem basic to some (especially those who are aware that what I described is just one approach to measurement) and a little overwhelming for others. The takeaway points are that (a) one wants the accumulated evidence obtained using a measurement instrument of employee engagement to demonstrate high reliability from sample to sample, and, hopefully, in samples that mimic the one of interest (e.g., health care, high tech, blue-collar labor); and (b) one wants substantial validity evidence for the measure including forms of convergent and divergent validity evidence, as well as criterion-related validity evidence, if the goal is to "predict" some criterion such as performance, well-being, or job satisfaction.

Those offering the measurement instrument should provide accumulated evidence of consistent reliability of scores and sufficient validity evidence to evaluate the quality of the engagement measure. Most vendors providing engagement solutions may not necessarily volunteer the information up front, but when asked, they should be able to provide it quite easily and without constraint or extra cost. Many who are not in the test construction business and instead in the management solution business may not be familiar with the basics of theory and techniques in psychological measurement, even though they are providing a measurement instrument to assess employee engagement. Their organization may not have the skilled personnel to collect data such as the construct validity evidence necessary for demonstrating their measure assesses engagement and not commitment, and scores from their measure correlate with scores on measures of well-being or performance. Thus, to assume everyone has the information and can readily provide it may be a faulty assumption.

What If Validity Information Is Not Available?

There are some measures for which validity evidence is simply not available in a format noted earlier (e.g., construct, convergent) or unobtainable because the measures are proprietary, and the vendors have not published their data. First, if you cannot get a hold of the validity information, try to find information about how the items were written or chosen for the measure (e.g., the story behind the creation of the survey). This information could provide some sense as to how well the items were constructed, whether they were developed based on a theoretical model of engagement, and whether the scale developers thought about how to distinguish these items and the overall scale from measures assessing other similar constructs. Second, track down information about how and whether the items have been used in an instrument elsewhere, and what variables or constructs might have been correlated with the measure containing those or similar items. Correlations offer information about convergent and divergent validity evidence. Third, a number of my clients like using questions they feel better represents their work environment than those already available in public domain. The costs of some proprietary measures can be prohibitive, so developing their own measure seems like a good next move, as does modifying existing measures to fit the organizational norms. Construct validity evidence begins at the design stage; thus, writing items based on a theoretical framework, having subject matter experts review the items, collecting data to modify and improve the scale, and collecting convergent and divergent validity evidence before putting the measure into practice or surveying the entire organization all contribute to accumulating construct validity evidence.

When not given the opportunity to conduct preliminary qualitative studies to assess the culture and language of the organization, I have drawn from existing measures of engagement and related constructs to write items that have higher face validity for the organization and indirectly get at the theoretically proposed definitions (e.g., Kahn, 1990; Schaufeli, Bakker, & Salanova, 2006). I look into the scholarly literature for research on similar constructs and examine their scale items to determine how to assess engagement as separate from these scales. I include measures of other constructs that may seem similar to engagement, such as job involvement and passion, and during analyses, I run tests to assess the uniqueness of the items I claim are measuring engagement. I perform a pilot test for several reasons, including (but not limited to) collecting initial data to evaluate the quality of the homemade scale. I conduct exploratory and confirmatory factor analyses on all the study variables and, as a consequence, I modify items as needed. The collection of the full sample occurs because I know I have some preliminary evidence in support of the measure. There are other approaches to collecting validity evidence; interested readers can consult sources such as *Alternative Validation Strategies: Developing New and Leveraging Existing Validity Evidence* (McPhail, 2007).

My main goal in these situations is to be able to say, with confidence and data to back me up, that I have measured engagement and its associated constructs as best as possible. I am, therefore, confident the conclusions we make are about engagement, and actions taken as a result of the scores are going to be about engagement and not about something else. Organizations with whom I work seek results obtained using scientifically rigorous methods and results they can defend when asked why one intervention was chosen over another. Applications for various awards, such as the Malcolm Baldrige National Quality Award (www.nist.gov/baldrige/), require evidence of high-quality studies using well-developed measures within the organization. Regardless of the definition of engagement, the goal of using scientifically rigorous methods to assess engagement and its antecedents and consequences is a worthy one: find ways to confirm that what you want to measure is what is measured, and measured well.

Available Measures of Engagement

The Utrecht Work Engagement Scale

By far, the most widely used measure of employee engagement in the academic literature is the Utrecht Work Engagement Scale (UWES), based on Schaufeli et al.'s (2002) definition of engagement. The UWES was developed to assess the three dimensions of Schaufeli et al.'s definition: vigor, dedication, and absorption. The UWES has a history within the stress literature, specifically the burnout literature. Researchers wanting to assess engagement as an indicator of well-being use the UWES.

Grounded in positive psychology, Maslach and Leiter (1997) observed that people who were not burned out seemed engaged. Thus, their perspective was that engagement was the opposite of burnout and could be assessed using the Maslach Burnout Inventory (MBI; Maslach & Jackson, 1981) reverse scored. Thus, low scores on the MBI's three dimensions (exhaustion, cynicism, and inefficacy) translated into high scores on the three engagement components (vigor, dedication, and absorption, respectively). However, Schaufeli and Bakker (2003) determined they could not adequately measure employee engagement using the MBI burnout inventory. First, a direct opposite of inefficacy did not seem to fit conceptually with the idea of work engagement. Second, they argued because engagement and burnout were opposite constructs, thus perfectly negatively correlated, using the same instrument to measure them was psychometrically and conceptually problematic (Schaufeli & Bakker, 2003).

Therefore, the authors modified the MBI and created the UWES (Schaufeli, Salanova et al., 2002). They contended that although correlations between the MBI and the UWES were moderate to high between and across dimensions, the two scales assess distinct constructs. They modified the definition and measurement instrument, moving it away from its direct connection with burnout (although you can still find reference to it as the antipode of burnout), suggesting the two constructs, though related, are conceptually unique and experienced differently (Schaufeli & Bakker, 2003). Recent research supports their assertion (e.g., Nimon & Shuck, 2020). The result of Schaufeli and Bakker's work was a new definition of engagement comprising three dimensions – vigor, dedication, and absorption – which represent a persistent affective-cognitive state of mind. Further, they noted their three dimensions reflect their characterization of engagement as high levels of strong work identification, energy, and happiness, and as feeling enthusiastic and proud of one's work.

The UWES is a self-report questionnaire that assesses vigor with six items, dedication with five items, and absorption with six items. Respondents rate the frequency with which the items are experienced. Although the UWES test manual (Schaufeli & Bakker, 2003) reports confirmatory factor analyses demonstrate a better fit to a three-factor structure than a one-factor structure, their reported fit statistics are nearly identical for the 9-item version, and unacceptable for the 15-item and the 17-item version (fit indices are all below standard acceptable values; Hu & Bentler, 1999). There is no statistical test of difference in fit (e.g., chi-square difference test), and no item or scale factor loadings provided. The test manual reports on the development of the UWES; however, there are aspects of scale development missing. For instance, the selection of opposites of the dimensions of burnout are not explained in this manual, thus for this scale it is unknown whether the conversion was theoretical or based on what seemed to be the opposite construct. As Maslach and Jackson (1984) explain, the three-part definition of burnout was not derived from theory, and as such, neither is the engagement definition espoused by Schaufeli, Salanova et al. (2002). Because of the lack of strong conceptual foundation to the dimensions of engagement, and the lack of a priori theory that explains why these three new dimensions should be distinct, an exploratory factor analysis is justified, yet none is provided in the manual. Despite criticisms of the UWES (e.g., Cole, Walter, Bedeian, & O'Boyle, 2012; Wefald et al., 2012), Schaufeli and colleagues developed a 9-item version (Schaufeli et al., 2006) and a 3-item version (Schaufeli et al., 2019) of the UWES.

In the first edition of this book, I reported that the few researchers who used the UWES and who conducted exploratory analyses found the three dimensions were not distinct (e.g., Sonnentag, 2003; Storm & Rothmann, 2003). Others at that time reported varying results using both the 17-item and 9-item versions of the scale (Cole et al., 2012; Wefald et al., 2012). Since these earlier studies, many more have been published using the UWES-9 in particular, although all versions (17-item, 9-item, 3-item) are studied. For the 17- or 9-item version, some researchers found a two-factor structure (e.g., Jeanson & Michinov, 2020 deleted vigor because of low factor loadings), and some a one-factor structure (e.g., Meintjes & Hofmeyr, 2018). Most researchers conducted an overall confirmatory factor analysis of their study variables (usually as the measurement model within structural equation modeling) wherein the three UWES dimensions are considered separate scales, without considering them as a single measure of engagement (or second-order factor measure) even though they claim engagement is a higher-order construct (Auh, Menguc, Spyropoulou, & Wang, 2016; Tan, Wang, Qian, & Lu, 2020). The results vary across studies with many having to remove one or two items to achieve adequate fit (e.g., Olugbade & Karatepe, 2019). Many researchers do not conduct confirmatory factor analysis, or when they do, they fail to provide more than an overall model fit. It may be that the widespread use of the UWES has many researchers feeling a confirmatory factor analysis on the scale is no longer necessary.

The authors of the UWES can boast of its use in numerous countries and in a significant number of studies. Summarizing findings from studies using the UWES is challenging for three key reasons. First, not all studies employing the measure use all three dimension scales. Second, studies vary as to whether they assess engagement as a single score or three separate scores. Third, researchers vary the response scale between types of anchors (e.g., agree vs. frequency vs. applies/does not apply) and numerical range (e.g., 0 to 6, 1 to 5, and 1 to 7). What I can summarize about engagement assessed using the UWES is that it is positively correlated with anything that could be construed as a resource and negatively related to anything considered a stressor or demand. Thus, for example, engagement is positively correlated with leadership, support, aspects of the job characteristics theory, components of self-determination theory, and performance. Some researchers report small correlations between engagement with the UWES and age or sex, whereas others (most) report no significant correlation with either age or sex. Mean scores are typically around the median, as opposed to skewed positively or negatively, and standard deviations are usually between 0.85 to 1.2. In many cases, researchers do not report means and/or standard deviations. Theories most often employed when using the UWES are the JD-R model (the most highly used), conservation of resources theory, social exchange theory, and (as of late) self-determination theory coupled with the JD-R. Lastly, since the publication of the first edition of this book in 2015, researchers have used a few variations of the UWES to assess engagement in a number of countries, including Australia, Belgium, Brazil, China, Finland, France, Germany, Ghana, Iceland, India, Italy, Japan, the Netherlands, New Zealand, Nigeria, Pakistan, Poland, Romania, South Africa, South Korea, Spain, Switzerland, Taiwan, Turkey, and Vietnam.

The Job Engagement Scale

Another measure of employee engagement in the academic literature is the JES developed by Rich et al. (2010), designed to assess Kahn's (1990) definition of engagement. This measure assesses three dimensions of engagement Kahn proposed: affective, cognitive, and physical self-expression. Although Rich et al. published the scale over a decade ago, it has not enjoyed the same popularity as the UWES.

The measure was originally developed because none existed assessing Kahn's (1990) seminal conceptualization of engagement, and the UWES incorporates items that assess the antecedents of engagement as proposed by Kahn (e.g., items on challenge and meaningfulness). Thus, if one wishes to assess Kahn's perspective on engagement, the UWES is not the right measure to use. Based on an extensive review of the literature on the assessment of the dimensions of Kahn's engagement, Rich et al. developed a measure of 18 items, 6 per dimension. The scale was pilot tested and submitted to exploratory factor analysis. The authors subsequently modified the scale as needed based on the factor analysis results, and conducted a cross-validation study using a different sample. Substantial model testing in the form of confirmatory factor analyses with various model configurations supported a second-order structure, with the three dimensions as first-order factors. The authors recruited an additional sample in their 2010 study, and again, confirmatory factor analyses supported the second-order structure (see Rich et al. [2010] for details).

Rich et al. (2010) provided exploratory and confirmatory factor analysis evidence for this scale, demonstrating the three dimensions' distinctiveness and only moderate correlations with each other. Additionally, Rich et al. provided validity evidence for the distinctiveness of engagement from a number of other theoretical antecedents, consequences, and related constructs. Researchers using the JES report similar results; the JES consistently factors into three distinct dimensions. Engagement assessed using the JES is negatively related to burnout ($r = -.31$; Anthony-McMann, Ellinger, Astakhova, & Halbesleben, 2017) and work interruptions ($r = -.10$; Parke et al., 2018). The JES is positively related to authentic leadership and contextual performance ($b = .21$ and $b = .56$, respectively; Jiang & Shen, 2020); transformational and transactional leadership, as well as leader-member exchange ($r = .22$, $r = .19$, and $r = .18$, respectively; Lai et al., 2020); humble leadership ($r = .25$; Walters & Diab, 2016); supervisor-rated popularity ($r = .27$; Garden et al., 2018); and several management-related constructs, such as moral identity, psychological job ownership, and corporate social responsibility (e.g., He et al., 2019; Raza et al., 2021; L. Wang et al., 2019). Most studies with the JES have not reported correlations with age or gender. Of the two that have, one reported no significant relationships (Hammedi, Leclercq, Poncin, & Alkire, 2021), whereas the other reported a low correlation with age (e.g., Lai et al., 2020). Mean scores are not available in all studies. Researchers using the JES tend to use the scale as a single, multifaceted measure as opposed to separating the three dimensions into three separate scales (for exceptions, see Anthony-McMann et al., 2017; Črnjar, Dlačić, & Milfelner, 2020; Jiang & Shen, 2020). Additionally, researchers use either a 1–5 or 1–7 agree response scale; Rich et al. used a 1–5 scale. In perhaps the only intervention study using the JES, McGonagle et al. (2020) demonstrated that coaching improved engagement.

Job and Organization Engagement

Saks (2006) developed a measure of employee engagement that assess job (five items) and organizational engagement (six items) as two separate scales. At first glance, these scales seem to borrow somewhat from a number of constructs. For example, items assess the extent to which individuals are all-consumed by their job, they lose track of time (absorption, flow), and their involvement as an organizational member is the most exciting and is exhilarating (involvement, identification). Both scales include an item stating, "I am highly engaged in this [job or organization]" (Saks, 2006, p. 617). Saks provided evidence these scales were moderately correlated with each other ($r = .62$) but were considered separate (he offers an overview of factorial results to indicated separateness of scales from each other, but no detailed listing of factor loadings).

Saks proposed employees offer job and organizational engagement as part of a social exchange relationship (Blau, 1964) with the organization. His regression results suggest job engagement is related to job characteristics, job satisfaction, organizational commitment, citizenship behaviors beneficial to the organization, and organizational support, whereas organizational engagement is related to organizational support (more strongly than to job engagement), procedural justice, job satisfaction, organizational commitment, and citizenship behavior beneficial to both individuals and the organization. Thus, both scales are similarly related to other constructs, with just a few exceptions. Even though Saks's measures were designed to assess engagement as two forms of reciprocation (job and organization), some researchers combine the scales together and use a single engagement score representing both job and organization engagement (e.g., Mayuran & Kailasapathy, 2020; Santhanam & Srinivas, 2019). Other researchers use only one of the engagement scales, typically job engagement (e.g., Hai et al., 2020; Haldorai et al., 2020); though organization engagement only is occasionally assessed (e.g., Akingbola & van den Berg, 2019).

A couple of my clients believe employees are engaged in their job and/or their organization. They intuitively like the idea of engagement in one's specific job in which the focus is on completing tasks, as well as engagement in the organization, which they feel implies a kind of investment in the organization's goals. Organizational leaders and human resource managers emphasize the need for engagement to be aligned with meeting organizational goals; thus, having employees very energized and focused on task completion that is not in the direction the organization wants to go is inefficient and undesirable. Interestingly, although the idea of organizational engagement is appealing in some practitioner and organizational circles, a search through the Web of Science online database reveals not many researchers have used Saks's (2006) model or scales. Akingbola and van den Berg (2019) used both the JES as three separate scales and Saks's organization engagement scale. They found organization engagement was highly correlated with emotional engagement ($r = .71$) and moderately correlated with physical ($r = .49$) and cognitive ($r = .51$) engagement. Though they found a few differences in relationships between emotional and organization engagement and other study variables (i.e., value congruence), the two forms of engagement related to other constructs very similarly, suggesting Saks's organization engagement is very similar to the JES emotional engagement dimension. I report correlations between Saks's measures, the JES, and UWES in Table 3.4 in Chapter 3.

May et al.'s Measure

May, Gilson, and Harter (2004) introduced their three-component measure of engagement, along with made-up scales for assessing psychological meaningfulness, safety, and availability. Their three engagement components included physical, emotional, and cognitive, consistent with Kahn's proposed framework. Although their intentions were good, the psychological availability scale was actually a scale of self-efficacy (Bandura, 1997), representing self-confidence in one's ability to handle the work. As noted in Byrne, Peters, and Weston (2016), psychological availability "reflects the degree of freedom from nonwork distractions that would otherwise prevent one from fully expressing oneself at work (W. A. Kahn, personal communication, May 6, 2012)" (p. 1205). Viljevac, Cooper-Thomas, and Saks (2012) scrutinized the validity of May et al.'s measure compared to the UWES. They found the UWES was different from organizational commitment, but not that different from job involvement and intentions to stay. By comparison, May et al.'s measure was distinguishable from organizational commitment, but not job involvement or intentions to stay. Additionally, person–job fit and person–organization fit were more strongly related to the UWES than May et al.'s measure of engagement. The authors concluded, "both measures performed tolerably across the various analyses" (p. 3704). Most importantly, the authors found neither measure could be distinguished from job satisfaction.

Soane et al.'s Measure

Soane et al. (2012) developed a 9-item ISA (intellectual, social, affective) engagement measure that has not been used much by anyone other than the original authors. Like other measures of engagement, the ISA has three components: intellectual engagement, which is the same as cognitive engagement of the JES or May et al. scale or absorption of the UWES; social engagement, which is the most unique component relative to other engagement scales; and affective engagement, which has two affective items and one physical (vigor)–related item. Social engagement is represented by items about sharing work values, sharing work goals, and sharing work attitudes with colleagues. Soane et al. reported the ISA forms a single engagement score and is moderately related to turnover intentions ($r = -.49$) and weakly related to task performance ($r = .38$) and citizenship behaviors ($r = .31$).

Non-academic Engagement Scales

Because of the proprietary nature of non-academic scales, they are not used in the research literature except by individuals associated with the consulting organization sponsoring the measure or who have signed an agreement to use proprietary measures (e.g., Harter, Schmidt, & Hayes, 2002; Luthans & Peterson, 2002; Macey et al., 2009; Medlin & Green, 2009; Zhu, Avolio, & Walumbwa, 2009). Consulting firms such as Towers-Watson, Kenexa, Gallup Organization, Valtera (absorbed by Corporate Executive Board, which was later absorbed by Gartner), and the Hay Group, to name a few, all boast their own measures of employee engagement, but the proprietary nature of these surveys makes it difficult, if not impossible, for researchers to confirm the scales' ability to assess employee engagement. Likewise, the definition used by these consulting firms is, for the most part, unknown unless they provide a glimpse of their model on their websites, or if known, is quite different from academically derived definitions. It is important to state here that the goal may not always be to assess employee engagement itself, by itself, or to assess the academic versions of the construct; rather the goal may be to assess the work environment that potentially fosters engagement and the outcomes that result. For example, as previously mentioned, some vendors I reviewed admitted their measures did not assess engagement but assessed predictors or drives. If assessing drivers of engagement is the goal, a number of vendor solutions, to the best of my knowledge based on minimal review, are definitely worthy of consideration given what we currently know about what predicts engagement. Importantly, organizations want to know what they can change in the organization to increase their employees' behavior that facilitates meeting organizational goals. Thus, not only is it important to measure employee engagement, but it is also important to measure aspects of the work environment that may relate to engagement. It may also be the case once clear definitions are available for scrutiny, the proprietary measures may perform very well in assessing engagement.

Although the Gallup Organization's Q^{12} is considered proprietary, items from the measure have been published in public-domain research papers (Harter et al., 2002) with the copyright note that the items are not to be reprinted or reproduced without permission. Therefore, I will not reproduce the items here, but they are available in Harter et al.'s published paper. Harter et al. note employee engagement is defined as involvement in and satisfaction at work. They further note the Q^{12} demonstrates high convergent validity with measures of overall job satisfaction. A visual review of the items reveals that even though they do not ask about employee engagement, they appear to ask about aspects of the work environment that potentially foster engagement. For example, the survey items ask about the clarity of role expectations, job resources, feedback, supportive supervisors and coworkers, and job characteristics such as task significance. Researchers have examined all these concepts as antecedents to employee engagement; thus, the Q^{12} may be considered a very quick and surface snapshot of work dimensions considered positively related to engagement. In many situations, such a snapshot is quite valuable; however, it should be followed with more intensive efforts to pinpoint how and where to devote intervention time and effort. It is possible Gallup uses this very strategy. That said, without actually assessing employee engagement, one cannot be certain the interventions are having an effect on engagement.

Comparing Scales

Table 6.1 compares and contrasts measures and notes some of their validity evidence, allowing one to choose the scale that best fits the needs and has the available evidence to support its use. In the table, I include engagement measures I have had access to in the public domain, ranked in order of most frequently used to least frequently used (as far as I can tell from the published literature). The Q^{12} is reported last because it is a proprietary measure, yet I include it because its items have appeared in print in at least one public domain article (Harter et al., 2002) and at least one book (Buckingham & Coffman, 1999). Additionally, I reference it in this table because every 1–2 years, Gallup publishes their "state of the workplace" reports, in which they claim how engaged (or not) the workforce is. Their reports are based on data obtained using surveys that include the Q^{12}. Many who argue for the importance of an engaged workforce cite Gallup's reports; hence, the Q^{12} ends up being a reluctant contender.

My Own Research Comparing UWES to JES

Because the UWES and JES are the most well-known measures of engagement used in research, I focused most of my energy on comparing these two scales to each other. Using five different samples, two of my students, Janet Peters and James Weston, and I showed that the UWES and JES are different enough from each other that they are not assessing the exact same construct. That is, they

TABLE 6.1 Validity Evidence for Available Measures of Employee Engagement

Measure	Authors and Notes	Fundamentals	Validity Evidence
Utrecht Work Engagement Scale (UWES) Three versions exist: UWES-3, UWES-9, UWES-17	Schaufeli, Salanova et al. (2002)	3 dimensions (vigor, dedication, absorption), each producing a separate score that can be combined to create a single score; based on definition of engagement being opposite of burnout	*Factorial validity evidence:* Exploratory and confirmatory factor analyses indicate the 3 dimensions not clearly distinct from each other: sometimes 1, 2, or 3 dimensions emerge depending on the sample. Some researchers remove some offending items (varies by study) and a second-order structure fits best. *Convergent and divergent validity evidence:* Correlates with self-efficacy, need for achievement, positive affectivity, job satisfaction, organizational support; lacks sufficient divergent validity evidence. High correlations with organizational commitment and job involvement, task significance and variety, and conscientiousness, but not so high that engagement is considered the same as these constructs.
Job Engagement Scale (JES)	Rich et al. (2010)	3 dimensions (physical, cognitive, affective) combined to create a single scale score; based on Kahn's definition of engagement as expression of physical, cognitive, affective self when fully invested into the job role	*Factorial validity evidence:* Exploratory and confirmatory factor analyses indicating 3 dimensions are distinct from each other and form a second-order factor. *Convergent and divergent validity evidence:* Correlates with task performance, organizational citizenship behavior, perceived organizational support, perceived supervisory support, organizational commitment, and psychological meaningfulness.

(Continued)

TABLE 6.1 (Continued)

Measure	Authors and Notes	Fundamentals	Validity Evidence
Engagement Scale	May et al. (2004)	Based on Kahn (1990) designed to measure physical, cognitive, and emotional engagement.	*Factorial validity evidence:* Evidence failed to support the 3 dimensions as unique, thus authors used an overall scale score using only those items demonstrating internal consistency reliability and some balance across the 3 dimensions. No information available for scale item construction, or evidence of distinctiveness from other constructs in the study (i.e., no factorial validity evidence). *Convergent and divergent validity evidence:* Correlations reported are positive between engagement and meaningfulness, job enrichment, organizational commitment, and supervisor relations, and negative with outside activities such as volunteering in the community and turnover intentions.
Job engagement and organizational engagement	Saks (2006)	2 independent scales: one focused on engagement in the job and the other focused on engagement toward the organization; based on a social exchange relationship.	*Factorial validity evidence:* None provided. *Convergent and divergent validity evidence:* Both job and organizational engagement were equally correlated with organizational support, supervisory support, job satisfaction, citizenship behavior, and commitment.

Self-engagement (self-engagement is defined as "being personally responsible for and committed to one's performance"; Britt & Bliese, 2003, p. 247)	Britt (1999)	Measure of self-engagement as defined by Britt; not the same as employee or work engagement	Based on an integration of Kahn (1990), Kanungo's (1982) job involvement, Lodahl and Kejner's (1965) self-efficacy/job involvement concept, and commitment. Calls the combination of these 3 concepts the triangle model.	*Factorial validity evidence:* None provided. *Convergent and divergent validity evidence:* Positively correlates with perceived control and job training (Britt, 1999), and negatively correlates with work stress and psychological distress (Britt & Bliese, 2003). Does not correlate with citizenship behavior (Britt et al., 2012), even though many other studies show engagement is positively correlated with citizenship behavior (e.g., Christian, Garza, & Slaughter, 2011; Rich et al., 2010).
Q^{12} (items shown in Harter et al. [2002], but are noted as copyrighted)	Gallup Organization, reported in Harter et al. (2002)	measure of satisfaction with aspects of work that others have shown are related to engagement, but Gallup claims it measures engagement.	Based on criterion-keyed method of scale development, where items are chosen based on whether they are endorsed by those who considered their manager to be excellent and not endorsed by those who considered their manager to be weak.	*Factorial validity evidence:* None is available. *Convergent and divergent validity evidence:* Positively associated with customer satisfaction and turnover intentions (Harter et al., 2002). Correlations between satisfaction and engagement with other constructs were identical to one another (Harter et al., 2002), indicating these two constructs are probably not distinct.

do not relate to the same variables in the same way, and in some cases, they do not relate to the same variables at all. Thus, when evaluating their nomological networks (Cronbach & Meehl, 1955), we clarified they do not occupy exactly the same space in a single network. The UWES showed overlap with a number of different attitudes and had high correlations with most variables assessed, including stress, job performance, strains (e.g., headache), organizational commitment, job commitment, and burnout. The JES, in contrast, showed much less overlap and weaker correlations with the variables, except support and psychological safety – which was similar to the UWES. Overall, we concluded the UWES was assessing a much broader portion of the engagement nomological network than the JES (Byrne et al., 2016). We recommended using the UWES if what one wants is a broad sweeping assessment of job attitudes including engagement, and the JES for research and a more definitive assessment of engagement, and engagement only. Lastly, using a specific two-sample technique to examine construct-level relationships (not just measurement differences), we showed that engagement is different from the opposite of burnout, is an antecedent to burnout, and that psychological meaningfulness might actually be part of the engagement concept. Additional studies should replicate and extend our work.

Visual Comparison of the UWES Versus the JES Items

Neither the JES nor the UWES assesses engagement as a moment-to-moment phenomenon, a conceptualization of engagement Kahn (1990) put forth. Questions on both the JES and the UWES are phrased as a statement about how one is, or about one's perspective in general ("At work, I am absorbed in my job" and "In my job, I feel strong and vigorous," respectively). Hence, even though the JES is modeled after Kahn's moment-to-moment conceptualization of engagement, and the UWES is modeled after Schaufeli, Salanova et al.'s (2002) conceptualization of engagement as a persistent and stable state, neither seems to hit the mark. For example, one might expect items on the JES to be phrased in this manner: "At this moment, I am devoting a lot of energy to the tasks of my job." For the UWES, one might expect items to be phrased as, "In general, I am enthusiastic about my job." While it is easy to change items to specific the "time" component of the assessment, neither scale was developed aimed at the period specified in the definition. Thus, it is not clear exactly what role time plays with regard to engagement. That is, is engagement truly a moment-by-moment or persistent state, regardless of how the items on the scale are phrased?

The UWES was originally designed with a different rating scale than the JES, which may contribute to assessing a slightly different perception of the construct. Specifically, the UWES was originally designed to be used on a frequency scale ranging from "0 = Never" to "6 = Every day," in which people rate how often they feel what is described in the item. Since its original construction, however, researchers have used a variety of response scales, both in terms of anchor types and numerical values. The JES is designed to be assessed on an agreement scale ranging from "1 = Strongly disagree" to "5 = Strongly agree." It appears most researchers keep to this scaling, though some have extended the scale from 5 to 7 (1 to 7 total). While the numbers are often the same (i.e., 1 to 7), frequency response scales are qualitatively different from agreement scales.

Conclusion About Measures of Engagement

A common disadvantage of the engagement scales noted earlier is they all assume engagement is the same for every organization. Given the literature on organizational climate and culture, the predictors of employee engagement in terms of leadership styles, support, characteristics of the job, and individual sense of meaning and purpose in the job, it is unlikely a single engagement scale can work well in every organization. Organizational cultures differ, as do country cultures. It may be that some industry characteristic requires a different kind of assessment of employee engagement, and perhaps even a different definition of engagement. My own qualitative research findings in different health care organizations suggest engagement is not conceptualized identically from organization to organization, even though there may be some similarities.

The State of Measurement of Engagement

Where are we with the measurement of employee engagement? One can contend not very far, based on the preceding review; but that means there is room for improvement. There are a few scales in the academic literature, as noted earlier; however, they may not be ideal for every situation. A disadvantage of the extant measures is they are all questions used in surveys. Other ways of assessing engagement have yet to be explored. In Chapter 2, I note a new definition of employee engagement wherein I suggest rather than just physically engaged, people are physiologically engaged; their level of arousal may or may not be visible, and they themselves may not be fully cognizant of how aroused they are. None of the existing measures incorporates the possibility of physiological arousal without a physical outburst, such as what we might be able to assess using instrumentation other than a self-report survey. One could speculate that to assess physical engagement accurately, a different method than a questionnaire-based survey is needed. In an earlier study, not yet reviewed in this book, one of my students (Janet Peters) and I attempted to assess physical engagement using physiological measures; specifically, galvanic skin response and heart rate. This was a lab study in which we attempted to create or foster engagement within participants; we were unsuccessful. However, what is important about sharing this attempt to examine physical engagement is it may not be unreasonable to assume a physiological measure is the best way to assess that which is supposed to be physiologically arousing. Our failure may simply be an inability to manipulate engagement in a lab setting with student participants.

Additionally, when employee engagement is described within the practice environment, it is nearly always described as a behavioral observation; that is, we can *see* when an employee is engaged and when not. I have maintained, consistent with current research literature, employee engagement is a motivational state, and the effects of engagement may be observed in some employees, but perhaps not all. This may be particularly relevant in some occupations versus others. Thus, one could potentially include an observational measure to assess the consequences or effects of employee engagement, but not use it as the only source of data. This observational data would serve as non–self-report data that could be used in conjunction with other data on engagement obtained via surveys and physiological measures. Perhaps a corroboration of a variety of methods as suggested here is required to assess a construct that has affective, cognitive, and physical/physiological dimensions accurately.

What to Do to Measure Engagement?

With such need for more research in developing accurate and adequate measures of employee engagement, what should an organization that wants to assess employee engagement do today? There are at least a few approaches organizations can take. First, organizations can use the existing scales available in the academic literature, or a proprietary measure offered by a consulting firm. Look for measures with sufficient validity evidence that can be used reliably, allowing for comparison across organizational units. By using measures that have evidence of actually assessing employee engagement and not other constructs, such as organizational commitment, job involvement, or other antecedents or consequences of engagement (e.g., support or performance), the organization can be sure it is getting an assessment of engagement. For instance, you can get a quick snapshot of engagement using standard scales, such as the JES, which may provide a high-level view of engagement, enough to move the organization forward. However, to design specific interventions that address concerns within the organization that are preventing employees from becoming engaged may require a custom measure that effectively assesses employee engagement in that particular organization or another measure in addition to engagement to assess antecedent conditions of engagement and outcomes of interest.

Second, organizations can hire small consulting firms or independent consultants (sometimes researchers themselves) who have experience creating customized assessments for employee engagement to create custom measures. It is possible that large consulting firms can provide a certain amount of customization to their existing measures, sometimes with a price; however, these firms often provide benchmarking data that make customization of the actual engagement items impossible. You need to ask. The same scrutiny should apply: be sure the custom assessment is based on the use of rigorous scientific methods and gets at engagement, not just its antecedents or expected consequences.

Third, organizations might have internal expertise (e.g., internal industrial and organizational [IO] psychologists) to develop their own measures of engagement. If this is the best route for getting an affordable custom measure of engagement, follow good scale development practices, solicit review from subject matter experts, and conduct some internal validity studies before rolling out the measure to the entire organization. Lastly, consider collaborating with researchers to support your efforts.

The Last Word on Measuring Engagement

The purpose of research is to advance our understanding of a construct domain and continuously improve by questioning previous findings and building anew. Unfortunately, it seems that little progress has been made on improving measures of engagement over the last decade. There are two measures widely used: Gallup Q^{12} and the UWES. Gallup has proprietary rights to the Q^{12}, which is really more a measure of satisfaction with one's work environment than a measure of engagement itself. Although the UWES is widely used, the various criticisms put forth by several researchers (e.g., Byrne et al., 2016; Cole et al., 2012; Newman & Harrison, 2008; Wefald et al., 2012) remain unaddressed. Furthermore, it seems anything goes with how the UWES is altered to make it work within each study, including dropping items, using only one or two of the dimensions, combining dimensions, and changing response scales. Less frequently used measures include the JES and Saks's (2006) job and organizational engagement scales. The JES may be more appropriate for research than the UWES (Byrne et al., 2016), yet researchers have not taken to its use until the last 2 years or so (i.e., most papers using the JES have been published in the last 2–3 years). Only a handful of researchers have used Saks's measures. Regardless of how many studies exist about engagement, more are published claiming a lack of understanding of engagement and its measurement (e.g., Shuck et al., 2017).

Lastly, the assessment of employee engagement appears to be separate from the assessment of clinical engagement or student engagement. Clinical engagement refers to involvement and commitment toward health care treatment and effectiveness of health care delivery. Student engagement refers to the level of effort, sustained concentration or focus, persistence over time, enjoyment, and intention to finish school tasks that students feel and display in school and outside of school, working on educational tasks (e.g., homework; Brophy, Rohrkemper, Rashid, & Goldberger, 1983). Student engagement refers to behavioral and emotional components of student involvement and level of motivation in learning (Skinner & Belmont, 1993). Thus, at some level, employee engagement, student engagement, and to a small degree clinical engagement tap similar constructs: cognitive, emotional, and behavioral motivation. Thus far, scholars have treated these literatures separately, but there might be something gained by considering the commonalities.

WALK-AWAY POINTS

- Good measures produce reliability of scores and have validity evidence in support of their use.
- A number of employee engagement scales are available; however, based on the available evidence at the time of this writing, none is outstanding.
- A big opportunity exists for researchers to develop good measures of engagement with the collaboration of practitioners, to keep measures grounded in science yet usable for practice.
- Measures for cross-cultural use are sorely needed (see Chapter 9 for more on international studies).

PART III
Competitive Advantage

7

HOW DO WE IMPROVE EMPLOYEE ENGAGEMENT FOR COMPETITIVE ADVANTAGE?

Ulrich and Lake (1991) proposed "building better products or services, pricing goods or services lower than the competition, or incorporating technological innovations into research and manufacturing operations must today be supplemented by organizational capability – the firm's ability to manage people to gain competitive advantage" (p. 77). One can think of competitive advantage as the "ability to generate above normal returns relative to competitors" and the "social version of survival of the fittest" (Ployhart, 2012, p. 62). Although Ulrich and Lake's article may be considered a bit outdated today, their supposition remains valid.

To be competitive, today's businesses must be flexible, shifting their product lines quickly and generating new market demand before their current market declines. New technology and open trading across geographical borders have pushed customer-focused solutions to the surface and widened the range of providers, such that innovation (and not just product, but also process) is essential for survival (Teece, 2010). For organizations to respond to the market competition, they must have employees who are flexible and capable of adapting to change in support of the organization's mission; thus, organizations are increasingly focusing on human resources (human capital), not on just their technological advances (Jin, Hopkins, & Wittmer, 2010). Recruiting talented individuals is essential for sustainable competitive market advantage, and to do so organizations must present a positive corporate image that will meet the needs of talented individuals who are new to the workforce and also appeal to their sense of "fit" in the organization (Rau & Hyland, 2006). Furthermore, competition in the world market requires innovation – the intentional development or creation of novel ideas, idea promotion, and realization or application

DOI: 10.4324/9781003171133-10

of these new and novel ideas that benefit the group and/or organization (Amabile, Conti, Coon, Lazenby, & Herron, 1996; Janssen, 2000; Kanter, 1988; Scott & Bruce, 1994).

Scholars suggest that for companies to be innovative, competitive, and sustainable, they must have an engaged workforce (e.g., Byrne, Palmer, Smith, & Weidert, 2011; Macey, Schneider, Barbera, & Young, 2009; Ncube & Jerie, 2012; Rich, LePine, & Crawford, 2010). The hypothesis here is that engaged employees are more willing and able to change as needed by the organization than employees who are not engaged. Although no study has yet tested this specific hypothesis, a recent study reported positive correlations between employee engagement and willingness to support an organizational change intervention ($r = .37$, $p < .01$; van den Heuvel, Demerouti, Schreurs, Bakker, & Schaufeli, 2009). Research has linked employee engagement to innovative work behaviors (e.g., Agarwal, Datta, Blake-Beard, & Bhargava, 2012; Bhatnagar, 2012; Chughtai & Buckley, 2011; Ge & Sun, 2020; Montani, Vandenberghe, Khedhaouria, & Courcy, 2020; Tian & Zhang, 2020; Xu, Du, Lei, & Hipel, 2020), adding to the conclusion that engagement is essential for competitive advantage. The hypothesis that for organizations to compete in the world market they must have engaged employees is also supported by the research reviewed in previous chapters; engagement is positively correlated with job performance, task performance, and citizenship behavior (or extra-role behaviors). In addition, recent studies show support for engagement among teams and coworkers, potentially amplifying individual effects of engagement on competitiveness (e.g., Guchait, 2016; Waight & Edwards, 2020). For organizations to compete, they must produce, and this holds true around the globe.

Research to date suggests employees become engaged with (a) the right amount of resources; (b) an ability to manage work stressors; (c) trust to feel safe to fully invest themselves in the work task; (d) an interpersonal leader creating connection and a meaningful vision; (e) ability to create and find meaning in the work; (f) support and connection with others at work, allowing them to focus on the job and align themselves with the organization's values; and (g) job–organization and person–organization fit (e.g., Aryee, Walumbwa, Zhou, & Hartnell, 2012; Bakker & Demerouti, 2008; Berg, Dutton, & Wrzesniewski, 2013; Biswas & Bhatnagar, 2013; Z. Chen, Zhang, & Vogel, 2011; Christian, Garza, & Slaughter, 2011; Kahn, 1990; May, Gilson, & Harter, 2004; Zhu, Avolio, & Walumbwa, 2009).

One way to provide these seven components to employees is to have an organization with an organizational culture that supports these components and employees who proactively seek ways to become and stay engaged. Although the previous chapters refer to drivers and inhibitors of engagement, this chapter pulls them together, along with other factors not previously discussed (e.g., selection), to create the right climate for engaging employees and keeping them engaged.

An Organizational Culture for Engagement

Organizational culture refers to the combination of norms, behaviors, practices, and expectations of the organization by which employees come to understand and experience their workplace (Ostroff, Kinicki, & Muhammad, 2013; Ostroff, Kinicki, & Tamkins, 2003; Schein, 1990, 2000). Employees' experience of organizational culture tells them what to believe about the workplace, how to behave at work, what they will be rewarded for, the organization's values, and to what extent they become connected to the organization and its members (Jones & James, 1979; Rentsch, 1990; Schneider, 1990). Organizations with a culture for engagement maximize the probability their employees will be engaged at work because they have provided the resources and fostered the relationships that are believed to trigger engagement. In the following, I review a number of factors that research suggests can be manipulated to create a culture for engagement.

Trust

Substantial evidence shows that trust in the supervisor or leaders makes a big difference in employees' perception of work and their ability to perform on the job (Sousa-Lima, Michel, & Caetano, 2013). Trust also plays an important role in creating perceptions of psychological safety (i.e., Aryee, Budhwar, & Chen, 2002; Basit, 2017). The nature of the employee–organization exchange is based on social exchange theory (Blau, 1964), which suggests employees are obligated to reciprocate to an organization or leader who offers something of value, such as support. The social exchange relationship is predicated on trust, in which the organization trusts the employee to reciprocate and the employee trusts the organization to continue in this relationship once obligations are fulfilled. Trust is a necessary condition for vulnerability, in which employees and the representatives of the organization demonstrate a belief in each other's dependability, reliability, and competency and an emotional feeling of mutual caring (McAllister, 1995). The condition of trust translates into feeling safe to express one's competency on the job without negative consequences – a key aspect of perceived psychological safety (Kahn, 1990). Trust follows in climates of justice or fairness (e.g., Aryee et al., 2002; Byrne, Pitts, Wilson, & Steiner, 2012; Korsgaard, Schweiger, & Sapienza, 1995), and leaders have control over fairness procedures and outcomes (e.g., Bies & Moag, 1986; Byrne & Cropanzano, 2001). Researchers have recently found direct and indirect relationships between trust in the supervisor or leader and employee engagement (e.g., Basit, 2017; Holland, Cooper, & Sheehan, 2017), as well as an indirect relationship between authentic leadership and engagement via trust (D. Wang & Hsieh, 2013). People work harder and tend to respect a leader they consider competent (Justis, 1975), and they tend to trust a competent leader (Tan & Tan,

2000). Additionally, employees who trust their organization believe its leaders are competent and will take the organization in a beneficial direction (Tan & Tan, 2000). Thus, trust in both leader and organization is essential for employees to feel a fit and a willingness to be vulnerable to invest in their job roles. Lastly, employees who lack trust in their supervisor report feeling less psychological meaningfulness and availability, which inhibits their engagement (e.g., Roberts & David, 2017).

Interpersonal Leadership

Leadership characteristics that inspire interpersonal relations seem most related to employee engagement (Aryee et al., 2012; Hansen, Byrne, & Kiersch, 2014; Tuckey, Bakker, & Dollard, 2012; Yang et al., 2018). Interpersonal leaders can promote positive well-being in employees (Arnold, Turner, Barling, Kelloway, & McKee, 2007), which serves to increase perceptions of psychological availability (Kahn, 1990). Transformational leaders, in particular, tend to demonstrate interpersonal characteristics that positively relate to engagement, such as personally recognizing employees' efforts, conveying caring and an appreciation for employees, and connecting employees' goals with those of the organization, thereby increasing their feelings of value and significance (Bass, 1985; Rafferty & Griffin, 2004; Walumbwa, Avolio, & Zhu, 2008). Transformational leaders inspire their followers to seek and create meaning at work by aligning their goals with those of the organization (Bass, 1985; Yukl, 2010). Researchers have shown the effectiveness of leadership development programs in increasing transformational leadership behaviors (W. Brown & May, 2012; Parry & Sinha, 2005).

Similarly, authentic leaders, those whose actions are consistent with their internal beliefs and who remain true to themselves, including sharing vulnerabilities (Avolio, Gardner, Walumbwa, Luthans, & May, 2004), promote trust and engagement in their followers (Hassan & Ahmed, 2011). The willingness to be vulnerable and encourage open criticism in the spirit of improvement sets up the authentic leader to create a climate for psychological safety, paving the way for engagement (Kahn, 1990). Walumbwa, Christensen, and Muchiri (2013) suggest transformational leaders can promote engagement by influencing their followers' perceptions of meaningful work. They recommend a number of strategies including developing their employees' self-efficacy, and job redesign and describing work in ideological terms. Additional forms of leadership emphasizing interpersonal relations with employees include leader–member exchange, which has been shown to positively related to engagement (Burch & Guarana, 2014). Likewise, empowering leadership, which incorporates support and encouragement, is positively associated with engagement (Kim & Beehr, 2020).

Finding and Creating Meaning

Employees who perceive a fit between themselves and their jobs or organizations are more likely to find meaning in their work (Shamir, 1991). Shamir (1991) proposed a self-concept-based theory of motivation to explain why people seek meaning and ultimately become engaged at work. He suggested people need to self-express consistent with their self-concept, to maintain and enhance their self-esteem, and to increase the congruency of their self-concept and behavior. Doing so gives them a sense of meaning: they are behaving and expressing themselves in a manner consistent with their self-concept. Taking this perspective suggests employee engagement comes from within the employee, and therefore is not under the leader or manager's full control. Hence, engagement can be encouraged through job factors, social factors, organizational culture, and other work aspects that enable and help employees align their behavior with their self-concept.

Based on the self-concept theory (Shamir, 1991), self-concept–job fit refers to a congruence between individuals' feelings of their self-perception as derived from their work performance and their ideal self. Their performance on the job creates a self-perception of how they are doing, and what their knowledge, skills, and abilities are in performing the job; if this self-perception matches or is consistent with their identity or self-concept of how they should be able to perform on the job, they have self-concept–job fit (Scroggins & Benson, 2007). A lack of congruence is a lack of self-concept–job fit. When individuals feel they have self-concept–job fit, they have meaning at work; those who lack fit seek ways to create fit. Scroggins (2008) found self-concept–job fit was positively related to meaningful work, which in turn was related to job performance, and was negatively related to turnover intentions. Scroggins suggested self-concept–job fit can be developed via career planning and progression activities and by job redesign (Oldham & Hackman, 1980).

As reviewed extensively in Chapter 4, job crafting is another approach to job redesign and has shown to be effective in encouraging engagement. Job crafting refers to the process of redefining and reframing the way a job is designed to personally fit and work for the individual employee (Wrzesniewski & Dutton, 2001). By conceptualizing one's work tasks differently than they are now, and through changing the boundary conditions of the job (i.e., changing the tasks a bit, modifying how much time is spent on the various tasks, changing how one relates to others on the job, or changing how one sees the job tasks themselves), one can essentially craft the job to be more meaningful (Wrzesniewski & Dutton, 2001). By empowering the employee to job craft, the employee can create their own meaningful work structure within the boundaries of organizational demands (the authors are not advocating employees change the core deliverable or requirement of the job, such as to become an accountant when their job is customer service; Berg et al., 2013). Recent studies show support for job crafting positively relating to engagement (Meng et al., 2021). Chapter 4 also provides review of the JD-R version of job crafting, which through the increase of job resources shows positive correlations with work engagement.

Connection With Others

Friendship at work involves a voluntary and amiable relationship between two employees, which includes support for each other's social and emotional goals (Song & Olshfski, 2008). Humans have a "powerful, fundamental, and extremely pervasive" need for belongingness and relational bonds (Baumeister & Leary, 1995, p. 497). As such, friendship at work fulfills individuals' needs for belongingness and relatedness, thus promoting individual health and well-being (H. Reis, Sheldon, Gable, Roscoe, & Ryan, 2000). Additionally, friendship offers individuals a sense of security and positive social validation (i.e., via reciprocity), thereby facilitating development of each individual's positive self-concept (Bukowski, Motzoi, & Meyer, 2009). Friendship may also potentially foster engagement through Kahn's (1990) critical states (e.g., friendship in the workplace could promote perceived psychological safety). Friendship is a fundamental aspect of human life that gives meaning to life (Bukowski et al., 2009), and it appears friendship can enhance engagement. The Gallup Organization includes an item on their Q^{12} asking about having a best friend at work (see Buckingham & Coffman, 1999; Gebauer, Lowman, & Gordon, 2008; Harter et al., 2002). This item, most likely, works to predict employee outcomes because it captures to some extent this powerful need for belongingness.

Friends, coworkers, and others of close proximity in the workplace fulfill another important function: that of creating a social reality. Social information processing theory (Salancik & Pfeffer, 1978) suggests employees draw on past behavior, and their thoughts of what others around them think of them, to form their own attitudes, behaviors, and beliefs. These thoughts then help them adapt to their current situation and help to create the reality of their own past behavior and situations. Thus, people are constantly adapting based on the information in the social environment. Social information processing theory applied to engagement suggests employees may alter their perception of the meaningfulness of their work, and ultimately their engagement, through processing the information and social environment around them.

Virtual Work

Although proximity makes sense in a collocated or non-virtual work environment, connection with others in the virtual environment is essential for engagement and vice versa. Panteli, Yalabik, and Rapti (2019) determined employees can be engaged in virtual environments, but they rely heavily on asynchronous technology to connect with their teammates and that connection is essential. Many employees I interviewed during the COVID-19 pandemic forced work-from-home period noted how they remained connected with their peers and leaders through the use of technology – and not with just one platform or tool: video and/or audio conferencing, chats, email, and texting were all heavily utilized for the most engaged employees.

Incivility Threatens Inclusion

Connections with others work well when colleagues and leaders operate from a base of civility. Civility refers to the interpersonal behaviors that demonstrate respect for others (Andersson & Pearson, 1999). A lack of civility or incivility is related to employee stress outcomes (e.g., anxiety), lost productivity, and even worse, retaliation (Bies & Tripp, 2005; Skarlicki & Folger, 1997; Yamada, 2000). Those who are on the receiving end of incivility report greater psychological distress than those who are not (Cortina, Magley, Williams, & Langhout, 2001). We can hypothesize that a culture of incivility inhibits the development of engagement, because employees who are surrounded by incivility may spend tremendous energy coping with the stress these conflicting and negative interactions create. It is also possible employees who are otherwise surrounded by coworkers who are rude or disrespectful but who find friendship with those who are civil can experience engagement (i.e., the civility helps buffer the incivility). Indeed, researchers have explored how creating an empowering culture promotes civility and trust (e.g., Laschinger et al., 2012), which should promote psychological safety and ultimately engagement.

Recent theorizing in inclusivity and diversity suggests inclusion is grounded in the balance or tension between belongingness and uniqueness, in which one feels a strong sense of belongingness and fit yet is also appreciated and valued for their uniqueness (although this may be a particularly Western culture perspective; Shore et al., 2011). When defined this way, inclusivity refers to being accepted for oneself and being given the opportunity to express one's true self without fear of exclusion or isolation (i.e., psychological safety). Psychological safety is essential for engagement (Kahn, 1990). Furthermore, the need to feel unique, acknowledged for one's contribution and individuality seems particularly relevant for experiencing psychological meaningfulness – that what one does is meaningful in and of itself. Meaning is not just derived from the recognition the organization can give, but from the feeling that what one is doing is making an important contribution and that the "gain relative to the cost" of effort is worthwhile (Kahn, 1990). Lastly, not having to fight assimilation (being treated as an insider when you conform and downplay your uniqueness), exclusion (your uniqueness is not valued, so you are an outsider, but others are valued for their uniqueness and treated as insiders), or differentiation (treated as an outsider but uniqueness is valued; Shore et al., 2011) allows one to spend energy and attention on the job task, freeing cognitive and emotional loads for experiencing psychological availability (Kahn, 1990). Thus, inclusivity, being treated as an insider and encouraged to retain your uniqueness (Shore et al., 2011), may be a key organizational culture component that contributes to experienced psychological conditions necessary for engagement. A current limitation of this perspective of inclusivity is the emphasis on the individual, which is a perspective firmly based in the Western culture (I review different cultures in Chapter 9); therefore, this particular approach may not be as applicable to Eastern cultures, where individualism is not the central value. Research focused on addressing employee diversity shows positive correlations with creating an inclusive work environment and fostering engagement (e.g., Cenkci, Zimmerman, & Bircan, 2019; Downey, van der Werff, Thomas, & Plaut, 2015; James, McKechnie, & Swanberg, 2011; Luu, Rowley, & Vo, 2019; Randel, Dean, Ehrhart, Chung, & Shore, 2016; Randel et al., 2018). Inclusive work environments promote authenticity, which encourages engagement (G. Reis, Trullen, & Story, 2016).

Including Aging Workers

A number of recent studies on engagement of aging workers shows organizations might increase their competitive advantage by retaining older workers: they tend to be more engaged than younger workers. For example, Rudolph and Baltes (2017) found, across two studies, that older workers tended to take advantage of flexible work arrangements, which contributes to their higher levels of engagement as compared to younger workers. In their studies, older workers were those over 40 years of age (Study 1: $M = 42.13$ years, maximum 81 years; Study 2: $M = 51.72$ years, maximum 65 years).

Congruence Between Person and Organization or Job

Person–organization fit (P–O fit) may be a good example of a construct that reflects employees' perceptions of some of the right conditions for engagement. Specifically, P–O fit refers to the degree to which an employee's skills, needs, values, and personality are congruent with those required for the job (Chatman, 1989; Kristof-Brown, Zimmerman, & Johnson, 2005). When employees perceive strong P–O fit, they report high levels of engagement ($\beta = .48$; Biswas & Bhatnagar, 2013). Importantly, relative to perceived organizational support, fit contributes more to explaining the variance in engagement.

P–O fit can be taken into consideration when selecting and hiring employees, which may address popular writings suggesting employers hire engaged employees (C. Wright, 2012). In support, some have suggested fit with the organization or job is and can be used in making selection decisions (e.g., Cable & Judge, 1996; Sekiguchi & Huber, 2011). Research shows those with congruence between their values and needs with the organization or with their jobs are less likely to quit, tend to report higher job satisfaction, demonstrate higher levels of organizational commitment, and perform at a higher level than those with low fit (Kristof-Brown et al., 2005; Lauver & Kristof-Brown, 2001). Recent research provides preliminary evidence that suggests organizations could select employees with high potential for engagement by focusing on their P–O fit (e.g., Sørlie, Hetland, Dysvik, Fosse, & Martinsen, 2020).

Furthermore, various forms of fit have been identified, such as person–group, person–supervisor, and person–job (Kristof-Brown et al., 2005), all demonstrating slightly different relationships with employees' attitudes and behaviors. For example, person–job fit was more strongly related to job satisfaction than were other fits, and organizational commitment most strongly related to person–organization fit. These results indicate that ensuring a good congruence between employees and the organization at the time of hire and then ensuring a good fit between employees and their supervisor and team (or coworkers) may make a difference in the extent to which employees are able to develop and find meaningfulness in their work (Scroggins, 2008).

Likewise, employees who perceive alignment between their job tasks and the organization's strategic goals or priorities report higher levels of work engagement than do those who do not perceive alignment, and those higher levels were maintained over a 1- to 3-year period (Biggs, Brough, & Barbour, 2013). Based on their review of the literature, Jin et al. (2010) suggested, "organizations with superior human capital resources that are aligned with the overall organizational strategy will outperform their competition and have long-term success" (p. 941). The authors additionally offered that such competitive advantage is achieved because employees' skills and knowledge directly relate to productivity, employees with these skills and knowledge are scarce, the tacit knowledge developed by employees working in and with the organization make them imitable, and the combination of employees skills, abilities, and background experience with the organization make them non-substitutable.

Resources

Leaders and immediate managers are in a good position to provide resources, such as training, scheduling flexibility, help in the form of experts or more employees devoted to a project, or guidance on how to remove roadblocks preventing task completion (Eisenberger, Huntington, Hutchison, & Sowa, 1986; Graen & Uhl-Bien, 1995). Initial research into transformational leaders' effects on follower engagement suggests transformational leaders, those who lead by aligning subordinates' goals with those of the organization through an inspiring vision (Bass, 1985), promote employees' feelings of self-efficacy

(Lester, Hannah, Harms, Vogelgesang, & Avolio, 2011), which results in them feeling they have what they need to do the job and do it well. Thus, promoting self-efficacy may also be considered a type of resource (Bakker & Demerouti, 2008) that a leader can provide. Resources can come from other sources, such as coworkers who offer support (Byrne, Dik, & Chiaburu, 2008; Chiaburu, 2010; Sloan, 2012), or the job itself through job control or autonomy, access, opportunities for development, and job or skill variety (Crawford, LePine, & Rich, 2010).

In a recent study, my coauthors and I (Byrne, Peters, Rechlin, Smith, & Kedharnath, 2013) proposed resources could be divided into a few different types, two of which are those available on the job, such as autonomy and skill or task variety, and those from the leader, such as fairness and support. Our results indicated these forms of resources differentially related to engagement through their relationship with psychological meaningfulness and safety (which were both differentially related to engagement) and that engagement subsequently positively predicted job performance and negatively predicted turnover intentions. These findings suggest resources are not perceived as all having the same value, can come from various sources (Cooper-Thomas, Xu, & Saks, 2018; Kallioniemi et al., 2018), and do relate to the key conditions Kahn (1990) suggested are required for engagement.

Sufficient resources are implicated in the development of a culture for creativity, a precursor to innovation according to Amabile and colleagues (1996). Resources come in the form of an organizational culture that encourages creativity by providing fairness, rewards and recognition, a safe environment for sharing new ideas and obtaining constructive judgment, and leaders who develop a shared vision employees can support with their new ideas. Supervisors who are good role models by demonstrating support for the group, valuing individual contributions, and showing confidence in others' ability to develop new ideas are also considered a necessary resource for promoting employee creativity. Likewise, access to funds, materials, information, and necessary equipment are essential support for promoting creativity (Amabile et al., 1996). Though preliminary research shows a positive relationship between engagement and innovation (Bhatnagar, 2012; Chughtai & Buckley, 2011), no studies to date have examined employee engagement and creativity or engagement and the organizational culture recommended for promoting creativity.

Managing Work Stressors

Some employees demonstrate the ability to cope with stress and work overload more effectively than do others. For example, those with high resistance to stress or dispositional optimism (Baltes, Zhdanova, & Clark, 2011; Carver & Scheier, 1998; Collins, 2007; Holahan & Moos, 1985; Maas & Spinath, 2012) tend to fare better. However, aspects of the job, coworkers, and leaders' efforts can make managing excessive job demands and workload easier. For example, employees with job autonomy, work schedule flexibility, job control, and voice have the ability to accommodate personal stressors, such as family needs at home, by rescheduling their work obligations and pushing back when the workload or other negative aspects of the work environment are unreasonable (Baugher & Roberts, 2004). Providing the facilities for employees to balance their work demands enables them to manage their stress and become engaged at work (Richardsen, Burke, & Martinussen, 2006). Additionally, employees lacking the appropriate skills to do the job becomes a workload management problem (Freeney & Tiernan, 2009); hence, skill development can be a resource. A large number of publications exist for managing stress at work, including Quick, Murphy, and Hurrell (1992) and Rossi, Perrewé, and Sauter (2006); readers are encouraged to consult these and other published resources for more information on stress management.

Besides individually oriented approaches in stress management, however, managing work stress can also come in the form of a culture in which support for one another and from management is the norm and in which those with a high tolerance for stress or hardiness are selected into jobs where stress is the norm (because they can handle the stress, whereas others cannot). For example, military personnel selected for special forces should score higher on tests for stress resistance or psychological hardiness (Arendasy, Sommer, & Hergovich, 2007; Bartone et al., 2008). For jobs in which stress fluctuates or is not the key characteristic of the job (e.g., chronically high stressful conditions), it may not be as critical to select for psychological hardiness regarding achieving engagement.

Table 7.1 summarizes the various actions organizations can take to address factors of culture that have been empirically associated with promoting employee engagement.

TABLE 7.1 Actions Organizations Can Take to Create a Culture for Engagement

Factor	Actions
Connection	• Create a climate that promotes and encourages friendship • Matrix structures that require cross-team collaborations • Zero tolerance for incivility or discrimination • Employee ownership through open-book management or stock options
Congruence	• Fit with the organization and the job values and skills
Inclusivity	• Actively develop a diverse workplace • Have zero tolerance for incivility
Leadership	• Interpersonal and/or transformational • High accountability

(*Continued*)

TABLE 7.1 (Continued)

Factor	Actions
Managing work stressors	• Trustworthiness • Empowerment • Scheduling flexibility, workload distribution strategies, job control, voice to suggest process improvements, appropriate autonomy • Supervisory support • Job fit for stress-tolerant or hardy personalities
Meaning	• Career planning • Organizational mission or vision • Job crafting
Resources	• Training, scheduling flexibility, mentors or expert employees, organizational support • Transformational or interpersonal leaders who emphasize both vision and employee relations • Access to necessary information, equipment, or materials for creativity and job task completion
Trust	• Leadership trust • Transparent and frequent communication • Climate of justice or fairness

WHAT DOES A CULTURE FOR ENGAGEMENT POTENTIALLY LOOK LIKE?

Jaspreet chose to work for Gingo-Bird, a retailer that manufactures and sells all products related to birds. She loves birds and was drawn to apply for their opening when she heard Gingo-Bird is a fun place to work. A friend of Jaspreet's works for Gingo-Bird and talked often about how even though the organization is large and spread across a number of European locations, the employees feel connected because of the regular company gatherings, the local meetings and gatherings, and the opportunities to find mentors across the organization. Part of the job benefits are going to the company meetings held in different countries (France, Germany, Belgium, and the Netherlands). Being an animal lover, Jaspreet liked the organization's mission: "Protect, Promote, and Pamper Birds of All Feather." She also liked that reports about the company suggested that it "walks the talk" (does as it says it will do). Annual reports from the organization posted online showed their financials were solid, despite volatility in the overseas markets, and their leadership team was highly regarded. They adopted an open-book management practice from the United States (see Case, 1995; Stack, 1994), and employee ownership programs made Jaspreet feel that the organization was transparent in its policies and wanted employees to own and have input into how the organization should be run. Another aspect of the organization's statistics that appealed to Jaspreet were its reports on diversity: the company boasted high percentages of individuals from various ethnic and religious backgrounds, a wide range of age groups, individuals from several European and Asian cultures, and a relatively even balance of men and women on both the board and in leadership levels.

Since she was hired, Jaspreet has had some family issues and needed to take time off. Her boss and teammates were supportive and worked with her to develop a schedule that supported her needs yet also ensured the work was completed, and no one felt taken for granted. Jaspreet was able to shift her responsibilities to allow for more flextime, yet this also gave her the chance to continue contributing to the new ideas the team was developing for bird-games, which allowed them to compete for company rewards in best ideas. Team members attended classes when first hired to learn how to have healthy debates without turning the discussions into disrespectful competition. They learned how to agree to disagree and how to discuss sensitive topics as needed. When asked to participate in a longitudinal diary study of engagement, Jaspreet's ratings trend high.

Selecting for Engagement for Competitive Advantage

A logical question frequently asked is whether organizations can select for engagement, assuming competitive advantage for organizations can actually be achieved with engaged employees. Are some people predisposed to engagement such that one could select for this characteristic, ensuring an engaged workforce? I noted earlier how P–O fit may be a helpful factor in selection, but P–O fit is not a predisposition (i.e., not a trait).

According to Kahn (1990), engagement is not a stable trait or characteristic of an individual; it is a moment-to-moment experience that naturally fluctuates depending on the work context, individual (ability to be present or not; Kahn, 1992), and other factors of the work and job role itself. Although Schaufeli, Salanova et al. (2002) originally defined engagement as a stable and persistent state, recent studies into daily and weekly levels of engagement have shown this definition requires modification to conform more closely to Kahn's perspective (e.g., Bakker & Oerlemans, 2016; Breevaart et al., 2014). Macey and Schneider (2008) offered the only definition thus far that incorporates the concept of engagement as a trait – a stable individual difference characteristic that could be selected for in job application situations. The authors defined trait engagement as a positive orientation toward work indicated by proactive personality (e.g., tendency to influence or take charge of one's work environment), conscientiousness, trait positive affect, and autotelic personality (e.g., tendency to participate in activities for their own sake). Their argument is that people who score high on these traits are more likely to become engaged.

Macey et al. (2009) proposed employees with proactive or conscientious personality characteristics are likely to be positive and productive, resulting in engagement. As noted in Chapter 4, research has shown positive correlations between engagement and proactive personality (Cai, Cai, Sun, & Ma, 2018; Dikkers et al., 2010). Furthermore, Dikkers and colleagues (2010) found that proactive personality was positively related to higher scores in dedication and absorption 18 months after their initial assessment. Causation cannot be inferred because the two data points were self-report surveys with no intermediary intervention and no controls to isolate whether it was indeed the proactive personality that caused the increase in engagement. Nonetheless, these findings suggest the two constructs are related.

Correlations between engagement and conscientiousness ($r = .14$, $p < .05$) are not that high, according to Liao et al. (2013). Liao et al. examined person-situation interactions on engagement, namely, the effects of personality (i.e., neuroticism, agreeableness, conscientiousness, openness, and extraversion) on the relationship between quality of team member relations (team member exchange) and engagement (Schaufeli, Salanova et al., 2002) in a sample of 235 Chinese employees. Agreeableness had the highest correlation with engagement at $r = .22$, $p < .01$. Over a 3-month period, they found employees with high extraversion, low neuroticism, and low conscientiousness were more engaged when they experienced high-quality team member relationships. In contrast, Mostert and Rothmann (2006) found conscientiousness correlated at .38 ($p < .01$) and extraversion at .33 ($p < .05$) with engagement (Schaufeli, Salanova et al., 2002) in a sample of 1,794 South African police members (officers and staff), including Whites, Blacks, Coloreds (people of mixed white and black or Asian ancestry), and Indians. They concluded from regression analyses that employees reporting higher conscientiousness, emotional stability (low neuroticism), and extraversion reported higher engagement, even in their stressful job environment. Recently, H. Chen, Richard, Boncoeur, and Ford (2020) found conscientious moderated the relationship between engagement and emotional exhaustion. In their meta-analysis, Young, Glerum, Wang, and Joseph (2018) found that personality (Big Five, proactive personality, trait affectivity) accounted for 48% of the variance in engagement, indicating it might be possible to use personality in selecting workers likely to be engaged. They further conducted a relative weights analysis to determine which personality trait had the strongest effect on engagement and found positive trait affectivity ranked number one, followed by proactive personality, conscientiousness, and extraversion. They concluded that selection systems incorporating assessment of these traits may maximize hiring individuals primed for high engagement levels because these traits suggest effectiveness in self-regulation and energy expenditure – all necessary for engagement.

Although some initial research examining engagement and various personality traits shows positive correlations exist, it is unclear why or whether these correlations matter in determining or predicting a predisposition to engagement. For example, why would someone scoring low in conscientiousness or extraversion not be able to become engaged at work? Is it just that being conscientious predisposes a person to take advantage of resources and a climate for engagement more so than someone who is not predisposed?

Conclusion

No research today offers evidence providing the type of comprehensive and complex culture as described earlier that will ensure an engaged workforce and whether an engaged workforce secures competitive advantage. Such a study would be challenging to conduct, to say the least, given all the variables that would have to be simultaneously studied and the number of controls required to isolate which factor played what role in engagement and in competitive advantage. There are many case studies of organizational successes in improving engagement and competitive advantage offered by consulting firms such as Kenexa, Gallup, Towers-Watson, Deloitte, BlessingWhite, Inward Strategic, Hay Group, and Gagen MacDonald to name a small few.[1] However, none indicates how engagement was defined or measured (most hint or state that engagement is synonymous with job satisfaction), nor do they provide data regarding how they evaluated improvements. Thus, even though many report increases of 50% or more in engagement scores, organizational performance, or even financial gains, none provides the actual evidence.

Results from many individual studies as reviewed earlier, when taken together, suggest the noted factors independently support the right environment for engagement. Not all solutions are ripe for combining; it may be that some factors interact with others to set up conditions that are not as conducive to engagement as one might think. For example, research has shown that cynical employees, those who believe their voice is unheard and suggestions discarded, tend to view organizational support negatively (Byrne & Hochwarter, 2008). Those exhibiting cynicism in their study were not the same as those suffering burnout; rather, they were assessed as those who have given up trying to offer their positive suggestions to improve the organization (most likely from lack of psychological safety or perceived value).

---

1 There is no order to this list, and inclusion on the list is not representative of quality or size of offerings. It is simply an example list of consulting firms that offer engagement solutions and case studies of their reported successes.

WALK-AWAY POINTS

- Having engaged employees may be one way to achieve competitive advantage.
- Organizations may be able to select for personality characteristics that predispose employees to become engaged.
- Organizations can create a culture for engagement.
- There is a big need for empirical evidence that demonstrates that the actions recommended here and in other publications on culture for engagement are actually effective in building a culture that promotes engagement; engagement increases as a result, along with competitive advantage.

8

HOW DO WE USE ENGAGEMENT TO CREATE A HEALTHY AND THRIVING ORGANIZATION?

The study of psychology originally focused on understanding what prevents people from enjoying positive well-being, employing a medical model perspective on diagnosing and treating mental illness (Koch & Leary, 1985); many still focus their attention today on resolving negative experiences that have lasting psychological effects. However, since about the late 1940s and early 1950s, attention has also been placed on understanding and helping healthy people flourish. This positive approach to understanding the human existence, labeled positive psychology (M. P. Seligman & Csikszentmihalyi, 2000), has been active on both the individual and group levels. At the individual level of focus, researchers have studied individuals' traits that predispose them to happiness and hope, whereas at the group level, the focus is on how institutions promote citizenship, altruism, and a positive strong work ethic (Maddux, 2002).

Occupational health psychology has as a primary aim to identify and remove individual and organizational health risks (Quick & Tetrick, 2011; Tetrick, Quick, & Gilmore, 2012). Psychologists within this field focus on improvements to the workplace that eliminate or reduce stressors, prevent accidents and illness, and strive for healthy employees. Thus, one could describe occupational health psychology as an arm of psychology focused on the creation of healthy organizations (a term once reserved for describing the financial survivability of an organization; Graham, Howard, & Dougall, 2012), including creating healthy employees within.

Healthy and thriving organizations not only prevent health risks for employees, but they also grow their employees' health. Healthy organizations implement interventions specifically designed to create and protect the health and welfare of their employees (Cooper & Cartwright, 1994; Ganster, 1995), seeing employees as valuable renewable resources rather than expendable throwaways.

DOI: 10.4324/9781003171133-11

One approach to the study of employee engagement that has, to a degree, followed the history of psychology and trended toward the aim of occupational health psychology was launched by Maslach and colleagues (Maslach & Leiter, 1997; Maslach, Schaufeli, & Leiter, 2001). Maslach and her colleagues proposed that employee engagement was a movement away from burnout to the state in which burnout is not experienced – in essence, framing engagement as the opposite of burnout. We can describe their purpose as an attempt to find the construct space that captured what it meant to not be paying attention to the lack of fulfillment and personal connection only, but rather enjoying and fulfilling a positive existence marked by productivity and growth. This attempt to get away from or describe an opposite state of being, one that was positive as opposed to negative, was carried forward by Schaufeli, Salanova, González-Romá, and Bakker (2002) and other researchers studying occupational health.

Thus far, researchers using the theoretical approach focused on the relationship between engagement and stress have studied the effects of the work environment on employee engagement – whether stress conditions negatively affect levels of engagement. But what if we flipped that causal direction the other way around: why not consider how engaged employees create a healthy organization?

Engagement Contagion

Theory and research on contagions, shared cognitions, social information processing, and the perception–behavior link suggest engaged employees create engagement in those around them through a process I call *engagement contagion*. Others who are nearby those expressing their engagement at work "catch" the emotions, behaviors, and cognitions of engaged employees, thereby creating their own engagement. Thus, those who are fully expressing the characteristic state of employee engagement create engagement around them, increasing the number of employees who are engaged at work and ultimately creating a healthy and thriving organization.

I explain next how this engagement contagion effect occurs by first explaining emotional and social cognitions contagions, social information processing theory, and the perception–behavior link. The synergistic and simultaneous activation of these contagions and transference theories create the foundation for engagement contagion.

Emotional Contagion

Emotional contagion refers to a tendency to mimic and adopt the emotions of others (Hatfield, Cacioppo, & Rapson, 1993). It is the automatic (either conscious or unconscious) mimicry and synchronization of people's expressions, vocalizations, and behaviors with others that results in an emotional convergence (Hatfield et al., 1993; Hatfield, Cacioppo, & Rapson, 1994). As described by Hatfield et al. (1993), emotions are considered integrated packages of facial, vocal, and physical expressions of neurophysiological and nervous system activity that triggers various behaviors in response to the environment or one's thoughts. Thus, emotional contagion includes the mimicry of facial expressions, vocal tones, speech patterns, and body language of others. Mimicking others is not a new phenomenon in human history; in fact, research on how babies learn demonstrates that we begin mimicking the expressions of others shortly after birth (Hatfield et al., 1994; O'Toole & Dubin, 1968).

During conversation, people tend to synchronize their movements and expressions with others automatically, posturing and speaking similarly to one another without conscious awareness of doing so (Hatfield et al., 1993; Kendon, 1970; LaFrance & Broadbent, 1976). The physical act of mimicking creates changes in one's own body, resulting in the physical and affective experience of the emotion and not just mirroring the emotion. The physiological feedback from muscles, visceral, and glandular mechanisms creates the full experience of the emotion, making the emotion one's own (Adelmann & Zajonc, 1989; Hatfield et al., 1994). Similarly, vocal feedback in the form of rhythm, pauses, and intonation from mimicry influences one's experience of the emotion (Hatfield, Hsee, Costello, & Weisman, 1995). As a result of mimicry, people "catch" the emotions of others and experience them as fully as if they were originally their own (Hatfield et al., 1993). We cannot help ourselves: yawning elicits yawning, seeing someone in pain causes us to wince in as if we are in pain, and we mimic the facial expressions and behaviors we see on television (Bavelas et al., 1986; Hsee et al., 1990; Provine, 1986).

Cognitive Contagion

Shared Cognitions

Whereas emotional contagion is primarily unconscious, shared cognitions, the learned understanding of group members' knowledge and approaches (Barsade, 2002; Cannon-Bowers & Salas, 2001; Hatfield et al., 1993), are accomplished through language. Therefore, shared cognitions do not require face-to-face interactions and tend more toward a conscious process (Cannon-Bowers & Salas, 2001; Ilgen & Klein, 1988; Salancik & Pfeffer, 1978). Typically referred to with regard to teams or groups, shared cognitions include task-specific knowledge, task-related knowledge, team attitudes/beliefs and judgments, and knowledge of each other (Cannon & Edmondson, 2001; Cannon-Bowers & Salas, 2001; Klimoski & Mohammed, 1994). By understanding each other's expertise and by learning over time how members solve problems, group members can compensate for and support each other without first having to discuss the situation (Cannon-Bowers & Salas, 2001). Similarly, group members adjust their behavior to allow for the strengths of others to complement their own, maximizing group performance. What is shared is the understanding of the knowledge base or compatible knowledge, such that individuals can draw the same or a common interpretation from the situation, even if they do not each possess the exact same structure of information. One's understanding of how others think or what approach they use to think through problems or situations, essentially creating shared meaning, forms the shared cognition. Collective meaning is another descriptor for the product of social interactions that include shared perceptions, behaviors, norms, belief systems, and interpretations (Gruenfeld & Hollingshead, 1993; Zajonc & Adelmann, 1987).

Social Information Processing Theory

Social information processing theory (Salancik & Pfeffer, 1978), a special case of social cognition theories (Ilgen & Klein, 1988), suggests people construct and share thoughts, judgments, attitudes, and cognitions through their interactions with each other in their work environment. People spend considerable time together at work or in work interactions (and not necessarily face-to-face, although cues have a stronger impact when transmitted in face-to-face interactions; Ilgen & Klein, 1988), and this social context provides information and insight into people's attitudes and thoughts. Through a need to fit into and make sense of the social environment (Baumeister & Leary, 1995), people adapt their attitudes, behaviors, and beliefs accordingly, using the cues from others around them to determine how and in what way that adaptation should occur (Salancik & Pfeffer, 1978). Consequently, they take on each other's attitudes and judgments, forming a shared social cognition (Bateman, Griffin, & Rubinstein, 1987). Thus, shared social cognitions involve a process by which people share and construct memories, judgments, ideas, and thoughts, in general (Klimoski & Mohammed, 1994; Moreland, Argote, & Krishnan, 1996).

Many researchers have used a variety of terms for describing collective or shared cognitions (e.g., Cannon-Bowers, Salas, & Converse, 1993; Hardin & Higgins, 1996; Hutchins, 1991; Ickes & Gonzalez, 1994; Klimoski & Mohammed, 1994; Levine, Resnick, & Higgins, 1993; Resnick, Levine, & Teasley, 1991). To date, even though the term *shared cognitions* has been used in conjunction with emotional contagion, no definition of cognitive contagion appears to have been offered (Barsade, 2002; Hatfield et al., 1993). Therefore, drawing on the frameworks of shared cognitions, social information processing theory, and the concept of a contagion, I propose *cognitive contagion* is the shared creation of meaning, an understanding of how to make sense of the work tasks and work environment while drawing on compatible or shared knowledge structures. I further propose cognitive contagion is similar to emotional contagion in that one can adopt, synchronize, or absorb the cognitive approach, beliefs, and judgment patterns of others, in essence "catching" their perspective and way of thinking to create meaning of the work environment.

Cognitive contagion is different from emotional contagion in that shared cognitions are not transferred via mimicry. Instead, cognitive contagion occurs through the process of sharing judgments, ideas, and thoughts about problems and tasks at work and conveying emotionally infused thought patterns. Cognitive contagion passes or transmits cognitions through the behavioral and communication cues of others.

Emotional contagion can occur in groups where members of a group or individuals who work together influence the moods and judgments of those around them (Barsade, 2002). This group contagion effect results in collective emotions, which positively affect work outcomes (George, 1990, 2002). As a result, greater cognitive effort at work is displayed during complex reasoning and problem-solving tasks, and individuals tend to increase performance regardless of occupation (M. E. Seligman & Schulman, 1986; Staw, Sutton, & Pelled, 1994; Sullivan & Conway, 1989; T. Wright & Staw, 1999). Thus, the consequences of emotional and cognitive contagion combined are positive for both individuals and the organization.

Behavioral Contagion

A viable explanation for the transmission (i.e., infection) and adoption of others' behaviors is the perception-behavior link. Chartrand and Bargh (1999) noted that people take on the behaviors of others, called the chameleon effect, and explained this effect using the perception–behavior link (Bargh, Chen, & Burrows, 1996). Similar to mimicry, a key aspect of emotional contagion, the perception–behavior link states people unintentionally mimic the postures, expressions, and behaviors of others, unconsciously matching their behavior to others and changing how they interact in the social environment. Just perceiving how another behaves, not even interpreting or processing the social context as proposed by symbolic interactionism, is enough to trigger changing one's own behavior to match (Chartrand & Bargh, 1999). The process of thinking about acting in a particular way actually triggers the same regions of the brain that doing the behavior activates, which serves as an explanation for why visualization is so powerful (Suinn, 1984). The act of thinking about the behavior leads to a tendency to engage in the behavior because of the muscular response thinking triggers (Chartrand, Maddux, & Lakin, 2005).

Chartrand, Maddux, and Lakin (2005) noted that perceiving the actions of others triggers associated representations in memory that in turn make one likely to enact the same behaviors. They argued that the main difference between perception–behavior link and mimicry is that mimicry requires no interpretation or translation of traits into behaviors, whereas perceiving the actions of others leads to spontaneous attributions and activation of stereotypes. Thus, the invocation of trait constructs and stereotypes or schemas trigger such behaviors, a process that does not exist with simple mimicry. We can see evidence of this in the mimicking demonstrated by babies, who lack trait constructs and stereotypes on which to draw when mimicking their mother's or father's expressions or behavior. The difference is subtle, yet Chartrand et al. suggest it is important.

Substantial research evidence supports the perception–behavior link (Chartrand et al., 2005). The research evidence not only supports behavioral matching between people who care about one another, such as a mother and a child, but also between strangers. For example, Chartrand and Bargh (1999) conducted a lab study wherein they placed strangers with confederates. Half of the participants were first with a confederate who rubbed her face and then later with a confederate who shook her foot during the sessions. The other half of participants were exposed to the foot-shaking confederate first, followed by the face-rubbing confederate. Chartrand and Bargh found participants demonstrated the same behaviors as their confederates, shaking their foot with the foot-shaking confederate *and* rubbing their face with the face-rubbing confederate. At the end of the study, the researchers asked participants about their behaviors, and none noticed either the confederates' behaviors or their own mimicry of the behaviors. The authors also found participants mimicked confederates they reportedly did not like, demonstrating that the perception–behavior link is not simply about adopting behaviors from those you like.

Combining Contagions to Make Engagement Contagion

The dominant definition of engagement in the research literature is that it comprises three parts: affective (dedication), cognitive (absorption), and physical or physiological (vigor). Using this definition, engagement has integrated, interdependent components, and as such, engagement contagion relies on the synergistic integration of key theories and research to explain how these three components are transmitted and caught by others. The transmission of affective, cognitive, and physical/physiological does not occur in isolation; however, it helps to break the three apart to explain how the transmission or "infection" occurs.

To date, no one has described engaged employees as apathetic, zombielike, or foggy-brained. Rather, engaged employees are described as expressing enthusiasm, energy, playfulness, and generally displaying positive attitudes (Kahn, 1990; Schaufeli, Salanova et al., 2002). Engaged employees are characterized as expressive, vigorous, energetic, cognitively focused, empathetic, and active (Kahn, 1990; Macey et al., 2009; Saks, 2006; Schaufeli, Salanova et al., 2002). Because of how visible emotions are in comparison to what one may be thinking (which can be expressed to some degree) or whether one is internally physiologically aroused (if strong enough, we may be very active behaviorally), engagement may be more strongly transmitted through its emotional component than its cognitive or physiological components, although all three operate in synergy and are transmitted simultaneously.

Transmitting Affect

Through their interactions with others at work, engaged employees transmit their positive emotions, their physiological arousal associated with their emotions, and their sense of meaning and interpretation of what is meaningful at work. In doing so, employees who are around those who are engaged "catch" engagement through the mechanism of engagement contagion. Unless one deliberately runs away from, avoids, argues with, fights, or purposefully ignores and resists engaged employees, the engaged employee's emotions are visible and can infect others. Even skeptical coworkers or colleagues who question the validity of the engaged employee's thoughts may become engaged themselves by diving into a heated debate or disagreement about the ideas, demonstrating their own fully focused and embraced attention on their viewpoint. Engaged employees express enthusiasm and excitement that can be caught by others, as explained by emotional contagion. Emotional contagion infuses in others an emotional response, influencing cognitions, attitudes, and behaviors (Hatfield et al., 1993).

Transmitting Cognition

Employee engagement also includes a cognitive component, to which cognitive contagion applies. Engaged employees share their focus, cognitive absorption, and persistence in problem-solving, such that others working with them and around them are infected and pulled into that problem-solving space. Through conversation, brainstorming, hearing how one makes meaning from the work environment and job tasks, and exploring thought processes together, the engaged employee infects others with a shared cognition and shared meaning of the work. Not adopting the mental models, the schemas or thinking engaged employees bring to the table while focused and in a state of flow would require ignoring the engaged employee, not joining in the problem-solving space, and removing oneself from the active discussion or brainstorming.

Transmitting Physiology

Lastly, engaged employees are physiologically aroused, excited, and energetic; they express an arousal level even if they are not physically darting around a room. Engaged employees might convey their internal arousal by punctuating their words, talking fast, purposefully increasing or decreasing their volume to make a point, demonstrating fast reaction or response times with comments or actions, using expressive body language, and varying their intonations. Moreover, energy intensifies emotions, such that high arousal levels are associated with high energy emotions: heart rate is accelerated, skin conductance is high, and facial activity increases indicating affective involvement (Jacob et al., 1999). Through the perception–behavior link, engaged employees infect others with an aroused physiology, matching pace, body language, and expressions.

Working in Groups

Employees who are engaged most likely connect with others at work. Research suggests connection and relations with others promotes engagement within individuals, as do friends and close coworker relations (Kahn, 1990). Relationships at work provide support that facilitates becoming engaged (Bakker & Demerouti, 2008). People are attracted to emotionally expressive people (H. Friedman, Riggio, & Casella, 1988). This means engaged employees are not work hermits; they attract and interact positively and frequently with others at work. Moreover, expectations for working together increases mimicking (Lakin & Chartrand, 2003), which suggests engaged colleagues activate engagement contagion on a consistent and ongoing basis; it is not a one-time infection.

In summary, engagement contagion occurs through the mechanisms of emotional, cognitive, and physiological contagions and is unique in that it synergistically combines these other forms of contagion to infect others.

Why Some May Not Catch Engagement From Others

Dynamic social impact theory (Latané, 1997) suggests when people work together, even minimally, there is a natural tendency toward consolidation (as the proportion of the people who hold a minority perspective shrinks, the diversity in the group shrinks), clustering (people become more similar to those near them than to those farther away), and continuing diversity (a few holding minority views persist within the group). Evidence supports these natural tendencies (e.g., Latané & L'Herrou, 1996), indicating shared cognitions and behaviors are natural and common phenomena when people participate in groups or work with others. Those who do not catch engagement may make up the minority group or the minority perspective.

There may be several reasons why engagement contagion is not fully passed on to others. Some reasons may be motivational, situational, or dispositional. Like those in Latané's (1997) continuing diversity group, some may purposefully choose to remain uninfected.

Motivational

Those who do not catch engagement to its fullest extent may be motivated to deflect the emotional or behavioral influences of others because they have instrumental reasons, such as political battles or retaliatory behavior, not being excited or involved in the tasks or project, or for purposefully shutting down and withdrawing from work. If people have a reason for not wanting to be a part of a team or group, part of a solution, or open to the excitement of others, they may be less inclined to pay attention to the emotions of others and to the thoughts or comments from others and may not notice others' behaviors. In this case, the mechanisms of emotional and cognitive contagion and perception–behavior links are deflected and unable to have their effect.

Reasons for deflecting engagement from others may also include depression or emotional exhaustion, which affects one's motivation to participate at work (Maslach & Leiter, 1997). As long as people interpret their work environment as supporting their feelings of competence and a sense of relatedness, they should feel self-determined and intrinsically motivated (Ryan & Deci, 2000). However, when external motivators, in particular introjected regulation (attempts to push guilt) or external regulation (attempts to get compliance), are used, feelings of being controlled reduce motivation and lead to less intrinsic motivation to perform (Ryan & Deci, 2000). Therefore, if engagement contagion feels staged or pushed by the organization, which could occur in a training session or a team-building intervention, results may lead to less engagement than otherwise would be achieved through natural interactions.

Situational

Researchers studying emotional contagion have shown people who we considered our opponents are unlikely to infect us (McHugo et al., 1985), suggesting it is possible to deflect absorbing others' emotions, cognitions, and behaviors. Thus, a possible situational boundary condition to engagement contagion may be where interactions involve individuals with whom one has a conflicting or negative relationship, such as opponents, enemies, or nemeses.

Sensitivity to rejection (Mehrabian & Ksionzky, 1970), a determinant of affiliative behavior, refers to a tendency to struggle with interactions with others over a fear of rejection and strong desire for belongingness. High sensitivity to rejection, hypothesized to stem from attachment issues with parental figures (hence, situational; Butler, Doherty, & Potter, 2007), would lead one to avoid extensive contact with others (this does not require that contact be face-to-face), making engagement contagion challenging and less likely.

Dispositional

There may be personality traits, such as neuroticism or emotional instability, that when expressed result in withdrawing from others at work or avoiding strong connection with others. For example, individuals strongly endorsing facets of neuroticism, such as self-consciousness or depression, may struggle with work relationships (Costa & McCrae, 1992, 2009).

Another personality trait, social anxiety (called *social phobia* in the *Diagnostic and Statistical Manual of Mental Disorders* [DSM-IV, 1994]), can manifest itself in different ways and refers to a persistent fear of social or performance situations. Shyness may be considered related to social phobia (Van Ameringen, Mancini, & Oakman, 1998); thus, not all anxiety issues have to manifest themselves at a clinically diagnostic level such as social phobia. For those who are either very shy or experience a manageable yet challenging level of social anxiety, interactions with others become very uncomfortable and difficult and, thus, are kept to a minimum, reducing opportunity for engagement contagion.

Weakened Effect of Engagement Contagion?

The engagement contagion effect is strongest for employees working in similar occupations and units as compared to those working in different fields of study. Namely, for the cognitive contagion effect of engagement contagion to work, employees must understand each other's work environment and fundamental knowledge base. Thus, lawyers working with nurses are unlikely to cognitively infect each other because they do not understand each other's workload, tasks, and content language. It may be possible to transmit one's enthusiasm and physical energy for work in general, but shared meaning and thinking are less likely and weaker across occupational boundaries.

One could hypothesize engagement contagion may be weakened for workers from different countries who do not share a common language. However, my own experience suggests that this hypothesis needs extensive testing. When I visited Russia in 2012 and 2013, although the university leaders told me that they felt their students and faculty members were more excited and bubbling with energy for research because of my visit and because of being around me, we could not share our thinking about research because we could not speak each other's language. Our communication was through interpreters, and that boundary through which we spoke prevented our ability to share direct meaning, understanding, problem-solving strategies, or ways of thinking about our fields of interest. Language is critical to cognitive contagion, and language barriers constrain or prohibit shared meaning through cognitive contagion. What I found particularly fascinating, however, was that even though I could not speak Russian and my contemporaries could not speak English, we seemed to understand each other's intention through our emotional expressions, excitement, and touch. By connecting on all other levels, our shared feelings and energy seemed to provide us some feeling of shared meaning, even if not as fully as if we could understand each other's words. It felt almost as if we could actually understand each other's words at times; however, once the interpreter translated our words, we realized what we thought was said was not. Instead, what we seemed to accurately understand was the emotion (e.g., positive, affiliative, excited), the intent of the thoughts and content (e.g., making progress, collaboration, resolving differences), and the behavioral messages (e.g., energy, impatience to get started, impatience to understand each other).

In addition to language barriers, one could hypothesize physical boundaries to accurately perceiving behavior, such as virtual work environments (even those that incorporate audio-visual communication mechanisms) that may weaken the engagement contagion effect. Although employees can perceive each other's behaviors, expressions, and vocal tones across virtual work boundaries when audio-visual communication media are available, the strength of contagion effect is dependent on the quality of transmission. One must be able to adequately see behaviors, body language, and expressions to mimic or match them. However, recent research on the use of digital avatars (computerized representation of people) has shown that animated avatars mimicking their communication partner's nonverbal cues (i.e., head movements) were more persuasive and likable than were non-mimicking avatars (Bailenson & Yee, 2005).

Can You Train Others to Catch Engagement?

Organizational consultants, no doubt, want an answer to the next logical question: "Can it be trained?" That is, can you train engaged employees to "infect" others around them, or train employees to catch engagement? Hatfield et al. (1993) proposed people cannot consciously mirror others without coming across as phony because of the amount of time it takes to synchronize one's movements. When done unconsciously, mimicry and synchronization of facial expressions, movements, postures, and vocal intonations can occur very quickly (Hatfield et al., 1994). The research on mimicking avatars suggests, however, that some learned mimicry may be sufficient for at least low amounts of engagement contagion.

In support, recent research in digital mimicry suggests people cannot decipher faked mimicry from general behaviors (Bailenson & Yee, 2005). The implications of the digital chameleon effect studies are that people can be taught to mimic others, which has promise for the idea of training employees to catch engagement. By mimicking the behaviors and emotions of engaged employees, and collaborating on projects where the engaged employees share their thought processes and problem-solving approaches, non-engaged employees may be exposed to the engagement contagion. A challenge with any training that is not necessarily voluntary on the part of the employee is motivation; in this case, training to mimic others need not be positioned as a training program in how to become engaged.

Chartrand et al. (2005) suggested rapport, goals to affiliate, interdependent self-construals, and perspective taking act as facilitators of non-conscious mimicry, which I argue are therefore facilitators of engagement contagion. People use body language to convey liking and to build rapport (Scheflen, 1964).

Thus, posture sharing, an indicator of rapport, leads to behavioral mimicry (Chartrand et al., 2005), which leads to engagement contagion. Likewise, rapport increases posture sharing (LaFrance & Broadbent, 1976), again leading to engagement contagion.

In a series of experiments, Lakin and Chartrand (2003) exposed a group of participants to words related to goal affiliation (e.g., friends, together) and a control group to neutral words, and exposed another group to an explicit goal of affiliating with another person and a control group to neutral words. Participants in the two experimental groups were asked to complete a fairly mundane distractor task before being asked to watch a live feed of a person in the next room (a confederate) with whom they would soon be working. The confederate touched her face throughout the live feed, which resulted in participants (who were being videotaped) mimicking her behavior. Independent coders watched these video recordings of participants and measured the extent to which they mimicked the face-touching behavior of the confederate. Results showed that those who were exposed to the goal affiliation words and the explicit goal of affiliation touched their faces more than those in the control group who were exposed to neutral words prior to the mundane task. Lakin and Chartrand's results confirmed that individuals mimic more when given an implicit or explicit goal to affiliate, suggesting that goals to affiliate (whether implicit or explicit) lead to increased mimicry. Thus, I propose an implicit or explicit goal to affiliate with an engaged employee will result in higher levels of or a stronger likelihood of engagement contagion. Lakin and Chartrand's results have implications for training programs in producing engagement contagion.

Training programs can be conducted globally within non–U.S. countries. Construals of the self are how people view themselves relative to others, whether as independent, self-contained, and autonomous as in the Western view, or as interdependent, related, or part of a larger social world as in the Eastern or African view (Markus & Kitayama, 1991; see more in Chapter 9). Those with an interdependent self-construal tend to seek harmonious relationships, connection, and meaning in being identified with others (Markus & Kitayama, 1991). In a series of studies, Chartrand and colleagues (van Baaren, Maddux, Chartrand, de Bouter, & van Knippenberg, 2003) demonstrated those with an interdependent self-construal were more likely to match the behavior of confederates than were those with an independent self-construal. Consistent with rapport and goals to affiliate, interdependent self-construals facilitate engagement contagion.

Furthermore, training across cultures can also be effective. Chartrand et al. (2005) suggest that perspective taking facilitates mimicry. The ability to see things from another's point of view makes one susceptible to the influence of mimicry; by focusing attention on perceiving what others perceive, one adopts their viewpoint and experiences their emotions, thoughts, and intentions toward specific behaviors. Indeed, Chartrand and Bargh (1999) found those who scored high on an empathy scale (perspective taking is a component of empathy) were more likely to mimic compared to those scoring lower on the measure of empathy.

Lastly, training others to catch engagement may involve training them on how to build rapport with others (Utay & Utay, 1999), helping them to set goals for affiliation, taking others' perspective (Ray & Ray, 1986), and developing an appreciation for a self-construal other than one's own (Constantine, 2001).

Benefits to the Organization of Engagement Contagion

Positive affect leads to collaborative and supportive prosocial behavior (George & Brief, 1992), which increases prosocial behavior in others as a result of social exchange relationships at work (Blau, 1964). Likewise, engagement contagion will increase prosocial behavior between individuals because of the exchange of the emotional and physical aspects of engagement via emotional and physiological contagion (e.g., Chartrand & Bargh, 1999; Chartrand et al., 2005; van Baaren et al., 2004). The promotion of prosocial behavior results in higher employee performance, reduced turnover intentions and withdrawal behaviors, and higher organizational-level performance and customer satisfaction (N. Podsakoff, Whiting, Podsakoff, & Blume, 2009).

Engaged employees experience positive emotions, which serve to broaden their ability to cope with higher levels of stress, enabling them to maintain high levels of engagement even when working in otherwise stressful conditions (Fredrickson et al., 2003). Thus, engagement may promote a healthy organization by helping employees to cope with stress and through engagement contagion, passing engagement along to others, making them more capable of coping with stress. Leaders supervising engaged employees are more capable of leading and moving their workforce to achieve innovation and higher levels of performance because engaged employees infect their colleagues with such desires and capabilities.

WHAT DOES ENGAGEMENT CONTAGION LOOK LIKE?

Elsabee Krüger is a new doctoral student at Ludwig-Maximilians Universität München, also known as the University of Munich, Germany. She has chosen to work with one of the professors in the graduate school of systemic neurosciences, mainly because of his enthusiasm about his research topic. There are other, more well-known professors in the same department, but she was drawn to this professor because of his high energy. Although she has never been that interested in research per se, she finds that when she and her advisor meet to discuss how they will design their studies, what recent publications have come out in print, and to which conferences they will submit their current research findings, she is drawn into his high-energy, nearly nervous behavior and excited speech. Normally a soft-spoken, somewhat slow to speak person, Elsabee becomes a new person when working with her advisor: she is animated, loud at times, anxious to speak, and just as excited as he is. The enthusiasm and passion of her advisor is contagious, and it is not just Elsabee who "catches" it; the other students on the research team are the same. In fact, a key differentiator between her advisor's research team and all others in their department is their team is excited, energetic, and very research active. One could argue the excitement over the research area has nothing to do with engagement contagion; students entering doctoral programs are, in general, excited about advancing into their new careers. But how then do we explain the excitement and energy displayed by those students who dislike research, struggle with it, and have no aspirations for research-oriented careers, but who become completely engaged in the academic track when working with this advisor? The most notable characteristic about this advisor is his engagement: he is completely engaged in his work, and he infects the students with whom he works with engagement. As we look further into the graduate school, we see that other students who are office mates of those who work with Elsabee's advisor are also engaged at work.

WALK-AWAY POINTS

- Engagement is contagious. Engagement contagion incorporates emotional, behavioral, and cognitive contagions.
- Engaged employees *can make* a more engaged and healthy organization by infecting others with the ability to do more, be excited, and cope with work challenges beyond what they could do without catching engagement.
- Employees can be taught to infect each other and how to catch engagement from others around them, and leaders of engaged employees can capitalize on engagement contagion, creating a more productive and innovative workforce.

PART IV

The New Frontiers of Employee Engagement

9

SHINING AN INTERNATIONAL LIGHT

Is Engagement the Same Everywhere?

The practical reality of the worldwide marketplace is that engagement crosses cultural boundaries in very complex ways. Take, for example, the following real organizational situations (names and exact countries changed):

> Jian-Xi Guo is the vice president of southeastern Asia sales with an international company. He is based in China and manages several regional sales managers including Hitesh Dhingra in India, Hae Sim Kwon in Korea, Seo-yeon Daeng in Malaysia, and Loi Pham in Vietnam, not to mention sales managers in Thailand, Indonesia, and Japan. Some of his managers are from countries that dislike one another and have multiple cultures within their country. They all work for a U.S.-based organization, and as such, they are expected to conform to the norms prescribed by U.S. culture during their interactions with each other and their U.S. colleagues. In a similar situation, Matías González is the vice president for sales in South America for a company based in Brazil. He lives in Argentina. He manages sales managers in Chile, Bolivia, Brazil, Peru, and Colombia. Like Jian-Xi, he is challenged with supervising people from a number of different cultures, all working for the same organization.

What can we tell Jian-Xi and Matías about how to foster engagement within their sales groups and across their diverse management teams? Not only do they and their staff have country cultures to deal with, but they also have an organizational culture that transcends the country cultures, and as managers, they are expected to abide by the organizational norms. At this time, there seems to be little we can tell these managers about how to foster engagement in their situations; there simply is

DOI: 10.4324/9781003171133-13

not much research on engagement, not to mention how to deal with the interaction of country culture and organizational culture, across the globe.

I originally structured this chapter to share what was known about engagement across the globe between 2002 and 2013. None of those studies, and none since, however, adequately addresses the challenges outlined in the preceding scenarios. What is known today is a good place to start, and I challenge the research community to develop and grow our knowledge so that we have answers for people such as Jian-Xi, Matías, and others in similar situations.

What Do We Know So Far About Engagement Internationally?

A number of studies looking at employee engagement have incorporated international samples. In the first edition of this book, I tapped into 48 different studies published between 2002 and 2013 (as indexed in electronic databases such as PsycINFO and Academic Search Premier). Since then, hundreds of additional studies have been conducted around the globe, far too many to provide a detailed chart. For example, a search and categorization in Web of Science of studies published between January 2020 and April 2021 with work or employee engagement in the abstract returned the following results by country: 19.4% United States, 15.3% China, 7.5% India, 6.7% Netherlands, 5.5% England and Australia each, 5.2% Spain, 4.5% Italy and Pakistan each, 4% South Africa, and another 84 countries at 3% and below. The Web of Science geography report has limitations: the countries are categorized by author affiliation as opposed to where the study data were actually collected. This means if there are three authors on a paper, one affiliated with a university in France, one in India, and the other with a university in China, the study will be counted in those three countries, even if the data were collected in Italy. To find which country the samples were actually from, I reviewed 389 published studies between 2020 and 2021, which actually incorporated engagement as a variable in the research rather than just using the term in the abstract. The rank order and percentages reported in Web of Science appear similar to my mapping despite the limitations with how studies are categorized by geography. In my review of 389 studies, researchers reported on samples from the United States (20%), China (11%), India (6.7%), Pakistan (3.6%), Korea (3.1%), the Netherlands (2.8%), Japan (2.3%), Spain (2%), and Italy (2%), with the remaining 49 countries at much lower percentages than these top nine.

Despite the increase in number of published international studies since 2013, very few incorporated equivalence testing or examined cultural nuances to determine whether engagement is understood similarly across cultures. Test translation and adaptation should follow an agreed-upon process with standards, such as that documented by the International Test Commission (2017). After one verifies the construct is understood in the same way across cultures and languages (typically achieved using focus groups and interviews; International Test Commission, 2017), one can begin equivalence testing. Equivalence testing refers to assessing whether the scales actually measure the same construct across samples, which indicates the scales and items have the same meaning across cultures (Brett, Tinsley, Janssens, Barsness, & Lytle, 1997). Researchers wanting to examine the equivalency of measures across countries use an established procedure (Brett et al., 1997), ranging from least restrictive in how equivalent measures should be to most restrictive. Specifically, least restrictive means the measures have the same number of dimensions and factor patterns, but not necessarily the same values. More restrictive includes the criteria for the least restrictive, but adds invariance of factors loadings. The most restrictive adds invariance of error variances and factor variance-covariance matrices on top of the same number of dimensions and factor patterns, and invariance of factor loadings (see Byrne et al. [2004] and Meyers et al. [2019] for an example). This invariance testing, however, only tells you if the measure in one language shows the similar configuration and assessment as another language; it does not tell you if that construct actually exists or is understood to be the same construct. For example, suppose I have two samples in my study, one from Pakistan and the other from the United States. Both samples respond favorably to the items from the JES physical engagement dimension. As an example, two of the items are "I work with intensity on my job" and "I try my hardest to perform well on my job." Suppose that in Pakistan, instead of these items representing a construct called engagement, respondents recognize these items as a construct called work-hard. The invariance testing will not tell me the items are not representing engagement in the Pakistan sample; all the invariance testing tells me is that the items hold together in the Pakistan sample the same way they do in a U.S. sample. If I am a researcher in Pakistan, I will interpret these results as saying the scale effectively measures work-hard the same in both countries. If I am a researcher in the United States, I will interpret these results as saying the scale effectively measures engagement in both countries. Cultural nuances like presented in this example seem lost and altogether missing in the international research conducted on engagement.

In the first edition of the book, Figure 9.1 showed the average engagement scores reported in 31 of the 48 studies (not all studies reported means)[1] on a scale from 0 to 6 using the UWES-17. Unfortunately, however, there is no consistency to the response scales used or the version of the UWES (9 or 17 version). Additionally, many studies dropped items here and there to improve fit, and frequently measured engagement using fewer than all three dimensions. Quite a number of studies have no means reported, and some do not report the response scales. Only a handful of the recent international studies used the JES or Saks's measures.

1 Special thanks to James Weston, Xuan Zheng, and Jackie Benson for their help coding international studies of employee engagement that provided the data for Figure 9.1 in the first edition of this book.

I found visualizing the means of engagement as reported on the UWES across countries in a graph/chart like Figure 9.1 gave me some global perspective. I found it interesting that across all the studies I was finding the mean engagement score was always above the median and often at least one response anchor above; standard deviations, when reported, were about the same as well. This was true regardless of which response scale the researchers used and may be a result of the positive phrasing of engagement measures. Assuming others find a rough visualization helpful, I kept Figure 9.1 from the first edition of the book but modified it to include more scores and countries in studies published since 2013. Thus, in this edition, Figure 9.1 shows engagement scores on any version of the UWES (mostly UWES-9), with response scales transformed to position the mean on a scale of 0 to 6. I roughly averaged across studies per country (in alphabetical order), so that each bar on the graph represents a mean score across a number of studies, but only studies I could find (or had access to) and only those that reported mean scores, standard deviations, and response scales. Thus, the data are not precise: the graph offers a high-level picture of engagement as measured using the UWES across a variety of countries. Shimazu, Schaufeli, Miyanaka, and Iwata (2010) reported a more accurate comparison of studies using the UWES-9 capitalizing on a database owned and maintained by Schaufeli. In exchange for using the UWES, Schaufeli requests you provide your research data for the database. There appears to be no public access to this database, but perhaps those who use the measure are given access to the database. In Shimazu et al.'s paper, mean scores on the UWES were all above the median except for Japan. Their chart looks remarkably similar to Figure 9.1, with a couple of exceptions, though it does not cover as many countries as are represented in Figure 9.1.

Although more studies exist than covered here, evident from Figure 9.1 is most studies report engagement scores above the midpoint (3 = sometimes/a few times a month, 4 = often/once a week), on a scale of 0 (never) to 6 (always/every day). A vertical bar on the figure indicates the midpoint. Additionally, at a glance, Figure 9.1 shows engagement varies somewhat across countries, with some countries reporting higher engagement scores than others. For example, engagement scores in Japan seem quite a bit lower than scores in the United Kingdom. It seems that regardless of where one conducts an engagement study, employees report experiencing engagement often/once a week or more and/or agree they are engaged (anchor labels depend on which response scale is used).

The challenge with using and interpreting these types of data is the visual comparisons across countries are actually cross-national and not necessarily across *cultures*, although cross-national and cross-cultural comparisons are often correlated (Javidan, House, & Dorfman, 2004). Several cultures can exist within one country, and cultures can cross country boundaries, which are not reflected in any of these studies. Again, it is important for me to repeat that Figure 9.1 is not precise. Because of how researchers reported their data (or did

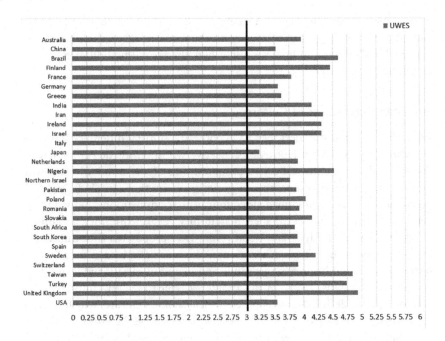

FIGURE 9.1   Chart of International Studies Published in English Between 2002 and 2021 ($N = 200$)

not report), it was simply not possible for me to actually calculate and convert the response scales and averages across the hundreds of studies. Thus, Figure 9.1 is a high-level visual to illustrate approximately how average engagement scores are generally above the median and vary across countries.

What Does This Mean for Engagement on an International Level?

Digging deeper than a rough visual, we know very little about whether or how engagement truly varies (or does not) from country to country or whether it is a concept that retains its conceptualization across countries; cross-cultural studies (not just studies in different countries) are sorely needed. Although the data in Figure 9.1 might suggest engagement scores are similar, we cannot draw a firm conclusion without actual cross-cultural comparisons. In the studies I found published since 2013, there seemed only a few cross-culture comparisons of engagement scores. I call attention to these studies as I review more on culture later.

We can hypothesize country differences in engagement based on theory and findings on constructs related to engagement. The literature on cross-cultural psychology and cross-cultural research is extensive, and even a brief review here cannot adequately capture its depth or breadth. Therefore, only a brief and selective review is offered here, with the focus on theoretical models and studies that shed light on how we might hypothesize cultural differences with employee engagement.

Hofstede Dimensions of Culture

In general, when researchers seek to hypothesize cultural differences between constructs, many rely on Hofstede's collective works. Hofstede (1980) defined country culture as "the collective programming of the mind which distinguishes the members of one human group from another" (p. 260), and proposed cultures can be described along four primary dimensions: individualism versus collectivism, power distance, masculinity versus femininity, and uncertainty avoidance. Hofstede and Bond (1988) later proposed a fifth dimension: long-term versus short-term orientation. Culture can also be defined as a set of norms, beliefs, and behaviors that guide and maintain society and its products and people (Triandis, 1994). In this chapter, I refer to *country* culture (see the aforementioned definition), as opposed to *organizational* culture, which refers to the experience of employees within an organization, and the norms and beliefs that guide organizational behavior (Schein, 1990; Schneider, 2000).

Hofstede (1980) developed his dimensions based on data collected in one large U.S.-based multinational corporation (later revealed to be IBM) across its 40 country locations. Data were collected at two time points (Time 1: 1967–1969, Time 2: 1971–1973), and participants in each country received the survey in their native language (versions in 20 languages were made available; Hofstede, 1980). Each of the 40 countries was given a score on each of Hofstede's dimensions (excluding long-term vs. short-term). After several other validation studies incorporating 10 more countries (e.g., Hofstede, 1983), Hofstede settled on the four dimensions, which, as noted earlier, were later extended to five (adding short-term orientation) by Hofstede and Bond (1984).

Individualism/Collectivism

Individualism versus collectivism, probably the most popular and recognized component of culture, has been considered a unidimensional, bipolar construct, with individualism occupying the one pole and representing individuals who prefer to operate on their own and be considered distinct and unique. Individualism embraces the idea of freedom of speech, autonomy, little attachment to the in-group, and little attention to contextual factors (M. Erez, 1994; Triandis, 1994). In contrast, collectivism is represented by a value for in-group solidarity, preference to do things in a group or with others, subordinate personal goals for those of the group, and preference to be considered like others and nondistinct (M. Erez, 1994; Triandis, 1994). Collectivism embraces attention to social relations and contextual factors that influence behavior. Although generally considered opposites, research shows the two poles can coexist; thus, they are not exclusive of one another. They may be best viewed as a probability for behavior in one direction or the other, depending on the situation (see Kâğitçibaşi, 1994).

Originally proposed as a country or societal level construct, research has shown cultural differences along this dimension also exist at the individual level. However, as Kâğitçibaşi (1994) pointed out, a lack of clarity between macro- and micro-level views of individualism and collectivism resulted in conceptual confusion that sparked the creation of other terms for this dimension at the individual (micro) level of analyses. Specifically, Triandis, Leung, Villareal, and Clack (1985) delineated individualism versus collectivism as idiocentric versus allocentric (respectively) at the individual level (as opposed to a group- or country-level construct in Hofstede's work). Triandis and colleagues assumed individuals vary *within* countries on their level of idiocentrism and allocentrism. Results across three studies showed that allocentric values include cooperation, equality, and honesty, whereas idiocentric values include competition and social recognition (Triandis et al., 1985).

Another way to view the individualism/collectivism dimension of culture is using Kâğitçibaşi's (1987) terms: culture of separateness and culture of relatedness. Culture of separateness captures the independent, individualistic view that one is distinct from others and the environment. Culture of relatedness reflects the interdependent, collectivistic, or group-oriented perspective; one is intertwined with others and the environment and prefers to be related to others rather than distinct from others.

An example of one of the few studies I found using Hofstede's (1980) cultural framework, specifically collectivism, is by Garczynski, Waldrop, Rupprecht, and Grawitch (2013). They hypothesized Indian participants would differ from American participants on engagement because the Indian culture is more collective than the American, which provides more resources and social support. Their results were consistent with their hypothesis: Indian participants rated engagement significantly higher than did American participants ($M = 5.41$ vs. $M = 4.54$, respectively).

Power Distance

Power distance refers to the preference for, or acceptance of, an unequal distribution of authority, resources, and power. In societies with a large power distance, the norm is to accept formal orders and mandatory in-role job performance expectations, and to respect hierarchy. In contrast, societies with a small power distance believe everyone should have equal rights, everyone relies on each other as opposed to being dependent on those in positions of authority, and superiors are accessible to those beneath them in the hierarchical chain

(Hofstede, 1980). Within organizations, Hofstede (2001) described power distance as "a measure of the interpersonal power or influence between B and S as perceived by the less powerful of the two, S" (p. 83), where B stands for boss and S stands for subordinate. Hofstede's (1980) power-distance construct is considered a property or description of a society, whereas Schwartz and colleagues (S. Schwartz, 1992; S. Schwartz & Bilsky, 1987, 1990) have defined power as a personal value associated with wealth and authority over guiding others' lives (e.g., "it is important to me to be rich"; Davidov, Schmidt, & Schwartz, 2008).

Masculinity/Femininity

Masculinity/femininity may be Hofstede's most controversial dimension, mainly because of the label. Hofstede (2001) contended that societies hold assumptions and normative beliefs over what behaviors, values, and choices are most indicative of women and men. According to Hofstede, masculinity reflects the extent to which the society values dominance, assertiveness, and money. Hofstede (1980) suggested the label came from the difference between how men and women tended to score in terms of their value of these items: within nearly all groups he studied, men reported more positive values for dominance and assertiveness than did the women. As others summarize this dimension (e.g., M. Erez, 1994), men within masculine cultures are expected to be aggressive, tough, and focus on success, and women are expected to be modest and soft-spoken. Relying on sex roles (roles tied to biological functions as opposed to gender, which is tied to societal functions), Hofstede (2001) proposed that because women bear children and tend to be responsible for the first months of feeding and direct care, they are naturally more oriented toward taking care of people and connecting with others. Men, lacking the ability to bear children, are concerned with economic support for the family and for achievement. In support, Tannen (1990), a sociolinguist, proposed communication styles of men and women differ significantly; essentially women talk to connect and to build community, whereas men talk to convey information and achieve separateness. Although described in ways suggesting this dimension is non-distinguishable from individualism/collectivism, Hofstede (2001) provided empirical evidence of the distinctiveness of the dimensions. He argued masculinity/femininity "is about ego enhancement versus relationship enhancement, regardless of group ties" (p. 293). Lastly, to clarify further, Hofstede (2001) suggested masculinity refers to a society wherein the gender roles are distinct, with men expected to be assertive and women expected to be nurturing. Femininity refers to a society in which gender roles are overlapping, where expectations for both men and women are that they be modest and caring.

In a recent study, Lo Presti, Kertechian, and Landolfi (2020) examined engagement as an outcome of workload in Canadian and Italian employees. Using Hofstede's country scoring, where Italy is rated more masculine than

Canada, the authors hypothesized the Italian participants would report higher engagement than the Canadian participants because masculine cultures are competitive and achievement oriented. Their results were consistent with their supposition: Italians rated their engagement level significantly higher than the Canadians did ($M = 4.51$ vs. $M = 3.17$, respectively).

Uncertainty Avoidance

Uncertainty avoidance describes how much ambiguity about the future a culture can tolerate before it feels threatened. When uncertainty avoidance is strong, people tend to gravitate to more rules, structure, career stability versus changeability, and are not tolerant of new ideas or deviant behaviors. By using rules, standard operating procedures, and contracts, organizations can avoid (to a degree) the uncertainty of the future. Hofstede (1980) suggested societies with strong uncertainty avoidance tend to experience high levels of anxiety and aggression, resulting in a strong internal drive to work hard. Additionally, he offered that religious prescriptions, bureaucracy, traditions, and rituals (e.g., business meetings, training programs, memos, and reports) are all mechanisms for coping with the uncertainty of the future (Hofstede, 2001). Hofstede (2001) emphasized uncertainty avoidance is not the same as risk avoidance. He proposed risk is a probability function specific to an event, whereas uncertainty is a diffuse feeling with no associated probability. Uncertainty avoidance is about ambiguity; hence, cultures with high or strong uncertainty avoidance adopt traditions, ceremonies, plans, structure, and rules to remove ambiguity and thereby reduce uncertainty. Based on existing models of engagement, it seems unlikely that engagement levels would differ across cultures with high versus low uncertainty avoidance.

Long-Term Versus Short-Term Orientation

Influenced by his collaborations with Bond in Hong Kong, Hofstede added a fifth dimension called long-term versus short-term orientation. Long-term versus short-term orientation is about perspective taking in reference to time. Long-term orientation refers to focusing on the future and participating in practices, such as persistence or thriftiness, which support sustenance in the future. A short-term orientation is the opposite of long-term orientation, in which the focus is on the immediate or present moment. Ignoring the future ramification of today's decisions and sacrificing the future for today's gain are behaviors indicative of a short-term orientation. Hofstede (2001) defined long-term orientation as a "fostering of virtues oriented towards future rewards, in particular, perseverance and thrift. Its opposite pole, Short Term Orientation, stands for the fostering of virtues related to the past and present, in particular, respect for tradition, preservation of 'face' and fulfilling social obligations"

(p. 359). Low long-term-oriented (i.e., short-term-oriented) cultures are characterized by expectations for fast response, value of leisure time, lack of value for persistence as a personality trait, spending, and reciprocity of greetings and gifts. High long-term-oriented cultures are characterized by persistence and perseverance, thriftiness, saving, and a value for personal adaptability.

Other Theoretical Perspectives

In efforts to advance Hofstede's work, power distance has been combined with the individualism/collectivism dimension and referred to as horizontal versus vertical orientations, resulting in four cells of a 2 × 2 matrix (Singelis, Triandis, Bhawuk, & Gelfand, 1995; Triandis, 1995). According to Torelli and Shavitt (2010),[2] vertical individualistic cultures (e.g., United States) are characterized by people attempting to be unique and seeking power and status through competition with everyone (regardless of in-group or out-group). Having a vertical individualistic orientation is correlated with using power to benefit oneself at the expense of others (Torelli & Shavitt, 2010); thus, it may be consistent with politicized organizational climates (see organizational politics; Ferris, Russ, & Fandt, 1989). People in horizontal individualistic cultures (e.g., Sweden) value distinctiveness and separateness but do not seek status. Vertical collectivistic cultures (e.g., Japan) are characterized by people seeking to fulfill the in-group's goals, obeying authority, and competing with the out-group. Lastly, people in horizontal collectivistic cultures (e.g., Israel) tend to emphasize connection, goal congruency, and responsibility for others but fail to subordinate to authority. Having a horizontal collectivistic orientation is positively associated with using one's power to help others (Torelli & Shavitt, 2010).

Individualism versus collectivism has also been framed as the independent versus interdependent self-construal (Markus & Kitayama, 1991). Self-construal refers to one's self schema or the cognitive framework one holds about the self. A schema is a stable mental or cognitive structure or organization that explains and represents our knowledge about a concept (S. Fiske & Taylor, 1991); thus, a self-schema is the cognitive representation of what we know and understand about who we are and how we fit into the world. Self-schemata are derived from past experiences and are socially constructed using information others provide about the self (Markus, 1977). According to Markus and Kitayama (1991), an independent self-construal refers to thinking of the self as independent of the surrounding environment and from others. The self becomes the target and referent for all experiences (cognitive, emotional, physical), such that actions and

---

2 Remember from Chapter 2 that employee engagement is a state of motivation, wherein one is psychologically present (i.e., in the moment) and psychophysiologically aroused, is focused on the job and organizational goals, and is in a state wherein one brings all of oneself (emotionally, physiologically, cognitively) together to transform work into meaningful and purposeful accomplishment.

feelings are generated from within and are not situationally bound or connected with others. In this context, actions are seen as self-serving. To the contrary, the interdependent self-construal describes one's experience in relation to others, situationally bound, and interdependent or intertwined with the surrounding context. One's actions are seen as other-serving and in connection with others. Western Europe and the United States exemplify the independent view of the self; in contrast, Asian cultures as well as African and Latin American cultures exemplify the interdependent view (Markus & Kitayama, 1991). Akin to people with a collectivistic orientation, those with an interdependent orientation do not seek to connect with *everyone*; rather, their desire for group connection is within their own group, the in-group, as opposed to members of the out-group.

Markus and Kitayama (1991) suggest one's self-construal has significant implications for motivation. With the independent self, motivation is self-directed, expressing one's internal needs and competency, and is self-enhancing, self-consistent, self-affirming, self-verifying, and self-determined. In contrast, with the interdependent self, motivation is other-directed, expresses social motives, and is other-referent; one is driven to achieve connection and consistency with others, and to affirm others. These differences also have implications for engagement. Specifically, affiliation, connection, and fulfilling the desires of the group may be more influential in promoting engagement among those with an interdependent self-construal than among those with an independent self-construal who may be more likely to seek autonomy, self-fulfillment, and self-significance. Thus, research showing core job dimensions, such as autonomy, which are positively relating to engagement (e.g., Christian, Garza, & Slaughter, 2011; Menguc, Auh, Fisher, & Haddad, 2013), may not hold up in interdependent cultures, in which the search for autonomy is of less value. Although engagement is not the same as motivation, engagement has motivational principles and is often defined as a motivational state (e.g., Macey & Schneider, 2008; Rich, LePine, & Crawford, 2010). Thus, studies about motivation and cultural effects on motivation may translate to effects on engagement.

Conclusion Regarding Typologies

Although I have briefly described only two popular typologies of culture, most definitions of culture focus on the shared meaning of norms that are adaptive and transmitted over time (Triandis, 1994). The two primary typologies offered here were chosen because of their potential for deriving hypotheses for how we might consider the effects of culture on employee engagement. Readers interested in more in-depth and broader reviews of culture may look at Cross and Gore (2012); Triandis et al. (1985, 1993); A. Fiske, Kitayama, Markus, and Nisbett (1998); Markus, Kitayama, and Heiman (1996); Ronen and Shenkar (1985, 2013); and Oyserman, Coon, and Kemmelmeier (2002).

Cross-Cultural Findings for Constructs Similar to Engagement

Before using the theoretical frameworks reviewed earlier to develop hypotheses about how engagement may vary across cultures, a quick look at several empirical cross-culture findings on constructs similar to engagement such as motivation, job involvement, commitment, and organizational citizenship behaviors (OCBs) may prove useful. Although few studies have been conducted, those that have been done provide some valuable insight.

Motivation

Employee engagement is considered a motivational state; therefore, cultural studies examining various motivational states may provide insight into how engagement may (or may not) vary across cultures. In the following three studies, research has shown that cultural perspective affects the interpretation of the situation, goals, and expected outcomes of motivation, which provides information about designing interventions and implications for the study of engagement.

First, research has shown that both Chinese and U.S. individuals are intrinsically motivated by challenging situations, but for Chinese individuals the challenge must be well within their level of mastery to positively affect their intrinsic motivation, otherwise it becomes a negative factor. In contrast, U.S. individuals are motivated by challenge even when the challenge is extreme (Moneta, 2004). Similarly, people from collectivistic/high power–distance cultures (i.e., Singapore) are more motivated by moderately challenging, achievable goals than are people from individualistic/low power–distance cultures (i.e., Israel; Kurman, 2001). They do not seek the desire to stand out either in achieving a hard goal or failing to achieve one.

Second, B. Kim, Williams, and Gill (2003) examined goal orientation between young athletes (ages 11–16 years) in the United States and South Korea. The authors explored whether student athletes would differ on their goal orientation and intrinsic motivation because of their independent and interdependent culture perspectives. The authors assessed task and ego goal orientations, in which task goal orientation refers to choosing goals that are challenging, exerting maximum effort to achieve those goals, and persisting in the face of difficulty. Ego goal orientation refers to choosing goals that preserve the ego, accomplished by choosing easily achieved goals that require little effort; high ego goal orientation results in quickly giving up when it appears failure is imminent (B. Kim et al., 2003). Results from B. Kim et al.'s study showed American athletes reported high task goal orientation and low ego goal orientation, and the two orientations were negatively correlated. The American athletes reported higher intrinsic motivation than did the Korean athletes. In comparison, Korean athletes reported moderately high task goal orientation and average ego goal orientation (higher than American athletes), but the two orientations were positively (although not strongly) correlated. For both athlete groups, task orientation was positively related to intrinsic motivation. The authors suggested in their findings that the Korean athletes have both task and ego goal orientations because of the school sport system. Specifically, the Korean students compete in athletics to gain entry into high school, and such competition naturally promotes a strong social comparison, which ultimately boosts an ego orientation (i.e., competition to preserve one's ego relative to how one sees oneself compared to others). Hence, their goal orientation did not necessarily determine or strongly relate to their intrinsic motivation, but rather it changed their interpretation of the goal. Choosing the challenging goal and needing to persist were necessary for entry into high school, thus not a task goal per se but rather an ego goal: they wanted to get into school to fit in with their peers. Kim et al.'s findings suggest the actual construct of intrinsic motivation itself may not differ along cultural lines, but how one interprets or frames the antecedents of intrinsic motivation may differ. Thus, just assessing intrinsic motivation between the American and Korean athletes would have resulted in similar scores and no cultural difference effects; measures of the antecedent to motivation, however, would not produce the same scores.

Third, choice is often studied in the context of motivation, especially in studies of intrinsic motivation, and when placed under the cross-cultural lens provides additional perspective to the findings reviewed earlier. In a study of Asian children (Chinese and Japanese, 7–9 years) compared to American children (7–9 years), Lepper, Sethi, Dialdin, and Drake (1997) examined whether being assigned to a choice by one's mother, selecting one's own choice, or having no choice on a task was more motivating. The task was solving various anagrams, and motivation was assessed by the time spent and number of anagrams solved. Asian children scored highest on the mother-assigned choice condition and lowest on the no-choice condition. In contrast, American children scored highest on the free-choice option and lowest on the mother-assigned choice. Similarly, Iyengar and Lepper (1999) found personal choice (autonomy) positively affected intrinsic motivation for Anglo-Americans, whereas it was less important for Asian Americans, who were more intrinsically motivated by choices made for them by authority figures or peers. J. Miller and Bersoff (1994) suggest from an interdependent perspective, the choice of others is not inconsistent with one's own desires; thus, in the Lepper et al. study, one might conclude that the Asian children did not view their own choice as being in conflict with the choice assigned by their mother.

The implications for engagement of these combined studies are engagement scores may be similar across cultures, but the antecedents or how the antecedents are framed and interpreted may differ. Such differences are important to understand because even if the engagement scores are the same, how we get them differs: interventions designed for one culture will not work in another.

Furthermore, many interventions are implemented in organizations as a no-choice event; that is, employees are required to attend the workshops or training sessions put in place to increase engagement scores. Thus, applying equivalent reasoning to the choice studies reviewed earlier suggests that employees holding an interdependent perspective may be less put off by an organization's choice to send them to training to increase employee engagement as compared to employees who are independent and may view such efforts as being assigned the choice of whether to be engaged or not. Being given a choice reflects the opportunity for self-expression – a decision that mirrors the independent self (Iyengar & DeVoe, 2003; Iyengar & Lepper, 1999); hence, for the employees from an independent/individualistic culture, being assigned the intervention may not result in the desired effect on engagement levels.

Other influences on motivation and other forms of motivation have been studied cross-culturally, and the results of those studies may also provide insight into studying engagement cross-culturally. For example, S. Schwartz and Bilsky (1990) determined people from Hong Kong can experience both a strong need for achievement and a strong need for interdependence. Historically, the need for achievement has been considered indicative of an independent or individualistic value system, marked by a drive for mastery and power (Hilgard, 1987). Schwartz and Bilsky speculated that in Hong Kong the need for achievement may be experienced as a drive to do what is expected. Thus, their Hong Kong sample seemed to dissolve any potential inconsistency between the need for achievement (independent/individualism) and need for fulfilling others' expectations (interdependence/collectivism) by considering the results of the need for achievement relative to their culture (expectation vs. demonstration of independence). The study showed that the need for achievement should not be automatically associated with independent/individualistic cultures.

Individuals with an independent versus interdependent self-construal tend toward a promotion as opposed to a prevention motive, respectively (Heine et al., 2001; A. Lee, Aaker, & Gardner, 2000). A promotion motive refers to a motivational pattern marked by the pursuit of ideals and toward gains, whereas a prevention motive refers to a pattern marked by avoiding losses and meeting obligations. These motivational patterns are activated by one's self-construal, which has an impact on individuals' social perceptions and behaviors (A. Lee et al., 2000). Thus, according to Heine et al. (2001) and A. Lee et al. (2000), the tendency is for people with an independent self-construal to pursue ideals and advancement, whereas those with an interdependent self-construal take the conservative route avoiding risk. This seems a somewhat broad overstatement and deserves additional research; however, the implication for engagement research is that different cultural perspectives may trigger different motives, influencing the degree to which engagement is manifested in advancing behaviors (e.g., job performance to get ahead) versus maintenance behaviors (e.g., OCBs in the form of voice extra-role behaviors; Van Dyne & LePine, 1998).

Organizational antecedents of motivation include leadership and core job dimensions; thus, cross-cultural research examining these constructs is particularly relevant for considering how engagement may vary cross-culturally. Leadership is considered a predictor of engagement, and when looked at through the cross-cultural lens within motivation studies, leadership could provide insights into engagement across cultures. For example, Misumi (1989, 1995) and colleagues (Misumi & Peterson, 1985a, 1985b) collectively demonstrated Japanese leaders who are both transactional or performance oriented and personally caring of their employees in and outside of work were considered the most effective, as compared to those leaders who were task oriented only and who separated personal matters from work-related matters. In their review of Misumi and colleagues' findings, Markus and Kitayama (1991) suggested in interdependent cultures such as Japan, employees' personal attachment to their leader is more important in fostering motivation than are the strong independent leadership skills and characteristics considered essential of good leaders in independent cultures such as the United States. However, Misumi and colleagues' findings suggest leaders who are balanced in both transactional and relational tasks will fare better than those focused only on personal attachments. Misumi and his colleagues did not study American leaders, and therefore, the converse of this hypothesis may not necessarily be appropriate.

Job characteristics theory (Hackman & Oldham, 1976) has been used to explain predictors of engagement (e.g., Kahn, 1990), and cross-cultural research on the effects of job characteristics on motivation may shed light on what can be expected with regard to engagement. Specifically, core job dimensions – job autonomy and task complexity – were shown to increase initiative-taking behaviors in both East and West Germany (Frese, Kring, Soose, & Zempel, 1996). Research has shown that core job dimensions, in general, were positively related to motivation in Dutch, Bulgarian, and Hungarian samples, although comparatively, autonomy had a more pronounced effect on responsibility in the Netherlands than in the other two countries (Roe, Zinovieva, Dienes, & Ten Horn, 2000). Notably in Roe et al.'s (2000) study, core job dimensions did not influence psychological meaningfulness or job involvement in the same way across the Netherlands, Bulgaria, and Hungry. Their results suggest that engagement may not be fostered in the same way between independent or individualistic cultures such as the Netherlands as it is in interdependent or collectivistic cultures such as Bulgaria or Hungary (although Hofstede, 1980, 2001, did not examine former communist countries, he suggested most communist countries would rate collectivism higher over individualism). Roe et al. considered Bulgaria and Hungary different from the Netherlands because of the countries' differing "political, cultural, and economic" (2000, p. 660) views. A conclusion from these studies on core job dimensions is that autonomy, task identity, and skill variety may influence engagement levels more in individualistic/independent cultures than in collectivistic/interdependent cultures, where the desire to be known, distinct, and decide for oneself (essentially what core job dimensions provide) are not as highly valued as in individualistic cultures.

Implications of Cross-Cultural Motivation Research for Engagement

The cross-culture literature reviewed here implies that how one interprets predictors or antecedents of motivation determines whether motivation is fostered, and those interpretations rely heavily on one's cultural framework. Extrapolating from this literature suggests it may be engagement itself is viewed similarly from culture to culture, but what fosters it is culturally influenced. For example, achievement motivation as assessed using the Achievement Motivation Inventory appears invariant across country samples, implying achievement motivation is interpreted to have the same meaning from country to country (see Byrne et al., 2004). However, as noted by Schwartz and Bilsky (1990), what achievement motivation results in (fulfillment of expectations of group vs. demonstration of independence) may vary by culture. Similarly, what fosters motivation, such as the type of leader behavior displayed, the job characteristics (high autonomy or not; free choice or assigned), and type of goal (easy vs. challenging) may vary by culture, or at least how these ante-cedents are interpreted may differ, thereby ultimately affecting the level of motivation displayed.

Another broad conclusion from the motivation research and current engage-ment literature is much of what we currently know about antecedents to engagement are grounded in the individualistic/independent, low power dis-tance, masculine, and high tolerance for ambiguity culture perspectives. Con-cepts such as autonomy, freedom of speech (as with psychological safety), and being in control of creating one's own meaning, as well as feeling significant are all values representative of these culture dimensions.

Commitment, Job Involvement, and Citizenship Behaviors

As noted in Chapter 3, employee engagement has been confused, at times, with organizational commitment, job involvement, and OCBs. Although enough accumulated research has demonstrated these constructs are distinct (see Chap-ters 2 and 3), they still overlap and share some of the same antecedents. Thus, examining cross-cultural research on organizational commitment, job involve-ment, and citizenship behaviors may provide insight into the development of hypotheses about engagement across cultures.

In a study of South Koreans in comparison to German participants, Stein-metz, Park, and Kabst (2011) set out to evaluate the predictive validity of need for achievement, the need for affiliation, and the need for power regarding job involvement and organizational commitment. After first determining the two countries' cultures differed (South Korea scored higher on power distance and collectivism than Germany), the authors reported scores on job involvement (M = 2.06, 2.46) and organizational commitment (M = 2.53, 2.11) for the South Korean and German samples, respectively. Using structural equation modeling, the authors demonstrated the three needs were similarly related (nearly identical path coefficients and standard errors) to both job involvement and commitment in each country. Specifically, need for achievement was positively related to both involvement and commitment (β = .27 and β = .33, respectively) in both the South Korean and German samples. The need for affiliation was unrelated to both outcomes in both samples, and the need for power was only positively related to job involvement (β = .36) in both samples. The study findings indicate that for this sample of 209 South Korean and 198 German executive MBA students and alumni, there are no significant cross-cultural differences in how the three needs predict job involvement and commitment. The authors concluded interventions designed to motivate employees to be more involved and committed at work, via their need for achievement and power, should be universal across cultures that differ on collectivism and power distance. The authors did not examine the other Hofstede dimensions of culture.

Similarly, an examination of job involvement across an Indian and U.S. sample also showed predictors of job involvement do not vary between the two cultures (Sekaran, 1981). Sekaran examined 20 predictors including demographic variables, personality characteristics such as need for achievement and affiliation, and core job dimensions such as autonomy.

Although the results suggest there are no differences across culture for predictors of job involvement and commitment, country differences are not necessarily reflective of cultural differences, though they are related (Javidan et al., 2004). Looking at multiple cultures within one country, Cohen (2007) examined job involvement, organizational commitment, and OCBs in northern Israel, a region the author divided into at least five different cultural groups: secular Jews, Orthodox Jews, kibbutz members, Druze, and Arabs. Cohen's results are detailed, and one must read the study to see the specific results; but I summarize a few findings relevant to my review. The cultural groups differed significantly in their ratings of Hofstede's (1980) four original dimensions (excluding time orientation), indicating they should be considered different cultures from each other. Druze and Arabs rated highest on collectivism, whereas kibbutz members and secular Jews could be considered more individualistic given their significantly lower ratings on collectivism than the other groups. Arabs were highest in power distance, and kibbutz members were lowest. Arabs and Druze were highest in masculinity, whereas kibbutz members were lowest (indicating high femininity scores). Lastly, secular Jews were highest in uncertainty avoidance, and kibbutz members were lowest. Results for analysis of variance comparisons of mean scores on job involvement, organizational commitment, and OCBs indicated some of the cultures differed from one another on their job attitude scores, though not all. For example, on organizational commitment, the secular Jews differed from the kibbutz members, but not from the Orthodox Jews. For job involvement, the secular Jews differed from all other groups, but the other groups did not significantly differ from each other (e.g., Arabs did not score job involvement significantly different from Druze). Ratings of citizenship behavior, specifically altruism and conscientiousness, differed across cultures. Finally, Cohen (2007) concluded from his findings that collectivism is strongly related to citizenship behaviors, namely, altruism and civic virtue.

Overall, Cohen's (2007) results indicate that scores on job involvement, commitment, and OCBs *do* differ by culture. Using regression analysis, Cohen additionally determined collectivism was positively related to altruism and civic virtue, and low power distance was related to higher levels of conscientiousness. Because the focus of his study was primarily on OCBs and in-role job performance, Cohen did not run regression analyses on job involvement or commitment with culture because his primary goal was to examine predictors of OCB and in-role performance.

OCBs have been compared across cultures, even though what constitutes extra-role behaviors may vary across cultures (e.g., Lam, Hui, & Law, 1999). Research has shown that Canadians, in general, demonstrate fewer OCBs than do those in Iran or Turkey (Kabasakal, Dastmalchian, & Imer, 2011). OCB was assessed by three dimensions: helping, civic virtue, and sportsmanship. In the same study, Iranians' scores were higher on helping behaviors, whereas the Turkish participants scored highest on civic virtue OCBs. In Cohen's (2007) study, OCB was assessed by three dimensions – altruism, civic virtue, and conscientiousness – and levels of each dimension varied by cultural group (although not all groups were significantly different from each other). Whether OCB is defined using Organ's (1988) or Williams and Anderson's (1991) definition matters, and which dimensions of OCB are measured makes a difference in how results are interpreted.

In summary, the findings reviewed from a number of cross-cultural studies examining organizational commitment, job involvement, and OCBs are mixed. The constructs were not all assessed using the same instruments or in the same manner (e.g., one overall score combining dimensions versus dimensions separated into individual scores). Perhaps the clearest pattern of results is antecedents to job attitudes did not seem to vary across countries, but levels of the job attitudes themselves did vary by culture. This pattern suggests a number of conclusions: (a) what predicts job attitudes may not vary by country; (b) we have not yet examined predictors expected to vary by country; (c) we have not yet examined contrasting cultures, or we are looking at irrelevant dimensions of culture (these studies were across country and did not comment on culture per se); or (d) the meaning of the actual job attitude itself varies by culture. It may be that organizational commitment does not quite mean the same thing across countries or cultures and our failure to examine scale invariance in every cross-cultural study hides this issue. In my trips to Russia in 2012 and 2013, after many hours of conversation and presentations, while trying to understand what employee engagement is in Russia, I finally determined engagement may not be the same between the United States and Russia, and this has implications for understanding what is engagement, if anything, in Russia.

Implications for Employee Engagement Overall

In the preceding review, I offered several implications of the cross-cultural research findings in other areas of organizational behavior related to engagement. In this next section, I develop several propositions about what employee engagement may look like across cultures. I relied on the two theoretical frameworks of culture described earlier in this chapter, in addition to the overall patterns of findings from empirical literature applicable to engagement. For this discussion, I rely on the current dominant definitions of employee engagement (Kahn, 1990; Schaufeli, Salanova, González-Romá, & Bakker, 2002) and leverage the extant literature in engagement on what predicts or fosters engagement levels.

Employees in individualistic cultures value work and their role at work, viewing outside demands such as family as distractions to personal achievement. Work is given more emphasis than is leisure, and meaningfulness is achieved through one's role and accomplishment at work, as opposed to one's contribution to society (Spector et al., 2007). In contrast, employees in collectivistic cultures view their connection with others as central to their personal fulfillment, and work is a means to serving one's value in the group. Becoming completely absorbed at work to the detriment of outside distraction (e.g., requests for help from others in the group) may be considered more of an individualistic value than a collectivistic one. Because of the difference in focus of the individualistic versus collectivistic perspective, one could hypothesize those in individualistic cultures are more engaged at work than those in collectivistic cultures.

In support of work playing a central role at the expense of family, Spector and colleagues (2007) showed the association between work demands and work interference with family was stronger in individualistic cultures than collectivistic cultures. However, one could also maintain that because of the social support those in collectivistic cultures receive from their social network and the sense of communal meaningfulness one can derive from working with others to achieve a common goal (goal of the unit or organization), employees from collectivistic cultures are more engaged at work than are those from individualistic cultures who shun support as a sign of lack of independence. Consequently, I propose two competing propositions:

Proposition 1a: Individualistic cultures where autonomy, one's significance, achieving meaningfulness for the self, and one's personal achievement is valued, report higher employee engagement than collectivistic cultures where fitting into the group, serving the meaningfulness of others, and social relations are valued above self-promotion.

Proposition 1b: Collectivistic cultures valuing social support, connection at work, and the meaningfulness of community are more engaged than their individualistic counterparts because they receive support to offset job demands.

High power-distance cultures probably have organizations supporting a steep hierarchy (i.e., many levels of management) because of their acceptance and expectation for authority and inequality. In such organizations, subordinates are unlikely to speak out or feel safe expressing their ideas (M. Erez, 1994). Thus, they would report low psychological safety, which is one of Kahn's (1990) psychological states leading to engagement; hence, engagement is probably lower in organizations based in high power-distance cultures than in low power-distance cultures:

Proposition 2: High or large power-distance cultures in which following orders, doing what you are told versus what you think, and working without clear task identity or significance report lower employee engagement than do low or small power-distance cultures where equal rights for everyone, voice opportunity, and the ability to step outside of the line of authority to do something that would create greater meaning are valued.

Organizations in masculine cultures endorse strong masculine gender roles in which promotional opportunities are favored for men over women, higher salaries for men over women are preferred under the assumption men are the main source of household income, and work is emphasized over family, judgment over intuition, assertiveness over consideration, and results over process (M. Erez, 1994). As such, we might hypothesize social support in masculine cultures is minimal, and transactional leadership may be preferred over transformational or servant leadership, in which one focuses on the relationship and development of employees more so than on just getting the job done. Consequently, one would expect employee engagement to be higher in feminine cultures than in masculine cultures because of the support, community, and relational components of feminine cultures, components shown as positively related to engagement. I note, that my hypothesis runs counter to Lo Presti et al.'s (2020) findings of respondents in a masculine culture rating their engagement higher than those in a feminine culture.

Proposition 3: Cultures rated as masculine, in which the culture is aggressive, work is stressed over family and family-life balance, and the focus of work is on ego enhancement may inhibit employee engagement, resulting in lower scores than do feminine cultures, in which opportunities are equal, balance between work and family is encouraged (promoting psychological availability), and a focus on meaningfulness may be more valued.

M. Erez (1994) suggested that in cultures with high uncertainty avoidance, organizations put efforts in place to formalize rules, regulations, and control employee actions. In organizations with many constraints on employees, autonomy is most likely limited. Furthermore, regulated work environments may stifle employees' ability to derive meaningfulness from the work because efforts to feel valued may be seen as working outside regulations. One could hypothesize, as a result of such control, that engagement would be lower than in cultures where uncertainty avoidance is low. Furthermore, current research on engagement suggests autonomy is important to promoting high levels of engagement. Having the freedom to choose to invest oneself into the work role is constrained in a culture of high uncertainty avoidance. Freedom of choice, however, is a value of the independent self-construal. Thus, those with an interdependent self-construal may not feel as constrained in a high uncertainty avoidance culture as may those with an independent self-construal. Therefore, self-construal and uncertainty avoidance interact to determine employee engagement levels:

> *Proposition 4*: In cultures with high uncertainty avoidance, in which formal rules, structure, and tight policies are in place to minimize ambiguity, employee engagement may be stifled because of the inability to create a meaningful workplace. However, the effects of uncertainty avoidance on engagement are moderated by one's self-construal.

Hofstede and Bond's (1984) fifth dimension of culture, short-term versus long-term orientation, is a challenging dimension to tie to engagement. A culture of long-term orientation focuses on the future, on the sustainability of effort, gains over the long run, high persistence, and perseverance. Although both Kahn's (1990) and Schaufeli, Salanova et al.'s (2002) definitions of engagement incorporate persistence and perseverance, neither is time based. Neither suggests a trade-off of the present for the future, which is indicative of a long-term versus short-term orientation. The thriftiness of the long-term orientation, the holding back of resources for a future need, may be counterproductive to engagement, which requires giving all of oneself in the present moment. Kahn (1992) proposed psychological presence is an essential antecedent to engagement. Thus, holding back and conserving would appear to be the opposite of employee engagement. Therefore, we could hypothesize engagement should be higher in short-term-oriented cultures. In contrast, though, researchers relying on the conservation of resources theory maintain that conserving and accumulating job resources, which can be achieved by holding back resources consistent with the theory's suppositions, results in higher engagement (e.g., Hakanen, Perhoniemi, & Toppinen-Tanner, 2008; Harju,

Hakanen, & Schaufeli, 2016). Thus, we could also hypothesize that long-term-oriented cultures, in which conserving resources and seeking to accumulate more resources is the norm, will lead to higher engagement.

> *Proposition 5a*: Short-term-oriented cultures in which giving all your effort for the immediate need encourage higher levels of employee engagement than do long-term-oriented cultures, in which conserving resources for the future encourages not giving all your effort to the immediate role performance.
>
> *Proposition 5b*: Long-term-oriented cultures in which conserving resources for the future encourage higher engagement levels than do short-term-oriented cultures.

The preceding propositions assume employee engagement is defined using either Kahn's (1990) or Schaufeli, Salanova et al.'s (2002) conceptualization. If, instead, I use my definition offered in Chapter 2,[3] cultural effects on employee engagement may diminish. Specifically, by providing a target for motivation, in particular *the goals of the organization*, both individualistic and collectivistic cultures have equal influence because how the goal is defined seems to matter in motivation (as concluded from the review of the literature in this chapter). Another component of my definition, *focus*, refers to alignment with organizational goals, goals established within a particular culture. Thus, the meaning of the goal itself may differ across cultures, but focusing on the goal does not, as just identified in the prior literature reviewed; hence, engagement would remain the same. My version of *focus* is different from Schaufeli, Salanova et al.'s (2002) conceptualization, where focus is a part of absorption or flow, requiring detachment from others or time. Other elements of my definition, *psychophysiological arousal* and *physiological arousal*, as opposed to vigor or physical activity, allow for conservative expression of engagement, such as might occur in collectivistic/interdependent cultures in which one wishes to blend in with the group. For the expression of one's *affective and cognitive self* in transforming work into meaningful accomplishment, it is similar. By specifically incorporating the idea of *transforming* work activity into what the individual finds meaningful, my definition allows for meaningfulness to be culturally based. Specifically, in collectivistic cultures, *meaningfulness* is in service to the goals of the group versus one's own significance. Likewise, *purposeful accomplishment* may be completing the assigned goal. Lastly, in contrast to the other more culture-free aspects of the definition, the incorporation of *psychological presence* may suggest engagement would be higher in short-term versus long-term-oriented cultures because one must direct all attention and energy to the moment rather than to the future.

In defense of existing definitions of engagement, my definition of engagement incorporates components of the two most dominant definitions, Kahn's (1990)

---

3 The example countries in this paragraph to represent the different combinations of individualism/ collectivism by vertical/horizontal were taken directly from Torelli and Shavitt (2010).

and Schaufeli, Salanova et al.'s (2002). Thus, one could contend their definitions should be as culturally free as mine, and mine is not completely culture-free (i.e., not biased toward one culture versus another). I agree with this criticism, although other aspects of Kahn's and Schaufeli, Salanova, et al.'s definitions render them potentially less flexible to cultural requirements. Specifically, the perspective and framing of their definitions ties them to a number of the cultural dimensions identified by Hofstede (1980). For example, Kahn's foundation of the job characteristics theory, which suggests core job dimensions lead to psychological states that then lead to motivation, is somewhat problematic from a cross-cultural perspective. The core job dimensions of autonomy, task significance, and task identity suggest an independent/individualistic orientation. Psychological states such as psychological safety, which refers to the freedom to express oneself honestly and without career threat, is inherently a low power-distance, individualistic, and possibly masculine value. Likewise, Schaufeli, Salanova, et al.'s definition is based on original conceptualizations of engagement as the opposite of burnout (Maslach & Leiter, 1997), an experience grounded in how an individual withdraws from the environment, others, and the self. Consequently, Schaufeli, Salanova et al.'s conceptualization of engagement relies on expressions of energy and connection as a way of demonstrating the opposite of withdrawal and depression. Schaufeli, Salanova et al.'s definition also relies heavily on concepts of value in individualistic cultures, such as self-absorption and intense focus on the job at the expense of all others around. Both definitions, Kahn's (1990) and Schaufeli, Salanova et al.'s (2002), in addition to my own, could be modified to accommodate a cross-cultural perspective, if research evidence suggests engagement has the same meaning around the globe.

WHAT I LEARNED ABOUT ENGAGEMENT FROM NON-U.S. COUNTRIES

In the first edition of this book, I reported on several visits to a number of countries in the last several years. My visits involved presenting on employee engagement and exploring whether the concept exists or is understood in these countries. The countries included the United Kingdom, France, Russia, and South Africa. My observations that follow are all bounded by my limited exposure in each country.

In France and South Africa, the academicians I spoke with had heard of employee engagement, but very few were studying the construct. Their understanding of engagement was limited to the opposite of burnout, the definition grounding the UWES, the only measure they knew of for assessing engagement. Non-academics with whom I spoke in France thought that engagement was the same as commitment. Since then, researchers in France and South Africa have published a significant number of studies in English on engagement using the UWES. None of those studies reported an examination of whether the concept of engagement is the same as understood in the United States. In the United Kingdom, my audience had heard of engagement but not in much detail. Most of the individuals who spoke with me after my talks were primarily interested in whether engagement was a fad or a long-lasting area of study. Since then, a few researchers in the United Kingdom have reported on studies of engagement. I was left with the impression in both France and the United Kingdom, engagement is not as big of a phenomenon as it appears in the United States, but also it was not being ignored. In the United States, talks about engagement and, perhaps more important, *how* you engage employees seemed in vogue. I did not get that impression in the United Kingdom or France.

In Russia, both academicians and practitioners with whom I spoke had either never heard of engagement or, if they had (which was rare), they had heard of the "opposite of burnout" definition from a few papers on the UWES translated into Russian. I found the Russians with whom I interacted, including non-academic business leaders, to be fascinated with the concept. I have found no published studies on engagement in Russia.

Lastly, in South Africa, a few academicians with whom I spoke knew of the concept, and I found a few papers published in the South African journals; if engagement was defined at all, it was the opposite of burnout and relied on using the UWES. The practitioners with whom I spoke were not interested in the concept; they struggled with broader concepts relating to fairness in selection, diversity of cultures within organizations, and the very large disparity of income levels within a single business unit. Since then, a few more studies of engagement in South Africa have appeared in journals.

A potential cultural weakness of all the definitions, including my own and several others I reviewed in Chapter 2, is they are all derived from or based on studies of the individual, separate from the social environment, situational influences, and their values, thus placing the individual as the central reference point. On one hand, because engagement is an individual-level construct, it makes sense that the construct would be studied from an individual's point of view. On the other hand, this self-referent approach to identifying the concept removes interpretations of engagement as placed in something other than an individualistic, low power-distance, low uncertainty avoidance, masculine concept. Engagement may be more socially and situationally dependent than current conceptualizations allow.

Conclusion

Researchers have made progress in studying engagement internationally. There exist a substantial number of studies looking at employee engagement in different countries, though not cross-country or cross-cultural. Additionally, all but a handful of researchers relied on an already translated version of the UWES-9 for assessing engagement. As reviewed in Chapter 6, the UWES is a broad measure of engagement, which includes several additional overlapping constructs, such as commitment, stress, job involvement, and positive affect (see Byrne, Peters, & Weston, 2016; Newman & Harrison, 2008; Wefald, Mills, Smith, & Downey, 2011). The substantial overlap with a number of other constructs makes it challenging to evaluate whether the studies in other countries are getting at engagement, per se, or at some of the other constructs contained within this broad construct with fuzzy boundaries. The contribution of these various studies to engagement would be greater if the focal construct was better isolated from potential antecedents or consequences of engagement, such as with the JES (see Byrne et al., 2016). The primary contribution of nearly all the international studies published since 2013 appears most in service to other literature, such as stress and well-being, high performance work systems, or leadership. In a large proportion of these studies, engagement serves as one of a few mediators, thus providing an explanation for relationships between other constructs (e.g., human resource management systems and organization performance). The secondary contribution, at best, is identifying a new antecedent to engagement or providing additional support for an already studied antecedent. Most antecedents include another form of a job resource, form of leadership (good or bad), or industry specific construct such as religious spirituality. Most of the studies have the JD-R and/or conservation of resources as the theoretical framework.

While the study authors would, no doubt, claim they are making a contribution to the engagement literature by studying old and new antecedents to engagement in their country or with their unique sample (e.g., dairy farmers, parents with children with disabilities), the advancement to understanding engagement would be enhanced with consideration of unique norms within those countries. For example, in one of the few studies to consider cultural differences, Kotera, Van Laethem, and Ohshima (2020) examined Dutch and Japanese employees' mental health shame and engagement. The authors hypothesized that based on Japan's culture of shame, Japanese employees would likely underestimate or downplay mental health distress. In contrast, the authors suggested the Dutch culture was not as shame based and would therefore be more likely to estimate accurate levels of mental health distress. The authors further proposed that since engagement is closely related to mental health, they anticipated differences between Japanese and Dutch workers on engagement levels. Furthermore, previous studies (e.g., Shimazu et al., 2010) showed Japanese employees suppress positive emotions, whereas Dutch employees' self-enhance positive emotions, which should result in higher engagement reported by Dutch over Japanese study participants. Indeed, Kotera et al. (2020) found Dutch participants reported higher mental health distress and higher engagement than did the Japanese participants.

One could conclude the accumulation of research on engagement across countries and samples, showing similar means, suggests engagement is universal. I beg to differ a little on this broad and overarching conclusion. First, I have concerns regarding the quality of assessment of engagement. Second, I turn once again to my experience in Russia to contend that although the words in a survey might translate from one language to another, it does not mean the same construct is assessed. In Russia, the word *engagement* was consistently translated into the words "job involvement." But job involvement is not the same as engagement, although there is construct overlap. It may be that there is a construct in Russia that is the same as engagement; they just do not call it engagement and, therefore, we are unable to make an accurate translation. This translation dilemma is not isolated to Russia. For example, Tran et al. (2020) noted that some items from the UWES simply did not translate into Vietnamese. The phrase "strong and vigorous" was replaced with a Vietnamese phrase meaning "physically and mentally healthy, good at verbal communication, and lively." Researchers conducting the translations do make every effort to find the meaning of the words from one culture to the other; however, the focus is on translating the words, not necessarily on determining if the construct exists and then evaluating the best set of items to assess that culture specific construct.

To advance our understanding of engagement across cultures, engagement needs to be defined and understood from within each country's (and culture's) perspective. For example, there are 11 official languages in South Africa, with each reflecting a unique culture. China is geographically divided along east–west and north–south lines, essentially creating at least four different regions and four different cultures – and this does not capture the 55 minority groups or more than 200 dialects (see Gundling & Zanchettin [2007] for more details on China and six other countries). Does engagement exist as a concept within these different cultures? To study engagement across countries and within these countries and cultures, accurate and careful translation cannot be overlooked, which means more than just translating the survey words: the concept must be understood before it can be assessed. Additionally, to provide answers for Jian-Xi and Matías, studies of the interaction between cultures across countries, and country cultures with organizational culture, are necessary.

WALK-AWAY POINTS

- Little cross-cultural research on engagement exists.
- Cross-cultural studies of related concepts provide some insight into whether engagement will vary by culture; what fosters engagement may vary because of how work environment, goals, leadership, and meaningfulness are interpreted across cultures.
- Studies assessing cross-cultural comparisons are sorely needed, as are studies of interactions between cultures and organizational culture.
- Language is culturally defined and grounded; translations are critical to how we understand and study engagement cross-culturally and cross-nationally.

10

THE PARADOX OF EMPLOYEE ENGAGEMENT

Is There a Dark Side?

Employee engagement is considered a positive state and one that organizations desire of every employee. As noted in the beginning of Chapter 2, financial gains and losses attributed to engagement and disengaged employees, respectively, are too much for human resource managers and organizational leaders to ignore. As such, their focus on engagement thus far has been toward maximizing it and finding ways to ensure employees are consistently and constantly engaged. Research to date has followed suit by examining positive outcomes of engagement, focusing on the benefits of engaged employees, such as customer satisfaction and organizational productivity (e.g., Harter, Schmidt, & Hayes, 2002); commitment and turnover intentions (e.g., Karatepe, 2013); and job, task, and extra-role performance (e.g., Rich, LePine, & Crawford, 2010; Saks, 2006). Recent studies show engagement is positively associated with willingness to change and higher financial performance (e.g., Ghlichlee & Bayat, 2021; Vakola, Petrou, & Katsaros, 2021). For those employees who do not "appear" engaged, leadership and organizational interventions have been, and are being designed, to "fix" their perceived lack of engagement (e.g., see various websites for consulting perspectives; Macey, Schneider, Barbera, & Young, 2009). All of the above assume that low, inconsistent, not continuous, or less than obvious engagement are all bad (e.g., Gallup Organization, 2002, 2013a; Gebauer, Lowman, & Gordon, 2008). But is it really beneficial to have everyone engaged, all the time, at the highest intensity level? George (2010) suggests that it is not. Instead, she and others (e.g., Macey & Schneider, 2008) contend continuous engagement comes at a cost to the employee, a cost in the form of burnout and work–life conflict (Sonnentag, 2003). Organizations may suffer a negative cost as well, as employees' turnover intentions may increase at high levels of engagement (e.g., Caesens, Stinglhamber, & Marmier, 2016).

DOI: 10.4324/9781003171133-14

Research has shown that forms of recovery, as simple as a lunch break (Bosch, Sonnentag, & Pinck, 2018), are valuable in maintaining employee well-being and high levels of engagement throughout the workday and workweek (e.g., Berga & Muzikante, 2017; Erks, Allen, Harland, & Prange, 2020; Kim, Cho, & Park, 2021; Kühnel, Zacher, de Bloom, & Bledow, 2017; McGrath, Cooper, Garrosa, Sanz, & Cheung, 2017). Thus, the implication of these studies are that too much engagement may be unhealthy.

In this chapter, I review the literature that says too much engagement is not in the organization's best interest; there is a dark side to engagement. When does engagement come at the expense of other highly desirable organizational constructs? This chapter explores this fundamental question.

Too Much Engagement

Researchers have begun to question whether employees can become too engaged (Halbesleben, Harvey, & Bolino, 2009; Schaufeli, Taris, & Bakker, 2006; van Beek, Taris, & Schaufeli, 2011; Van Wijhe, Peeters, & Schaufeli, 2011). This question comes on the heels of Pierce and Aguinis's (2013) principle of the Too-Much-of-a-Good-Thing effect, which says positive antecedents in excess result in harmful outcomes. The principle explains research findings of curvilinear relationships between constructs previously shown to have linear relationships only. For example, researchers showed the relationship between job performance and turnover intentions is curvilinear (U-shaped) rather than linear (e.g., Salamin & Hom, 2005).

Researchers speculate employees who are engaged frequently, over long periods of time, or at very high levels of intensity, may eventually become burned out (e.g., Halbesleben, Harvey, & Bolino, 2009). Thus, people who work at intense levels of concentration for consecutive periods, with little rest in between, demonstrate emotional exhaustion and mental fatigue (Schaufeli, Taris et al., 2006). However, other researchers have maintained that rather than employee engagement leading to such negative outcomes, when employees work obsessively and to their own detriment, they are no longer demonstrating engagement; instead, they are demonstrating workaholism (Schaufeli, Taris et al., 2006).

Workaholism

Various definitions of a workaholic or workaholism exist (see Burke, 2009), although most tend to include the notions of self-imposed demands that are compulsive, excessive, neglectful of other areas of life, unhealthy, and crippling (Burke, 2009). Workaholism was originally patterned after the term *alcoholism* (Oates, 1968), to capture the addictive and negative consequences of excessive work. However, few tend to consider workaholism in the same light as alcoholism, which falls under substance-related disorders, a category of mental disorders listed in the *Diagnostic and Statistical Manual of Mental Disorders* (DSM-IV, 1994). Alcoholism is a substance-related mental disorder, whereas workaholism is not considered a mental disorder. Workaholics tend to feel driven to work because of an internal sense of guilt when not working or an inner pressure to keep on working. Thus, working because it is enjoyable or fulfilling is not what characterizes workaholism (Spence & Robbins, 1992); however, others disagree and characterize workaholics as enjoying work but unable to disengage (McMillan & O'Driscoll, 2006; Ng, Sorensen, & Feldman, 2007). In studies comparing workaholics with individuals who are considered enthusiastic about their jobs (thus exhibiting some of the same work involvement tendencies), workaholics scored higher on scales of perfectionism, job stress, and inability to delegate (Spence & Robbins, 1992). Contrary to popular belief, working a lot (hour per week) is not necessarily characteristic of workaholics (Burke, 2009).

Although workaholics may report losing track of time while working, their lack of ability to track time is not the same as flow. Flow is often described as part of engagement (Kahn, 1990; Schaufeli, Salanova, González-Romá, & Bakker, 2002) because of the intensity of focus and absorption, but it is not considered a component of workaholism (Burke & Matthiesen, 2004). As described in Chapter 3, flow is experienced as enjoyable and being lost in the pleasure of just doing the activity for the sake of doing it; there is no guilt or pressure to do the task (Csikszentmihalyi & Rathunde, 1993) like there is with workaholism. Workaholism is pathological; it is an unpleasant, anxiety-provoking, all-consuming phenomenon with detrimental consequences (Clark, Michel, Zhdanova, Pui, & Baltes, 2016).

Some researchers have suggested that "good" workaholics demonstrate high levels of engagement (Schaufeli, Taris, & Bakker, 2006). Across several studies, Schaufeli and colleagues (2007; Schaufeli, Taris, & van Rhenen, 2008) determined engagement and workaholism, when operationalized as working excessively and compulsively, were similar yet distinct. In support, Mazzetti, Schaufeli, and Guglielmi (2018), and Di Stefano and Gaudiino (2019) demonstrated engagement (measured using the UWES) and workaholism are distinct constructs. Schaufeli and colleagues (2007, 2008) measured working compulsively with items that capture working without enjoyment, feeling obligated to work, and feeling compelled to work rather than wanting to work. Working excessively was measured with items focusing on working beyond what others do, being overcommitted to work, and unable to take breaks from work. The authors concluded from their findings that good workaholism can be operationalized as work engagement, even though they found correlations of only .27 between work engagement (measured using the UWES) and working excessively (which was correlated at .57 with working compulsively). However, whether called good or not, overcommitment at work is positively related to burnout (Philp, Egan, & Kane, 2012). A good workaholic might be better labeled an overly enthusiastic worker (Wojdyło, 2015).

Like Spence and Robbins (1992); K. Scott, Moore, and Miceli (1997); and others, Schaufeli et al. (2008) divided their sample into multiple types of workaholics, with some displaying positive characteristics (enjoyment) and others displaying negative characteristics (guilt, lack of enjoyment). Across the various types of workaholics, those displaying more positive characteristics may be considered more like engaged workers, suggesting potential construct overlap. However, although some have suggested workaholism has positive characteristics, workaholics create tense work environments around them, pushing others to work more (Machlowitz, 1980; K. Scott et al., 1997; Seybold & Salomone, 1994).

To refer to workaholism as "good" or "functional" might be treating a pathologically harmful construct as pleasant, creating confusion for researchers who aim to study the negative health consequences of workaholism (Wojdyło, 2015). Scholars, such as Clark (2018) and Wojdyło (2015), provide ample argument for why workaholism is not an appropriate term to use when describing too much engagement or over-engagement. Recently, Clark, Smith, and Haynes (2020) resolved several inconsistencies in the conceptualization of workaholism and proposed a multidimensional definition comprising an inner pressure/compulsion to work, persistent and uncontrollable thoughts about work, feeling negative when not working, and working to excess beyond requirements or expectations. Using five samples, they developed and tested a new 16-item measure to assess their multidimensional definition, in addition to providing extensive validity evidence for their measure relative to existing measures of workaholism.

Passion

Descriptions of workaholism and compulsive work seem similar to obsessive passion (see Vallerand & Houlfort, 2003). Passion is not typically considered a construct of excess or compulsivity; however, Vallerand and colleagues (Vallerand, 2008; Vallerand & Houlfort, 2003) proposed that individuals can demonstrate either *harmonious* or *obsessive* passion toward several activities, including work. Harmonious passion is defined as willing involvement in a task without the compelling need to do the task at all times (Vallerand, 2008). Obsessive passion, in contrast, refers to "rigid persistence toward the activity" (Vallerand, 2008, p. 2), describing an individual who becomes dependent on the activity such that their normal functioning is impaired by the obsessive need for continuous involvement in the activity. Working at the task may provide a boost to the ego and satisfy a need for feeling important, yet it controls the individual. Thus, obsessive passion is compulsive, whereas harmonious passion is considered "in harmony with other aspects of the person's life" (Vallerand, 2008, p. 2). Others have defined passion as incorporating a synthesis of one's affective and cognitive self-perception toward the job (e.g., Ho, Wong, & Lee, 2011). Although compulsive behaviors describe workaholism and obsessive passion, the compulsive behaviors are not indicative of a mental disorder, such as obsessive-compulsive mental disorder, a type of anxiety disorder (see the *Diagnostic and Statistical Manual of Mental Disorders* [DSM-IV, 1994], published by the American Psychiatric Association).

Across a series of studies conducted in three different countries, Burke and colleagues (Burke, Burgess, & Oberklaid, 2003; Burke & Matthiesen, 2004; Burke, Richardsen, & Martinussen, 2004) examined the relationship between passion and addiction to work (e.g., compulsive work). Results from all three studies showed passion and addiction demonstrated opposite relationships with outcomes; passion was positively related to satisfaction and health outcomes, whereas addiction was negatively related to both. The authors concluded that obsessive passion and addiction may be considered opposite constructs to one another.

In terms of the relationship between passion and engagement, studies have shown that harmonious and obsessive passion are distinct constructs from engagement and related to engagement (e.g., Trépanier, Fernet, Austin, Forest, & Vallerand, 2014). Specifically, harmonious passion was positively related to engagement, whereas obsessive passion demonstrated no significant relationship to engagement (engagement was assessed using only the vigor component of the UWES). Moreover, both forms of passion were shown to mediate the relationship between job resources and job demands with engagement and burnout (see Trépanier et al., 2014). Using the JES in Study 1 and the UWES in Study 2, Birkeland and Buch (2015) found some overlap between harmonious passion and engagement and obsessive passion and workaholism; however, their overall evidence supports distinction between passion, engagement, and workaholism. Ho and Astakhova (2018) used Saks's (2006) measures of job and organization engagement and showed both harmonious and obsessive passion were related to organization engagement more than job engagement, though all correlations were moderate to high ($r = .38$ to $r = .57$). Tóth-Király, Morin, and Salmela-Aro (2020) study provides longitudinal evidence that engagement does not predict change over time in workaholism, nor vice versa, indicating the two constructs are distinct. Additionally, consistent with prior studies, engagement was positively associated with harmonious passion. Moreover, the authors showed that increases in engagement did not create or increase the risk of becoming a workaholic. Increases in workaholism were associated with reductions in employees' level of engagement, consistent with running out of steam from excessive workloads.

In sum, neither workaholism nor passion reflects the idea of too much engagement. As found in the studies reviewed earlier, engagement appears to be a separate construct from workaholism and passion.

If "Too Engaged" Is Not Workaholism or Passion, Then What Is It?

In her chapter on too much engagement, George (2010) suggested high levels of engagement interfere with conscious decision-making and problem-solving processes. Specifically, she argued when an employee is in a state of high engagement, problem-solving is limited because conscious thinking cannot access as much information as the nonconscious mind. Relying on the works of Wilson and colleagues (Wilson, 2002; Wilson, Dunn, Bybee, Hyman, & Rotondo, 1984; Wilson & Kraft, 1993a, 1993b; Wilson & Schooler, 1991), she concluded:

> high levels of engagement are necessary to acquire the knowledge and information relevant to decisions and judgments that come up on a job. When actually making complex decisions and judgments, perhaps, too much engagement and weighing pros and cons may be dysfunctional.
>
> *(George, 2010, p. 257)*

The argument here is when one allows the nonconscious mind to problem-solve and make decisions – essentially following one's "gut" (George, 2010, p. 256) – the greater capacity of the nonconscious mind is accessed and responds in a divergent, less restricted processing manner (Dijksterhuis & Nordgren, 2006; Dijksterhuis & van Olden, 2006; Wilson, 2002). Because most behavior is primarily nonconscious, driven by nonconscious thoughts and feelings, and performed automatically based on activated schemas, scripts, and predispositions (e.g., George, 2009; Glaser & Kihlstrom, 2005; Uleman & Bargh, 1989), using conscious thought to behave inhibits and limits access to the adaptive and accumulated knowledge stored in the nonconscious. One's thoughts, feelings, and behaviors can become faster, richer, and less structured or constrained if conscious intent is set aside. However, herein lies the problem according to George (2010); engagement has been defined as *conscious* thoughts, feelings, and behaviors (e.g., Kahn, 1990; Schaufeli, Salanova et al., 2002).

Assuming George's (2010) reasoning is correct, that conscious engagement can be dysfunctional in decision-making, creative work, and complex problem-solving, too much engagement can be detrimental to an organization. Some research has shown that better decisions are indeed made when relying on one's gut as opposed to simply relying on conscious problem-solving (Wilson, 2002; Wilson et al., 1984; Wilson & Kraft, 1993a, 1993b; Wilson & Schooler, 1991); therefore, organizations would benefit from fluctuating levels of employee engagement – precisely what George (2010) reasoned is most beneficial for employees themselves.

George (2010) further proposed that although engagement has been defined as a positive affective state, negative affect may be just as important to experience during moments of engagement. She suggested negative affect signals a problem exists that must be solved, mobilizing the mind and body to work on changing behavior or changing the situation (Damasio, 1999; Frijda, 1988; George, 2009). Thus, if engagement is limited to a positive affective state only, as is suggested in its definition (Kahn, 1990; Schaufeli, Martínez, Marques Pinto, Salanova, & Bakker, 2002), being engaged all the time may not be particularly beneficial to an organization. George's (2010) arguments are compelling in suggesting that how engagement is currently defined renders it a concept organizations should not want to continually push for from every employee at all times. Research on work recovery suggests employees need to periodically detach from work to replenish resources and energy (Sonnentag & Fritz, 2015), and studies show that micro-breaks enhance engagement (Steidle, Gonzalez-Morales, Hoppe, Michel, & O'Shea, 2017), further supporting the supposition that too much engagement is bad.

The Paradox of Engagement

There are other concerns for the dark side of engagement (i.e., engagement is not always good), even if we retain its current definition. As reviewed in earlier chapters in this book, researchers have shown engagement is associated with commitment, job involvement, and extra-role behaviors (e.g., Christian, Garza, & Slaughter, 2011; Karatepe, 2013). Although these outcomes are generally considered good for the organization, when taken to an extreme they become negative. For example, employees who are engaged in their current jobs and projects may become so committed to the project their commitment becomes rigid, so much so that changes become unacceptable. Siegrist et al. (2004) proposed *over-commitment to work* occurs when employees seek high job demands and extend their work efforts beyond what is expected of the organization, all in an effort to obtain approval. A similar construct in terms of high commitment, *goal commitment*, refers to an "attachment to or determination to reach a goal" (Locke & Latham, 1990, p. 125). Employees with high goal commitment are characterized as persistent, resisting distractions, and keeping to the goal even in the face of obstacles that would, under all other circumstances, deter others (Bipp & Kleinbeck, 2011). These characterizations are not unlike what has been attributed to engaged employees; engaged employees are characterized as persistent even when faced with challenges and can be so absorbed they lose track of time and filter out all distractions. Persistence to the point of not knowing when to stop or not stopping even when the organization wants you to becomes obsessive passion and a negative outcome for the organization. Likewise, failing to pay attention to important issues, including personal needs, borders on workaholic behavior that cannot be considered positive or good.

Workaholics are considered over-involved in their work, essentially taking job involvement to an extreme (Ng et al., 2007) and developing an irrational commitment to excessive work (Cherrington, 1980). Job involvement and workaholism are positively correlated (Mudrack & Naughton, 2001), such that when employees become excessively involved in their jobs, they become compulsive and rigid in their thinking and ability to change (Mudrack, 2004).

Employees with high job involvement tend to demonstrate obsessive-compulsive behaviors (Schwartz, 1982), but not necessarily to levels of impairment as with a personality disorder (Macdonald & de Silva, 1999). Like job involvement, although extra-role behaviors are beneficial to an organization (P. Podsakoff & MacKenzie, 1997), when taken to the extreme – such as demonstrated at the expense of the actual job requirements or in lieu of what is required on the job – they become negative.

Like other researchers, Shimazu, Schaufeli, Kubota, Watanabe, and Kawakami (2018) maintained that being too engaged leads to work–home interference because of the excess time and effort over-engaged employees spend at work. They further argued that over-engagement leads to psychological distress (e.g., irritability, anxiety, depression) because of chronic arousal and sustained psychophysiological arousal. Thus, the authors proposed too much engagement is bad. They did not assess psychophysiological arousal; however, the more engaged the employee, the more psychological distress they reported, though this distress disappeared over time. Contrary to their hypotheses, they concluded, "except for short-term effect on psychological distress, no dark side of work engagement was observed" (p. 14).

How the Paradox Supposedly Occurs

The organization plays a role in moving engagement from a good mental state that brings about positive outcomes to a state wherein the results are paradoxically negative for the organization. For example, just as pay-for-performance plans result in employees' overly focusing on their in-role job behaviors (i.e., only what is directly and formally expected; Deckop, Mangel, & Cirka, 1999), over-rewarding and overemphasizing engagement to get citizenship behaviors results in attention focused on extra-role behaviors to the detriment of in-role performance behaviors (Bergeron, 2007). Research has shown when workaholic behaviors are reinforced by the organization, employees are more likely to develop workaholic tendencies (e.g., Burke, 2001; Harpaz & Snir, 2003; Ng et al., 2007; Snir & Harpaz, 2004).

Similarly, individuals who become too focused on their own work and are rewarded for doing so fail to make contributions to teamwork necessary for successful team performance (Pfeffer, 1998). Overemphasis on individual employee engagement is likely to cause employees to refrain from helping their teammates (Deming, 1986; Pfeffer, 1998) because doing so takes away from their concentration, their mindful presence on their work, and their ability to express themselves in their work role – unless it is clear their work role subsumes being a collaborative team player. In individualistic countries, in particular, the focus of performance appraisal and work settings is on the individual as opposed to the team (Cable & Judge, 1996); hence, few employees are likely to see their primary role as being a team player.

It is widely known in organizations that what you focus on or reward is what you get (Hitt, 1995). Thus, engaged employees who are reinforced for their engagement levels may fall into extreme goal commitment and excessive attention to extra-role behaviors because they are rewarded for these behaviors. Some might argue, however, that engagement is a motivational state much like intrinsic motivation or it actually incorporates intrinsic motivation (Chalofsky & Krishna, 2009; Salanova & Schaufeli, 2008; Schaufeli et al., 2008), and therefore, external rewards inhibit and reduce motivational drive (Deci, Koestner, & Ryan, 1999; Deci & Ryan, 1985). Even though engagement may share conceptual space with intrinsic motivation and is positively related ($r = .35$; Rich et al., 2010), it has been shown to be distinct from intrinsic motivation (Rich et al., 2010). Therefore, it is unlikely rewards or reinforcement for being engaged will reduce levels of engagement.

WHAT DOES THE DARK SIDE OF ENGAGEMENT LOOK LIKE?

Panya works for Pine Investments and regularly helps others, offering to stay late or take on additional work that is not hers. She goes above and beyond on her own projects, ensuring customers are very happy with the solutions; they regularly provide positive ratings on her, sending in comments about how she remembers their kids' names and birthdays and about how she takes time to chat with them beyond the scheduled appointment slot.

Panya is known for championing new service products, especially the ones she likes. She works with marketing to make the brochures personal, almost as if she owns the product. Panya is well rewarded for her performance: she is considered one of the top paid employees and receives many accolades from the bosses. Panya would rate herself very engaged; she is energetic at work and energized by what she is doing. She is focused at work, feeling fulfilled by the accomplishments and from the meaningfulness she derives from helping others at work. Panya's engagement at work, however, makes others feel pressured to be as busy, excited, and as attached to the work role as she. Her teammates have stopped asking her for help because she gets so into the project that she takes over, forgetting that they asked for help and did not ask her to do it for them. Panya is highly rewarded for being the last-minute hero, but the supervisors overlook how that takes away from the contribution of all the others on the team who worked just as hard but earlier and for longer periods before the due date. Additionally, Panya considers herself a workaholic in the positive sense – she loves her job and that is why she works intensely at it – but others view her work habits as competitive. Because she loves what she does, Panya tends to agree to everything that comes her way, creating a workload bottleneck at times and difficulty for the boss to balance the workload across team members.

Recently, a project on which Panya put in overtime and excessive personal attention was cancelled. Panya was not willing to let go of the project and accept the cancellation decision; after all, she was enjoying the project and felt that it was the right thing for the organization to do. Her inability to let go created a lot of difficulty for the team, the boss, and herself. Because she was so into the project, she could not see that it really was best for the organization to cancel the project. Panya thinks she is doing what the organization wants from her because they keep talking about how critical it is that employees are engaged, and she is rewarded for her high engagement scores.

Panya's work involves focusing on a variety of tasks, but because Panya becomes engaged at work in the tasks she finds most meaningful, she loses sight of the big picture and the need to get all the tasks done. This results in unintended workflow and workload problems. Panya is so absorbed in what she is doing at work that she fails to see what she is not doing and how her engagement is not always best for the organization.

Conclusion

Engagement is considered a positive mental state of motivation, and thus far, positive outcomes have been associated with the construct. However, some researchers suggest there is a dark side to engagement, an unintended paradox wherein engagement is not necessarily always good for organizations. Organizations, consultants, and researchers, thus far, have not considered the possibility that engagement needs to be managed appropriately, and fluctuations in levels of engagement can be productive and necessary at the individual, group, and organizational levels. Recent research on engagement and recovery suggest that some recognize ongoing engagement may not be possible or may not be healthy (e.g., Sonnentag, Mojza, Demerouti, & Bakker, 2012; Steidle et al., 2017; ten Brummelhuis & Bakker, 2012).

Researchers can contribute to understanding engagement by examining the potential for unintended consequences of engaged employees, organizational policies, and actions that promote and reinforce engagement at the expense of managed workloads. Thus far, only a handful of studies exist clearly separating engagement from workaholism or passion. Longitudinal studies may help shed light on whether, over time, engagement leads to workaholism or whether harmonious passion over time leads to obsessive passion that then filters into either engagement and/or workaholism. Shimazu et al. (2018) suggested not; however, more studies are needed.

EMPLOYEES' REFLECTIONS

In one of my engagement consulting projects, an employee I interviewed reflected on workaholism and engagement: "There are times when I really have to look at myself and say okay, am I a workaholic, or am I? Is this just where I thrive? I think prior . . . I probably would have labeled myself as a workaholic, but now I think it's really your perspective. It's not about what I have to do, it's about what I want to do."

It may be that after much research, we might find there really is no dark side to engagement. However, like constructs introduced long before engagement, such as citizenship behaviors, more sounds better until we ponder whether there is a dark side and what it looks like.

WALK-AWAY POINTS

- Theoretical discourse has likened too much engagement to workaholism and obsessive passion; too much engagement has been related to burnout.
- For all intents and purposes, engagement is desirable in employees and can contribute to productive and positive results for the organization, but there is a dark side when engagement is not necessarily beneficial.
- Fluctuations and changes in engagement levels may be productive and necessary for both employees and their organizations.

11

SUMMING IT ALL UP

Where Do We Go From Here?

Grasping the ideas within an entire book is challenging, especially if one only reads a few chapters here and there. In this chapter, I summarize the general ideas and contributions of the book and offer perspectives on next steps in the employee engagement landscape.

The Current State of the Field

In Parts I and II of the book, I reviewed where we are today with understanding employee engagement. Current, dominant, definitions of engagement (e.g., Kahn, 1990; Macey & Schneider, 2008; Schaufeli, Salanova, González-Romá, & Bakker, 2002) suggest engaged employees:

1. Feel vigorous, demonstrating high levels of energy and persistence at work
2. Are dedicated, experiencing enthusiasm, pride, and significance in their work
3. Are absorbed in their work to the point of intense concentration, whereby they lose track of time and display an inability to stop working
4. Are mindful and present in their work roles
5. Are expressive emotionally, physically, and authentically
6. Can be stable in their levels of engagement or fluctuate from moment to moment or across other variants of time (e.g., day to day, across activities)
7. Experience their engagement in a process whereby their individual characteristics (e.g., personality) lead to them to feel engaged, all of which translate into performance behaviors on the job and positive psychological attitudes.

Employee/work engagement is different from other psychological constructs studied in the organizational sciences. It is a unique construct from job perfor

DOI: 10.4324/9781003171133-15

mance, organizational citizenship behavior, job involvement, job satisfaction, organizational commitment, intrinsic motivation, flow, and happiness. Different from these other constructs, engagement proposes employees invest themselves completely (emotionally, mentally, and physiologically) into their work roles and toward achieving the goals of the organization. With engagement, the head and the heart are aligned: individuals' harmonious passion follows their thinking, and their thinking follows their passion. Scholars and practitioners have described engaged workers as valuing their work and feeling they are doing what makes them most fulfilled and internally rewarded, while intellectually doing work fitting of their skills and capabilities. Engaged employees transform their work from day-to-day tasks that may be mechanical, automatic, and in some cases dehumanizing (Haslam, 2006) into something from which they derive meaning and purpose, and the organization thrives. Finally, employee engagement may synergistically incorporate intrinsic motivation, flow, involvement, passion, and physiological arousal, which result in behavioral displays of their engagement in the form of performance, citizenship behavior, satisfaction, happiness, and commitment.

Understanding what engagement is and how it is different from other known and understood constructs within the organizational sciences allows researchers and consultants to explore how to encourage engagement within organizations. Organizations and employees themselves contribute to whether they enter into a state of engagement. For example, leadership approaches such as full range, transformational, empowering, supportive, and interpersonal and applications of emotional intelligence are organizational interventions supporting the promotion of engagement in followers. Organizational changes to the immediate work environment, such as job redesign efforts in which attention is focused on providing core job dimensions of the job characteristics theory, job rotation and enrichment, and greater team interdependency in collectivistic societies can facilitate engagement. Additionally, employees gain psychological availability when provided with sufficient job resources offsetting the many job demands with which they struggle and are challenged. Most job resources come from the organization; however, others such as social connections and coworker support come from employees themselves. Likewise, enabling employees themselves to mentally job redesign through job crafting has been theorized and shown to facilitate engagement.

With some ideas of how to help employees become engaged, there is still the challenge of what to do about those who simply are not engaged (or not engaged often). What prevents employees from being engaged at work? Many researchers and practitioners refer to disengagement to define what engagement is or why engaged employees are so valuable to the organization (usually framed using lost and gained finances), but disengagement itself is rarely, if ever, defined. Kahn (1990) seems to be one of the few authors to explicitly define disengagement, and yet few researchers have taken up the charge to study and pursue what is disengagement and how it manifests itself in organizations. Burnout has been put forth as a possible construct capturing the idea of disengagement, but burnout fails to reflect a state that is not dysfunctional and also not energetic. Reflections on my own findings from qualitative work on exploring the idea of disengagement and what it means for people at work reveals that disengagement is different from burnout. Based on my research and on the theoretical and empirical work on engagement thus far, I offered in Chapter 5 a number of organizational and individual factors that appear to play a role in inhibiting employee engagement.

In Chapter 6, I offered a crash course in psychometrics, conveying what makes for a good measure of engagement and how to evaluate measures to determine if they are good. The consequences of poorly assessing engagement are grave for clarifying and understanding the construct. Namely, incorrect and/or less than accurate conclusions are drawn about engagement (or what we think is engagement), and correcting those conclusions later becomes very challenging, to say the least. Poor assessment means not really measuring engagement but measuring something else in its stead. Poor measurement is grave for organizational interventions as well. With poor measurement, organizational interventions may point to issues and changes other than what will have the intended consequence on engagement, and the domino effect continues. Having struggled myself when first starting in this field of study to find a good measure of engagement, and having been asked by colleagues, students, and clients to help them with assessing engagement, I decided it was essential in this book to provide a thorough review of existing measures of engagement. The accurate measurement of employee engagement is an area in need of attention. Developing measures, accumulating evidence, and then tweaking to improve those measures is necessary for understanding the construct of engagement and for developing effective interventions. Despite some initial evidence, there is no consensus on whether engagement is a fluctuating state beyond minor moment-to-moment changes, stable and consistent over time, or the same across all cultures. Without proper measures and rigorous study methods, we are not able to answer these questions.

Scholars suggest engaged employees create competitive advantage for organizations, and the development of a culture for engagement is essential toward this end. In my consulting work, clients often ask me whether they can select employees for engagement – is there a measure or a way to choose who is most likely to be an engaged employee? Researchers have not empirically studied whether engagement is a personality characteristic, which would require a longitudinal study with many points of assessment across a variety of situations. Researchers also have not yet established whether engagement is fully determined by situational characteristics or rather an interaction between person and situation. Lastly, I have not been able to find studies examining engagement within a selection context, such as within an actual longitudinal experimental (or quasi-experimental) predictive study. Therefore, I would not feel confident endorsing the measurement of a job candidate's engagement level, assuming this level will remain constant throughout their employment or even be their long-running average level of engagement. There is simply not enough data to support such an endorsement. It may be possible, though, to select employees based on stable attributes, such as conscientiousness, trait affectivity, and proactive personality (e.g., Cai, Cai, Sun, & Ma, 2018; Inceoglu & Warr, 2011; H. Kim, Shin, & Swanger, 2009; Young, Glerum, Wang, & Joseph, 2018), which research has shown are positively associated with engagement and also other welcome organizational constructs (e.g., performance).

Future: A Path Forward

In Part III of the book, I focused on how employee engagement can be a competitive advantage for organizations by drawing attention to the future of the field. I proposed a number of research agendas that advance the scientific study of employee engagement while creating a path for how organizations can consider fostering employee engagement to promote their employees' well-being, as well as their own (Chapter 7 was devoted to creating an organizational climate and culture for engagement).

Part IV of the book reflects the new frontiers of employee engagement. In Chapter 9, I focused on engagement around the globe, reviewing what we know about engagement internationally, and more importantly, I exposed the gaps in our understanding and challenges with filling those gaps. In Chapter 10, I reviewed the paradox of engagement, the idea that engagement may not always be a good thing for employees or their organizations. I also explained how workaholism is not the same as a "dark side" of engagement, as others have suggested.

Measuring Engagement: Getting It Right

The path forward in engagement requires good measures, as highlight in Chapter 6. The Utrecht Work Engagement Scale (UWES; Schaufeli & Bakker, 2003) has been widely circulated, yet a few studies examining the validity of the measure questioned the short form (Wefald, Mills, Smith, & Downey, 2012) and whether the UWES (regardless which form) measures a different construct than burnout (Cole, Walter, Bedeian, & O'Boyle, 2012). Researchers have steered away from the idea of engagement as the opposite of burnout, including the UWES's authors Schaufeli and Bakker (see Schaufeli, Salanova et al., 2002). Recently, Nimon and Shuck (2020) conducted secondary analyses of Cole et al.'s (2012) correlations and concluded the UWES was measuring something different from the Maslach Burnout Inventory, a well-known measure of burnout and the original template for the UWES. The widespread use of the UWES has resulted in substantial cumulative evidence of its ability to assess one or more of its dimensions: vigor, dedication, absorption – all dependent on which version of the UWES is used (e.g., UWES-17, UWES-9, UWES-3) or which dimension is isolated out of the measure (i.e., many researchers only assess one or two dimensions). As noted in Chapter 6, there are numerous variations on how the UWES is used, between the 17-, 9-, and 3-item versions; different numbers of dimensions used in any study; some items deleted from the measure; and several different types of response scales.

Other engagement measures, such as the job engagement scale (Rich, LePine, & Crawford, 2010) and Saks's (2006) job and organizational engagement scales, have less accumulated validity evidence than the UWES as of this date. However, less validity evidence thus far does not render these measures useless or poor; the evidence that does exist for them is solid. Finally, practitioners using their own non-academic measures tend not to provide psychometric evidence of their measures' validity, and their proprietary nature renders them both non-verifiable and inaccessible.

In sum, the opportunity exists for continuing to develop good measures of engagement, measures with accumulated, verifiable, validity evidence to support their use. Some researchers may be satisfied at this point with using the UWES. Others, wanting a refined or more narrow assessment of engagement, without the inclusion of potential antecedents or outcomes built into the measure, may prefer a scale like the JES (e.g., Byrne, Peters, & Weston, 2016) or continue their own scale development. What is most important is knowing what your measure assesses and confirming it does that well.

Using Engagement to Create Thriving Organizations

There is no lack of interest in employee engagement. To date, it has most frequently been studied in the context of well-being and overall health of employees. Turning this focus outward, in Chapter 8 I discussed how we can use employee engagement to create healthy and thriving organizations by introducing the idea of engagement contagion. Through the synergistic integration of emotional, cognitive, and behavioral contagions, I argued for engagement contagion as a means for how engaged employees create other engaged employees in the organization, eventually creating a healthy and thriving organization in which employees are engaged and self-reinforcing.

Although a few studies examining crossover of engagement exist (e.g., Bakker, Demerouti, & Schaufeli, 2005; Bakker, Shimazu, Demerouti, Shimada, & Kawakami, 2011; Bakker & Xanthopoulou, 2009), crossover is not engagement contagion. Specifically, crossover refers to the "dyadic, interindividual transmission of well-being between closely related individuals" (the exact phrase appears in both Bakker et al., 2011, p. 112, and Bakker & Xanthopoulou, 2009, p. 1563). As described in detail in Chapter 8, engagement contagion is a very different concept from crossover. As of yet, there are no studies examining engagement contagion, nor whether engagement contagion relates to the development of a thriving organization.

Cross-Cultural Studies of Engagement

Since the release of the first edition of this book, a substantial number of studies with engagement as one of the variables of study have relied on international samples. I specifically say "engagement as one of the variables of study" rather than "engagement studies" because nearly every international study was situated within a different literature than engagement (e.g., mental health, hospitality, nursing, leadership). A small number of those studies incorporated a sample from two or more different countries; however, the studies did not include a statistical comparison of engagement scores across cultures. Those that did were not oriented toward identifying or understanding whether or why engagement scores would be similar or different across cultures. One could claim that studies specifically designed to examine the validity of the UWES count for this purpose, as the mean scores of engagement are compared as a way of determining whether the UWES can be used in that country (e.g., Schaufeli, Shimazu, Hakanen, Salanova, & De Witte, 2019; Tran et al., 2020). I review my concern with studies across international samples in Chapter 9.

Most of the recent international studies appear to adopt the dominant academic definitions of engagement without first examining if those definitions make sense given the country norms and values. In a small handful of cases, researchers have compared scores across *countries*, but this is not necessarily the same as *cross-cultural* research. Chapter 9 was solely dedicated to shining a spotlight on the international perspective of engagement. The field of cross-cultural psychology is vast, and trying to squeeze in a comprehensive review of all theories and relevant empirical findings in cross-cultural psychology would be impossible. Instead, I used two well-known taxonomies of culture to offer suggestions for how engagement may vary (or not) by culture, and developed specific propositions that can be studied across cultures.

The Questionable Paradox of Engagement

Regardless of where researchers study engagement, they rely on definitions of engagement as a positive concept that no organization can do without. In Chapter 10, I asked the question, "But what if engagement is not always a good thing for organizations?" I reviewed research suggesting a *dark side* of engagement, a paradox wherein engagement, otherwise thought to be the solution to all that ails an organization, comes at the expense of several other highly desirable organizational constructs. The dark side of engagement is not the same as "too engaged," which some researchers have contended is the same as workaholism, burnout, and limited cognitive processing. A few recent studies have demonstrated the uniqueness of workaholism from engagement (e.g., Di Stefano & Gaudiino, 2019; Mazzetti, Schaufeli, & Guglielmi, 2018) and further clarified key conceptual differences (Clark, 2018). By incorporating the problem-solving signals that negative affectivity activates (George, 2010), engaged employees may become more aware of situations that need transforming and debates that need to be held to improve the work environment and work product. Whether there is such a thing as too much engagement or whether the dark side of engagement exists are empirical questions, ones that researchers can explore.

Other Considerations

The Stability (or Not) of Engagement

A gap in our understanding of engagement still exists in not knowing whether engagement is a moment-to-moment, intense, and short-lived experience (cf. emotion), a relatively stable state (cf. mood), a very stable state (cf. attitude), or a trait or individual difference characteristic (cf. personality). Opportunities exist for empirical research in answering the fundamental question: What is the "time" associated with engagement? Although there are studies in which researchers used diary sampling and experience sampling to assess engagement at various points in time, those studies did not seek to answer the questions of how and when engagement varied; the focus of the research was on whether resources and recovery time affect engagement measured once a day or once at the end of the week (e.g., Bakker & Bal, 2010; Petrou, Demerouti, Peeters, Schaufeli, & Hetland, 2012; Sonnentag, 2003; Xanthopoulou, Bakker, Demerouti, & Schaufeli, 2009; Xanthopoulou, Bakker, Heuven, Demerouti, & Schaufeli, 2008). Sonnentag, Dormann, and Demerouti (2010) provide a review of day-level and week-level studies conducted by themselves and their colleagues. However, like those listed above, studies reviewed in Sonnentag et al. (2010) primarily advance an understanding of how resources during the day relate to employees' responses to questions about their engagement. Studies wherein engagement is measured at two different time points does not provide insight into whether engagement fluctuates or not because it is not clear what is happening to engagement between time points or before/after time points. If, for example, engagement is relatively consistent within a narrow range of variability but fluctuates with dramatic work events, unless you just happened to measure engagement at one of those inflection points, you will not see much variability. You would conclude, incorrectly, that engagement does not fluctuate and may be more trait-like.

Research has shown that positive emotions on one day indirectly affect engagement the next day (Bledow, Schmitt, Frese, & Kühnel, 2011; Ouweneel, Le Blanc, Schaufeli, & van Wijhe, 2012; Sonnentag, Mojza, Demerouti, & Bakker, 2012). A recent study (Reis, Arndt, Lischetzke, & Hoppe, 2016) provides some insight into the variability of engagement within a day by examining whether work engagement (measured using the UWES) varies as much as emotions, which are short-lived, intense experiences (Davidson et al., 1994). In an experience sampling study, Reis et al. (2016) found that although employees' perception of their engagement levels, specifically vigor and absorption, varied within days and between days, they fluctuated less than emotions within days. Their results suggest engagement may be more like a mood (relatively stable and milder compared to an emotion; Davidson et al., 1994) than an emotion, but not as stable as an attitude or trait. Also using experience sampling, Weston (2016), a former student of mine, examined within-day and between-day variability in employee engagement (assessed using the JES) for his master's thesis. He found that although employees' afternoon engagement levels were significantly related to their morning engagement levels, other predictors of engagement, such as affect and stress, had a larger effect on individuals' current engagement than their previous levels of engagement. His results suggest that relatively little variance in current engagement levels can be explained by immediate preceding engagement levels, providing support for the conclusion that engagement may be more like a mood than an emotion. Though all these initial studies are promising and provide initial evidence indicating engagement is akin to a mood (i.e., somewhat stable with minor fluctuations throughout the day), much more research is required to examine fluctuations of engagement. One goal with this line of study is to determine whether engagement is stable enough to be used as a true predictor (not statistical only) of future performance.

Theory of Purposeful Work Behavior

Barrick, Mount, and Li (2013) proposed a theory of purposeful work behavior. The authors suggested that a motivational process results from the interaction of individual characteristics (i.e., personality) and situational characteristics (e.g., social and job environment), which leads to various work outcomes such as job satisfaction and performance behaviors (citizenship behavior, task performance). I have simplified the model in Figure 11.1 for illustration purposes.

Essentially, the model says person-by-situation effects on motivation are channeled through high-level achievement goals and experienced meaningfulness derived from work, resulting in motivated behavior. Barrick et al. (2013) proposed that one's personality is a key determinant of motivated behavior, which when combined with and understood in the context of the situational constraints and offerings results in a behavior set unique to each individual. When the situation allows for the full expression of one's personality, the more motivational drive is experienced: one can pursue one's goals as desired.

The authors stated, "a basic assumption in the theory of purposeful work behavior is that employee behavior is purposeful or directed toward the attainment of goals" (Barrick et al., 2013, p. 135). Goals, or personal agendas, as the authors refer to them, whether conscious or not, are important in the model as they specify toward what an individual is motivated. Personal agendas can

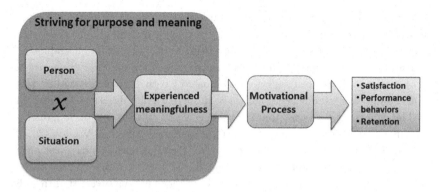

FIGURE 11.1 Adapted Model From Barrick et al.'s (2013) Theory of Purposeful Work Behavior

include communion (affiliation), status, autonomy, or achievement, and each is associated with one or more specific personality traits and situational characteristics. For example, if one strives for status, extraversion becomes more relevant over conscientiousness, openness to experience, emotional stability, or agreeableness, and the situation must support task significance, feedback from others, and the opportunity for power and influence.

The model holds promise for potentially explaining engagement. Other models, such as my own research reviewed in Chapter 4, are similar to the Barrick et al. (2013) model in that they consider the importance of contextual variables, and the development of psychological meaningfulness and feelings of purpose, which translate into outcomes via motivational processes. A number of researchers seem to be converging on the idea that various factors of the environment and person explain their striving for meaning and purpose, which results in motivational behavior (e.g., Kahn & Fellows, 2013; Lent, 2013).

Building on previous theoretical models and empirical findings of engagement reviewed in this book, an all-encompassing model of engagement might look (in its simplest form) like Figure 11.2.

The results of the interaction between personal environment, work environment, and person combine to predict engagement at work. I describe here what might fit into each block of the model (Figure 11.2).

Personal environment refers to the environment around the person, outside of the job. It might include:

- Social support and acceptance (e.g., family, friends)
- Life sustenance (consider the lower levels of Maslow's hierarchy: adequate money for living, comfortable place to live both in terms of house/roof over the head and community/country, adequate food, physical safety, health)
- Cognitive load (too much on your mind prevents you from being able to think or focus).

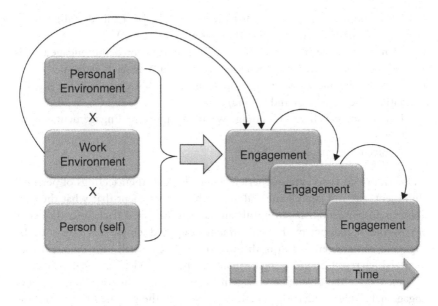

FIGURE 11.2   Z. Byrne's Proposed Model of Employee Engagement

Work environment refers to anything having to do with the workplace itself. It might include:

- Leadership (relational, transactional, visionary)
- Organizational vision
- Fit (between your values and those of the job and organization)
- Job dimensions (skill variety, task variety, autonomy when appropriate for culture)
- Meaningfulness (may include affiliation, meeting esteem needs, fulfilling ideals)
- Competence (ability to develop and demonstrate skills and capability)
- Growth (to build self-efficacy and keep learning)
- Reinforcement that engagement is desirable and highly regarded
- New and future oriented (work on something new as opposed to something that has no future)
- Resources, such as equipment to do your job, time to do it, communications to understand the job requirements
- Social support and acceptance (e.g., coworker support, friends at work)
- Culture (country, ethnic or religious, and organizational).

Person (self) refers to what the person brings to the workplace. This might include:

- Sense of calling – called to do the work
- Personality

- Head and heart alignment (what I feel about the job coincides/aligns with how I think about the job; I'm doing the "right" thing)
- Identification with the occupation, organization, or being engaged (it is part of your identity, who you are – you are an "engaged" person)
- Need for belongingness (my engagement fits with the norms of the organization; therefore, I fit and belong)
- Instrumental (Where am I going? What's my purpose? Engagement gets me there)
- Choice to be engaged.

Furthermore, as individuals experience engagement, their feelings of personal alignment, fit, and competence, along with reinforcement that what they are doing is instrumental, meaningful, and achievable, feed back into the work environment and personal environment. Engaged employees *choose* to be engaged, and are reinforced both internally and externally for their engagement, which results in more engagement. Thus, the model is cyclical, reflecting to some degree the idea of an engagement process – a self-sustaining model of engagement. The model additionally incorporates the passage of time and the idea that engagement in one moment affects engagement in the next moment, but it still recognizes that engagement may occur in chunks as opposed a single continuous stream of focus, energy, and thought.

EMPLOYEES' REFLECTIONS

I think someone who is truly engaged doesn't get there because someone else has facilitated that. I really believe that they get there because they have made a decision that this is for me and this is what I'm going to dig into because this is what I want to do and this is what I *choose* to do, and I see the possibilities.

Conclusion

When I wrote the first edition of this book, I stated that the study of employee engagement is still in its infancy. That is no longer true: engagement research has come a long way in a short time, though there is more to do. Even though evidence is accumulating, more can be done to clarify whether or how engagement can be fostered, managed, and utilized in organizations. Progress in several fundamental areas must be made to move these efforts forward. Table 11.1 lists (in alphabetical order) some of the areas of engagement in which progress has been made, as well as areas left to be explored, and the associated challenges or gaps still existing in those areas.

In this book, I have provided an up-to-date, comprehensive review of the theoretical and empirical works on employee engagement from a variety of perspectives, including academic and practice (though not as extensively as the academic view). It is my hope the chapters in this book provide essential knowledge and understanding of engagement as we understand it today and, importantly, spark conversation, research, and challenges to the ideas to move the field toward the future.

TABLE 11.1 Areas of Engagement With Their Respective Challenges and/or Gaps

Area	Challenges	Sub-challenges
Construct Consensus	Groups of engagement researchers ignoring or not having access to others' research	Academic and publication reward system
		Journal publication timing and review processes, including reviewers
Contagion	Measurement	Isolating infection from other ways of becoming engaged
	How to encourage	
Creating culture to foster engagement	Empirical evidence supporting effectiveness of solutions	Quasi-experimentation
		Too many variables
	Measuring change	
Cross-culture	Construct equivalence	Language barriers
	Measurement	
Dark side	Is there a dark side?	Isolating dark side of engagement from speculated but not legitimate constructs (e.g., workaholism)
	Measurement	What is the tipping point?
Definition	Consensus	
	Capturing time component	Measurement
	Cross-cultural	Translation
	Maintaining uniqueness or distinctiveness	
	Reflecting static concept or dynamic process concept	Measuring constantly changing construct
	Trait engagement	
	Is it on a continuum?	
	Multifocal engagement?	Isolating the foci

(Continued)

TABLE 11.1 (Continued)

Area	Challenges	Sub-challenges
Disengagement	Defining Measurement	What is the tipping point?
	Relationship with financial performance of organization	Measurement
Interventions	Collaboration with industry	Proof of utility of engagement to warrant an intervention
	Evaluation of effectiveness	Measurement
	Think outside the current boxes (e.g., beyond JD-R model)	Academic and publication reward system
Measurement	Improving existing measures	What adjustments or modifications are acceptable?
	Creating new and better measures	Requires clear definition
	Culturally free measures	Translation
	Multidimensional or unidimensional?	
	Long versus short	What is too long?
	Summing, averaging, or moment based	Stability of engagement
Shrinking science– practice gap	Should it be shrunk? Are practice and science talking about the same concept?	Specificity on language in practice
		Utility of research
Team engagement	Definition	What makes it different from engagement of individuals who just happened to be in a team?
	Measurement	Do you need agreement, like with climate constructs?
Theory development	Developing a new theory versus using existing theories	What other explanations might exist for engagement that are beyond the boundaries of current researchers' agendas?

WALK-AWAY POINTS

- We have developed a base of knowledge in employee engagement, a base that still has many holes. At this point, engagement appears to be a new construct, although it shares conceptual space with other similar and related constructs.
- There may be a dark side to engagement that suggests that it is not the answer to all that ails organizations today.
- The advancement of our understanding of engagement would progress faster and further if practice and academe were to join hands and collaborate more.
- Advancement of the field requires good measures, convergent on a clear definition, and evaluation studies of organizational interventions.
- Cross-cultural research (not just research in another country) is necessary to determine if engagement is a unique and relevant construct across the globe, or only unique to one or more cultures.

REFERENCES

Aboramadan, M., & Dahleez, K. A. (2020). Leadership styles and employees' work outcomes in nonprofit organizations: The role of work engagement. *Journal of Management Development, 39*(7/8), 869–893. http://dx.doi.org/10.1108/JMD-12-2019-0499

Adelmann, P. K., & Zajonc, R. B. (1989). Facial efference and the experience of emotion. *Annual Review of Psychology, 40*(1), 249–280. http://dx.doi.org/10.1146/annurev.ps.40.020189.001341

Adkins, C. L., Russell, C. J., & Werbel, J. D. (1994). Judgments of fit in the selection process: The role of work value congruence. *Personnel Psychology, 47*(3), 605–623. http://dx.doi.org/10.1111/j.1744-6570.1994.tb01740.x

AERA, APA, & NCME. (1999). *Standards for educational and psychological testing.* American Educational Research Association, American Psychological Association, National Council on Measurement in Education. Washington, DC: American Educational Research Association.

Agarwal, U. A., & Bhargava, S. (2013). Effects of psychological contract breach on organizational outcomes: Moderating role of tenure and educational levels. *Vikalpa: The Journal for Decision Makers, 38*(1), 13–25.

Agarwal, U. A., Datta, S., Blake-Beard, S., & Bhargava, S. (2012). Linking LMX, innovative work behaviour and turnover intentions: The mediating role of work engagement. *The Career Development International, 17*(3), 208–230. http://dx.doi.org/10.1108/13620431211241063

Ahearne, M., Mathieu, J., & Rapp, A. (2005). To empower or not to empower your sales force? An Empirical examination of the influence of leadership empowerment behavior on customer satisfaction and performance. *Journal of Applied Psychology, 90*(5), 945–955. http://dx.doi.org/10.1037/0021-9010.90.5.945

Ajzen, I. (2001). Nature and operation of attitudes. *Annual Review of Psychology, 52*(1), 27–58. http://dx.doi.org/10.1146/annurev.psych.52.1.27

Akhtar, R., Boustani, L., Tsivrikos, D., & Chamorro-Premuzic, T. (2015). The engageable personality: Personality and trait EI as predictors of work engagement. *Personality and Individual Differences, 73*, 44–49. http://dx.doi.org/10.1016/j.paid.2014.08.040

Akingbola, K., & van den Berg, H. A. (2019). Antecedents, consequences, and context of employee engagement in nonprofit organizations. *Review of Public Personnel Administration, 39*(1), 46–74. http://dx.doi.org/10.1177/0734371X16684910

Alarcon, G. M., & Lyons, J. B. (2011). The relationship of engagement and job satisfaction in working samples. *Journal of Psychology: Interdisciplinary and Applied, 145*(5), 463–480. http://dx.doi.org/10.1080/00223980.2011.584083

Albrecht, S. L. (2015). Challenge demands, hindrance demands, and psychological need satisfaction: Their influence on employee engagement and emotional exhaustion. *Journal of Personnel Psychology, 14*(2), 70–79. http://dx.doi.org/10.1027/1866-5888/a000122

Albrecht, S. L., Breidahl, E., & Marty, A. (2018). Organizational resources, organizational engagement climate, and employee engagement. *The Career Development International, 23*(1), 67–85. http://dx.doi.org/10.1108/CDI-04-2017-0064

Albrecht, S. L., & Marty, A. (2020). Personality, self-efficacy and job resources and their associations with employee engagement, affective commitment and turnover intentions. *The International Journal of Human Resource Management, 31*(5), 657–681. http://dx.doi.org/10.1080/09585192.2017.1362660

Alderfer, C. P. (1972). *Existence, relatedness, and growth: Human needs in organizational settings.* New York, NY: The Free Press.

Alfes, K., Veld, M., & Fürstenberg, N. (2020). The relationship between perceived high-performance work systems, combinations of human resource well-being and human resource performance attributions and engagement. *Human Resource Management Journal,* 1–24. http://dx.doi.org/10.1111/1748-8583.12310

Allen, K., van Someren, G., & Gutierrez, S. (2020). What's age got to do with it? You may be surprised! *Industrial and Organizational Psychology: Perspectives on Science and Practice, 13*(3), 403–407. http://dx.doi.org/10.1017/iop.2020.68

Allen, N. J., & Meyer, J. P. (1990). The measurement and antecedents of affective, continuance and normative commitment to the organization. *Journal of Occupational Psychology, 63*(1), 1–18. http://dx.doi.org/10.1111/j.2044-8325.1990.tb00506.x

Allen, R. W., Madison, D. L., Porter, L. W., Renwick, P. A., & Mayes, B. T. (1979). Organizational politics. *California Management Review, 22*(1), 77–83.

Allport, G. W. (1961). *Pattern and growth in personality.* New York, NY: Holt, Rinehart, and Winston.

Alpers, G. W., Adolph, D., & Pauli, P. (2011). Emotional scenes and facial expressions elicit different psychophysiological responses. *International Journal of Psychophysiology, 80*(3), 173–181. http://dx.doi.org/10.1016/j.ijpsycho.2011.01.010

Amabile, T. M., Conti, R., Coon, H., Lazenby, J., & Herron, M. (1996). Assessing the work environment for creativity. *Academy of Management Journal, 39*(5), 1154–1184. http://dx.doi.org/10.2307/256995

Andersson, L. M., & Pearson, C. M. (1999). Tit for tat? The spiraling effect of incivility in the workplace. *Academy of Management Review, 24*(3), 452–471. http://dx.doi.org/10.5465/AMR.1999.2202131

Andreassen, C., Ursin, H., & Eriksen, H. R. (2007). The relationship between strong motivation to work, "workaholism," and health. *Psychology & Health, 22*(5), 615–629. http://dx.doi.org/10.1080/14768320600941814

Anthony-McMann, M. P. E., Ellinger, A. D., Astakhova, M., & Halbesleben, J. R. B. (2017). Exploring different operationalizations of employee engagement and their relationships with workplace stress and burnout. *Human Resource Development Quarterly, 28*(2), 163–195. http://dx.doi.org/10.1002/hrdq.21276

Arendasy, M., Sommer, M., & Hergovich, A. (2007). Statistical judgment formation in personnel selection: A study in military aviation psychology. *Military Psychology, 19*(2), 119–136. http://dx.doi.org/10.1080/08995600701323418

Arnetz, J. E., Sudan, S., Fitzpatrick, L., Cotten, S. R., Jodoin, C., & Chang, C. (Daisy), & Arnetz, B. B. (2018). Organizational determinants of bullying and work disengagement among hospital nurses. *Journal of Advanced Nursing, 75*(6), 1229–1238. http://dx.doi.org/10.1111/jan.13915

Arnold, K. A., Turner, N., Barling, J., Kelloway, E. K., & McKee, M. C. (2007). Transformational leadership and psychological well-being: The mediating role of meaningful work. *Journal of Occupational Health Psychology, 12*(3), 193–203. http://dx/doi.org/10.1037/1076-8998.12.3.193

Aryee, S., Budhwar, P. S., & Chen, Z. X. (2002). Trust as a mediator of the relationship between organizational justice and work outcomes: Test of a social exchange model. *Journal of Organizational Behavior, 23*(3), 267–286. http://dx.doi.org/10.1002/job.138

Aryee, S., Walumbwa, F. O., Zhou, Q., & Hartnell, C. A. (2012). Transformational leadership, innovative behavior, and task performance: Test of mediation and moderation processes. *Human Performance, 25*(1), 1–25. http://dx.doi.org/10.1080/08959285.2011.631648

Ashforth, B. E., & Kreiner, G. E. (2013). Profane or profound? Finding meaning in dirty work. In B. J. Dik, Z. S. Byrne, & M. F. Steger (Eds.), *Purpose and meaning in the workplace* (pp. 127–130). Washington, DC: American Psychological Association.

Ashforth, B. E., & Mael, F. (1989). Social identity theory and the organization. *The Academy of Management Review, 14*(1), 20–39. http://dx.doi.org/10.2307/258189

Ashmos, D. P., & Duchon, D. (2000). Spirituality at work. *Journal of Management Inquiry, 9*(2), 134–146. http://dx.doi.org/10.1177/105649260092008

Aslam, U., Muqadas, F., Imran, M. K., & Rahman, U. U. (2018). Investigating the antecedents of work disengagement in the workplace. *Journal of Management Development, 37*(2), 149–164. http://dx.doi.org/10.1108/JMD-06-2017-0210

Auh, S., Menguc, B., Spyropoulou, S., & Wang, F. (2016). Service employee burnout and engagement: The moderating role of power distance orientation. *Journal of the Academy of Marketing Science, 44*(6), 726–745. http://dx.doi.org/10.1007/s11747-015-0463-4

Avolio, B. J. (1999). *Full leadership development: Building the vital forces in organizations.* Thousand Oaks, CA: Sage.

Avolio, B. J. (2011). *Full range leadership development* (2nd ed.). Thousand Oaks, CA: Sage.

Avolio, B. J., & Bass, B. M. (1994). Evaluate the impact of transformational leadership training at individual, group, organizational and community levels. *Final Report to the W.K. Kellogg Foundation.* Binghamton University, Binghamton, NY.

Avolio, B. J., & Bass, B. M. (Eds.). (2002). *Developing potential across a full range of leadership: Cases on transactional and transformational leadership.* Mahwah, NJ: Lawrence Erlbaum Associates Publishers.

Avolio, B. J., Gardner, W. L., Walumbwa, F. O., Luthans, F., & May, D. R. (2004). Unlocking the mask: A look at the process by which authentic leaders impact follower attitudes and behaviors. *The Leadership Quarterly, 15*(6), 801–823. http://dx.doi.org/10.1016/j.leaqua.2004.09.003

Azeem, M. U., Bajwa, S. U., Shahzad, K., & Aslam, H. (2020). Psychological contract violation and turnover intention: The role of job dissatisfaction and work disengagement. *Employee Relations, 42*(6), 1291–1308. http://dx.doi.org/10.1108/ER-09-2019-0372

Azen, R., & Budescu, D. V. (2003). The dominance analysis approach for comparing predictors in multiple regression. *Psychological Methods*, *8*(2), 129–148. http://dx.doi.org/10.1037/1082-989X.8.2.129

Baethge, A., Junker, N. M., & Rigotti, T. (2020). Does work engagement physiologically deplete? Results from a daily diary study. *Work & Stress*. http://dx.doi.org/10.1080/02678373.2020.1857466

Bailenson, J. N., & Yee, N. (2005). Digital chameleons: Automatic assimilation of nonverbal gestures in immersive virtual environments. *Psychological Science*, *16*(10), 814–819. http://dx.doi.org/10.1111/j.1467-9280.2005.01619.x

Bailey, C., Yeoman, R., Madden, A., Thompson, M., & Kerridge, G. (2019). A review of the empirical literature on meaningful work: Progress and research agenda. *Human Resource Development Review*, *18*(1), 83–113. http://dx.doi.org/10.1177/1534484318804653

Bakker, A. B. (2009). Building engagement in the workplace. In R. J. Burke & C. L. Cooper (Eds.), *The peak performing organization* (pp. 50–72). Oxford: Routledge.

Bakker, A. B. (2010). Engagement and "job crafting": Engaged employees create their own great place to work. In S. L. Albrecht (Ed.), *Handbook of employee engagement: Perspectives, issues, research and practice* (pp. 229–244). Northampton, MA: Edward Elgar.

Bakker, A. B., & Bal, P. (2010). Weekly work engagement and performance: A study among starting teachers. *Journal of Occupational and Organizational Psychology*, *83*(1), 189–206. http://dx.doi.org/10.1348/096317909X402596

Bakker, A. B., & Demerouti, E. (2008). Towards a model of work engagement. *The Career Development International*, *13*(3), 209–223. http://dx.doi.org/10.1108/13620430810870476

Bakker, A. B., Demerouti, E., & Schaufeli, W. B. (2005). The crossover of burnout and work engagement among working couples. *Human Relations*, *58*(5), 661–689. http://dx.doi.org/10.1177/0018726705055967

Bakker, A. B., Hakanen, J. J., Demerouti, E., & Xanthopoulou, D. (2007). Job resources boost work engagement, particularly when job demands are high. *Journal of Educational Psychology*, *99*(2), 274–284. http://dx.doi.org/10.1037/0022-0663.99.2.274

Bakker, A. B., & Oerlemans, W. G. M. (2016). Momentary work happiness as a function of enduring burnout and work engagement. *Journal of Psychology: Interdisciplinary and Applied*, *150*(6), 755–778. http://dx.doi.org/10.1080/00223980.2016.1182888

Bakker, A. B., & Oerlemans, W. G. M. (2019). Daily job crafting and momentary work engagement: A self-determination and self-regulation perspective. *Journal of Vocational Behavior*, *112*, 417–430. http://dx.doi.org/10.1016/j.jvb.2018.12.005

Bakker, A. B., Rodríguez-Muñoz, A., & Vergel, A. I. S. (2016). Modelling job crafting behaviours: Implications for work engagement. *Human Relations*, *69*(1), 169–189. http://dx.doi.org/10.1177/0018726715581690

Bakker, A. B., Schaufeli, W. B., Leiter, M. P., & Taris, T. W. (2008). Work engagement: An emerging concept in occupational health psychology. *Work & Stress*, *22*(3), 187–200. http://dx.doi.org/10.1080/02678370802393649

Bakker, A. B., Shimazu, A., Demerouti, E., Shimada, K., & Kawakami, N. (2011). Crossover of work engagement among Japanese couples: Perspective taking by both partners. *Journal of Occupational Health Psychology*, *16*(1), 112–125. http://dx.doi.org/10.1037/a0021297

Bakker, A. B., Tims, M., & Derks, D. (2012). Proactive personality and job performance: The role of job crafting and work engagement. *Human Relations*, *65*(10), 1359–1378. http://dx.doi.org/10.1177/0018726712453471

Bakker, A. B., & van Wingerden, J. (2021). Do personal resources and strengths use increase work engagement? The effects of a training intervention. *Journal of Occupational Health Psychology*, *26*(1), 20–30. http://dx.doi.org/10.1037/ocp0000266

Bakker, A. B., & Xanthopoulou, D. (2009). The crossover of daily work engagement: Test of an actor: Partner interdependence model. *Journal of Applied Psychology, 94*(6), 1562–1571. http://dx.doi.org/10.1037/a0017525

Bal, P. M., & De Lange, A. H. (2015). From flexibility human resource management to employee engagement and perceived job performance across the lifespan: A multisample study. *Journal of Occupational and Organizational Psychology, 88*(1), 126–154. http://dx.doi.org/10.1111/joop.12082

Baltes, B. B., Zhdanova, L. S., & Clark, M. A. (2011). Examining the relationships between personality, coping strategies, and work–family conflict. *Journal of Business and Psychology, 26*(4), 517–530. http://dx.doi.org/10.1007/s10869-010-9207-0

Bandura, A. (1997). *Self-efficacy: The exercise of control.* New York: Freeman.

Bargh, J. A., Chen, M., & Burrows, L. (1996). Automaticity of social behavior: Direct effects of trait construct and stereotype activation on action. *Journal of Personality and Social Psychology, 71*(2), 230–244. http://dx.doi.org/10.1037/0022-3514.71.2.230

Barling, J., Weber, T., & Kelloway, E. K. (1996). Effects of transformational leadership training on attitudinal and financial outcomes: A field experiment. *Journal of Applied Psychology, 81*, 827–832. http://dx.doi.org/10.1037/0021-9010.81.6.827

Barrick, M. R., Mount, M. K., & Li, N. (2013). The theory of purposeful work behavior: The role of personality, higher-order goals, and job characteristics. *The Academy of Management Review, 38*(1), 132–153. http://dx.doi.org/10.5465/amr.2010.0479

Barsade, S. G. (2002). The ripple effects: Emotional contagion and its influence on group behavior. *Administrative Science Quarterly, 47*(4), 644–675. http://dx.doi.org/10.2307/3094912

Bartone, P. T., Roland, R. R., Picano, J. J., & Williams, T. J. (2008). Psychological hardiness predicts success in U.S. Army Special Forces candidates. *International Journal of Selection and Assessment, 16*(1), 78–81. http://dx.doi.org/10.1111/j.1468-2389.2008.00412.x

Basit, A. A. (2017). Trust in supervisor and job engagement: Mediating effects of psychological safety and felt obligation. *Journal of Psychology, 151*(8), 701–721. http://dx.doi.org/10.1080/00223980.2017.1372350

Bass, B. M. (1985). *Leadership and performance beyond expectations.* New York: The Free Press.

Bass, B. M. (1998). *Transformational leadership: Industrial, military, and educational impact.* Mahwah, NJ: Lawrence Erlbaum Associates.

Bass, B. M., & Avolio, B. J. (1990). *Transformational leadership development: Manual for the multifactor leadership questionnaire.* Palo Alto, CA: Consulting Psychologist Press.

Bateman, T. S., & Crant, J. (1993). The proactive component of organizational behavior: A measure and correlates. *Journal of Organizational Behavior, 14*(2), 103–118. http://dx.doi.org/10.1002/job.4030140202

Bateman, T. S., Griffin, R. W., & Rubinstein, D. (1987). Social information processing and group-induced shifts in responses to task design. *Group & Organization Studies, 12*(1), 88–108. http://dx.doi.org/10.1177/105960118701200107

Bateman, T. S., & Organ, D. W. (1983). Job satisfaction and the good soldier: The relationship between affect and employee "citizenship." *Academy of Management Journal, 26*(4), 587–595. http://dx.doi.org/10.2307/255908

Baugher, J. E., & Roberts, J. (2004). Workplace hazards, unions, and coping styles. *Labor Studies Journal, 29*(2), 83–106.

Baumeister, R. F. (1991). *Meanings in life.* New York, NY: Guilford Press. http://dx.doi.org/10.1207/s15327965pli0704_2

Baumeister, R. F., & Leary, M. R. (1995). The need to belong: Desire for interpersonal attachments as a fundamental human motivation. *Psychological Bulletin, 117*(3), 497–529. http://dx.doi.org/10.1037/0033-2909.117.3.497

Baumeister, R. F., & Vohs, K. D. (2002). The pursuit of meaningfulness in life. In C. R. Snyder & S. J. Lopez (Eds.), *The handbook of positive psychology* (pp. 608–619). New York: Oxford University Press.

Bavelas, J. B., Black, A., Lemery, C. R., & Mullett, J. (1986). "I show how you feel": Motor mimicry as a communicative act. *Journal of Personality and Social Psychology, 50*(2), 322–329. http://dx.doi.org/10.1037/0022-3514.50.2.322

Becherer, R. C., Morgan, F. W., & Richard, L. M. (1982). The job characteristics of industrial salespersons: Relationships to motivation and satisfaction. *Journal of Marketing, 46*, 125–135. http://dx.doi.org/10.2307/1251368

Becker, H. S. (1960). Notes on the concept of commitment. *American Journal of Sociology, 66*, 32–40. http://dx.doi.org/10.1086/222820

Becker, T. E. (1992). Foci and bases of commitment: Are they distinctions worth making? *Academy of Management Journal, 35*(1), 232–244. http://dx.doi.org/10.2307/256481

Beehr, T. A., & Gupta, N. (1978). A note on the structure of employee withdrawal. *Organizational Behavior & Human Performance, 21*(1), 73–79.

Behson, S. J., Eddy, E. R., & Lorenzet, S. J. (2000). The importance of the critical psychological states in the job characteristics model: A meta-analytic and structural equations modeling examination. *Current Research in Social Psychology, 5*(12), 170–189.

Berg, J. M., Dutton, J. E., & Wrzesniewski, A. (2013). Job crafting and meaningful work. In B. J. Dik, Z. S. Byrne, & M. F. Steger (Eds.), *Purpose and meaning in the workplace.* (pp. 81–104). Washington, DC: American Psychological Association.

Berg, J. M., Grant, A. M., & Johnson, V. (2010). When callings are calling: Crafting work and leisure in pursuit of unanswered occupational callings. *Organization Science, 21*(5), 973–994. http://dx.doi.org/10.1287/orsc.1090.0497

Berga, L., & Muzikante, I. (2017). What should we do after work to feel engaged the next day? relationship between daily work engagement, psychological detachment from work and off-job activities. *Baltic Journal of Psychology, 18*(1/2), 23–39.

Bergeron, D. M. (2007). The potential paradox of organizational citizenship behavior: Good citizens at what cost? *Academy of Management Review, 32*(4), 1078–1095. http://dx.doi.org/10.5465/AMR.2007.26585791

Berlyne, D. E. (1966). Curiosity and exploration. *Science, 153*, 25–33. http://dx.doi.org/10.1126/science.153.3731.25

Bhatnagar, J. (2012). Management of innovation: Role of psychological empowerment, work engagement and turnover intention in the Indian context. *The International Journal of Human Resource Management, 23*(5), 928–951. http://dx.doi.org/10.1080/09585192.2012.651313

Bies, R. J. (1987). The predicament of injustice: The management of moral outrage. In L. L. Cummings & B. M. Staw (Eds.), *Research in organizational behavior* (Vol. 9, pp. 289–319). Greenwich, CT: JAI Press.

Bies, R. J., & Moag, J. S. (1986). Interactional justice: Communication criteria of fairness. In R. J. Lewicki, B. H. Sheppard, & M. H. Bazerman (Eds.), *Research on negotiation in organizations* (Vol. 1, pp. 43–55). Greenwich, CT: JAI Press.

Bies, R. J., & Tripp, T. M. (2005). The study of revenge in the workplace: Conceptual, ideological, and empirical issues. In S. Fox & P. E. Spector (Eds.), *Counterproductive work behavior: Investigations of actors and targets* (pp. 65–81). Washington, DC: American Psychological Association. http://dx.doi.org/10.1037/10893-003

Biggs, A., Brough, P., & Barbour, J. P. (2013). Strategic alignment with organizational priorities and work engagement: A multi-wave analysis. *Journal of Organizational Behavior*, Advanced online publication. http://dx.doi.org/10.1002/job.1866

"Enhancing work-related attitudes and work engagement: A quasi-experimental study of the impact of an organizational intervention": Correction to Biggs, Brough, & Barbour (2013). (2014). *International Journal of Stress Management, 21*(1), 68. http://dx.doi.org/10.1037/a0035865

Bilotta, I., Cheng, S. K., Ng, L. C., Corrington, A. R., Watson, I., Paoletti, J., . . . King, E. B. (2021). Remote communication amid the coronavirus pandemic: Optimizing interpersonal dynamics and team performance. *Industrial and Organizational Psychology, 14*, 36–40. http://dx.doi.org/10.1017/iop.2021.10

Binning, J. F., & Barrett, G. V. (1989). Validity of personnel decisions: A conceptual analysis of the inferential and evidential bases. *Journal of Applied Psychology, 74*(3), 478–494. http://dx.doi.org/10.1037/0021-9010.74.3.478

Bipp, T., & Kleinbeck, U. (2011). The effect of neuroticism in the process of goal pursuit. *Personality and Individual Differences, 51*(4), 454–459. http://dx.doi.org/10.1016/j.paid.2011.04.014

Birkeland, I. K., & Buch, R. (2015). The dualistic model of passion for work: Discriminate and predictive validity with work engagement and workaholism. *Motivation and Emotion, 39*(3), 392–408. http://dx.doi.org/10.1007/s11031-014-9462-x

Biswas, S., & Bhatnagar, J. (2013). Mediator analysis of employee engagement: Role of perceived organizational support, P-O Fit, organizational commitment and job satisfaction. *Vikalpa: The Journal For Decision Makers, 38*(1), 27–40.

Blau, P. M. (1964). *Exchange and power in social life.* New York: Wiley & Sons.

Bledow, R., Schmitt, A., Frese, M., & Kühnel, J. (2011). The affective shift model of work engagement. *Journal of Applied Psychology, 96*(6), 1246–1257. http://dx.doi.org/10.1037/a0024532

Borman, W. C., & Motowidlo, S. J. (1997). Task performance and contextual performance: The meaning for personnel selection research. *Human Performance, 10*(2), 99–109. http://dx.doi.org/10.1207/s15327043hup1002_3

Bosch, C., Sonnentag, S., & Pinck, A. S. (2018). What makes for a good break? A diary study on recovery experiences during lunch break. *Journal of Occupational & Organizational Psychology, 91*(1), 134–157. http://dx.doi.org/10.1111/joop.12195

Breevaart, K., & Bakker, A. B. (2018). Daily job demands and employee work engagement: The role of daily transformational leadership behavior. *Journal of Occupational Health Psychology, 23*(3), 338–349. http://dx.doi.org/10.1037/ocp0000082

Breevaart, K., Bakker, A. B., Demerouti, E., & Derks, D. (2016). Who takes the lead? A multi-source diary study on leadership, work engagement, and job performance. *Journal of Organizational Behavior, 37*(3), 309–325. http://dx.doi.org/10.1002/job.2041

Breevaart, K., Bakker, A. B., Hetland, J., Demerouti, E., Olsen, O. K., & Espevik, R. (2014). Daily transactional and transformational leadership and daily employee engagement. *Journal of Occupational and Organizational Psychology, 87*(1), 138–157. http://dx.doi.org/10.1111/joop.12041

Brett, J. M., Tinsley, C. H., Janssens, M., Barsness, Z. I., & Lytle, A. L. (1997). New approaches to the study of culture in industrial/organizational psychology. In P. C. Earley & M. Erez (Eds.), *New perspectives on international industrial/organizational psychology* (pp. 75–129). San Francisco, CA: New Lexington Press.

Bretz, R. D., Ash, R. A., & Dreher, G. F. (1989). Do people make the place? An examination of the attraction-selection-attrition hypothesis. *Personnel Psychology, 42*(3), 561–581. http://dx.doi.org/10.1111/j.1744-6570.1989.tb00669.x

Britt, T. W. (1999). Engaging the self in the field: Testing the triangle model of responsibility. *Personality and Social Psychology Bulletin, 25*(6), 696–706.

Britt, T. W., & Bliese, P. D. (2003). Testing the stress-buffering effects of self engagement among soldiers on a military operation. *Journal of Personality, 71*(2), 245–266.

Britt, T. W., McKibben, E. S., Greene-Shortridge, T. M., Odle-Dusseau, H. N., & Herleman, H. A. (2012). Self-engagement moderates the mediated relationship between organizational constraints and organizational citizenship behaviors via rated leadership. *Journal of Applied Social Psychology, 42*(8), 1830–1846. http://dx.doi.org/10.1111/j.1559-1816.2012.00920.x

Brooke, P. P., Russell, D. W., & Price, J. L. (1988). Discriminant validation of measures of job satisfaction, job involvement, and organizational commitment. *Journal of Applied Psychology, 73*(2), 139–145. http://dx.doi.org/10.1037/0021-9010.73.2.139

Brophy, J., Rohrkemper, M., Rashid, H., & Goldberger, M. (1983). Relationships between teachers' presentations of classroom tasks and students' engagement in those tasks. *Journal of Educational Psychology, 75*(4), 544–552. http://dx.doi.org/10.1037/0022-0663.75.4.544

Brown, A., Kitchell, M., O'Neill, T., Lockliear, J., Vosler, A., Kubek, D., & Dale, L. (2001). Identifying meaning and perceived satisfaction within the context of work. *Work, 16,* 219–226.

Brown, K., & Ryan, R. M. (2003). The benefits of being present: Mindfulness and its role in psychological well-being. *Journal of Personality and Social Psychology, 84*(4), 822–848. http://dx.doi.org/10.1037/0022-3514.84.4.822

Brown, S. B. (1996). A meta-analysis and review of organizational research on job involvement. *Psychological Bulletin, 20,* 235–255. http://dx.doi.org/10.1037//0033-2909.120.2.235

Brown, S. P., & Leigh, T. W. (1996). A new look at psychological climate and its relationship to job involvement, effort, and performance. *Journal of Applied Psychology, 81,* 358–368. http://dx.doi.org/10.1037/0021-9010.81.4.358

Brown, T. A. (2006). *Confirmatory factor analysis for applied research.* New York, NY: Guilford Press.

Brown, W., & May, D. (2012). Organizational change and development: The efficacy of transformational leadership training. *Journal of Management Development, 31*(6), 520–536. http://dx.doi.org/10.1108/02621711211230830

Brunetto, Y., Teo, S. T., Shacklock, K., & Farr-Wharton, R. (2012). Emotional intelligence, job satisfaction, well-being and engagement: Explaining organisational commitment and turnover intentions in policing. *Human Resource Management Journal, 22*(4), 428–441. http://dx.doi.org/10.1111/j.1748-8583.2012.00198.x

Buckingham, M., & Coffman, C. (1999). *First, break all the rules: What the world's greatest managers do differently.* New York, NY: Simon & Schuster.

Bui, H. T. M., Zeng, Y., & Higgs, M. (2017). The role of person-job fit in the relationship between transformational leadership and job engagement. *Journal of Managerial Psychology, 32*(5), 373–386. http://dx.doi.org/10.1108/JMP-05-2016-0144

Buitendach, J. H., Bobat, S., Muzvidziwa, R. F., & Kanengoni, H. (2016). Work engagement and its relationship with various dimensions of work-related well-being in the public transport industry. *Psychology and Developing Societies, 28*(1), 50–72. http://dx.doi.org/10.1177/0971333615622895

Bukowski, W. M., Motzoi, C., & Meyer, F. (2009). Friendship as process, function, and outcome. In K. H. Rubin, V. M. Bukowski, & B. Laursen (Eds.), *Handbook of peer interactions, relationships, and groups* (pp. 217–231). New York: Guilford Press.

Burch, T. C., & Guarana, C. L. (2014). The comparative influences of transformational leadership and leader: Member exchange on follower engagement. *Journal of Leadership Studies, 8*(3), 6–25. http://dx.doi.org/10.1002/jls.21334

Burke, R. J. (2001). Workaholism in organizations: The role of organizational values. *Personnel Review, 30*(6), 637–645. http://dx.doi.org/10.1108/EUM0000000005977

Burke, R. J. (2009). Working to live or living to work: Should individuals and organizations care? *Journal of Business Ethics, 84*, 167–172. http://dx.doi.org/10.1007/s10551-008-9703-6

Burke, R. J. (2010). Flow, work satisfaction and psychological well-being at the workplace. *IUP Journal of Soft Skills, 4*(1/2), 37–48.

Burke, R. J., Burgess, Z., & Oberklaid, F. (2003). Workaholism and divorce among Australian psychologists. *Psychological Reports, 93*(1), 91–92.

Burke, R. J., & Matthiesen, S. (2004). Workaholism among Norwegian journalists: Antecedents and consequences. *Stress & Health: Journal of the International Society for the Investigation of Stress, 20*(5), 301–308. http://dx.doi.org/10.1002/smi.1025

Burke, R. J., Richardsen, A. M., & Martinussen, M. (2004). Workaholism among Norwegian senior managers: New research directions. *International Journal of Management, 21*(4), 415–426.

Burns, J. M. (1978). *Leadership*. New York: Harper and Row. http://dx.doi.org/10.1177/1745691610393980

Burtaverde, V., & Iliescu, D. (2019). Emic vs etic frame of reference personality assessment in the prediction of work-related outcomes. *Career Development International, 24*(7), 686–701. http://dx.doi.org/10.1108/CDI-10-2018-0273

Busse, R., & Regenberg, S. (2019). Revisiting the "authoritarian versus participative" leadership style legacy: A new model of the impact of leadership inclusiveness on employee engagement. *Journal of Leadership & Organizational Studies, 26*(4), 510–525. http://dx.doi.org/10.1177/1548051818810135

Butler, J., Doherty, M. S., & Potter, R. M. (2007). Social antecedents and consequences of interpersonal rejection sensitivity. *Personality & Individual Differences, 43*(6), 1376–1385. http://dx.doi.org/10.1016/j.paid.2007.04.006

Byrne, Z. S., & Cropanzano, R. (2001). History of organizational Justice: The founders speak. In R. Cropanzano (Ed.), *Justice in the workplace (Volume II): From theory to practice* (pp. 3–26). Mahwah, NJ: Lawrence Erlbaum Associates.

Byrne, Z. S., Dik, B. J., & Chiaburu, D. S. (2008). Alternatives to traditional mentoring in fostering career success. *Journal of Vocational Behavior, 72*(3), 429–442. http://dx.doi.org/10.1016/j.jvb.2007.11.010

Byrne, Z. S., & Hochwarter, W. A. (2008). Perceived organizational support and performance. *Journal of Managerial Psychology, 23*(1), 54–72. http://dx.doi.org/10.1108/02683940810849666

Byrne, Z. S., Mueller-Hanson, R. A., Cardador, J. M., Thornton III, G. C., Schuler, H., Frintrup, A., & Fox, S. (2004). Measuring achievement motivation: Tests of equivalency for English, German, and Israeli versions of the achievement motivation inventory. *Personality and Individual Differences, 37*, 203–217. Http://dx.doi.org/10.1016/j.paid.2003.08.012

Byrne, Z. S., Palmer, C. E., Smith, C. L., & Weidert, J. M. (2011). The engaged employee face of organizations. In M. A. Sarlak (Ed.), *The new faces of organizations in the 21st century* (Vol. 1, pp. 93–135). Canada: NAISIT.

Byrne, Z. S., Peters, J. M., & Drake, T. (2014). *Measurement of employee engagement: The Utrecht Work Engagement Scale versus the Job Engagement Scale.* Unpublished manuscript.

Byrne, Z. S., Peters, J. M., Rechlin, A., Smith, C. L., & Kedharnath, U. (2013). *Fostering employee engagement through job control and work-related leader support.* Unpublished manuscript.

Byrne, Z. S., Peters, J. M., & Weston, J. W. (2016). The struggle with employee engagement: Measures and construct clarification using five samples. *Journal of Applied Psychology, 101*(9), 1201–1227. http://dx.doi.org/10.1037/apl0000124

Byrne, Z. S., Pitts, V. E., Wilson, C. M., & Steiner, Z. J. (2012). Trusting the fair super visor: The role of supervisory support in performance appraisals. *Human Resource Manage ment Journal, 22*(2), 129–147. http://dx.doi.org/10.1111/j.1748-8583.2012.00193.x

Cable, D. M., & Judge, T. A. (1996). Person: Organization fit, job choice decisions, and organizational entry. *Organizational Behavior and Human Decision Processes, 67*(3), 294–311. http://dx.doi.org/10.1006/obhd.1996.0081

Caesens, G., Stinglhamber, F., & Marmier, V. (2016). The curvilinear effect of work engagement on employees' turnover intentions. *International Journal of Psychology, 51*(2), 150–155. http://dx.doi.org/10.1002/ijop.12131

Cai, D., Cai, Y., Sun, Y., & Ma, J. (2018). Linking empowering leadership and employee work engagement: The effects of person-job fit, person-group fit, and proactive personality. *Frontiers in Psychology, 9.* http://dx.doi.org/10.3389/fpsyg.2018.01304

Campbell, A. (1976). Subjective measures of well-being. *American Psychologist, 31*(2), 117–124. http://dx.doi.org/10.1037/0003-066X.31.2.117

Campbell, J. P. (1990). Modeling the performance prediction problem in industrial and organizational psychology. In M. D. Dunnette & L. M. Hough (Eds.), *Handbook of industrial and organizational psychology* (Vol. 1, 2nd ed., pp. 687–732). Palo Alto, CA: Consulting Psychologists Press.

Campbell, J. P., Dunnette, M. D., Lawler, E. E., & Weick, K. E. (1970). *Managerial behavior, performance, and effectiveness.* New York: McGraw-Hill.

Campbell, J. P., McHenry, J. J., & Wise, L. L. (1990). Modeling job performance in a population of jobs. *Personnel Psychology, 43*(2), 313–333. http://dx.doi.org/10.1111/j.1744-6570.1990.tb01561.x

Cannon, M. D., & Edmondson, A. C. (2001). Confronting failure: Antecedents and consequences of shared beliefs about failure in organizational work groups. *Journal of Organizational Behavior, 22*(2), 161–177.

Cannon-Bowers, J. A., & Salas, E. (2001). Reflections on shared cognition. *Journal of Organizational Behavior, 22*(2), 195–202. http://dx.doi.org/10.1002/job.82

Cannon-Bowers, J. A., Salas, E., & Converse, S. (1993). Shared mental models in expert team decision making. In N. J. Castellan (Ed.), *Individual and group decision making: Current issues* (pp. 221–246). Hillsdale, NJ: Lawrence Erlbaum Associates.

Carnegie Foundation for the Advancement of Teaching. (2009). Retrieved May 7, 2009, from www.carnegiefoundation.org/classifications/index.asp?key=1213

Caruso, D. R., Mayer, J. D., & Salovey, P. (2002). Emotional intelligence and emotional leadership. In R. E. Riggio, S. E. Murphy, & F. J. Pirozzolo (Eds.), *Multiple intelligences and leadership* (pp. 55–74). Mahwah, NJ: Lawrence Erlbaum Associates.

Carver, C., & Scheier, M. (1998). *On the self regulation of behavior.* New York, NY: Cambridge University Press.

Cascio, W. F. (1998). *Applied psychology in human resource management.* Upper Saddle River, NJ: Prentice Hall.

Case, J. (1995). *Open-book management: The coming business revolution.* New York, NY: HarperBusiness.

Cavanaugh, M. A., Boswell, W. R., Roehling, M. V., & Boudreau, J. W. (2000). An empirical examination of self-reported work stress among U.S. managers. *Journal of Applied Psychology, 85*(1), 65–74. http://dx.doi.org/10.1037/0021-9010.85.1.65

Cenkci, A. T., Zimmerman, J., & Bircan, T. (2019). The effects of employee resource groups on work engagement and workplace inclusion. *International Journal of Organizational Diversity, 19*(2), 1–19. http://dx.doi.org/10.18848/2328-6261/cgp/v19i02/1-19

Cesário, F., & Chambel, M. J. (2017). Linking organizational commitment and work engagement to employee performance. *Knowledge & Process Management, 24*(2), 152–158. http://dx.doi.org/10.1002/kpm.1542

Chalofsky, N., & Krishna, V. (2009). Meaningfulness, commitment, and engagement: The intersection of a deeper level of intrinsic motivation. *Advances in Developing Human Resources, 11*, 189–203. http://dx.doi.org/10.1177/1523422309333147

Champoux, J. E. (1991). A multivariate test of the job characteristics theory of work motivation. *Journal of Organizational Behavior, 12*(5), 431–446. http://dx.doi.org/10.1002/job.4030120507

Chan, A. W., Snape, E., & Redman, T. (2011). Multiple foci and bases of commitment in a Chinese workforce. *The International Journal of Human Resource Management, 22*(16), 3290–3304. http://dx.doi.org/10.1080/09585192.2011.586866

Chartrand, T. L., & Bargh, J. A. (1999). The chameleon effect: The perception: Behavior link and social interaction. *Journal of Personality and Social Psychology, 76*(6), 893–910. http://dx.doi.org/10.1037/0022-3514.76.6.893

Chartrand, T. L., Maddux, W. W., & Lakin, J. L. (2005). Beyond the perception-behavior link: The ubiquitous utility and motivational moderators of nonconscious mimicry. In R. R. Hassin, J. S. Uleman, & J. A. Bargh (Eds.), *The new unconscious* (pp. 334–361). New York, NY: Oxford University Press.

Chatman, J. A. (1989). Improving interactional organizational research: A model of person-organization fit. *Academy of Management Review, 14*(3), 333–349. http://dx.doi.org/10.5465/AMR.1989.4279063

Chatman, J. A. (1991). Matching people and organizations: Selection and socialization in public accounting firms. *Administrative Science Quarterly, 36*(3), 459–484. http://dx.doi.org/10.2307/2393204

Chawla, D. S. (2021). Zoom fatigue saps grant reviewers' attention. *Nature, 590*(7844), 172. http://dx.doi.org/10.1038/d41586-021-00161-5

Chen, C.-C., & Chiu, S.-F. (2009). The mediating role of job involvement in the relationship between job characteristics and organizational citizenship behavior. *Journal of Social Psychology, 149*, 474–494. http://dx.doi.org/10.3200/SOCP.149.4.474-494

Chen, H., Richard, O. C., Boncoeur, O. D., & Ford, D. L., Jr. (2020). Work engagement, emotional exhaustion, and counterproductive work behavior. *Journal of Business Research, 114*, 30–41. http://dx.doi.org/10.1016/j.jbusres.2020.03.025

Chen, Z., Zhang, X., & Vogel, D. (2011). Exploring the underlying processes between conflict and knowledge sharing: A work-engagement perspective. *Journal of Applied Social Psychology, 41*(5), 1005–1033. http://dx.doi.org/10.1111/j.1559-1816.2011.00745.x

Cheng, B., Jiang, D., & Riley, J. H. (2003). Organizational commitment, supervisory commitment and employee outcomes in the Chinese context: Proximal hypothesis or global hypothesis? *Journal of Organizational Behavior, 24*(3), 313–334. http://dx.doi.org/10.1002/job.190

Cherniss, C., Grimm, L. G., & Liautaud, J. P. (2010). Process-designed training: A new approach for helping leaders develop emotional and social competence. *Journal of Management Development, 29*(5), 413–431. http://dx.doi.org/10.1108/02621711011039196

Cherrington, D. J. (1980). *The work ethic.* New York: American Management Association.

Chiaburu, D. S. (2010). The social context of training: Coworker, supervisor, or organizational support? *Industrial & Commercial Training, 42*(1), 53–56. http://dx.doi. org/10.1108/00197851011013724

Christian, M. S., Garza, A. S., & Slaughter, J. E. (2011). Work engagement: A quantitative review and test of its relations with task and contextual performance. *Personnel Psychology, 64*, 89–136. http://dx.doi.org/10.1111/j.1744-6570.2010.01203.x

Christian, M. S., Garza, A. S., & Slaughter, J. E. (2014). "Work engagement: A quantitative review and test of its relations with task and contextual performance": Erratum. *Personnel Psychology, 67*(1), 309–311. http://dx.doi.org/10.1111/peps.12070

Chughtai, A., & Buckley, F. (2011). Work engagement: Antecedents, the mediating role of learning goal orientation and job performance. *The Career Development International, 16*(7), 684–705. http://dx.doi.org/10.1108/13620431111187290

CIPD. (2009). *Employee engagement.* Retrieved April 27, 2009, from www.cipd.co.uk/ hr-topics/employee-engagement.aspx

Clark, M. A. (2018). *What is employee engagement & why does it matter.* Retrieved from www. glasdoor.com/employers/blog/what-is-employee-engagement-why-does-it-matter/

Clark, M. A., Michel, J. S., Zhdanova, L., Pui, S. Y., & Baltes, B. B. (2016). All work and no play? A meta-analytic examination of the correlates and outcomes of workaholism. *Journal of Management, 42*(7), 1836–1873. http://dx.doi.org/10.1177/0149206314522301

Clark, M. A., Smith, R. W., & Haynes, N. J. (2020). The multidimensional workaholism scale: Linking the conceptualization and measurement of workaholism. *Journal of Applied Psychology, 105*(11), 1281–1307. http://dx.doi.org/10.1037/apl0000484.supp (Supplemental).

Clore, G. L., Schwarz, N., & Conway, M. (1994). Affective causes and consequences of social information processing. In R. S. Wyer & T. K. Srull (Eds.), *Handbook of social cognition* (pp. 323–417). Hillsdale, NJ: Erlbaum.

Cochran, D. S., David, F. R., & Gibson, C. (2008). A framework for developing an effective mission statement. *Journal of Business Strategies, 25*(2), 27–39.

Cohen, A. (2007). One nation, many cultures: A cross-cultural study of the relationship between personal cultural values and commitment in the workplace to in-role performance and organizational citizenship behavior. *Cross-Cultural Research: The Journal of Comparative Social Science, 41*(3), 273–300.

Cohen, J. (1988). *Statistical power analysis for the behavioral sciences* (2nd ed.). Hillsdale, NJ: Lawrence Erlbaum Associates.

Cole, M. S., Walter, F., Bedeian, A. G., & O'Boyle, E. H. (2012). Job burnout and employee engagement: A meta-analytic examination of construct proliferation. *Journal of Management, 38*(5), 1550–1581. http://dx.doi.org/10.1177/0149206311415252

Collins, S. (2007). Social workers, resilience, positive emotions and optimism. *Practice: Social Work in Action, 19*(4), 255–269. http://dx.doi.org/10.1080/09503150701728186

Conger, J. A., & Kanungo, R. N. (1988). The empowerment process: Integrating theory and practice. *Academy of Management Review, 13*(3), 471–482. http://dx.doi.org/ 10.5465/AMR.1988.4306983

Constantine, M. G. (2001). Multicultural training, self-construals, and multicultural competence of school counselors. *Professional School Counseling, 4*(3), 202–207.

Coo, C., & Salanova, M. (2018). Mindfulness can make you happy-and-productive: A mindfulness controlled trial and its effects on happiness, work engagement and performance. *Journal of Happiness Studies, 19*(6), 1691–1711. http://dx.doi.org/10. 1007/s10902-017-9892-8

Cooper, C. L., & Cartwright, S. (1994). Healthy mind: Healthy organization: A proactive approach to occupational stress. *Human Relations, 47*(4), 455–471. http://dx.doi.org/10.1177/001872679404700405

Cooper-Thomas, H. D., Xu, J., & Saks, A. M. (2018). The differential value of resources in predicting employee engagement. *Journal of Managerial Psychology, 33*(4–5), 326–344. http://dx.doi.org/10.1108/JMP-12-2017-0449

Cortina, L. M., & Magley, V. J. (2009). Patterns and profiles of response to incivility in the workplace. *Journal of Occupational Health Psychology, 14*(3), 272–288. http://dx.doi.org/10.1037/a0014934

Cortina, L. M., Magley, V. J., Williams, J., & Langhout, R. (2001). Incivility in the workplace: Incidence and impact. *Journal of Occupational Health Psychology, 6*(1), 64–80. http://dx.doi.org/10.1037/1076-8998.6.1.64

Costa, P. T., & McCrae, R. R. (1992). The five-factor model of personality and its relevance to personality disorders. *Journal of Personality Disorders, 6*(4), 343–359. http://dx.doi.org/10.1521/pedi.1992.6.4.343

Costa, P. T., & McCrae, R. R. (2009). The five-factor model and the NEO inventories. In J. N. Butcher (Ed.), *Oxford handbook of personality assessment* (pp. 299–322). New York, NY: Oxford University Press. http://dx.doi.org/10.1093/oxfordhb/9780195366877.013.0016

Costantini, A., Ceschi, A., Viragos, A., De Paola, F., & Sartori, R. (2019). The role of a new strength-based intervention on organisation-based self-esteem and work engagement: A three-wave intervention study. *Journal of Workplace Learning, 31*(3), 194–206. http://dx.doi.org/10.1108/JWL-07-2018-0091

Crawford, E. R., LePine, J. A., & Rich, B. L. (2010). Linking job demands and resources to employee engagement and burnout: A theoretical extension and meta-analytic test. *Journal of Applied Psychology, 95*(5), 834–848. http://dx.doi.org/10.1037/a0019364

Črnjar, K., Dlačić, J., & Milfelner, B. (2020). Analysing the relationship between hotels' internal marketing and employee engagement dimensions. *Trziste/Market, 32*, 49–65. http://dx.doi.org/10.22598/mt/2020.32.spec-issue.49

Cronbach, L. J. (1951). Coefficient alpha and the internal structure of tests. *Psychometrika, 16*, 297–334.

Cronbach, L. J., & Meehl, P. E. (1955). Construct validity in psychological tests. *Psychological Bulletin, 52*, 281–302. http://dx.doi.org/10.1037/h0040957

Cross, S. E., & Gore, J. S. (2012). Cultural models of the self. In M. R. Leary & J. Tangney (Eds.), *Handbook of self and identity* (2nd ed., pp. 587–614). New York, NY: Guilford Press.

Csikszentmihalyi, M. (1990). *Flow: The psychology of optimal experience.* New York, NY: Harper Perennial.

Csikszentmihalyi, M. (1996). *Creativity: Flow and the psychology of discovery and invention.* New York: HarperCollins.

Csikszentmihalyi, M. (1997). *Finding flow: The psychology of engagement with everyday life.* New York, NY: Basic Books.

Csikszentmihalyi, M., Abuhamdeh, S., & Nakamura, J. (2005). Flow. In A. Elliot & C. S. Dweck (Eds.), *Handbook of competence and motivation* (pp. 598–608). New York, NY: Guilford.

Csikszentmihalyi, M., & Kleiber, D. A. (1991). Leisure and self-actualization. In B. L. Driver, P. J. Brown, & G. L. Peterson (Eds.), *Benefits of leisure* (pp. 91–102). State College, PA: Venture.

Csikszentmihalyi, M., & Rathunde, K. (1993). The measurement of flow in everyday life: Toward a theory of emergent motivation. *Nebraska Symposium on Motivation, 40*, 57–97.

Dalal, R. S., Baysinger, M., Brummel, B. J., & LeBreton, J. M. (2012). The relative importance of employee engagement, other job attitudes, and trait affect as predictors of job performance. *Journal of Applied Social Psychology, 42,* E295–E325. http://dx.doi.org/10.1111/j.1559-1816.2012.01017.x

Dalal, R. S., Brummel, B. J., Wee, S., & Thomas, L. L. (2008). Defining employee engagement for productive research and practice. *Industrial and Organizational Psychology: Perspectives on Science and Practice, 1*(1), 52–55. http://dx.doi.org/10.1111/j.1754-9434.2007.00008.x

Dale Carnegie Organization. (2007). *Beyond rules of engagement: How can organizational leaders build a culture that supports high engagement?* Retrieved from www.dalecarnegie.com/imap/white_papers/employee_engagement_white_paper/

Damasio, A. (1999). *The feeling of what happens: Body and emotion in the making of consciousness.* Fort Worth, TX: Harcourt College.

Dane, E. (2011). Paying attention to mindfulness and its effects on task performance in the workplace. *Journal of Management, 37*(4), 997–1018. http://dx.doi.org/10.1177/0149206310367948

Danner, F., & Lonky, E. (1981). A cognitive-developmental approach to the effects of rewards on intrinsic motivation. *Child Development, 52*(3), 1043–1052. http://dx.doi.org/10.2307/1129110

Davidov, E., Schmidt, P., & Schwartz, S. H. (2008). Bringing values back in: The adequacy of the European social survey to measure values in 20 countries. *Public Opinion Quarterly, 72*(3), 420–445. http://dx.doi.org/10.1093/poq/nfn035

Davidson, R. J., Ekman, P., Frijda, N. H., Goldsmith, H. H., Kagan, J., Lazarus, R., . . . Clark, L. A. (1994). How are emotions distinguished from moods, temperament, and other related affective constructs? In P. Ekman & R. J. Davidson (Eds.), *The nature of emotion: Fundamental questions* (pp. 49–96). Oxford: Oxford University Press.

de Beer, L. T., Rothmann, S., Jr., & Mostert, K. (2016). The bidirectional relationship between person-job fit and work engagement: A three-wave study. *Journal of Personnel Psychology, 15*(1), 4–14. http://dx.doi.org/10.1027/1866-5888/a000143

de Beer, L. T., Rothmann, S. Jr., & Pienaar, J. (2012). A confirmatory investigation of a job demands-resources model using a categorical estimator. *Psychological Reports, 111*(2), 528–544. http://dx.doi.org/10.2466/01.03.10.PR0.111.5.528-544

Deci, E. L. (1975). *Intrinsic motivation.* New York: Plenum.

Deci, E. L., Koestner, R., & Ryan, R. M. (1999). A meta-analytic review of experiments examining the effects of extrinsic rewards on intrinsic motivation. *Psychological Bulletin, 125,* 627–668. http://dx.doi.org/10.1037/0033-2909.125.6.627

Deci, E. L., & Ryan, R. M. (1980). The empirical exploration of intrinsic motivational processes. In L. Berkowitz (Ed.), *Advances in experimental social psychology* (Vol. 13, pp. 39–80). New York: Academic Press.

Deci, E. L., & Ryan, R. M. (1985). *Intrinsic motivation and self-determination in human behavior.* New York: Plenum.

Deckop, J. R., Mangel, R., & Cirka, C. C. (1999). Getting more than you pay for: Organizational citizenship behavior and pay-for-performance plans. *Academy of Management Journal, 42*(4), 420–428. http://dx.doi.org/10.2307/257012

Demerouti, E., Bakker, A. B., de Jonge, J., Janssen, P. M., & Schaufeli, W. B. (2001). Burnout and engagement at work as a function of demands and control. *Scandinavian Journal of Work, Environment & Health, 27*(4), 279–286. http://dx.doi.org/10.5271/sjweh.615

Deming, W. E. (1986). *Out of the crisis.* Cambridge, MA: MIT Center for Advanced Engineering Study.

Demirtas, O., Hannah, S. T., Gok, K., Arslan, A., & Capar, N. (2017). The moderated influence of ethical leadership, via meaningful work, on followers' engagement, organizational identification, and envy. *Journal of Business Ethics, 145*(1), 183–199. http://dx.doi.org/10.1007/s10551-015-2907-7

Deutsch, M. (1985). *Distributive justice: A social-psychological perspective.* New Haven, CT: Yale University Press.

de Wind, A., Leijten, F. R. M., Hoekstra, T., Geuskens, G. A., Burdorf, A., & van der Beek, A. J. (2017). "Mental retirement?" Trajectories of work engagement preceding retirement among older workers. *Scandinavian Journal of Work, Environment & Health, 43*(1), 34–41. http://dx.doi.org/10.5271/sjweh.3604

Dijksterhuis, A., & Nordgren, L. F. (2006). A Theory of unconscious thought. *Perspectives on Psychological Science (Wiley-Blackwell), 1*(2), 95–109. http://dx.doi.org/10.1111/j.1745-6916.2006.00007.x

Dijksterhuis, A., & van Olden, Z. (2006). On the benefits of thinking unconsciously: Unconscious thought can increase post-choice satisfaction. *Journal of Experimental Social Psychology, 42*(5), 627–631. http://dx.doi.org/10.1016/j.jesp.2005.10.008

Dik, B. J., Byrne, Z. S., & Steger, M. J. (Eds.). (2013). *Purpose and meaning in the workplace.* Washington, DC: American Psychological Association.

Dikkers, J. E., Jansen, P. W., de Lange, A. H., Vinkenburg, C. J., & Kooij, D. (2010). Proactivity, job characteristics, and engagement: A longitudinal study. *The Career Development International, 15*(1),59–77.http://dx.doi.org/10.1108/13620431011020899

Di Stefano, G., & Gaudiino, M. (2019). Workaholism and work engagement: How are they similar? How are they different? A systematic review and meta-analysis. *European Journal of Work and Organizational Psychology, 28*(3), 329–347. http://dx.doi.org/10.1080/1359432X.2019.1590337

Douglas, S. K., & Roberts, R. A. (2020). Older and more engaged: The influence of an employee's age on work engagement. *Journal of Business Diversity, 20*(4), 73–84. http://dx.doi.org/10.33423/jbd.v20i4.3198

Downey, S. N., van der Werff, L., Thomas, K. M., & Plaut, V. C. (2015). The role of diversity practices and inclusion in promoting trust and employee engagement. *Journal of Applied Social Psychology, 45*(1), 35–44. http://dx.doi.org/10.1111/jasp.12273

Dubbelt, L., Demerouti, E., & Rispens, S. (2019). The value of job crafting for work engagement, task performance, and career satisfaction: Longitudinal and quasi-experimental evidence. *European Journal of Work and Organizational Psychology, 28*(3), 300–314. http://dx.doi.org/10.1080/1359432X.2019.1576632

Duchon, D., & Plowman, D. A. (2005). Nurturing the spirit at work: Impact on work unit performance. *The Leadership Quarterly, 16*(5), 807–833. http://dx.doi.org/10.1016/j.leaqua.2005.07.008

Duffy, E. (1957). The psychological significance of the concept of "arousal" or "activation." *Psychological Review, 64*, 265–275. http://dx.doi.org/10.1037/h0048837

Dunham, R. B., Smith, F. J., & Blackburn, R. S. (1977). Validation of the index of organizational reactions with the JDI, the MSQ, and faces scales. *Academy of Management Journal, 20*(3), 420–432. http://dx.doi.org/10.2307/255415

Dvir, T., Eden, D., Avolio, B. J., & Shamir, B. (2002). Impact of transformational leadership on follower development and performance: A field experiment. *Academy of Management Journal, 45*(4), 735–744. http://dx.doi.org/10.2307/3069307

Eagly, A. H., & Chaiken, S. (1998). Attitude structure and function. In D. T. Gilbert, S. T. Fiske, & G. Lindzey (Eds.), *The handbook of social psychology* (Vols. 1 and 2, 4th ed., pp. 269–322). New York, NY: McGraw-Hill.

Eagly, A. H., & Chaiken, S. (2007). The advantages of an inclusive definition of attitude. *Social Cognition, 25*(5), 582–602.

Edwards, C. C. (2009). The pursuit of happiness [human resource management]. *Engineering & Technology (17509637), 4*(4), 76–79. http://dx.doi.org/10.1049/et.2009.0419

Eisenberger, R., Huntington, R., Hutchison, S., & Sowa, D. (1986). Perceived organizational support. *Journal of Applied Psychology, 71*(3), 500–507. http://dx.doi.org/10.1037/0021-9010.71.3.500

Eisenberger, R., Stinglhamber, F., Vandenberghe, C., Sucharski, I., & Rhoades, L. (2002). Perceived supervisor support: Contributions to perceived organizational support and employee retention. *Journal of Applied Psychology, 87*, 565–573.

Ekman, P. (1992). Are there basic emotions? *Psychological Review, 99*, 550–553. http://dx.doi.org/10.1037/0033-295X.99.3.550

Eldor, L., Harpaz, I., & Westman, M. (2020). The work/nonwork spillover: The enrichment role of work engagement. *Journal of Leadership & Organizational Studies, 27*(1), 2134. http://dx.doi.org/10.1177/1548051816647362

Erez, M. (1994). Toward a model of cross-cultural industrial and organizational psychology. In H. C. Triandis, M. D. Dunnette, & L. M. Hough (Eds.), *Handbook of industrial and organizational psychology* (Vol. 4, 2nd ed., pp. 559–607). Palo Alto, CA: Consulting Psychologists Press.

Erks, R. L., Allen, J. A., Harland, L. K., & Prange, K. (2020). Do volunteers volunteer to do more at work? The relationship between volunteering, engagement, and OCBs. *Voluntas: International Journal of Voluntary & Nonprofit Organizations*, 1–14. http://dx.doi.org/10.1007/s11266-020-00232-7

Fairhurst, K., & May, C. (2006). What general practitioners find satisfying in their work: Implications for health care system reform. *Annals of Family Medicine, 4*(6), 500–505. http://dx.doi.org/10.1370/afm.565

Fairlie, P. (2011). Meaningful work, employee engagement, and other key employee outcomes: Implications for human resource development. *Advances in Developing Human Resources, 13*(4), 508–525. http://dx.doi.org/10.1177/1523422311431679

Faupel, S., & Süß, S. (2019). The effect of transformational leadership on employees during organizational change: An empirical analysis. *Journal of Change Management, 19*(3), 145–166. http://dx.doi.org/10.1080/14697017.2018.1447006

Fazi, L., Zaniboni, S., Estreder, Y., Truxillo, D., & Fraccaroli, F. (2019). The role of age in the relationship between work social characteristics and job attitudes. *Journal of Workplace Behavioral Health, 34*(2), 77–95. http://dx.doi.org/10.1080/15555240.2019.1597632

Ferris, G. R., Frink, D. D., Beehr, T. A., & Gilmore, D. C. (1995). Political fairness and fair politics: The conceptual integration of divergent constructs. In R. S. Cropanzano & K. M. Kacmar (Eds.), *Organizational politics, justice, and support: Managing the social climate of the workplace* (pp. 21–36). Westport, CT: Quorum books.

Ferris, G. R., & Kacmar, K. (1992). Perceptions of organizational politics. *Journal of Management, 18*(1), 93.

Ferris, G. R., Russ, G. S., & Fandt, P. M. (1989). Politics in organizations. In R. A. Giacalone & P. Rosenfeld (Eds.), *Impression management in the organization* (pp. 143–170). Hillsdale, NJ: Lawrence Erlbaum Associates.

Fine, G., & Holyfield, L. (1996). Secrecy, trust, and dangerous leisure: Generating group cohesion in voluntary organizations. *Social Psychology Quarterly, 59*(1), 22–38. http://dx.doi.org/10.2307/2787117

Fine, M. (1983). The social context and a sense of injustice: The option to challenge. *Representative Research in Social Psychology, 13*, 15–33.

Fine, S., Horowitz, I., Weigler, H., & Basis, L. (2010). Is character good enough? The effects of situational variables on the relationship between integrity and counterproductive work behaviors. *Human Resource Management Review, 20*, 73–84.

Fineman, S. (1983). Work meanings, non-work, and the taken-for-granted. *Journal of Management Studies, 20*(2), 143–157.

Fisher, C. D. (1978). The effects of personal control, competence, and extrinsic reward systems on intrinsic motivation. *Organizational Behavior and Human Performance, 21*, 273–288. http://dx.doi.org/10.1016/0030-5073(78)90054-5

Fiske, A., Kitayama, S., Markus, H., & Nisbett, R. E. (1998). The cultural matrix of social psychology. In D. T. Gilbert, S. T. Fiske, & G. Lindzey (Eds.), *The handbook of social psychology* (Vols. 1 and 2, 4th ed., pp. 915–981). New York, NY: McGraw-Hill.

Fiske, S. T., & Taylor, S. E. (1991). *Social cognition* (2nd ed.). New York, NY: McGraw-Hill.

Flade, P. (2003). Great Britain's workforce lacks inspiration. *Gallup Management Journal Online*, 1–3.

Fleck, S., & Inceoglu, I. (2010). A comprehensive framework for understanding and predicting engagement. In S. L. Albrecht (Ed.), *Handbook of employee engagement: Perspectives, issues, research and practice* (pp. 31–42). Northampton, MA: Edward Elgar. http://dx.doi.org/10.4337/9781849806374.00009

Fletcher, L. (2019). How can personal development lead to increased engagement? The roles of meaningfulness and perceived line manager relations. *The International Journal of Human Resource Management, 30*(7), 1203–1226. http://dx.doi.org/10.1080/09585192.2016.1184177

Forest, J., Mageau, G. A., Sarrazin, C., & Morin, E. M. (2011). "Work is my passion": The different affective, behavioural, and cognitive consequences of harmonious and obsessive passion toward work. *Canadian Journal of Administrative Sciences, 28*(1), 17–30. http://dx.doi.org/10.1002/cjas.170

Francaro, K. E. (2007). The consequences of micromanaging. *Contract Management, 47*(7), 4–8.

Frank, L. L., & Hackman, J. (1975). A failure of job enrichment: The case of the change that wasn't. *Journal of Applied Behavioral Science, 11*(4), 413–436. http://dx.doi.org/10.1177/002188637501100404

Frankl, V. E. (1967). *Psychotherapy and existentialism: Selected papers on logotherapy.* New York, NY: Washington Square Press.

Frankl, V. E. (1978). *The unheard cry for meaning: Psychotherapy and humanism.* New York, NY: Washington Square Press. http://dx.doi.org/10.1037/h0086035

Frankl, V. E. (1984). *Man's search for meaning* (3rd ed.). New York, NY: First Washington Square Press (Original work published in 1963).

Frederick, D. E., & VanderWeele, T. J. (2020). Longitudinal meta-analysis of job crafting shows positive association with work engagement. *Cogent Psychology, 7*(1). http://dx.doi.org/10.1080/23311908.2020.1746733

Fredricks, J. A., Blumenfeld, P. C., & Paris, A. H. (2004). School engagement: Potential of the concept, state of the evidence. *Review of Educational Research, 74*(1), 59–109. http://dx.doi.org/10.3102/00346543074001059

Fredrickson, B. L. (2001). The role of positive emotions in positive psychology: The broaden-and-build theory of positive emotions. *American Psychologist, 56*, 218–226. http://dx.doi.org/10.1037/0003-066X.56.3.218

Fredrickson, B. L., Tugade, M. M., Waugh, C. E., & Larkin, G. R. (2003). What good are positive emotions in crisis? A prospective study of resilience and emotions following the terrorist attacks on the United States on September 11th, 2001. *Journal of Personality And Social Psychology, 84*(2), 365–376. http://dx.doi.org/10.1037/0022-3514.84.2.365

Freeney, Y. M., & Tiernan, J. (2009). Exploration of the facilitators of and barriers to work engagement in nursing. *International Journal of Nursing Studies, 46*(12), 1557–1565. http://dx.doi.org/10.1016/j.ijnurstu.2009.05.003

Frese, M., Kring, W., Soose, A., & Zempel, J. (1996). Personal initiative at work: Differences between East and West Germany. *Academy of Management Journal, 39*, 37–63.

Friedman, H. S., Riggio, R. E., & Casella, D. F. (1988). Nonverbal skill, personal charisma, and initial attraction. *Personality and Social Psychology Bulletin, 14*(1), 203–211. http://dx.doi.org/10.1177/0146167288141020

Friedman, S. D., Christensen, P., & DeGroot, J. (1998). Work and life: The end of the zero-sum game. *Harvard Business Review, 76*(6), 119–129.

Frijda, N. H. (1987). Emotion, cognitive structure, and action tendency. *Cognition & Emotion, 1*, 115–143. http://dx.doi.org/10.1080/02699938708408043

Frijda, N. H. (1988). The laws of emotion. *American Psychologist, 43*(5), 349–358. http://dx.doi.org/10.1037/0003-066X.43.5.349

Gagné, M., Senécal, C. B., & Koestner, R. (1997). Proximal job characteristics, feelings of empowerment, and intrinsic motivation: A multidimensional model. *Journal of Applied Social Psychology, 27*(14), 1222–1240. http://dx.doi.org/10.1111/j.1559-1816.1997.tb01803.x

Gallup Organization. (2002, April 15). The high cost of disengaged employees. *Gallup Management Journal*, 1–2. Retrieved from http://gmj.gallup.com

Gallup Organization. (2013a). *State of the American workplace: Employee engagement insights for U.S. business leaders.* Retrieved from www.gallup.com/strategicconsulting/163007/state-american-workplace.aspx

Gallup Organization. (2013b). *State of the global workplace: Employee engagement insights for business leaders worldwide.* Retrieved from www.gallup.com/file/strategicconsulting/164735/State%20of%20the%20Global%20Workplace%20Report%202013.pdf

Gallup Organization. (2017a). *State of the American workplace.* Retrieved from www.gallup.com/workplace/238085/state-american-report-2017.aspx

Gallup Organization. (2017b). *State of the global workplace.* Gallup Press.

Ganster, D. C. (1995). Interventions for building healthy organizations: Suggestions from the stress research literature. In L. R. Murphy, J. R. Hurrell, S. L. Sauter, & G. Keita (Eds.), *Job stress interventions* (pp. 323–336). Washington, DC: American Psychological Association. http://dx.doi.org/10.1037/10183-021

Garczynski, A. M., Waldrop, J. S., Rupprecht, E. A., & Grawitch, M. J. (2013). Differentiation between work and nonwork self-aspects as a predictor of presenteeism and engagement: Cross-cultural differences. *Journal of Occupational Health Psychology, 18*(4), 417–429. http://dx.doi.org/10.1037/a0033988

Garden, R., Hu, X., Zhan, Y., & Wei, F. (2018). The role of workplace popularity: Links to employee characteristics and supervisor-rated outcomes. *Journal of Leadership & Organizational Studies, 25*(1), 19–29. http://dx.doi.org/10.1177/1548051817712876

Ge, Y., & Sun, X. (2020). The relationship of employees' strengths use and innovation: Work engagement as a mediator. *Social Behavior and Personality: An International Journal, 48*(5), 1–6. http://dx.doi.org/10.2224/sbp.9083

Gebauer, J., Lowman, D., & Gordon, J. (2008). *Closing the engagement gap: How great companies unlock employee potential for superior results.* New York: Portfolio.

George, J. M. (1990). Personality, affect, and behavior in groups. *Journal of Applied Psychology, 75*(2), 107–116. http://dx.doi.org/10.1037/0021-9010.75.2.107

George, J. M. (2002). Affect regulation in groups and teams. In R. G. Lord, R. J. Klimoski, & R. Kanfer (Eds.), *Emotions in the workplace: Understanding the structure and role of emotions in organizational behavior* (pp. 182–217). San Francisco, CA: Jossey-Bass.

George, J. M. (2009). The illusion of will in organizational behavior research: Nonconscious processes and job design. *Journal of Management, 35*(6), 1318–1339. http://dx.doi.org/10.1177/0149206309346337

George, J. M. (2010). More engagement is not necessarily better: The benefits of fluctuating levels of engagement. In S. L. Albrecht (Ed.), *Handbook of employee engagement: Perspectives, issues, research and practice* (pp. 253–263). Northampton, MA: Edward Elgar.

George, J. M., & Brief, A. P. (1992). Feeling good-doing good: A conceptual analysis of the mood at work-organizational spontaneity relationship. *Psychological Bulletin, 112*(2), 310–329. http://dx.doi.org/10.1037/0033-2909.112.2.310

Gerards, R., de Grip, A., & Baudewijns, C. (2018). Do new ways of working increase work engagement? *Personnel Review, 47*(2), 517–534. http://dx.doi.org/10.1108/PR-02-2017-0050

Ghlichlee, B., & Bayat, F. (2021). Frontline employees' engagement and business performance: The mediating role of customer-oriented behaviors. *Management Research Review, 44*(2), 290–317. http://dx.doi.org/10.1108/MRR-11-2019-0482

Ghosh, D., Sekiguchi, T., & Fujimoto, Y. (2020). Psychological detachment: A creativity perspective on the link between intrinsic motivation and employee engagement. *Personnel Review, 49*(9), 1789–1804. http://dx.doi.org/10.1108/PR-12-2018-0480

Gibbons, J. (2006). *Employee engagement: A review of current research and its implications.* Ottawa, Ontario, Canada: Conference Board of Canada.

Gillet, N., Huart, I., Colombat, P., & Fouquereau, E. (2013). Perceived organizational support, motivation, and engagement among police officers. *Professional Psychology: Research and Practice, 44*(1), 46–55. http://dx.doi.org/10.1037/a0030066

Gillet, N., Morin, A. J. S., Jeoffrion, C., & Fouquereau, E. (2020). A person-centered perspective on the combined effects of global and specific levels of job engagement. *Group & Organization Management, 45*(4), 556–594. http://dx.doi.org/10.1177/1059601119899182

Glaser, J., & Kihlstrom, J. F. (2005). Compensatory automaticity: Unconscious volition is not an oxymoron. In R. R. Hassin, J. S. Uleman, & J. A. Bargh (Eds.), *The new unconscious* (pp. 171–195). New York, NY: Oxford University Press.

Glerum, D. R. (2021). Tainted heroes: The emergence of dirty work during pandemics. *Industrial and Organizational Psychology, 14*, 41–44. http://dx.doi.org/10.1017/iop.2021.5

Goffman, E. (1961). *Encounters: Two studies in the sociology of interaction.* Indianapolis, IN: Bobbs-Merrill.

Gong, Y., Wu, Y., Huang, P., Yan, X., & Luo, Z. (2020). Psychological empowerment and work engagement as mediating roles between trait emotional intelligence and job satisfaction. *Frontiers in Psychology, 11.* http://dx.doi.org/10.3389/fpsyg.2020.00232

Gordon, H. J., Demerouti, E., Le Blanc, P. M., Bakker, A. B., Bipp, T., & Verhagen, M. A. M. T. (2018). Individual job redesign: Job crafting interventions in healthcare. *Journal of Vocational Behavior, 104*, 98–114. http://dx.doi.org/10.1016/j.jvb.2017.07.002

Graen, G. B., & Uhl-Bien, M. (1995). Relationship-based approach to leadership: Development of Leader-Member Exchange (LMX) theory of leadership over 25 years: Applying a multi-level multi-domain perspective. *The Leadership Quarterly, 6*(2), 219–247. http://dx.doi.org/10.1016/1048-9843(95)90036-5

Graham, H., Howard, K. J., & Dougall, A. (2012). The growth of occupational health psychology. In R. J. Gatchel & I. Z. Schultz (Eds.), *Handbook of occupational health and wellness* (pp. 39–59). New York, NY: Springer Science + Business Media. http://dx.doi.org/10.1007/978-1-4614-4839-6_3

Green, K. W. (2010). Impact of recession-based workplace anxiety. *International Journal of Management & Enterprise Development, 9*(3), 213–232.

Gregory, B. T., Albritton, M., & Osmonbekov, T. (2010). The mediating role of psychological empowerment on the relationships between P-O fit, job satisfaction, and in-role performance. *Journal of Business and Psychology, 25*(4), 639–647. http://dx.doi.org/10.1007/s10869-010-9156-7

Griffin, M. A., Parker, S. K., & Neal, A. (2008). Is behavioral engagement a distinct and useful construct? *Industrial and Organizational Psychology: Perspectives on Science and Practice, 1*(1), 48–51. http://dx.doi.org/10.1111/j.1754-9434.2007.00007.x

Gronlund, N. E., & Linn, R. L. (1990). *Measurement and evaluation in teaching* (6th ed.). New York, NY: Macmillan.

Groysberg, B., & Slind, M. (2012). Leadership is a conversation. *Harvard Business Review, 90*(6), 76–84.

Gruenfeld, D. H., & Hollingshead, A. B. (1993). Sociocognition in work groups: The evolution of group integrative complexity and its relation to task performance. *Small Group Research, 24*(3), 383–405. http://dx.doi.org/10.1177/1046496493243006

Guchait, P. (2016). The mediating effect of team engagement between team cognitions and team outcomes in service-management teams. *Journal of Hospitality & Tourism Research, 40*(2), 139–161. http://dx.doi.org/10.1177/1096348013495698

Guest, R. H. (1964). Better utilization of skills through job design. *Management of Personnel Quarterly, 3*(3), 3–11.

Guion, R. M., & Gibson, W. M. (1988). Personnel selection and placement. *Annual Review of Psychology, 39*, 349–374. http://dx.doi.org/10.1146/annurev.ps.39.020188.002025

Guion, R. M., & Landy, F. J. (1972). The meaning of work and the motivation to work. *Organizational Behavior & Human Performance, 7*(2), 308–339. http://dx.doi.org/10.1016/0030-5073(72)90020-7

Gundling, E., & Zanchettin, A. (2007). *Global diversity: Winning customers and engaging employees within world markets*. Boston, MA: Nicholas Brealey International.

Guo, J., Qiu, Y., & Gan, Y. (2020). Workplace incivility and work engagement: The chain mediating effects of perceived insider status, affective organizational commitment and organizational identification. *Current Psychology: A Journal for Diverse Perspectives on Diverse Psychological Issues*. Published online. http://dx.doi.org/10.1007/s12144-020-00699-z

Hackman, J., & Lawler III, E. E. (1971). Employee reactions to job characteristics. *Journal of Applied Psychology, 55*(3), 259–286.

Hackman, J., & Oldham, G. R. (1975). Development of the job diagnostic survey. *Journal of Applied Psychology, 60*(2), 159–170. http://dx.doi.org/10.1037/h0076546

Hackman, J., & Oldham, G. R. (1976). Motivation through the design of work: Test of a theory. *Organizational Behavior & Human Performance, 16*(2), 250–279.

Hai, S., Wu, K., Park, I.-J., Li, Y., Chang, Q., & Tang, Y. (2020). The role of perceived high-performance HR practices and transformational leadership on employee engagement and citizenship behaviors. *Journal of Managerial Psychology, 35*(6), 513–526. http://dx.doi.org/10.1108/JMP-03-2019-0139

Hakanen, J. J., Bakker, A. B., & Schaufeli, W. B. (2006). Burnout and work engagement among teachers. *Journal of School Psychology, 43*, 495–513.

Hakanen, J. J., Peeters, M. C. W., & Schaufeli, W. B. (2018). Different types of employee well-being across time and their relationships with job crafting. *Journal of Occupational Health Psychology, 23*(2), 289–301. http://dx.doi.org/10.1037/ocp0000081

Hakanen, J. J., Perhoniemi, R., & Toppinen-Tanner, S. (2008). Positive gain spirals at work: From job resources to work engagement, personal initiative and work-unit innovativeness. *Journal of Vocational Behavior, 73*(1), 78–91. http://dx.doi.org/10.1016/j.jvb.2008.01.003

Hakanen, J. J., Schaufeli, W. B., & Ahola, K. (2008). The job demands-resources model: A three-year cross-lagged study of burnout, depression, commitment, and work engagement. *Work & Stress, 22*(3), 224–241. http://dx.doi.org/10.1080/02678370802379432

Hakanen, J. J., Seppälä, P., & Peeters, M. C. W. (2017). High job demands, still engaged and not burned out? The role of job crafting. *International Journal of Behavioral Medicine, 24*(4), 619–627. http://dx.doi.org/10.1007/s12529-017-9638-3

Halbesleben, J. R. B. (2010). A meta-analysis of work engagement: Relationships with burnout, demands, resources, and consequences. In A. B. Bakker & M. P. Leiter (Eds.), *Work engagement: A handbook of essential theory and research* (pp. 102–117). New York, NY: Psychology Press.

Halbesleben, J. R. B., Harvey, J., & Bolino, M. C. (2009). Too engaged? A conservation of resources view of the relationship between work engagement and work interference with family. *Journal of Applied Psychology, 94*(6), 1452–1465. http://dx.doi.org/10.1037/a0017595

Halbesleben, J. R. B., & Wheeler, A. R. (2008). The relative roles of engagement and embeddedness in predicting job performance and intention to leave. *Work & Stress, 22*(3), 242–256. http://dx.doi.org/10.1080/02678370802383962

Halbesleben, J. R. B., Wheeler, A. R., & Shanine, K. K. (2013). The moderating role of attention-deficit/hyperactivity disorder in the work engagement: Performance process. *Journal of Occupational Health Psychology, 18*(2), 132–143. http://dx.doi.org/10.1037/a0031978

Haldorai, K., Kim, W. G., Phetvaroon, K., & Li, J. (Justin). (2020). Left out of the office "tribe": The influence of workplace ostracism on employee work engagement. *International Journal of Contemporary Hospitality Management, 32*(8), 2717–2735. http://dx.doi.org/10.1108/IJCHM-04-2020-0285

Halgin, D. S., Gopalakrishnan, G. M., & Borgatti, S. P. (2015). Structure and agency in networked, distributed work: The role of work engagement. *American Behavioral Scientist, 59*(4), 457–474. http://dx.doi.org/10.1177/0002764214556807

Halinski, M., & Harrison, J. A. (2020). The job resources-engagement relationship: The role of location. *International Journal of Public Sector Management, 33*(6/7), 681–695. http://dx.doi.org/10.1108/IJPSM-12-2019-0303

Hall, D. T. (1996). Implications: The new role of the career practitioner. In D. T. Hall & Associates (Eds.), *The career is dead, long live the career, a relational approach to careers* (pp. 314–336). San Francisco, CA: Jossey-Bass.

Hallberg, U., & Schaufeli, W. B. (2006). "Same" but different: Can work engagement be discriminated from job involvement and organizational commitment? *European Journal of Psychology, 11*, 119–127.

Hammedi, W., Leclercq, T., Poncin, I., & Alkire, L. (2021). Uncovering the dark side of gamification at work: Impacts on engagement and well-being. *Journal of Business Research, 122*, 256–269. http://dx.doi.org/10.1016/j.jbusres.2020.08.032

Hansen, A. M., Byrne, Z. S., & Kiersch, C. E. (2014). How interpersonal leadership relates to employee engagement. *Journal of Managerial Psychology, 29*(8), 953–972.

Hardin, C. D., & Higgins, E. (1996). Shared reality: How social verification makes the subjective objective. In R. M. Sorrentino & E. Higgins (Eds.), *Handbook of motivation and cognition, Vol. 3: The interpersonal context* (pp. 28–84). New York, NY: Guilford Press.

Harju, L. K., Hakanen, J. J., & Schaufeli, W. B. (2016). Can job crafting reduce job boredom and increase work engagement? A three-year cross-lagged panel study. *Journal of Vocational Behavior, 95–96*, 11–20. http://dx.doi.org/10.1016/j.jvb.2016.07.001

Harpaz, I., & Snir, R. (2003). Workaholism: Its definition and nature. *Human Relations, 56*(3), 291–319. http://dx.doi.org/10.1177/0018726703056003613

Harris, G. E., & Cameron, J. E. (2005). Multiple dimensions of organizational identification and commitment as predictors of turnover intentions and psychological well-being. *Canadian Journal of Behavioural Science/Revue Canadienne Des Sciences Du Comportement, 37*(3), 159–169. http://dx.doi.org/10.1037/h0087253

Harrison, A. (2012). 5 steps to employee engagement: Improving your goals for organizational success. *Public Relations Tactics, 19*(11), 10.

Harrison, D. A., Newman, D. A., & Roth, P. L. (2006). How important are job attitudes? Meta-analytic comparisons of integrative behavioral outcomes and time sequences. *Academy of Management Journal, 49*(2), 305–325. http://dx.doi.org/10.5465/AMJ.2006.20786077

Harter, J. K., Schmidt, F. L., & Hayes, T. L. (2002). Business-unit-level relationship between employee satisfaction, employee engagement, and business outcomes: A meta-analysis. *Journal of Applied Psychology, 87*(2), 268–279.

Haslam, N. (2006). Dehumanization: An integrative review. *Personality and Social Psychology Review, 10*, 252–264. http://dx.doi.org/10.1207/s15327957pspr1003_4

Hassan, A., & Ahmed, F. (2011). Authentic leadership, trust and work engagement. *World Academy of Science, Engineering & Technology, 80*, 750–756.

Hatfield, E., Cacioppo, J. T., & Rapson, R. L. (1993). Emotional contagion. *Current Directions in Psychological Science (Wiley-Blackwell), 2*(3), 96–99. http://dx.doi.org/10.1111/1467-8721.ep10770953

Hatfield, E., Cacioppo, J. T., & Rapson, R. L. (1994). *Emotional contagion.* New York, NY: Cambridge University Press.

Hatfield, E., Hsee, C. K., Costello, J., & Weisman, M. (1995). The impact of vocal feedback on emotional experience and expression. *Journal of Social Behavior & Personality, 10*(2), 293–312.

Hawkes, A. J., Biggs, A., & Hegerty, E. (2017). Work engagement: Investigating the role of transformational leadership, job resources, and recovery. *Journal of Psychology: Interdisciplinary and Applied, 151*(6), 509–531. http://dx.doi.org/10.1080/00223980.2017.1372339

Hay Group. (2010). *The road to performance: Leveraging employee research to achieve business success.* Retrieved April 27, 2009, from www.haygroup.com/ww/downloads/details.aspx?ID=20768

He, H., Chao, M. M., & Zhu, W. (2019). Cause-related marketing and employee engagement: The roles of admiration, implicit morality beliefs, and moral identity. *Journal of Business Research, 95*, 83–92. http://dx.doi.org/10.1016/j.jbusres.2018.10.013

Heil, G., Bennis, W., & Stephens, D. C. (2000). *Douglas McGregor, revisited: Managing the human side of the enterprise.* New York, NY: John Wiley.

Heine, S. J., Kitayama, S., Lehman, D. R., Takata, T., Ide, E., Leung, C., & Matsumoto, H. (2001). Divergent consequences of success and failure in Japan and North America: An investigation of self-improving motivations and malleable selves. *Journal of Personality and Social Psychology, 81*(4), 599–615. http://dx.doi.org/10.1037/0022-3514.81.4.599

Hernandez, M., & Guarana, C. L. (2018). An examination of the temporal intricacies of job engagement. *Journal of Management, 44*(5), 1711–1735. http://dx.doi.org/10.1177/0149206315622573

Hernaus, T., Vujčić, M. T., & Aleksić, A. (2017). Changing work engagement: The longitudinal effect of a job redesign intervention among public sector employees. *Strategic Management, 22*(2), 3–8.

Herndon, F. (2008). Testing mindfulness with perceptual and cognitive factors: External vs. internal encoding, and the cognitive failures questionnaire. *Personality and Individual Differences, 44*(1), 32–41. http://dx.doi.org/10.1016/j.paid.2007.07.002

Hershcovis, M., Turner, N., Barling, J., Arnold, K. A., Dupré, K. E., Inness, M., . . . Sivanathan, N. (2007). Predicting workplace aggression: A meta-analysis. *Journal of Applied Psychology, 92*(1), 228–238. http://dx.doi.org/10.1037/0021-9010.92.1.228

Herzberg, F., Mausner, B., & Snyderman, B. B. (1959). *The motivation to work.* New York, NY: Wiley.

Hilgard, E. R. (1987). *Psychology in America: A historical survey.* San Diego, CA: Harcourt Brace Jovanovich.

Hirschfeld, R. R., & Thomas, C. H. (2008). Representations of trait engagement: Integration, additions, and mechanisms. *Industrial and Organizational Psychology: Perspectives on Science and Practice, 1*(1), 63–66. http://dx.doi.org/10.1111/j.1754-9434.2007.00011.x

Hitt, W. D. (1995). The learning organization: Some reflections on organizational renewal. *Leadership & Organization Development Journal, 16*(8), 17–25. http://dx.doi.org/10.1108/01437739510097996

Ho, V. T., & Astakhova, M. N. (2018). Disentangling passion and engagement: An examination of how and when passionate employees become engaged ones. *Human Relations, 71*(7), 973–1000. http://dx.doi.org/10.1177/0018726717731505

Ho, V. T., Wong, S., & Lee, C. (2011). A tale of passion: Linking job passion and cognitive engagement to employee work performance. *Journal of Management Studies, 48*(1), 26–47. http://dx.doi.org/10.1111/j.1467-6486.2009.00878.x

Hobfoll, S. E. (1989). Conservation of resources: A new attempt at conceptualizing stress. *American Psychologist, 44*(3), 513–524. http://dx.doi.org/10.1037/0003-066X.44.3.513

Hobfoll, S. E., & Shirom, A. (2001). Conservation of resources theory: Applications to stress and management in the workplace. In R. T. Golembiewski (Ed.), *Handbook of organizational behavior* (2nd ed., pp. 57–80). New York, NY: Marcel Dekker.

Hobson, C. J., Delunas, L., & Kesic, D. (2001). Compelling evidence of the need for corporate work/life balance initiatives: Results from a national survey of stressful life-events. *Journal of Employment Counseling, 38*(1), 38–44.

Hofstede, G. (1980). Motivation, leadership, and organization: Do American theories apply abroad? *Organizational Dynamics, 9,* 42–63.

Hofstede, G. (1983). Dimensions of national cultures in fifty countries and three regions. In J. B. Deregowski, S. Dziurawiec, & R. C. Annis (Eds.), *Expiscations in cross-cultural psychology* (pp. 335–355). Lisse, Netherlands: Swets & Zeitlinger.

Hofstede, G. (2001). *Culture's consequences: Comparing values, behaviors, institutions, and organizations across nations* (2nd ed.). Thousand Oaks, CA: Sage.

Hofstede, G., & Bond, M. H. (1984). Hofstede's culture dimensions: An independent validation using Rokeach's Value Survey. *Journal of Cross-Cultural Psychology, 15*(4), 417–433. http://dx.doi.org/10.1177/0022002184015004003

Hofstede, G., & Bond, M. H. (1988). The Confucius connection: From cultural roots to economic growth. *Organizational Dynamics, 16*(4), 5–21.

Holahan, C. J., & Moos, R. H. (1985). Life stress and health: Personality, coping, and family support in stress resistance. *Journal of Personality and Social Psychology, 49*(3), 739–747. http://dx.doi.org/10.1037/0022-3514.49.3.739

Holcombe, K. (2015). *Job crafting for work meaningfulness, identity, and engagement: The role of needs satisfaction.* Unpublished manuscript.

Holland, P., Cooper, B., & Sheehan, C. (2017). Employee voice, supervisor support, and engagement: The mediating role of trust. *Human Resource Management, 56*(6), 915–929. http://dx.doi.org/10.1002/hrm.21809

Holman, D. J., Axtell, C. M., Sprigg, C., Totterdell, P., & Wall, T. D. (2010). The mediating role of job characteristics in job redesign interventions: A serendipitous quasi-experiment. *Journal of Organizational Behavior, 31*(1), 84–105. http://dx.doi.org/10.1002/job.631

Hoppock, R. (1935). *Job satisfaction.* New York: Harper and Row.

Howard, J. H., Rechnitzer, P. A., & Cunningham, D. A. (1975). Coping with job tension-effective and ineffective methods. *Public Personnel Management, 4*(5), 317–325.

Howard, L. W., & Cordes, C. L. (2010). Flight from unfairness: Effects of perceived injustice on emotional exhaustion and employee withdrawal. *Journal of Business and Psychology, 25*(3), 409–428. http://dx.doi.org/10.1007/s10869-010-9158-5

Howell, J. M., & Frost, P. J. (1989). A laboratory study of charismatic leadership. *Organizational Behavior and Human Decision Processes, 43*(2), 243–269. http://dx.doi.org/10.1016/0749-5978(89)90052-6

Hsee, C. K., Hatfield, E., Carlson, J. G., & Chemtob, C. (1990). The effect of power on susceptibility to emotional contagion. *Cognition and Emotion, 4*(4), 327–340. http://dx.doi.org/10.1080/02699939008408081

Hu, J., He, W., & Zhou, K. (2020). The mind, the heart, and the leader in times of crisis: How and when COVID-19-triggered mortality salience relates to state anxiety, job engagement, and prosocial behavior. *Journal of Applied Psychology, 105*(11), 1218–1233. http://dx.doi.org/10.1037/apl0000620.supp (Supplemental).

Hu, L., & Bentler, P. M. (1999). Cutoff criteria for fit indexes in covariance structure analysis: Conventional criteria versus new alternatives. *Structural Equation Modeling, 6*, 1–55.

Hulin, C. L., & Judge, T. A. (2003). Job attitudes. In W. C. Borman, D. R. Ilgen, & R. J. Klimoski (Eds.), *Handbook of psychology: Industrial and organizational psychology* (Vol. 12, pp. 255–276). Hoboken, NJ: John Wiley & Sons.

Hulshof, I. L., Demerouti, E., & Le Blanc, P. M. (2020). Providing services during times of change: Can employees maintain their levels of empowerment, work engagement and service quality through a job crafting intervention? *Frontiers in Psychology, 11.* http://dx.doi.org/10.3389/fpsyg.2020.00087

Hutchins, E. (1991). The social organization of distributed cognition. In L. B. Resnick, J. M. Levine, & S. D. Teasley (Eds.), *Perspectives on socially shared cognition* (pp. 283–307). Washington, DC: American Psychological Association. http://dx.doi.org/10.1037/10096-012

Ickes, W., & Gonzalez, R. (1994). "Social" cognition and social cognition: From the subjective to the intersubjective. *Small Group Research, 25*(2), 294–315. http://dx.doi.org/10.1177/1046496494252008

Ilgen, D. R., & Klein, H. J. (1988). Organizational behavior. *Annual Review of Psychology, 40*, 327–351. http://dx.doi.org/10.1146/annurev.ps.40.020189.001551

Ilies, R., Liu, Y., Liu, X.-Y., & Zheng, X. (2017). Why do employees have better family lives when they are highly engaged at work? *Journal of Applied Psychology, 102*(6), 956–970. http://dx.doi.org/10.1037/apl0000211

Inceoglu, I., & Warr, P. (2011). Personality and job engagement. *Journal of Personnel Psychology, 10*(4), 177–181. http://dx.doi.org/10.1027/1866-5888/a000045

International Test Commission. (2017). *The ITC guidelines for translating and adapting tests* (2nd ed.). Retrieved from www.InTestCom.org

Irvine, D. (2009, May 8). *Employee engagement: What it is and why you need it.* Retrieved June 7, 2009, from www.businessweek.com/bwdaily/dnflash/content/may2009/db2009058_952910.htm

Isen, A. M. (2000). Positive affect and decision making. In M. Lewis & J. M. Haviland-Jones (Eds.), *Handbook of emotion* (pp. 417–435). New York, NY: Guilford Press.

Iyengar, S. S., & DeVoe, S. E. (2003). Rethinking the value of choice: Considering cultural mediators of intrinsic motivation. In V. Murphy-Berman & J. J. Berman (Eds.), *Cross-cultural differences in perspectives on the self* (pp. 146–191). Lincoln: University of Nebraska Press.

Iyengar, S. S., & Lepper, M. R. (1999). Rethinking the value of choice: A cultural perspective on intrinsic motivation. *Journal of Personality and Social Psychology, 76,* 349–366.

Jacob, R. G., Thayer, J. F., Manuck, S. B., Muldoon, M. F., Tamres, L. K., Williams, D. M., . . . Gatsonis, C. (1999). Ambulatory blood pressure responses and the circumplex model of mood: A 4-day study. *Psychosomatic Medicine, 61*(3), 319–333.

James, J. B., McKechnie, S., & Swanberg, J. (2011). Predicting employee engagement in an age-diverse retail workforce. *Journal of Organizational Behavior, 32*(2), 173–196. http://dx.doi.org/10.1002/job.681

Janssen, O. (2000). Job demands, perceptions of effort-reward fairness and innovative work behaviour. *Journal of Occupational and Organizational Psychology, 73*(3), 287–302. http://dx.doi.org/10.1348/096317900167038

Javidan, M., House, R. J., & Dorfman, P. W. (2004). A nontechnical summary of GLOBE findings. In R. J. House, P. J. Hanges, M. Javidan, P. W. Dorfman, & V. Gupta (Eds.), *Culture, leadership, and organizations: The GLOBE study of 62 societies* (pp. 29–48). Thousand Oaks, CA: Sage.

Jeanson, S., & Michinov, E. (2020). What is the key to researchers' job satisfaction? One response is professional identification mediated by work engagement. *Current Psychology, 39*(2), 518–527. http://dx.doi.org/10.1007/s12144-017-9778-2

Jiang, H., & Shen, H. (2020). Toward a relational theory of employee engagement: Understanding authenticity, transparency, and employee behaviors. *International Journal of Business Communication,* Online First, 1–28. http://dx.doi.org/10.1177/2329488420954236

Jin, Y., Hopkins, M. M., & Wittmer, J. S. (2010). Linking human capital to competitive advantages: Flexibility in a manufacturing firm's supply chain. *Human Resource Management, 49*(5), 939–963. http://dx.doi.org/10.1002/hrm.20385

Johnson, J. W., & LeBreton, J. M. (2004). History and use of relative importance indices in organizational research. *Organizational Research Methods, 7,* 238–257.

Johnson, M. J., & Jiang, L. (2017). Reaping the benefits of meaningful work: The mediating versus moderating role of work engagement. *Stress and Health: Journal of the International Society for the Investigation of Stress, 33*(3), 288–297. http://dx.doi.org/10.1002/smi.2710

Jones, A. P., & James, L. R. (1979). Psychological climate: Dimensions and relationships of individual and aggregated work environment perceptions. *Organizational Behavior and Human Performance, 23,* 201–250.

Judge, T. A., Bono, J. E., Erez, A., & Locke, E. A. (2005). Core Self-evaluations and job and life satisfaction: The role of self-concordance and goal attainment. *Journal of Applied Psychology, 90*(2), 257–268. http://dx.doi.org/10.1037/0021-9010.90.2.257

Judge, T. A., & Kammeyer-Mueller, J. D. (2012). General and specific measures in organizational behavior research: Considerations, examples, and recommendations for researchers. *Journal of Organizational Behavior, 33*(2), 161–174. http://dx.doi.org/10.1002/job.764

Judge, T. A., Thoresen, C. J., Bono, J. E., & Patton, G. K. (2001). The job satisfaction: Job performance relationship: A qualitative and quantitative review. *Psychological Bulletin, 127*(3), 376–407. http://dx.doi.org/10.1037/0033-2909.127.3.376

Justis, R. T. (1975). Leadership effectiveness: A contingency approach. *Academy of Management Journal, 18*(1), 160–167. http://dx.doi.org/10.2307/255636

Kabasakal, H., Dastmalchian, A., & Imer, P. (2011). Organizational citizenship behavior: A study of young executives in Canada, Iran, and Turkey. *The International Journal of Human Resource Management, 13*, 2703–2729. http://dx.doi.org/10.1080/0 9585192.2011.599943

Kâğitçibaşi, Ç. (1987). Individual and group loyalties: Are they compatible? In Ç. Kâğitçibaşi (Ed.), *Growth and progress in cross-cultural psychology* (pp. 94–103). Berwyn, PA: Swets North America.

Kâğitçibaşi, Ç. (1994). A critical appraisal of individualism and collectivism: Toward a new formulation. In U. Kim, H. C. Triandis, Ç. Kâğitçibaşi, S. Choi, & G. Yoon (Eds.), *Individualism and collectivism: Theory, method, and applications* (pp. 52–65). Thousand Oaks, CA: Sage.

Kahn, W. A. (1990). Psychological conditions of personal engagement and disengagement at work. *Academy of Management Journal, 33*, 692–724.

Kahn, W. A. (1992). To be fully there: Psychological presence at work. *Human Relations, 45*(4), 321–349. http://dx.doi.org/10.1177/00187267920450040

Kahn, W. A., & Fellows, S. (2013). Employee engagement and meaningful work. In B. J. Dik, Z. S. Byrne, & M. F. Steger (Eds.), *Purpose and meaning in the workplace* (pp. 105–126). Washington, DC: American Psychological Association.

Kallioniemi, M. K., Kaseva, J., Lunner Kolstrup, C., Simola, A., & Kymäläinen, H.-R. (2018). Job resources and work engagement among Finnish dairy farmers. *Journal of Agromedicine, 23*(3), 249–261. http://dx.doi.org/10.1080/1059924X.2018. 1470047

Kanfer, R. (1990). Motivation theory and industrial and organizational psychology. In M. D. Dunnette & L. M. Hough (Eds.), *Handbook of industrial and organizational psychology* (Vol. 1, pp. 75–170). Palo Alto, CA: Consulting Psychologists Press.

Kanste, O. (2011). Work engagement, work commitment and their association with well-being in health care. *Scandinavian Journal of Caring Sciences, 25*(4), 754–761. http://dx.doi.org/10.1111/j.1471-6712.2011.00888.x

Kanter, R. M. (1988). When a thousand flowers bloom: Structural, collective, and social conditions for innovation in organization. *Research In Organizational Behavior, 10*, 169–213.

Kanungo, R. N. (1982). Measurement of job and work involvement. *Journal of Applied Psychology, 67*, 341–249. http://dx.doi.org/10.1037//0021-9010.67.3.341

Karasek, R. A. (1979). Job demands, job decision latitude, and mental strain: Implications for job redesign. *Administrative Science Quarterly, 24*(2), 285–308.

Karatepe, O. M. (2013). Perceptions of organizational politics and hotel employee outcomes: The mediating role of work engagement. *International Journal of Contemporary Hospitality Management, 25*(1), 82–104.

Karatepe, O. M., Keshavarz, S., & Nejati, S. (2012). Do core self-evaluations mediate the effect of coworker support on work engagement? A study of hotel employees in Iran. *Journal of Hospitality and Tourism Management, 17*(1), 61–71.

Karl, K. A., O'Leary-Kelly, A. M., & Martocchio, J. J. (1993). The impact of feedback and self-efficacy on performance in training. *Journal of Organizational Behavior, 14*(4), 379–394.

Katz, D. (1964). The motivational basis of organizational behavior. *Behavioral Science, 9*(2), 131–146. http://dx.doi.org/10.1002/bs.3830090206

Kelley, H. H. (1984). Interdependence theory and its future. *Representative Research in Social Psychology, 14*(2), 2–15.

Kendon, A. (1970). Movement coordination in social interaction: Some examples described. *Acta Psychologica, Amsterdam, 32*(2), 101–125. http://dx.doi.org/10.1016/0001-6918(70)90094-6

Kenexa Research Institute. (2009). *The impact of employee engagement.* Retrieved from www.kenexa.com/getattachment/8c36e336-3935-4406-8b7b-777f1afaa57d/The-Impact-of-Employee-Engagement.aspx

Kim, B., Williams, L., & Gill, D. L. (2003). A cross-cultural study of achievement orientation and intrinsic motivation in young USA and Korean athletes. *International Journal of Sport Psychology, 34*(2), 168–184.

Kim, H. J., Shin, K. H., & Swanger, N. (2009). Burnout and engagement: A comparative analysis using the Big Five personality dimensions. *International Journal of Hospitality Management, 28*(1), 96–104.

Kim, K.-S. (2019). The influence of hotels high-commitment HRM on job engagement of employees: Mediating effects of workplace happiness and mental health. *Applied Research in Quality of Life, 14*(2), 507–525. http://dx.doi.org/10.1007/s11482-018-9626-z

Kim, M., & Beehr, T. A. (2020). The long reach of the leader: Can empowering leadership at work result in enriched home lives? *Journal of Occupational Health Psychology, 25*(3), 203–213. http://dx.doi.org/10.1037/ocp0000177

Kim, S., Cho, S., & Park, Y. (2021). Daily microbreaks in a self-regulatory resources lens: Perceived health climate as a contextual moderator via microbreak autonomy. *Journal of Applied Psychology.* Advance online publication. http://dx.doi.org/http://dx.doi.org/10.1037/apl0000891

King, L. A., Hicks, J. A., Krull, J. L., & Del Gaiso, A. K. (2006). Positive affect and the experience of meaning in life. *Journal of Personality and Social Psychology, 90*(1), 179–196. http://dx.doi.org/10.1037/0022-3514.90.1.179

Kirkpatrick, S. A., & Locke, E. A. (1996). Direct and indirect effects of three core charismatic leadership components on performance and attitudes. *Journal of Applied Psychology, 81*(1), 36–51.

Klatt, M., Steinberg, B., & Duchemin, A.-M. (2015). *Mindfulness in Motion* (MIM): An onsite Mindfulness Based Intervention (MBI) for chronically high stress work environments to increase resiliency and work engagement. *Journal of Visualized Experiments, 101*, e52359, 1–11. http://dx.doi.org/10.3791/52359

Klimoski, R., & Mohammed, S. (1994). Team mental model: Construct or metaphor? *Journal of Management, 20*(2), 403–438. http://dx.doi.org/10.1016/0149-2063(94)90021-3

Kline, T. J. B. (2005). *Psychological testing: A practical approach to design and evaluation.* Thousand Oaks, CA: Sage.

Koch, S., & Leary, D. E. (1985). *A century of psychology as science.* Washington, DC: American Psychological Association. http://dx.doi.org/10.1037/10117-000

Kokubun, K., Ogata, Y., Koike, Y., & Yamakawa, Y. (2020). Brain condition may mediate the association between training and work engagement. *Scientific Reports, 10*(1), 1–13. http://dx.doi.org/10.1038/s41598-020-63711-3

Kooij, D. T. A. M., Nijssen, H., Bal, P. M., & Kruijssen, D. T. F. van der. (2020). Crafting an interesting job: Stimulating an active role of older workers in enhancing their daily work engagement and job performance. *Work, Aging & Retirement, 6*(3), 165–174. http://dx.doi.org/10.1093/workar/waaa001

Korsgaard, M., Schweiger, D. M., & Sapienza, H. J. (1995). Building commitment, attachment, and trust in strategic decision-making teams: The role of procedural justice. *Academy of Management Journal, 38*(1), 60–84. http://dx.doi.org/10.2307/256728

Kotera, Y., Van Laethem, M., & Ohshima, R. (2020). Cross-cultural comparison of mental health between Japanese and Dutch workers: Relationships with mental health shame, self-compassion, work engagement and motivation. *Cross Cultural & Strategic Management, 27*(3), 511–530. http://dx.doi.org/10.1108/CCSM-02-2020-0055

Kottke, J. L., & Sharafinski, C. E. (1988). Measuring perceived supervisory and organizational support. *Educational and Psychological Measurement, 48*, 1075–1079.

Kramer, R. M. (1994). The sinister attribution error: Paranoid cognition and collective distrust in organizations. *Motivation and Emotion, 18*(2), 199–230. http://dx.doi.org/10.1007/BF02249399

Kramer, R. M. (1999). Trust and distrust in organizations: Emerging perspectives, enduring questions. *Annual Review of Psychology, 50*, 569–598. http://dx.doi.org/10.1146/annurev.psych.50.1.569

Kristof-Brown, A. L., Zimmerman, R. D., & Johnson, E. C. (2005). Consequences of individuals' fit at work: A meta-analysis of person-job, person-organization, person-group, and person-supervisor fit. *Personnel Psychology, 58*(2), 281–342. http://dx.doi.org/10.1111/j.1744-6570.2005.00672.x

Kühnel, J., Sonnentag, S., & Westman, M. (2009). Does work engagement increase after a short respite? The role of job involvement as a double-edged sword. *Journal of Occupational and Organizational Psychology, 82*(3), 575–594. http://dx.doi.org/10.1348/096317908X349362

Kühnel, J., Zacher, H., de Bloom, J., & Bledow, R. (2017). Take a break! Benefits of sleep and short breaks for daily work engagement. *European Journal of Work & Organizational Psychology, 26*(4), 481–491. http://dx.doi.org/10.1080/1359432X.2016.1269750

Kuijpers, E., Kooij, D. T. A. M., & van Woerkom, M. (2020). Align your job with yourself: The relationship between a job crafting intervention and work engagement, and the role of workload. *Journal of Occupational Health Psychology, 25*(1), 1–16. http://dx.doi.org/10.1037/ocp0000175

Kurman, J. (2001). Self-regulation strategies in achievement settings: Culture and gender differences. *Journal of Cross-Cultural Psychology, 32*, 491–503.

Lacey, J. L., Bateman, D. E., & VanLehn, R. (1953). Autonomic response specificity: An experimental study. *Psychomatic Medicine, 15*, 8–21.

LaFrance, M., & Broadbent, M. (1976). Group rapport: Posture sharing as a nonverbal indicator. *Group & Organization Studies, 1*(3), 328–333. http://dx.doi.org/10.1177/105960117600100307

Lai, F.-Y., Tang, H.-C., Lu, S.-C., Lee, Y.-C., & Lin, C.-C. (2020). Transformational leadership and job performance: The mediating role of work engagement. *SAGE Open, (January–March)*, 1–11. http://dx.doi.org/10.1177/2158244019899085

Lakin, J. L., & Chartrand, T. L. (2003). Using nonconscious behavioral mimicry to create affiliation and rapport. *Psychological Science, 14*(4), 334–339. http://dx.doi.org/10.1111/1467-9280.14481

Lam, S. S. K., Hui, C., & Law, K. S. (1999). Organizational citizenship behavior: Comparing perspectives of supervisor and subordinates across four international samples. *Journal of Applied Psychology, 84*, 594–601.

Lambert, S. J. (1991). The combined effects of job and family characteristics on the job satisfaction, job involvement, and intrinsic motivation of men and women workers. *Journal of Organizational Behavior, 12*, 341–363. http://dx.doi.org/10.1002/job.4030120408

Landells, E. M., & Albrecht, S. L. (2019). Perceived organizational politics, engagement, and stress: The mediating influence of meaningful work. *Frontiers in Psychology, 10.* http://dx.doi.org/10.3389/fpsyg.2019.01612

Laschinger, H. K. S., Leiter, M. P., Day, A., Gilin-Oore, D., & Mackinnon, S. P. (2012). Building empowering work environments that foster civility and organizational trust. *Nursing Research, 61*(5), 316–325. http://dx.doi.org/10.1097/NNR.0b013e318265a58d

Latané, B. (1997). Dynamic social impact: The societal consequences of human interaction. In C. McGarty & S. Haslam (Eds.), *The message of social psychology: Perspectives on mind in society* (pp. 200–220). Malden, MA: Blackwell.

Latané, B., & L'Herrou, T. (1996). Spatial clustering in the conformity game: Dynamic social impact in electronic groups. *Journal of Personality and Social Psychology, 70*(6), 1218–1230. http://dx.doi.org/10.1037/0022-3514.70.6.1218

Lauver, K. J., & Kristof-Brown, A. (2001). Distinguishing between employees' perceptions of person-job and person-organization fit. *Journal of Vocational Behavior, 59*(3), 454–470. http://dx.doi.org/10.1006/jvbe.2001.1807

Lavigna, B. (2013). Improving employee engagement: The special case of the public service. *PA Times, 36*(1), 11–12.

Lawler, E. E., & Hall, D. T. (1970). Relationship of job characteristics to job involvement, satisfaction, and intrinsic motivation. *Journal of Applied Psychology, 54*(4), 305–312. http://dx.doi.org/10.1037/h0029692

Lawler, E. E., Hackman, J., & Kaufman, S. (1973). Effects of job redesign: A field experiment. *Journal of Applied Social Psychology, 3*(1), 49–62. http://dx.doi.org/10.1111/j.1559-1816.1973.tb01294.x

Lazarus, R. S. (1991). *Emotion and adaptation.* New York: Oxford University Press.

Lazarus, R. S., & Folkman, S. (1984). *Stress, appraisal, and coping.* New York: Springer.

LeBreton, J. M., Hargis, M. B., Griepentrog, B., Oswald, F. L., & Ployhart, R. E. (2007). A multidimensional approach for evaluating variables in organizational research and practice. *Personnel Psychology, 60*(2), 475–498. http://dx.doi.org/10.1111/j.1744-6570.2007.00080.x

Lee, A. Y., Aaker, J. L., & Gardner, W. L. (2000). The pleasures and pains of distinct self-construals: The role of interdependence in regulatory focus. *Journal of Personality and Social Psychology, 78*, 1122–1134.

Lee, C.-H., Wang, M.-L., & Liu, M.-S. (2017). When and how does psychological voice climate influence individual change readiness? The mediating role of normative commitment and the moderating role of work engagement. *Frontiers in Psychology, 8*, 1–11. http://dx.doi.org/10.3389/fpsyg.2017.01737

Lee, K., & Allen, N. J. (2002). Organizational citizenship behavior and workplace deviance: The role of affect and cognitions. *Journal of Applied Psychology, 87*(1), 131–142. http://dx.doi.org/10.1037/0021-9010.87.1.131

Lee, W., Reeve, J., Xue, Y., & Xiong, J. (2012). Neural differences between intrinsic reasons for doing versus extrinsic reasons for doing: An fMRI study. *Neuroscience Research, 73*(1), 68–72. http://dx.doi.org/10.1016/j.neures.2012.02.010

Lench, H. C., Flores, S. A., & Bench, S. W. (2011). Discrete emotions predict changes in cognition, judgment, experience, behavior, and physiology: A meta-analysis of experimental emotion elicitations. *Psychological Bulletin, 137*, 834–855. http://dx.doi.org/10.1037/a0024244

Lent, R. W. (2013). Promoting meaning and purpose at work: A social-cognitive perspective. In B. J. Dik, Z. S. Byrne, & M. F. Steger (Eds.), *Purpose and meaning in the workplace* (pp. 151–170). Washington, DC: American Psychological Association.

LePine, J. A., Erez, A., & Johnson, D. E. (2002). The nature and dimensionality of organizational citizenship behavior: A critical review and meta-analysis. *Journal of Applied Psychology, 87*(1), 52–65. http://dx.doi.org/10.1037/0021-9010.87.1.52

Lepper, M. R., Sethi, S., Dialdin, D., & Drake, M. (1997). Intrinsic and extrinsic motivation: A developmental perspective. In S. S. Luthar, J. A. Burack, D. Cicchetti, & J. R. Weisz (Eds.), *Developmental psychopathology: Perspectives on adjustment, risk, and disorder* (pp. 23–50). New York, NY: Cambridge University Press.

Lerner, J. S., & Keltner, D. (2000). Beyond valence: Toward a model of emotion-specific influences on judgment and choice. *Cognition & Emotion, 14*, 473–493. http://dx.doi.org/10.1080/026999300402763

Lester, P. B., Hannah, S. T., Harms, P. D., Vogelgesang, G. R., & Avolio, B. J. (2011). Mentoring impact on leader efficacy development: A field experiment. *Academy of Management Learning & Education, 10*(3), 409–429. http://dx.doi.org/10.5465/amle.2010.0047

Levine, J. M., Resnick, L. B., & Higgins, E. (1993). Social foundations of cognition. *Annual Review of Psychology, 44*, 585–612. http://dx.doi.org/10.1146/annurev.ps.44.020193.003101

Lewin, K. (1946). Action research and minority problems. *Journal of Social Issues, 2*(4), 34–46. http://dx.doi.org/10.1111/j.1540-4560.1946.tb02295.x

Lewin, K. (1947). Frontiers in group dynamics. II: Channels of group life, social planning and action research. *Human Relations, 1*, 143–153. http://dx.doi.org/10.1177/001872674700100201

Li, Y. (2019). Leadership styles and knowledge workers' work engagement: Psychological capital as a mediator. *Current Psychology: A Journal for Diverse Perspectives on Diverse Psychological Issues, 38*(5), 1152–1161. http://dx.doi.org/10.1007/s12144-018-9968-6

Liao, F., Yang, L., Wang, M., Drown, D., & Shi, J. (2013). Team-member exchange and work engagement: Does personality make a difference? *Journal of Business & Psychology, 28*(1), 63–77. http://dx.doi.org/10.1007/s10869-012-9266-5

Lichtenthaler, P. W., & Fischbach, A. (2019). A meta-analysis on promotion- and prevention-focused job crafting. *European Journal of Work and Organizational Psychoogy, 28*(1), 30–50. http://dx.doi.org/10.1080/1359432X.2018.1527767

Linnenbrink, E. A., & Pintrich, P. R. (2010). Achievement goal theory and affect: An asymmetrical bidirectional model. *Educational Psychologist, 37*(2), 69–78. http://dx.doi.org/10.1207/S1532698SEP3702_2

Liu, D., Chen, Y., & Li, N. (2021). Tackling the negative impact of COVID-19 on work engagement and taking charge: A multi-study investigation of frontline health workers. *Journal of Applied Psychology.* Advance online publication. http://dx.doi.org/10.1037/apl0000866

Liu, J., & Cho, S. (2018). Interaction effect of display rules and emotional intelligence on hotel managers' and non-managers' work engagement. *International Journal of Contemporary Hospitality Management, 30*(3), 1903–1919. http://dx.doi.org/10.1108/IJCHM-02-2017-0063

Locke, E. A. (1976). The nature and causes of job satisfaction. In M. D. Dunnette (Ed.), *Handbook of industrial and organizational psychology* (pp. 1297–1349). Chicago: Rand McNally College Pub. Co.

Locke, E. A., & Latham, G. P. (1990). *A theory of goal setting & task performance.* Englewood Cliffs, NJ: Prentice-Hall.

Locke, E. A., Smith, P., Kendall, L. M., Hulin, C. L., & Miller, A. M. (1964). Convergent and discriminant validity for areas and methods of rating job satisfaction. *Journal of Applied Psychology, 48*(5), 313–319. http://dx.doi.org/10.1037/h0043202

Lodahl, T. M., & Kejner, M. (1965). The definition and measurement of job involvement. *Journal of Applied Psychology, 49*(1), 24–33.

Lo Presti, A., Kertechian, S. K., & Landolfi, A. (2020). Does the association between workload and work engagement depend on being workaholic? A cross-cultural study on Italian and Canadian employees. *Electronic Journal of Applied Statistical Analysis, 13*(3), 589–611. http://dx.doi.org/10.1285/i20705948v13n3p589

Luria, G., & Torjman, A. (2009). Resources and coping with stressful events. *Journal of Organizational Behavior, 30*(6), 685–707. http://dx.doi.org/10.1002/job.v30:610.1002/job.551

Luthans, F., Avolio, B. J., Avey, J. B., & Norman, S. M. (2007). Positive psychological capital: Measurement and relationship with performance and satisfaction. *Personnel Psychology, 60*(3), 541–572. http://dx.doi.org/10.1111/j.1744-6570.2007.00083.x

Luthans, F., & Peterson, S. J. (2002). Employee engagement and manager self-efficacy: Implications for managerial effectiveness and development. *Journal of Management Development, 5*, 376–387.

Luu, T. T., Rowley, C., & Vo, T. T. (2019). Addressing employee diversity to foster their work engagement. *Journal of Business Research, 95*, 303–315. http://dx.doi.org/10.1016/j.jbusres.2018.08.017

Maas, H., & Spinath, F. M. (2012). Personality and coping with professional demands: A behavioral genetics analysis. *Journal of Occupational Health Psychology, 17*(3), 376–385. http://dx.doi.org/10.1037/a0027Ml

Macdonald, A. M., & de Silva, P. (1999). The assessment of obsessionality using the Padua Inventory: Its validity in a British non-clinical sample. *Personality and Individual Differences, 27*(6), 1027–1046. http://dx.doi.org/10.1016/S0191-8869(99)00036-7

Macey, W. H., & Schneider, B. (2008). The meaning of employee engagement. *Industrial and Organizational Psychology: Perspectives on Science and Practice, 1*, 3–30.

Macey, W. H., Schneider, B., Barbera, K. M., & Young, S. A. (2009). *Employee engagement: Tools for analysis, practice, and competitive advantage.* Chichester: Blackwell.

Macgowan, M. J. (2000). Evaluation of a measure of engagement for group work. *Research on Social Work Practice, 10*(3), 348–361.

Machlowitz, M. (1980). *Workaholics: Living with them, working with them.* Reading, MA: Addison-Wesley.

Mackay, M. M., Allen, J. A., & Landis, R. S. (2017). Investigating the incremental validity of employee engagement in the prediction of employee effectiveness: A meta-analytic path analysis. *Human Resource Management Review, 27*(1), 108–120. http://dx.doi.org/10.1016/j.hrmr.2016.03.002

Maddux, J. E. (2002). Stopping the "Madness": Positive psychology and the deconstruction of the illness ideology and the DSM. In C. R. Snyder & S. J. Lopez (Eds.), *Handbook of positive psychology* (pp. 13–25). New York, NY: Oxford University Press.

Mael, F. A., & Tetrick, L. E. (1992). Identifying organizational identification. *Educational and Psychological Measurement, 52*(4), 813–824. http://dx.doi.org/10.1177/0013164492052004002

Maguire, M. A. (1983). The effects of context on attitude measurement: The case of job satisfaction. *Human Relations, 36*(11), 1013–1030. http://dx.doi.org/10.1177/001872678303601104

Mäkikangas, A. (2018). Job crafting profiles and work engagement: A person-centered approach. *Journal of Vocational Behavior, 106*, 101–111. http://dx.doi.org/10.1016/j.jvb.2018.01.001

Malinowska, D., & Tokarz, A. (2020). The moderating role of Self Determination Theory's general causality orientations in the relationship between the job resources and work engagement of outsourcing sector employees. *Personality and Individual Differences, 153*. http://dx.doi.org/10.1016/j.paid.2019.109638

Manning, S. G. (2015). *The development and validation of a measure of disengagement.* Unpublished thesis, Colorado State University. ProQuest Dissertations 1597892.

Markus, H. (1977). Self-schemata and processing information about the self. *Journal of Personality and Social Psychology, 35*(2), 63–78. http://dx.doi.org/10.1037/0022-3514.35.2.63

Markus, H., & Kitayama, S. (1991). Culture and the self: Implications for cognition, emotion, and motivation. *Psychological Review, 98*(2), 224–253.

Markus, H., Kitayama, S., & Heiman, R. J. (1996). Culture and "basic" psychological principles. In E. Higgins & A. W. Kruglanski (Eds.), *Social psychology: Handbook of basic principles* (pp. 857–913). New York, NY: Guilford Press.

Maslach, C. (1982). *Burnout: The cost of caring.* Englewood Cliffs, NJ: Prentice Hall.

Maslach, C. (2003). Job burnout: New directions in research and intervention. *Current Directions in Psychological Science (Wiley-Blackwell), 12*(5), 189–193. http://dx.doi.org/10.1111/1467-8721.01258

Maslach, C., & Jackson, S. E. (1981). The measurement of experienced burnout. *Journal of Occupational Behavior, 2*(2), 99–113.

Maslach, C., & Jackson, S. E. (1984). Burnout in organizational settings. *Applied Social Psychology Annual, 5*, 133–153.

Maslach, C., & Leiter, M. P. (1997). *The truth about burnout: How organizations cause personal stress and what to do about it.* San Francisco, CA: Jossey-Bass.

Maslach, C., Schaufeli, W. B., & Leiter, M. P. (2001). Job burnout. *Annual Review of Psychology, 52*, 397–422.

Maslow, A. H. (1943). A theory of human motivation. *Psychological Review, 50*(4), 370–396. http://dx.doi.org/10.1037/h0054346

Maslow, A. H. (1968). *Towards a psychology of being.* New York, NY: Van Nostrand.

Maslow, A. H. (1998). *Maslow on management.* New York, NY: John Wiley.

Matthews, D. J. (2010, February). Trust me: Credible leadership delivers results. *Chief Learning Officer*, 28–31.

Mauno, S., Kinnunen, U., Mäkikangas, A., & Nätti, J. (2005). Psychological consequences of fixed-term employment and perceived job insecurity among health care staff. *European Journal of Work and Organizational Psychology, 14*(3), 209–237. http://dx.doi.org/10.1080/13594320500146649

Mauno, S., Kinnunen, U., & Ruokolainen, M. (2007). Job demands and resources as antecedents of work engagement: A longitudinal study. *Journal of Vocational Behavior, 70*(1), 149–171. http://dx.doi.org/10.1016/j.jvb.2006.09.002

May, D. R., Gilson, R. L., & Harter, L. M. (2004). The psychological conditions of meaningfulness, safety and availability and the engagement of the human spirit at work. *Journal of Occupational and Organizational Psychology, 77*, 11–37.

Mayer, J. D., Caruso, D. R., & Salovey, P. (2000). Selecting a measure of emotional intelligence: The case for ability scales. In R. Bar-On & J. A. Parker (Eds.), *The handbook of emotional intelligence: Theory, development, assessment, and application at home, school, and in the workplace* (pp. 320–342). San Francisco, CA: Jossey-Bass.

Mayer, J. D., & Salovey, P. (1995). Emotional intelligence and the construction and regulation of feelings. *Applied & Preventive Psychology, 4*(3), 197–208. http://dx.doi.org/10.1016/S0962-1849(05)80058-7

Mayuran, L., & Kailasapathy, P. (2020). To engage or not? Antecedents of employee engagement in Sri Lanka. *Asia Pacific Journal of Human Resources, 1.* http://dx.doi.org/10.1111/1744-7941.12270

Mazzetti, G., Schaufeli, W. B., & Guglielmi, D. (2018). Are workaholism and work engagement in the eye of the beholder? A multirater perspective on different forms of working hard. *European Journal of Psychological Assessment, 34*(1), 30–40. http://dx.doi.org/10.1027/1015-5759/a000318

McAllister, D. J. (1995). Affect- and cognition-based trust as foundations for interpersonal cooperation in organizations. *Academy of Management Journal, 38*(1), 24–59.

McCulloch, M. C., & Turban, D. B. (2007). Using person: Organization fit to select employees for high-turnover jobs. *International Journal of Selection and Assessment, 15*(1), 63–71. http://dx.doi.org/10.1111/j.1468-2389.2007.00368.x

McGonagle, A. K., Schwab, L., Yahanda, N., Duskey, H., Gertz, N., Prior, L., . . . Kriegel, G. (2020). Coaching for primary care physician well-being: A randomized trial and follow-up analysis. *Journal of Occupational Health Psychology, 25*(5), 297–314. http://dx.doi.org/10.1037/ocp0000180.supp (Supplemental).

McGrath, E., Cooper, T. H. D., Garrosa, E., Sanz, V. A. I., & Cheung, G. W. (2017). Rested, friendly, and engaged: The role of daily positive collegial interactions at work. *Journal of Organizational Behavior, 38*(8), 1213–1226. http://dx.doi.org/10.1002/job.2197

McGregor, I., & Little, B. R. (1998). Personal projects, happiness, and meaning: On doing well and being yourself. *Journal of Personality and Social Psychology, 74*(2), 494–512. http://dx.doi.org/10.1037/0022-3514.74.2.494

McHugo, G. J., Lanzetta, J. T., Sullivan, D. G., Masters, R. D., & Englis, B. G. (1985). Emotional reactions to a political leader's expressive displays. *Journal of Personality and Social Psychology, 49*(6), 1513–1529. http://dx.doi.org/10.1037/0022-3514.49.6.1513

McMillan, L. W., & O'Driscoll, M. P. (2006). Exploring new frontiers to generate an integrated definition of workaholism. In R. J. Burke (Ed.), *Research companion to working time and work addiction* (pp. 89–107). Northampton, MA: Edward Elgar.

McPhail, S. M. (Ed.). (2007). *Alternative validation strategies: Developing new and leveraging existing validity evidence.* Hoboken, NJ: John Wiley & Sons.

Medlin, B., & Green, K. W. (2009). Enhancing performance through goal setting, engagement, and optimism. *Industrial Management & Data Systems, 109,* 943–956.

Meglino, B. M., Ravlin, E. C., & Adkins, C. L. (1989). A work values approach to corporate culture: A field test of the value congruence process and its relationship to individual outcomes. *Journal of Applied Psychology, 74*(3), 424–432. http://dx.doi.org/10.1037/0021-9010.74.3.424

Mehrabian, A., & Ksionzky, S. (1970). Models for affiliative and conformity behavior. *Psychological Bulletin, 74*(2), 110–126. http://dx.doi.org/10.1037/h0029603

Meintjes, A., & Hofmeyr, K. (2018). The impact of resilience and perceived organisational support on employee engagement in a competitive sales environment. *South African Journal of Human Resource Management, 16*(1), N.PAG. http://dx.doi.org/10.4102/sajhrm.v16i0.953

Meng, Y., Wang, Y., & Tian, X. (2021). Job crafting paths for job engagement: An empirical study among Chinese social workers. *Human Service Organizations: Management, Leadership & Governance.* http://dx.doi.org/10.1080/23303131.2021.1873213

Menguc, B., Auh, S., Fisher, M., & Haddad, A. (2013). To be engaged or not to be engaged: The antecedents and consequences of service employee engagement. *Journal of Business Research, 66*, 2163–2170.

Mesurado, B., Richaud, M. C., & Mateo, N. J. (2016). Engagement, flow, self-efficacy, and eustress of university students: A cross-national comparison between the Philippines and Argentina. *Journal of Psychology, 150*(3), 281–299. http://dx.doi.org/10.10 80/00223980.2015.1024595

Meurs, J. A., & Perrewé, P. L. (2011). Cognitive activation theory of stress: An integrative theoretical approach to work stress. *Journal of Management, 37*(4), 1043–1068. http://dx.doi.org/10.1177/0149206310387303

Meyer, J. P., & Allen, N. J. (1991). A three-component conceptualization of organizational commitment. *Human Resource Management Review, 1*(1), 61–90.

Meyer, J. P., & Gagné, M. (2008). Employee engagement from a self-determination theory perspective. *Industrial and Organizational Psychology: Perspectives on Science and Practice, 1*(1), 60–62. http://dx.doi.org/10.1111/j.1754-9434.2007.00010.x

Meyer, J. P., Gagné, M., & Parfyonova, N. M. (2010). Toward an evidence-based model of engagement: What we can learn from motivation and commitment research. In S. L. Albrecht (Ed.), *Handbook of employee engagement: Perspectives, issues, research and practice* (pp. 62–73). Northampton, MA: Edward Elgar.

Meyer, J. P., Stanley, L. J., & Parfyonova, N. M. (2012). Employee commitment in context: The nature and implication of commitment profiles. *Journal of Vocational Behavior, 80*(1), 1–16. http://dx.doi.org/10.1016/j.jvb.2011.07.002

Meyers, M. C., Adams, B. G., Sekaja, L., Buzea, C., Cazan, A.-M., Gotea, M., Stefenel, D., & van Woerkom, M. (2019). Perceived organizational support for the use of employees' strengths and employee well-being: A cross-country comparison. *Journal of Happiness Studies, 20*(6), 1825–1841. http://dx.doi.org/10.1007/s10902-018-0026-8

Michela, J. L., & Vena, J. (2012). A dependence-regulation account of psychological distancing in response to major organizational change. *Journal of Change Management, 12*(1), 77–94. http://dx.doi.org/10.1080/14697017.2011.652376

Miles, R. H. (2001). Beyond the age of Dilbert: Accelerating corporate transformations by rapidly engaging all employees. *Organizational Dynamics, 29*(4), 313–321.

Miller, J. G., & Bersoff, D. M. (1994). Cultural influences on the moral status of reciprocity and the discounting of endogenous motivation. *Personality and Social Psychology Bulletin, 20*(5), 592–602. http://dx.doi.org/10.1177/0146167294205015

Miller, R. B., Greene, B. A., Montalvo, G. P., Ravindran, B., & Nichols, J. D. (1996). Engagement in academic work: The role of learning goals, future consequences, pleasing others, and perceived ability. *Contemporary Educational Psychology, 21*, 388–422.

Misumi, J. (1989). Research on leadership and group decision in Japanese organisations. *Applied Psychology: An International Review, 38*(4), 321–336. http://dx.doi.org/10.1111/j.1464-0597.1989.tb01211.x

Misumi, J. (1995). The development in Japan of the Performance-Maintenance (PM) theory of leadership. *Journal of Social Issues, 51*(1), 213–228. http://dx.doi.org/10.1111/j.1540-4560.1995.tb01319.x

Misumi, J., & Peterson, M. F. (1985a). *The behavioral science of leadership: An interdisciplinary Japanese research program.* Ann Arbor: University of Michigan Press.

Misumi, J., & Peterson, M. F. (1985b). The Performance-Maintenance (PM) theory of leadership: Review of a Japanese research program. *Administrative Science Quarterly, 30*(2), 198–223. http://dx.doi.org/10.2307/2393105

Mone, E. M., & London, M. (2010). *Employee engagement through effective performance management: A practical guide for managers.* New York, NY: Routledge/Taylor & Francis Group.

Moneta, G. B. (2004). The flow model of intrinsic motivation in Chinese: Cultural and personal moderators. *Journal of Happiness Studies, 5,* 181–217.

Montani, F., Vandenberghe, C., Khedhaouria, A., & Courcy, F. (2020). Examining the inverted U-shaped relationship between workload and innovative work behavior: The role of work engagement and mindfulness. *Human Relations, 73*(1), 59–93. http://dx.doi.org/10.1177/0018726718819055

Moreland, J. (2013). Improving job fit can improve employee engagement and productivity. *Employment Relations Today, 40*(1), 57–62. http://dx.doi.org/10.1002/ert.21400

Moreland, R. L., Argote, L., & Krishnan, R. (1996). Socially shared cognition at work: Transactive memory and group performance. In J. L. Nye & A. M. Brower (Eds.), *What's social about social cognition? Research on socially shared cognition in small groups* (pp. 57–84). Thousand Oaks, CA: Sage.

Morin, A. S., Vandenberghe, C., Boudrias, J., Madore, I., Morizot, J., & Tremblay, M. (2011). Affective commitment and citizenship behaviors across multiple foci. *Journal of Managerial Psychology, 26*(8), 716–738. http://dx.doi.org/10.1108/02683941111181798

Morin, E. M. (1995). Organizational effectiveness and the meaning of work. In T. C. Pauchant & Associates (Eds.), *In search of meaning: Managing for the health of our organizations, our communities, and the natural world* (pp. 29–64). San Francisco, CA: Jossey-Bass.

Moritz, B. (2014). How I did it . . . the U.S. Chairman of PwC on keeping millennials engaged. *Harvard Business Review, 92*(11), 41–44.

Mostert, K., & Rothmann, S. (2006). Work-related well-being in the South African police service. *Journal of Criminal Justice, 34*(5), 479–491. http://dx.doi.org/10.1016/j.jcrimjus.2006.09.003

Motowidlo, S. J. (2003). Job performance. In W. C. Borman, D. R. Ilgen, & R. J. Klimoski (Eds.), *Handbook of psychology: Industrial and organizational psychology* (Vol. 12, pp. 39–53). Hoboken, NJ: John Wiley & Sons.

Motowidlo, S. J., & van Scotter, J. R. (1994). Evidence that task performance should be distinguished from contextual performance. *Journal of Applied Psychology, 79*(4), 475–480. http://dx.doi.org/10.1037/0021-9010.79.4.475

Mowday, R. T., Steers, R. M., & Porter, L. W. (1979). The measurement of organizational commitment. *Journal of Vocational Behavior, 14*(2), 224–247. http://dx.doi.org/10.1016/0001-8791(79)90072-1

Mudrack, P. E. (2004). Job involvement, obsessive-compulsive personality traits, and workaholic behavioral tendencies. *Journal of Organizational Change Management, 17*(5), 490–508. http://dx.doi.org/10.1108/09534810410554506

Mudrack, P. E., & Naughton, T. J. (2001). The assessment of workaholism as behavioral tendencies: Scale development and preliminary empirical testing. *International Journal of Stress Management, 8*(2), 93–111. http://dx.doi.org/10.1023/A:1009525213213

Murphy, K. R. (1989). Dimensions of job performance. In R. F. Dillon & J. W. Pellegrino (Eds.), *Testing: Theoretical and applied perspectives* (pp. 218–247). New York, NY: Praeger.

Murphy, K. R. (1994). Toward a broader conception of jobs and job performance: Impact of changes in the military environment on the structure, assessment, and prediction of job performance. In M. G. Rumsey, C. B. Walker, & J. Harris (Eds.), *Personnel selection and classification* (pp. 85–102). Hillsdale, NJ: Lawrence Erlbaum Associates.

Myers, I. B., & McCauley, M. H. (1985). *Manual: A guide to the development and use of the Myers-Briggs type indicator.* Palo Alto, CA: Consulting Psychologist Press.

Nakamura, J., & Csikszentmihalyi, M. (2002). The concept of flow. In C. R. Snyder & S. J. Lopez (Eds.), *Handbook of positive psychology* (pp. 89–105). New York, NY: Oxford University Press.

Ncube, F., & Jerie, S. (2012). Leveraging employee engagement for competitive advantage in the hospitality industry: A comparative study of hotels A and B in Zimbabwe. *Journal of Emerging Trends In Economics & Management Sciences, 3*(4), 380–388.

Newman, D. A., & Harrison, D. A. (2008). Been there, bottled that: Are state and behavioral work engagement new and useful construct "wines"? *Industrial and Organizational Psychology: Perspectives on Science and Practice, 1*, 31–35. http://dx.doi.org/10.1111/j.1754-9434.2007.00003.x

Ng, T. H., Sorensen, K. L., & Feldman, D. C. (2007). Dimensions, antecedents, and consequences of workaholism: A conceptual integration and extension. *Journal of Organizational Behavior, 28*(1), 111–136.

Nielsen, K., Randall, R., Yarker, J., & Brenner, S.-O. (2008). The effects of transformational leadership on followers' perceived work characteristics and psychological well-being: A longitudinal study. *Work & Stress, 22*, 16–32. http://dx.doi.org/10.1080/02678370801979430

Nikolaou, I. (2003). Fitting the person to the organisation: Examining the personality-job performance relationship from a new perspective. *Journal of Managerial Psychology, 18*(7), 639–648. http://dx.doi.org/10.1108/02683940310502368

Nimon, K., & Shuck, B. (2020). Work engagement and burnout: Testing the theoretical continuums of identification and energy. *Human Resource Development Quarterly, 31*(3), 301–318. http://dx.doi.org/10.1002/hrdq.21379

Ning, W., & Alikaj, A. (2019). The influence of age on the job resources-engagement relationship. *International Journal of Organizational Analysis, 27*(4), 1218–1238. http://dx.doi.org/10.1108/IJOA-09-2018-1528

Nunnally, J. C., & Bernstein, I. (1994). *Psychometric theory* (3rd ed.). New York: McGraw-Hill.

Oates, W. (1968). On being a "workaholic." *Pastoral Psychology, 19*(8), 16–20. http://dx.doi.org/10.1007/BF01785472

Ochsner, K. N. (2007). How thinking controls feeling: A social cognitive neuroscience approach. In E. Harmon-Jones & P. Winkielman (Eds.), *Social neuroscience: Integrating biological and psychological explanations of social behavior* (pp. 106–133). New York, NY: Guilford Press.

Okurame, D. E. (2012). Linking work-family conflict to career commitment: The moderating effects of gender and mentoring among Nigerian civil servants. *Journal of Career Development, 39*(5), 423–442. http://dx.doi.org/10.1177/0894845310391903

Oldham, G. R., & Hackman, J. R. (1980). Work design in the organizational context. *Research in Organizational Behavior, 2*, 247–279.

Olesen, C., White, D., & Lemmer, I. (2007). Career models and culture change at Microsoft. *Organization Development Journal, 25*(2), P31–P35.

Olugbade, O. A., & Karatepe, O. M. (2019). Stressors, work engagement and their effects on hotel employee outcomes. *Service Industries Journal, 39*(3/4), 279–298. http://dx.doi.org/10.1080/02642069.2018.1520842

Oprea, B. T., Barzin, L., Vîrgă, D., Iliescu, D., & Rusu, A. (2019). Effectiveness of job crafting interventions: A meta-analysis and utility analysis. *European Journal of Work and Organizational Psychology, 28*(6), 723–741. http://dx.doi.org/10.1080/1359432X.2019.1646728

O'Reilly, C. A., & Chatman, J. (1986). Organizational commitment and psychological attachment: The effects of compliance, identification, and internalization on prosocial behavior. *Journal of Applied Psychology, 71*(3), 492–499. http://dx.doi.org/10.1037/0021-9010.71.3.492

Organ, D. W. (1977). A reappraisal and reinterpretation of the satisfaction-causes-performance hypothesis. *Academy of Management Review, 2*, 46–53. http://dx.doi.org/10.5465/AMR.1977.4409162

Organ, D. W. (1988). *Organizational citizenship behavior: The good soldier syndrome.* Lexington, MA: Lexington Books/D. C. Heath and Com.

Organ, D. W. (1997). Organizational citizenship behavior: It's construct clean-up time. *Human Performance, 10*, 85–97.

Organ, D. W., & Ryan, K. (1995). A meta-analytic review of attitudinal and dispositional predictors of organizational citizenship behavior. *Personnel Psychology, 48*(4), 775–802. http://dx.doi.org/10.1111/j.1744-6570.1995.tb01781.x

Ostroff, C., Kinicki, A. J., & Muhammad, R. S. (2013). Organizational culture and climate. In N. W. Schmitt, S. Highhouse, & I. B. Weiner (Eds.), *Handbook of psychology, Vol. 12: Industrial and organizational psychology* (2nd ed., pp. 643–676). Hoboken, NJ: John Wiley & Sons.

Ostroff, C., Kinicki, A. J., & Tamkins, M. M. (2003). Organizational culture and climate. In W. C. Borman, D. R. Ilgen, & R. J. Klimoski (Eds.), *Handbook of psychology: Industrial and organizational psychology* (Vol. 12, pp. 565–593). Hoboken, NJ: John Wiley & Sons.

O'Toole, R., & Dubin, R. (1968). Baby feeding and body sway: An experiment in George Herbert Mead's "taking the role of the other." *Journal of Personality and Social Psychology, 10*(1), 59–65. http://dx.doi.org/10.1037/h0026387

Ouweneel, E., Le Blanc, P. M., Schaufeli, W. B., & van Wijhe, C. I. (2012). Good morning, good day: A diary study on positive emotions, hope, and work engagement. *Human Relations, 65*(9), 1129–1154. http://dx.doi.org/10.1177/0018726711429382

Ouweneel, E., Schaufeli, W. B., & Le Blanc, P. M. (2013). Believe, and you will achieve: Changes over time in self-efficacy, engagement, and performance. *Applied Psychology: Health & Well-Being, 5*(2), 225–247. http://dx.doi.org/10.1111/aphw.12008

Oyserman, D., Coon, H. M., & Kemmelmeier, M. (2002). Rethinking individualism and collectivism: Evaluation of theoretical assumptions and meta-analyses. *Psychological Bulletin, 128*(1), 3–73.

Panteli, N., Yalabik, Z. Y., & Rapti, A. (2019). Fostering work engagement in geographically-dispersed and asynchronous virtual teams. *Information Technology & People, 32*(1), 2–17. http://dx.doi.org/10.1108/ITP-04-2017-0133

Park, C. L. (2010). Making sense of the meaning literature: An integrative review of meaning making and its effects on adjustment to stressful life events. *Psychological Bulletin, 136*(2), 257–301. http://dx.doi.org/10.1037/a0018301

Park, J. G., Kim, J. S., Yoon, S. W., & Joo, B.-K. (2017). The effects of empowering leadership on psychological well-being and job engagement: The mediating role of psychological capital. *Leadership & Organization Development Journal, 38*(3), 350–367. http://dx.doi.org/10.1108/LODJ-08-2015-0182

Parke, M. R., Weinhardt, J. M., Brodsky, A., Tangirala, S., & DeVoe, S. E. (2018). When daily planning improves employee performance: The importance of planning type, engagement, and interruptions. *Journal of Applied Psychology, 103*(3), 300–312. http://dx.doi.org/10.1037/apl0000278

Parry, K. W., & Sinha, P. N. (2005). Researching the trainability of transformational organizational leadership. *Human Resource Development International, 8*(2), 165–183. http://dx.doi.org/10.1080/13678860500100186

Patience, M. G., De Braine, R., & Dhanpat, N. (2020). Job demands, job resources, and work engagement among South African nurses. *Journal of Psychology in Africa, 30*(5), 408–416. http://dx.doi.org/10.1080/14330237.2020.1821315

Paullay, I. M., Alliger, G. M., & Stone-Romero, E. F. (1994). Construct validation of two instruments designed to measure job involvement and work centrality. *Journal of Applied Psychology, 79*(2), 224–228. http://dx.doi.org/10.1037/0021-9010.79.2.224

Pearce, I. A. (1982). The company mission as a strategic tool. *Sloan Management Review, 23*(3), 15–24.

Pedhazur, E., & Schmelkin, L. (1991). *Measurement, design, and analysis: An integrated approach.* Hillsdale, NJ: Lawrence Erlbaum.

Perschel, A. (2010). Work-life flow: How individuals, Zappos, and other innovative companies achieve high engagement. *Global Business & Organizational Excellence, 29*(5), 17–30.

Petrou, P., Bakker, A. B., & van den Heuvel, M. (2017). Weekly job crafting and leisure crafting: Implications for meaning-making and work engagement. *Journal of Occupational and Organizational Psychology, 90*(2), 129–152. http://dx.doi.org/10.1111/joop.12160

Petrou, P., Demerouti, E., Peeters, M. W., Schaufeli, W. B., & Hetland, J. (2012). Crafting a job on a daily basis: Contextual correlates and the link to work engagement. *Journal of Organizational Behavior, 33*(8), 1120–1141. http://dx.doi.org/10.1002/job.1783

Petrou, P., Demerouti, E., & Schaufeli, W. B. (2018). Crafting the change: The role of employee job crafting behaviors for successful organizational change. *Journal of Management, 44*(5), 1766–1792. http://dx.doi.org/10.1177/0149206315624961

Pfeffer, J. (1998). *The human equation: Building profits by putting people first.* Boston, MA: Harvard Business School Press.

Pfieffelmann, B., Wagner, S. H., & Libkuman, T. (2010). Recruiting on corporate web sites: Perceptions of fit and attraction. *International Journal of Selection and Assessment, 18*(1), 40–47. http://dx.doi.org/10.1111/j.1468-2389.2010.00487.x

Philip, J. (2021). A multi-study approach to examine the interplay of proactive personality and political skill in job crafting. *Journal of Management & Organization.* http://dx.doi.org/10.1017/jmo.2021.1

Philp, M., Egan, S., & Kane, R. (2012). Perfectionism, over commitment to work, and burnout in employees seeking workplace counselling. *Australian Journal of Psychology, 64*(2), 68–74. http://dx.doi.org/10.1111/j.1742-9536.2011.00028.x

Pierce, J. R., & Aguinis, H. (2013). The too-much-of-a-good-thing effect in management. *Journal of Management, 39*(2), 313–338. http://dx.doi.org/10.1177/0149206311410060

Piszczek, M. M., & Pimputkar, A. S. (2020). Flexible schedules across working lives: Age-specific effects on well-being and work. *Journal of Applied Psychology.* http://dx.doi.org/10.1037/apl0000844.supp (Supplemental).

Ployhart, R. E. (2008). The measurement and analysis of motivation. In R. Kanfer, G. Chen, & R. D. Pritchard (Eds.), *Work motivation: Past, present, and future* (pp. 17–61). New York, NY: Routledge/Taylor & Francis Group.

Ployhart, R. E. (2012). The psychology of competitive advantage: An adjacent possibility. *Industrial and Organizational Psychology: Perspectives on Science and Practice, 5*(1), 62–81. http://dx.doi.org/10.1111/j.1754-9434.2011.01407.x

Podsakoff, N. P., Whiting, S. W., Podsakoff, P. M., & Blume, B. D. (2009). Individual- and organizational-level consequences of organizational citizenship behaviors: A meta-analysis. *Journal of Applied Psychology, 94*(1), 122–141. http://dx.doi.org/10.1037/a0013079

Podsakoff, P. M., & MacKenzie, S. B. (1997). Impact of organizational citizenship behavior on organizational performance: A review and suggestions for future research. *Human Performance, 10*(2), 133–151. http://dx.doi.org/10.1207/s15327043hup1002_5

Podsakoff, P. M., MacKenzie, S. B., Lee, J., & Podsakoff, N. P. (2003). Common method biases in behavioral research: A critical review of the literature and recommended remedies. *Journal of Applied Psychology, 88*(5), 879–903. http://dx.doi.org/10.1037/0021-9010.88.5.879

Porter, L. W., & Lawler, E. E. III. (1968). *Managerial attitudes and performance.* Homewood, IL: Irwin-Dorsey.

Pratt, M. G., & Ashforth, B. (2003). Fostering meaningfulness in working and at work. In K. Cameron, J. E. Dutton, & R. E. Quinn (Eds.), *Positive organizational scholarship: Foundations of a new discipline* (pp. 309–327). San Francisco, CA: Berrett-Koehler.

Pratt, M. G., Pradies, C., & Lepisto, D. A. (2013). Doing well, doing good, and doing with: Organizational practices for effectively cultivating meaningful work. In B. J. Dik, Z. S. Byrne, & M. F. Steger (Eds.), *Purpose and meaning in the workplace* (pp. 173–196). Washington, DC: American Psychological Association.

Provine, R. R. (1986). Yawning as a stereotyped action pattern and releasing stimulus. *Ethology, 72*(2), 109–122. http://dx.doi.org/10.1111/j.1439-0310.1986.tb00611.x

Pryce-Jones, J. (2011). Has the recession made us less happy at work? *Manager: British Journal of Administrative Management, 73*, 26–27.

Putra, E. D., Cho, S., & Liu, J. (2017). Extrinsic and intrinsic motivation on work engagement in the hospitality industry: Test of motivation crowding theory. *Tourism & Hospitality Research, 17*(2), 228–241. http://dx.doi.org/10.1177/1467358415613393

Quick, J. C., Murphy, L. R., & Hurrell, J. J., Jr. (Eds.). (1992). *Stress & well-being at work: Assessments and interventions for occupational mental health.* Washington, DC: American Psychological Association.

Quick, J. C., & Tetrick, L. E. (2011). *Handbook of occupational health psychology* (2nd ed.). Washington, DC: American Psychological Association.

Rabenu, E., & Tziner, A. (2021). Back to routine after the coronavirus pandemic lockdown: A proposal from a psychological perspective. *Industrial and Organizational Psychology, 14*, 178–183. http://dx.doi.org/10.1017/iop.2021.23

Rabinowitz, S., & Hall, D. T. (1977). Organizational research on job involvement. *Psychological Bulletin, 84*, 265–268. http://dx.doi.org/10.1037/0033-2909.84.2.265

Rafferty, A. E., & Griffin, M. A. (2004). Dimensions of transformational leadership: Conceptual and empirical extensions. *The Leadership Quarterly, 15*, 329–354.

Rahmadani, V. G., Schaufeli, W. B., Ivanova, T. Y., & Osin, E. N. (2019). Basic psychological need satisfaction mediates the relationship between engaging leadership and work engagement: A cross-national study. *Human Resource Development Quarterly, 30*(4), 453–471. http://dx.doi.org/10.1002/hrdq.21366

Rampersad, H. (2006). Self-examination as the road to sustaining employee engagement and personal happiness. *Performance Improvement, 45*(8), 18–25. http://dx.doi.org/10.1002/pfi.005

Randel, A. E., Dean, M. A., Ehrhart, K. H., Chung, B., & Shore, L. (2016). Leader inclusiveness, psychological diversity climate, and helping behaviors. *Journal of Managerial Psychology, 31*(1), 216–234. http://dx.doi.org/10.1108/JMP-04-2013-0123

Randel, A. E., Galvin, B. M., Shore, L. M., Ehrhart, K. H., Chung, B. G., Dean, M. A., & Kedharnath, U. (2018). Inclusive leadership: Realizing positive outcomes through belongingness and being valued for uniqueness. *Human Resource Management Review*, *28*(2), 190–203. http://dx.doi.org/10.1016/j.hrmr.2017.07.002

Rau, B. L., & Hyland, M. M. (2006). Corporate teamwork and diversity statements in college recruitment brochures: Effects on attraction. *Journal of Applied Social Psychology*, *33*(12), 2465–2492. http://dx.doi.org/10.1111/j.1559-1816.2003.tb02776.x

Ravichandran, K. K., Arasu, R. R., & Kumar, S. S. (2011). The impact of emotional intelligence on employee work engagement behavior: An empirical study. *International Journal of Business & Management*, *6*(11), 157–169. http://dx.doi.org/10.5539/ijbm. v6n11p157

Ray, E. B., & Ray, G. B. (1986). Teaching conflict management skills in corporate training: A perspective-taking approach. *Communication Education*, *35*(3), 288–290. http://dx.doi.org/10.1080/03634528609388351

Raza, A., Farrukh, M., Iqbal, M. K., Farhan, M., & Wu, Y. (2021). Corporate social responsibility and employees' voluntary pro-environmental behavior: The role of organizational pride and employee engagement. *Corporate Social Responsibility & Environmental Management*, 1. http://dx.doi.org/10.1002/csr.2109

Reina-Tamayo, A. M., Bakker, A. B., & Derks, D. (2017). Episodic demands, resources, and engagement: An experience-sampling study. *Journal of Personnel Psychology*, *16*(3), 125–136. http://dx.doi.org/10.1027/1866-5888/a000177

Reinhardt, B. (1996). Factors affecting coefficient alpha: A mini Monte Carlo study. In B. Thompson (Ed.), *Advances in social science methodology* (pp. 3–20). Greenwich, CT: JAI Press.

Reio, T. G., Jr., & Sanders-Reio, J. (2011). Thinking about workplace engagement: Does supervisor and coworker incivility really matter? *Advances in Developing Human Resources*, *13*(4), 462–478. http://dx.doi.org/10.1177/1523422311430784

Reis, D., Arndt, C., Lischetzke, T., & Hoppe, A. (2016). State work engagement and state affect: Similar yet distinct concepts. *Journal of Vocational Behavior*, *93*, 1–10. http://dx.doi.org/10.1016/j.jvb.2015.12.004

Reis, G., Trullen, J., & Story, J. (2016). Perceived organizational culture and engagement: The mediating role of authenticity. *Journal of Managerial Psychology*, *31*(6), 1091–1105. http://dx.doi.org/10.1108/JMP-05-2015-0178

Reis, H. T., Sheldon, K. M., Gable, S. L., Roscoe, J., & Ryan, R. M. (2000). Daily well-being: The role of autonomy, competence, and relatedness. *Personality and Social Psychology Bulletin*, *26*(4), 419–435. http://dx.doi.org/10.1177/0146167200266002

Rentsch, J. R. (1990). Climate and culture: Interaction and qualitative differences in organizational meanings. *Journal of Applied Psychology*, *75*, 668–681.

Resick, C. J., Baltes, B. B., & Shantz, C. (2007). Person-organization fit and work-related attitudes and decisions: Examining interactive effects with job fit and conscientiousness. *Journal of Applied Psychology*, *92*(5), 1446–1455. http://dx.doi.org/10.1037/0021-9010.92.5.1446

Resnick, L. B., Levine, J. M., & Teasley, S. D. (1991). *Perspectives on socially shared cognition*. Washington, DC: American Psychological Association. http://dx.doi.org/10.1037/10096-000

Rheinberg, F. (2008). Intrinsic motivation and flow. In J. Heckhausen & H. Heckhausen (Eds.), *Motivation and action* (pp. 323–348). New York, NY: Cambridge University. http://dx.doi.org/10.1017/CBO9780511499821.014

Rich, B. L., LePine, J. A., & Crawford, E. R. (2010). Job engagement: Antecedents and effects on job performance. *Academy of Management Journal*, *53*, 617–635. http://dx.doi.org/10.5465/AMJ.2010.51468988

Richardsen, A. M., Burke, R. J., & Martinussen, M. (2006). Work and health outcomes among police officers: The mediating role of police cynicism and engagement. *International Journal of Stress Management, 13*, 555–574.

Roberts, J. A., & David, M. E. (2017). Put down your phone and listen to me: How boss phubbing undermines the psychological conditions necessary for employee engagement. *Computers in Human Behavior, 75*, 206–217. http://dx.doi.org/10.1016/j. chb.2017.05.021

Robinson, D., Perryman, S., & Hayday, S. (2004). *The drivers of employee engagement.* Brighton: Institute for Employment Studies.

Rodell, J. (2021). Volunteer programs that employees can get excited about. *Harvard Business Review, 99*(1), 94–101.

Roe, R. A. (1999). Work performance: A multiple regulation perspective. In C. L. Cooper & I. T. Robertson (Eds.), *International review of industrial and organizational psychology* (Vol. 14, pp. 231–335). New York, NY: John Wiley & Sons.

Roe, R. A., Zinovieva, I. L., Dienes, E., & Ten Horn, L. (2000). A comparison of work motivation in Bulgaria, Hungary, and the Netherlands: Test of a model. *Applied Psychology: An International Review, 49*, 658–687. http://dx.doi.org/10.1111/1464-0597.00039

Roethlisberger, F. J., & Dickson, W. J. (1939). *Management and the worker: An account of a research program conducted by the Western Electric Company, Hawthorne Works, Chicago.* Cambridge, MA: Harvard University Press.

Rofcanin, Y., Bakker, A. B., Berber, A., Gölgeci, I., & Las Heras, M. (2019). Relational job crafting: Exploring the role of employee motives with a weekly diary study. *Human Relations, 72*(4), 859–886. http://dx.doi.org/10.1177/0018726718779121

Rogers, C. (1959). A theory of therapy, personality, and interpersonal relationships as developed in the client-centered framework. In S. Koch (Ed.), *Psychology: A study of science* (Vol. 3, pp. 184–256). New York, NY: McGraw-Hill.

Rogers, C. (1961). *On becoming a person.* Boston, MA: Houghton Mifflin.

Ronen, S., & Shenkar, O. (1985). Clustering countries on attitudinal dimensions: A review and synthesis. *Academy of Management Review, 10*(3), 435–454. http://dx.doi. org/10.5465/AMR.1985.4278955

Ronen, S., & Shenkar, O. (2013). Mapping world cultures: Cluster formation, sources and implications. *Journal of International Business Studies, 44*(9), 867–897. http:// dx.doi.org/10.1057/jibs.2013.42

Rossi, A. M., Perrewé, P. L., & Sauter, S. L. (Eds.). (2006). *Stress and quality of working life: Current perspectives in occupational health.* Charlotte, NC: Information Age.

Rosso, B., Dekas, K., & Wrzesniewski, A. (2010). On the meaning of work: A theoretical integration and review. *Research in Organizational Behavior, 30*, 91–127. http://dx.doi.org/10.1016/j.riob.2010.09.001

Rothbard, N. P. (2001). Enriching or depleting? The dynamics of engagement in work and family roles. *Administrative Science Quarterly, 46*(4), 655–684. http://dx.doi.org/ 10.2307/3094827

Rothmann, S. S., & Joubert, J. M. (2007). Job demands, job resources, burnout and work engagement of managers at a platinum mine in the North West Province. *South African Journal of Business Management, 38*(3), 49–61.

Rudolph, C. W., Allan, B., Clark, M., Hertel, G., Hirschi, A., Kunze, F., . . . Zacher, H. (2021). Pandemics: Implications for research and practice in industrial and organizational psychology. *Industrial and Organizational Psychology, 14*, 1–35. http:// dx.doi.org/10.1017/iop.2020.48

Rudolph, C. W., & Baltes, B. B. (2017). Age and health jointly moderate the influence of flexible work arrangements on work engagement: Evidence from two empirical studies. *Journal of Occupational Health Psychology, 22*(1), 40–58. http://dx.doi.org/10.1037/a0040147

Russell, J. A. (1991). Culture and the categorization of emotions. *Psychological Bulletin, 110,* 426–450. http://dx.doi.org/10.1037/0033-2909.110.3.426

Ryan, R. M. (1982). Control and information in the intrapersonal sphere: An extension of cognitive evaluation theory. *Journal of Personality and Social Psychology, 43*(3), 450–461. http://dx.doi.org/10.1037/0022-3514.43.3.450

Ryan, R. M., & Deci, E. L. (2000). Self-determination theory and the facilitation of intrinsic motivation, social development, and well-being. *American Psychologist, 55,* 68–78.

Saks, A. M. (2006). Antecedents and consequences of employee engagement. *Journal of Managerial Psychology, 27,* 600–619.

Saks, A. M., & Ashforth, B. E. (2002). Is job search related to employment quality? It all depends on the fit. *Journal of Applied Psychology, 87*(4), 646–654. http://dx.doi.org/10.1037/0021-9010.87.4.646

Sakuraya, A., Shimazu, A., Imamura, K., & Kawakami, N. (2020). Effects of a job crafting intervention program on work engagement among Japanese employees: A randomized controlled trial. *Frontiers in Psychology, 11.* http://dx.doi.org/10.3389/fpsyg.2020.00235

Salamin, A., & Hom, P. W. (2005). In search of the elusive U-shaped performance-turnover relationship: Are high performing Swiss bankers more liable to quit? *Journal of Applied Psychology, 90*(6), 1204–1216. http://dx.doi.org/10.1037/0021-9010.90.6.1204

Salancik, G. R., & Pfeffer, J. (1978). A social information processing approach to job attitudes and task design. *Administrative Science Quarterly, 23*(2), 224–253. http://dx.doi.org/10.2307/2392563

Salanova, M., Lorente, L., Chambel, M. J., & Martínez, I. M. (2011). Linking transformational leadership to nurses' extra-role performance: The mediating role of self-efficacy and work engagement. *Journal of Advanced Nursing, 67*(10), 2256–2266. http://dx.doi.org/10.1111/j.1365-2648.2011.05652.x

Salanova, M., & Schaufeli, W. B. (2008). A cross-national study of work engagement as a mediator between job resources and proactive behavior: A cross-national study. *International Journal of Human Resources Management, 19,* 116–131.

Salovey, P., & Mayer, J. D. (1989). Emotional intelligence. *Imagination, Cognition and Personality, 9*(3), 185–211.

Santhanam, N., & Srinivas, S. (2020). Modeling the impact of employee engagement and happiness on burnout and turnover intention among blue-collar workers at a manufacturing company. *Benchmarking: An International Journal, 27*(2), 499–516. http://dx.doi.org/10.1108/BIJ-01-2019-0007

Sapolsky, R. M. (2004). *Why zebras don't get ulcers: The acclaimed guide to stress, stress-related diseases, and coping* (3rd ed.). New York: Holt.

Scarlett, K. (2009). *What is engagement?* Retrieved April 27, 2009, from www.scarlettsurveys.com/employee_engagement.cfm

Schaufeli, W. B., & Bakker, A. B. (2003). *Utrecht work engagement scale: Preliminary manual (Version 1, November 2003).* Unpublished document, Utrecht University.

Schaufeli, W. B., Bakker, A. B., & Salanova, M. (2006). The measurement of work engagement with a short questionnaire: A cross-national study. *Educational and Psychological Measurement, 66,* 701–716.

Schaufeli, W. B., & Enzmann, D. (1998). *The burnout companion to study and practice: A critical analysis.* London: Taylor & Francis.

Schaufeli, W. B., Martínez, I. M., Marques Pinto, A., Salanova, M., & Bakker, A. B. (2002). Burnout and engagement in university students: A cross national study. *Journal of Cross-Cultural Psychology, 33,* 464–481. http://dx.doi.org/10.1177/0022022102033005003

Schaufeli, W. B., Salanova, M., González-Romá, V., & Bakker, A. B. (2002). The measurement of engagement and burnout: A two sample confirmatory factor analytic approach. *Journal of Happiness Studies, 3,* 71–92.

Schaufeli, W. B., Shimazu, A., Hakanen, J., Salanova, M., & De Witte, H. (2019). An ultra-short measure for work engagement: The UWES-3 validation across five countries. *European Journal of Psychological Assessment, 35*(4), 577–591. http://dx.doi.org/10.1027/1015-5759/a000430

Schaufeli, W. B., Taris, T. W., & Bakker, A. B. (2006). Dr. Jekyll and Mr. Hide: On the differences between work engagement and workaholism. In R. Burke (Ed.), *Research companion to working time and work addiction* (pp. 193–252). Northampton, MA: Edward Elgar.

Schaufeli, W. B., Taris, T. W., & van Rhenen, W. (2008). Workaholism, burnout, and work engagement: Three of a kind or three different kinds of employee well-being? *Applied Psychology: An International Review, 57*(2), 173–203. http://dx.doi.org/10.1111/j.1464-0597.2007.00285.x

Scheflen, A. E. (1964). The significance of posture in communication systems. *Psychiatry: Journal for the Study of Interpersonal Processes, 27*(4), 316–331.

Schein, E. H. (1990). Organizational culture. *American Psychologist, 45,* 109–119.

Schein, E. H. (2000). Sense and nonsense about culture and climate. In N. M. Ashkanasy, C. P. M. Wilderom, & M. F. Peterson (Eds.), *Handbook of organizational culture & climate* (pp. xxiii–xxx). Thousand Oaks, CA: Sage.

Schleicher, D. J., Watt, J. D., & Greguras, G. J. (2004). Reexamining the job satisfaction-performance relationship: The complexity of attitudes. *Journal of Applied Psychology, 89,* 165–177. http://dx.doi.org/10.1037/0021-9010.89.165

Schneider, B. (1987). The people make the place. *Personnel Psychology, 40*(3), 437–453. http://dx.doi.org/10.1111/j.1744-6570.1987.tb00609.x

Schneider, B. (1990). The climate for service: An application of the climate construct. In B. Schneider (Ed.), *Organizational climate and culture* (pp. 383–412). San Francisco, CA: Jossey-Bass.

Schneider, B. (2000). The psychological life of organizations. In N. M. Ashkanasy, C. P. M. Wilderom, & M. F. Peterson (Eds.), *Handbook of organizational culture & climate* (pp. xvii–xxi). Thousand Oaks, CA: Sage.

Schohat, L. M., & Vigoda-Gadot, E. (2010). "Engage me once again": Is employee engagement for real, or is it "same lady-different dress"?. In S. L. Albrecht (Ed.), *Handbook of employee engagement: Perspectives, issues, research and practice* (pp. 98–107). Northampton, MA: Edward Elgar.

Schwartz, H. S. (1982). Job involvement as obsession-compulsion. *Academy of Management Review, 7*(3), 429–432. http://dx.doi.org/10.5465/AMR.1982.4285355

Schwartz, S. H. (1992). Universals in the content and structure of values: Theoretical advances and empirical tests in 20 countries. In M. P. Zanna (Ed.), *Advances in experimental social psychology* (Vol. 25, pp. 1–65). San Diego, CA: Academic Press. http://dx.doi.org/10.1016/S0065-2601(08)60281-6

Schwartz, S. H. (1994). Beyond individuals/collectivism: New cultural dimensions of values. In U. Kim, H. C. Triandis, C. Kagitcibasi, S. Choi, & G. Yoon (Eds.), *Individualism & collectivism: Theory, method, and application* (pp. 85–119). Thousand Oaks, CA: Sage.

Schwartz, S. H., & Bilsky, W. (1987). Toward a universal psychological structure of human values. *Journal of Personality and Social Psychology, 53*(3), 550–562. http://dx.doi.org/10.1037/0022-3514.53.3.550

Schwartz, S. H., & Bilsky, W. (1990). Toward a theory of the universal content and structure of values: Extensions and cross-cultural replications. *Journal of Personality and Social Psychology, 58*(5), 878–891. http://dx.doi.org/10.1037/0022-3514.58.5.878

Scott, K. S., Moore, K. S., & Miceli, M. P. (1997). An exploration of the meaning and consequences of workaholism. *Human Relations, 50*(3), 287–314. http://dx.doi.org/10.1023/A:1016986307298

Scott, S. G., & Bruce, R. A. (1994). Determinants of innovative behavior: A path model of individual innovation in the workplace. *Academy of Management Journal, 37*(3), 580–607. http://dx.doi.org/10.2307/256701

Scrima, F., Lorito, L., Parry, E., & Falgares, G. (2014). The mediating role of work engagement on the relationship between job involvement and affective commitment. *The International Journal of Human Resource Management, 25*(15), 2159–2173. http://dx.doi.org/10.1080/09585192.2013.862289

Scroggins, W. A. (2008). The relationship between employee fit perceptions, job performance, and retention: Implications of perceived fit. *Employee Responsibilities and Rights Journal, 20*(1), 57–71. http://dx.doi.org/10.1007/s10672-007-9060-0

Scroggins, W. A., & Benson, P. G. (2007). Self-concept-job fit: Expanding the person-job fit construct and implications for retention management. In D. J. Svyantek (Series Ed.), D. J. Svyantek, & E. McChrystal (Vol. Eds.), *Research in organizational science: Vol. 2. Refining familiar constructs: Alternative views in OB, HR and I/O* (pp. 211–232). Charlotte, NC: Information Age.

Seijts, G. H., & Crim, D. (2006). What engages employees the most or, the Ten C's of employee engagement. *Ivey Business Journal, 70*(4), 1–5.

Sekaran, U. (1981). Are U.S. organizational concepts and measures transferable to another culture? An empirical investigation. *Academy of Management Journal, 24,* 409–417.

Sekiguchi, T., & Huber, V. L. (2011). The use of person-organization fit and person-job fit information in making selection decisions. *Organizational Behavior & Human Decision Processes, 116*(2), 203–216. http://dx.doi.org/10.1016/j.obhdp.2011.04.001

Seligman, M. E., & Csikszentmihalyi, M. (2000). Positive psychology: An introduction. *American Psychologist, 55*(1), 5–14. http://dx.doi.org/10.1037/0003-066X.55.1.5

Seligman, M. E., & Schulman, P. (1986). Explanatory style as a predictor of productivity and quitting among life insurance sales agents. *Journal of Personality and Social Psychology, 50*(4), 832–838. http://dx.doi.org/10.1037/0022-3514.50.4.832

Seppälä, P., Hakanen, J. J., Tolvanen, A., & Demerouti, E. (2018). A job resources-based intervention to boost work engagement and team innovativeness during organizational restructuring: For whom does it work? *Journal of Organizational Change Management, 31*(7), 1419–1437. http://dx.doi.org/10.1108/JOCM-11-2017-0448

Seybold, K., & Salomone, P. R. (1994). Understanding workaholism: A review of causes and counseling approaches. *Journal of Counseling & Development, 73*(1), 4–9.

Shamir, B. (1991). Meaning, self and motivation in organizations. *Organization Studies, 12*(3), 405–424. http://dx.doi.org/10.1177/017084069101200304

Sheldon, K. M., & Elliot, A. J. (1998). Not all personal goals are personal: Comparing autonomous and controlled reasons for goals as predictors of effort and attainment. *Personality and Social Psychology Bulletin, 24*(5), 546–557. http://dx.doi.org/10.1177/0146167298245010

Sheldon, K. M., & Elliot, A. J. (1999). Goal striving, need satisfaction, and longitudinal well-being: The self-concordance model. *Journal of Personality and Social Psychology, 76*(3), 482–497. http://dx.doi.org/10.1037//0022-3514.76.3.482

Shepard, J. M. (1972). Alienation as a process: Work as a case in point. *Sociological Quarterly, 13*(2), 161–173.

Sherif, C. W. (1963). Social categorization as a function of latitude of acceptance and series range. *Journal of Abnormal and Social Psychology, 67*(2), 148–156. http://dx.doi.org/10.1037/h0043022

Shimazu, A., Schaufeli, W. B., Kubota, K., Watanabe, K., & Kawakami, N. (2018). Is too much work engagement detrimental? Linear or curvilinear effects on mental health and job performance. *PLoS One, 13*(12), 1–17. http://dx.doi.org/10.1371/journal.pone.0208684

Shimazu, A., Schaufeli, W. B., Miyanaka, D., & Iwata, N. (2010). Why Japanese workers show low work engagement: An item response theory analysis of the Utrecht Work Engagement Scale. *BioPsychoSocial Medicine, 4*(17). http://dx.doi.org/10.1186/1751-0759-4-17

Shipman, W. G., Heath, H. A., & Oken, D. (1970). Response specificity among muscular and autonomic variables. *Archives of General Psychiatry, 23*, 369–374.

Shore, L. M., Randel, A. E., Chung, B. G., Dean, M. A., Holcombe Ehrhart, K., & Singh, G. (2011). Inclusion and diversity in work groups: A review and model for future research. *Journal of Management, 37*(4), 1262–1289. http://dx.doi.org/10.1177/0149206310385943

SHRM. (n.d.). *Developing and sustaining employee engagement.* Retrieved from www.shrm.org/resourcesandtools/tools-and-samples/toolkits/pages/sustainingemployeeengagement.aspx

Shrotryia, V. K., & Dhanda, U. (2020). Exploring employee engagement using grounded theory: Experiences from best firms in India. *Vision (09722629), 24*(2), 171–183. http://dx.doi.org/10.1177/0972262920915070

Shuck, B., Osam, K., Zigarmi, D., & Nimon, K. (2017). Definitional and conceptual muddling: Identifying the positionality of employee engagement and defining the construct. *Human Resource Development Review, 16*(3), 263–293. http://dx.doi.org/10.1177/1534484317720622

Shuck, B., Reio, T. R., & Rocco, T. (2011). Employee engagement: An examination of antecedent and outcome variables. *Human Resource Development International, 14*(4), 427–445. http://dx.doi.org/10.1080/13678868.2011.601587

Siegrist, J. (1996). Adverse health effects of high-effort/low-reward conditions. *Journal of Occupational Health Psychology, 1*(1), 27–41. http://dx.doi.org/10.1037/1076-8998.1.1.27

Siegrist, J., Starke, D., Chandola, T., Godin, I., Marmot, M., Niedhammer, I., & Peter, R. (2004). The measurement of effort-reward imbalance at work: European comparisons. *Social Science & Medicine, 58*(8), 1483–1499. http://dx.doi.org/10.1016/S0277-9536(03)00351-4

Singelis, T. M., Triandis, H. C., Bhawuk, D., & Gelfand, M. J. (1995). Horizontal and vertical dimensions of individualism and collectivism: A theoretical and measurement refinement. *Cross-Cultural Research: The Journal of Comparative Social Science, 29*(3), 240–275. http://dx.doi.org/10.1177/106939719502900302

Singh, S., David, R., & Mikkilineni, S. (2018). Organizational virtuousness and work engagement: Mediating role of happiness in India. *Advances in Developing Human Resources, 20*(1), 88–102. http://dx.doi.org/10.1177/1523422317741885

Skarlicki, D. P., & Folger, R. (1997). Retaliation in the workplace: The roles of distributive, procedural, and interactional justice. *Journal of Applied Psychology, 82*(3), 434–443.

Skinner, E. A., & Belmont, M. J. (1993). Motivation in the classroom: Reciprocal effects of teacher behavior and student engagement across the school year. *Journal of Educational Psychology, 85*(4), 571–581. http://dx.doi.org/10.1037/0022-0663.85.4.571

Slemp, G. R., Zhao, Y., Hou, H., & Vallerand, R. J. (2020). Job crafting, leader autonomy support, and passion for work: Testing a model in Australia and China. *Motivation and Emotion.* http://dx.doi.org/10.1007/s11031-020-09850-6

Sloan, M. M. (2012). Unfair treatment in the workplace and worker well-being: The role of coworker support in a service work environment. *Work and Occupations, 39*(1), 3–34. http://dx.doi.org/10.1177/0730888411406555

Snir, R., & Harpaz, I. (2004). Attitudinal and demographic antecedents of workaholism. *Journal of Organizational Change Management, 17*(5), 520–536. http://dx.doi.org/10.1108/09534810410554524

Soane, E., Truss, C., Alfes, K., Shantz, A., Rees, C., & Gatenby, M. (2012). Development and application of a new measure of employee engagement: The ISA Engagement Scale. *Human Resource Development International, 15*(5), 529–547. http://dx.doi.org/10.1080/13678868.2012.726542

Song, S.-H., & Olshfski, D. (2008). Friends at work: A comparative study of work attitudes in Seoul City government and New Jersey state government. *Administration & Society, 40*(2), 147–169. http://dx.doi.org/10.1177/0095399707312827

Sonnentag, S. (2003). Recovery, work engagement, and proactive behavior: A new look at the interface between nonwork and work. *Journal of Applied Psychology, 88*(3), 518–528. http://dx.doi.org/10.1037/0021-9010.88.3.518

Sonnentag, S., Dormann, C., & Demerouti, E. (2010). Not all days are created equal: The concept of state work engagement. In A. B. Bakker & M. P. Leiter (Eds.), *Work engagement: A handbook of essential theory and research* (pp. 25–38). New York, NY: Psychology Press.

Sonnentag, S., & Fritz, C. (2015). Recovery from job stress: The stressor-detachment model as an integrative framework. *Journal of Organizational Behavior, 36*(S1), S72–S103. http://dx.doi.org/10.1002/job.1924

Sonnentag, S., Mojza, E. J., Demerouti, E., & Bakker, A. B. (2012). Reciprocal relations between recovery and work engagement: The moderating role of job stressors. *Journal of Applied Psychology, 97*(4), 842–853. http://dx.doi.org/10.1037/a0028292

Sørlie, H. O., Hetland, J., Dysvik, A., Fosse, T. H., & Martinsen, Ø. L. (2020). Person-organization fit in a military selection context. *Military Psychology, 32*(3), 237–246. http://dx.doi.org/10.1080/08995605.2020.1724752

Sosik, J. J., & Jung, D. I. (2010). *Full range leadership development: Pathways for people, profit, and planet.* New York, NY: Psychology Press, a Taylor & Francis Group.

Sosik, J. J., Juzbasich, J., & Chun, J. (2011). Effects of moral reasoning and management level on ratings of charismatic leadership, in-role and extra-role performance of managers: A multi-source examination. *The Leadership Quarterly, 22*(2), 434–450. http://dx.doi.org/10.1016/j.leaqua.2011.02.015

Sousa-Lima, M., Michel, J. W., & Caetano, A. (2013). Clarifying the importance of trust in organizations as a component of effective work relationships. *Journal of Applied Social Psychology, 43*(2), 418–427. http://dx.doi.org/10.1111/j.1559-1816.2013.01012.x

Spector, P. E., Allen, T. D., Poelmans, S. Y., Lapierre, L. M., Cooper, C. L., O'Driscoll, M., ... Widerszal-Bazyl, M. (2007). Cross-national differences in relationships of work demands, job satisfaction, and turnover intentions with work-family conflict. *Personnel Psychology, 60*(4), 805–835. http://dx.doi.org/10.1111/j.1744-6570.2007.00092.x

Spence, J. T., & Robbins, A. S. (1992). Workaholism: Definition, measurement, and preliminary results. *Journal of Personality Assessment, 58*(1), 160.

Stack, J. (1994). *The great game of business: Unlocking the power and profitability of open-book management.* New York, NY: Currency/Doubleday.

Staw, B. M., Sutton, R. I., & Pelled, L. H. (1994). Employee positive emotion and favorable outcomes at the workplace. *Organization Science, 5*(1), 51–71.

Steele, J. P., Rupayana, D. D., Mills, M. J., Smith, M. R., Wefald, A., & Downey, R. G. (2012). Relative importance and utility of positive worker states: A review and empirical examination. *Journal of Psychology: Interdisciplinary and Applied, 146*(6), 617–650. http://dx.doi.org/10.1080/00223980.2012.665100

Steger, M. F., Dik, B. J., & Duffy, R. D. (2012). Measuring meaningful work: The Work and Meaning Inventory (WAMI). *Journal of Career Assessment, 20*(3), 322–337. http://dx.doi.org/10.1177/1069072711436160

Steidle, A., Gonzalez-Morales, M. G., Hoppe, A., Michel, A., & O'Shea, D. (2017). Energizing respites from work: A randomized controlled study on respite interventions. *European Journal of Work and Organizational Psychology, 26*(5), 650–662. http://dx.doi.org/10.1080/1359432X.2017.1348348

Steinmetz, H., Park, Y., & Kabst, R. (2011). The relationship between needs and job attitudes in South Korea and Germany. *Journal of Managerial Psychology, 26*(7), 623–644. http://dx.doi.org/10.1108/02683941111164517

Stevens, M. (2013). Driving employee engagement for business success. *In Practice (0263841X), 35*(2), 91–93. http://dx.doi.org/10.1136/inp.f192

Storm, K. K., & Rothmann, S. S. (2003). A psychometric analysis of the Maslach Burnout Inventory-General Survey in the South African police service. *South African Journal of Psychology, 33*(4), 219–226. http://dx.doi.org/10.1177/008124630303300404

Studer, B., & Clark, L. (2011). Place your bets: Psychophysiological correlates of decision-making under risk. *Cognitive, Affective & Behavioral Neuroscience, 11*(2), 144–158. http://dx.doi.org/10.3758/s13415-011-0025-2

Suh, T., Houston, M. B., Barney, S. M., & Kwon, I. G. (2011). The impact of mission fulfillment on the internal audience: Psychological job outcomes in a services setting. *Journal of Service Research, 14*(1), 76–92. http://dx.doi.org/10.1177/1094670510387915

Suinn, R. M. (1984). Visual motor behavior rehearsal: The basic technique. *Scandinavian Journal of Behaviour Therapy, 13*(3), 131–142. http://dx.doi.org/10.1080/16506078409455701

Sullivan, M. J., & Conway, M. (1989). Negative affect leads to low-effort cognition: Attributional processing for observed social behavior. *Social Cognition, 7*(4), 315–337. http://dx.doi.org/10.1521/soco.1989.7.4.315

Tajfel, H. (1978). Social categorization, social identity, and social comparison. In H. Tajfel (Ed.), *Differentiation between social groups: Studies in the social psychology of intergroup relations* (pp. 61–76). New York, NY: Academic Press.

Tajfel, H., Billig, M. G., Bundy, R. P., & Flament, C. (1971). Social categorization and intergroup behaviour. *European Journal of Social Psychology, 1*(2), 149–178. http://dx.doi.org/10.1002/ejsp.2420010202

Tajfel, H., & Turner, J. C. (1979). An integrative theory of intergroup conflict. In W. Austin & S. Worchel (Eds.), *The social psychology of intergroup relations* (pp. 33–47). Monterey, CA: Brooks/Cole.

Tan, H. H., & Tan, C. S. (2000). Toward the differentiation of trust in supervisor and trust in organization. *Genetic, Social, and General Psychology Monographs, 126*(2), 241–260.

Tan, L., Wang, Y., Qian, W., & Lu, H. (2020). Leader humor and employee job crafting: The role of employee-perceived organizational support and work engagement. *Frontiers in Psychology, 11*, 1–14. http://dx.doi.org/10.3389/fpsyg.2020.499849

Tannen, D. (1990). *You just don't understand: Women and men in conversation.* New York, NY: William Morrow.

Taris, T. W., van Horn, J. E., Schaufeli, W. B., & Schreurs, P. G. (2004). Inequity, burnout and psychological withdrawal among teachers: A dynamic exchange model. *Anxiety, Stress & Coping: An International Journal, 17*(1), 103–122. http://dx.doi.org/10.1080/1061580031000151620

Teece, D. J. (2010). Business models, business strategy and innovation. *Long Range Planning: International Journal of Strategic Management, 43*(2–3), 172–194.

ten Brummelhuis, L. L., & Bakker, A. B. (2012). Staying engaged during the week: The effect of off-job activities on next day work engagement. *Journal of Occupational Health Psychology, 17*(4), 445–455. http://dx.doi.org/10.1037/a0029213

Tetrick, L. E., Quick, J., & Gilmore, P. L. (2012). Research in organizational interventions to improve well-being: Perspectives on organizational change and development. In C. Biron, M. Karanika-Murray, & C. Cooper (Eds.), *Improving organizational interventions for stress and well-being: Addressing process and context* (pp. 59–76). New York, NY: Routledge/Taylor & Francis Group.

Thierry, H. (1990). Intrinsic motivation reconsidered. In U. Kleinbeck, H.-H. Quast, H. Thierry, & H. Häcker (Eds.), *Work motivation* (pp. 67–82). Hillsdale, NJ: Lawrence Erlbaum Associates.

Thompson, B. (2004). *Exploratory and confirmatory factor analysis: Understanding concepts and applications.* Washington, DC: American Psychological Association. http://dx.doi.org/10.1037/10694-000

Tian, G., & Zhang, Z. (2020). Linking empowering leadership to employee innovation: The mediating role of work engagement. *Social Behavior and Personality: An International Journal, 48*(10), 1–8. http://dx.doi.org/10.2224/sbp.9320

Tims, M., & Bakker, A. B. (2010). Job crafting: Towards a new model of individual job redesign. *South African Journal of Industrial Psychology, 36*, 1–9.

Tims, M., Bakker, A. B., & Derks, D. (2013). The impact of job crafting on job demands, job resources, and well-being. *Journal of Occupational Health Psychology.* http://dx.doi.org/10.1037/a0032141

Torelli, C. J., & Shavitt, S. (2010). Culture and concepts of power. *Journal of Personality and Social Psychology, 99*(4), 703–723. http://dx.doi.org/10.1037/a0019973

Tóth-Király, I., Morin, A. J. S., & Salmela-Aro, K. (2021). A longitudinal perspective on the associations between work engagement and workaholism. *Work & Stress, 35*(1), 27–56. http://dx.doi.org/10.1080/02678373.2020.1801888

Tran, T. T. T., Watanabe, K., Imamura, K., Nguyen, H. T., Sasaki, N., Kuribayashi, K., . . . Kawakami, N. (2020). Reliability and validity of the Vietnamese version of the 9-item Utrecht Work Engagement Scale. *Journal of Occupational Health, 62*(1), 1–11. http://dx.doi.org/10.1002/1348-9585.12157

Tremblay, M., Cloutier, J., Simard, G., Chênevert, D., & Vandenberghe, C. (2010). The role of HRM practices, procedural justice, organizational support and trust in organizational commitment and in-role and extra-role performance. *The International Journal of Human Resource Management, 21*(3), 405–433. http://dx.doi.org/10.1080/09585190903549056

Trépanier, S., Fernet, C., Austin, S., Forest, J., & Vallerand, R. J. (2014). Linking job demands and resources to burnout and work engagement: Does passion underlie these differential relationships? *Motivation and Emotion.* http://dx.doi.org/10.1007/s11031-013-9384-z

Treviño, L. K., & Brown, M. E. (2005). The role of leaders in influencing unethical behavior in the workplace. In R. E. Kidwell, Jr., & C. L. Martin (Eds.), *Managing organizational deviance* (pp. 69–88). Thousand Oaks, CA: Sage.

Triandis, H. C. (1994). *Culture and social behavior.* New York: McGraw-Hill.

Triandis, H. C. (1995). *Individualism & collectivism.* Boulder, CO: Westview Press.

Triandis, H. C., Leung, K., Villareal, M. J., & Clack, F. L. (1985). Allocentric versus idiocentric tendencies: Convergent and discriminant validation. *Journal of Research in Personality, 19*(4), 395–415. http://dx.doi.org/10.1016/0092-6566(85)90008-X

Triandis, H. C., McCusker, C., Betancourt, H., Iwao, S., Leung, K., Salazar, J., . . . Zaleski, Z. (1993). An etic-emic analysis of individualism and collectivism. *Journal of Cross-Cultural Psychology, 24*(3), 366–383. http://dx.doi.org/10.1177/0022022193243006

Tricahyadinata, I., Hendryadi, S., Zainurossalamia, S., & Riadi, S. S. (2020). Workplace incivility, work engagement, and turnover intentions: Multi-group analysis. *Cogent Psychology, 7*(1), 1–16. http://dx.doi.org/10.1080/23311908.2020.1743627

Tsoumbris, P., & Xenikou, A. (2010). Commitment profiles: The configural effect of the forms and foci of commitment on work outcomes. *Journal of Vocational Behavior, 77*(3), 401–411. http://dx.doi.org/10.1016/j.jvb.2010.07.006

Tuckey, M. R., Bakker, A. B., & Dollard, M. F. (2012). Empowering leaders optimize working conditions for engagement: A multilevel study. *Journal of Occupational Health Psychology, 17*(1), 15–27. http://dx.doi.org/10.1037/a0025942

Tziner, A., Shkoler, O., & Bat Zur, B.-E. (2019). Revisiting work engagement from a moderated-mediation vantage point. *Journal of Work and Organizational Psychology, 35*(3), 207–215. http://dx.doi.org/10.5093/jwop2019a22

Uleman, J. S., & Bargh, J. A. (1989). *Unintended thought.* New York, NY: Guilford Press.

Ulrich, D., & Lake, D. (1991). Organization capability: Creating competitive advantage. *Executive (19389779), 5*(1), 77–92. http://dx.doi.org/10.5465/AME.1991.4274728

Ursin, H., & Eriksen, H. R. (2004). The cognitive activation theory of stress. *Psychoneuroendocrinology, 29*(5), 567–592. http://dx.doi.org/10.1016/S0306-4530(03)00091-X

Utay, J., & Utay, C. (1999). The ABC's of rapport building: An organizing strategy for training counselors. *Psychology: A Journal of Human Behavior, 36*(1), 34–39.

Vacha-Haase, T. (1998). Reliability generalization: Exploring variance in measurement error affecting score reliability across studies. *Educational and Psychological Measurement, 58*(1), 6–20. http://dx.doi.org/10.1177/0013164498058001002

Vakola, M., Petrou, P., & Katsaros, K. (2021). Work engagement and job crafting as conditions of ambivalent employees' adaptation to organizational change. *Journal of Applied Behavioral Science, 57*(1), 57–79. http://dx.doi.org/10.1177/0021886320967173

Vallerand, R. J. (2008). On the psychology of passion: In search of what makes people's lives most worth living. *Canadian Psychology, 49*, 1–13. http://dx.doi.org/10.1037/0708-5591.49.1.1

Vallerand, R. J., & Houlfort, N. (2003). Passion at work: Toward a new conceptualization. In S. W. Gilliland, D. D. Steiner, & D. P. Skarlicki (Eds.), *Emerging perspectives on values in organizations* (pp. 175–204). Greenwich, CT: Information Age.

Van Ameringen, M., Mancini, C., & Oakman, J. M. (1998). The relationship of behavioral inhibition and shyness to anxiety disorder. *Journal of Nervous and Mental Disease, 186*(7), 425–431. http://dx.doi.org/10.1097/00005053-199807000-00007

van Baaren, R. B., Holland, R. W., Kawakami, K., & van Knippenberg, A. (2004). Mimicry and prosocial behavior. *Psychological Science, 15*(1), 71–74. http://dx.doi. org/10.1111/j.0963-7214.2004.01501012.x

van Baaren, R. B., Maddux, W. W., Chartrand, T. L., de Bouter, C., & van Knippenberg, A. (2003). It takes two to mimic: Behavioral consequences of self-construals. *Journal of Personality and Social Psychology, 84*(5), 1093–1102. http://dx.doi. org/10.1037/0022-3514.84.5.1093

van Beek, I., Taris, T. W., & Schaufeli, W. B. (2011). Workaholic and work engaged employees: Dead ringers or worlds apart? *Journal of Occupational Health Psychology, 16*(4), 468–482. http://dx.doi.org/10.1037/a0024392

Vandenberghe, C., Bentein, K., & Stinglhamber, F. (2004). Affective commitment to the organization, supervisor, and work group: Antecedents and outcomes. *Journal of Vocational Behavior, 64*(1), 47–71. http://dx.doi.org/10.1016/S0001-8791(03) 00029-0

Van den Broeck, A., Vansteenkiste, M., De Witte, H., & Lens, W. (2008). Explaining the relationships between job characteristics, burnout, and engagement: The role of basic psychological need satisfaction. *Work & Stress, 22*(3), 277–294. http://dx.doi. org/10.1080/02678370802393672

van den Heuvel, M., Demerouti, E., Schreurs, B. J., Bakker, A. B., & Schaufeli, W. B. (2009). Does meaning-making help during organizational change?: Development and validation of a new scale. *The Career Development International, 14*(6), 508–533. http://dx.doi.org/10.1108/13620430910997277

Van Dyne, L., & LePine, J. A. (1998). Helping and voice extra-role behaviors: Evidence of construct and predictive validity. *Academy of Management Journal, 41*(1), 108–119. http://dx.doi.org/10.2307/256902

Van Eerde, W., & Thierry, H. (1996). Vroom's expectancy models and work-related criteria: A meta-analysis. *Journal of Applied Psychology, 81*(5), 575–586.

Van Knippenberg, D., & Sleebos, E. (2006). Organizational identification versus organizational commitment: Self-definition, social exchange, and job attitudes. *Journal of Organizational Behavior, 27*(5), 571–584. http://dx.doi.org/10.1002/job.359

Van Oosten, E. B., McBride-Walker, S. M., & Taylor, S. N. (2019). Investing in what matters: The impact of emotional and social competency development and executive coaching on leader outcomes. *Consulting Psychology Journal: Practice and Research, 71*(4), 249–269. http://dx.doi.org/10.1037/cpb0000141

Van Scotter, J., Motowidlo, S. J., & Cross, T. C. (2000). Effects of task performance and contextual performance on systemic rewards. *Journal of Applied Psychology, 85*(4), 526–535. http://dx.doi.org/10.1037/0021-9010.85.4.526

Vansteenkiste, M., Neyrinkck, B., Niemiec, C. P., Soenens, B., De Witte, H., & Van den Broeck, A. (2007). On the relations among work value orientations, psychological need satisfaction and job outcomes: A self-determination theory approach. *Journal of Occupational and Organizational Psychology, 80,* 251–277. http://dx.doi. org/10.1348/096317906X111024

Van Wijhe, C. I., Peeters, M. W., & Schaufeli, W. B. (2011). To stop or not to stop, that's the question: About persistence and mood of workaholics and work engaged employees. *International Journal of Behavioral Medicine, 18*(4), 361–372. http://dx.doi. org/10.1007/s12529-011-9143-z

van Wingerden, J., Bakker, A. B., & Derks, D. (2017). Fostering employee well-being via a job crafting intervention. *Journal of Vocational Behavior, 100,* 164–174. http:// dx.doi.org/10.1016/j.jvb.2017.03.008

Vasalampi, K., Salmela-Aro, K., & Nurmi, J. (2009). Adolescents' self-concordance, school engagement, and burnout predict their educational trajectories. *European Psychologist, 14*(4), 332–341. http://dx.doi.org/10.1027/1016-9040.14.4.332

Vecina, M. L., Chacón, F., Sueiro, M., & Barrón, A. (2012). Volunteer engagement: Does engagement predict the degree of satisfaction among new volunteers and the commitment of those who have been active longer? *Applied Psychology: An International Review, 61*(1), 130–148. http://dx.doi.org/10.1111/j.1464-0597.2011.00460.x

Veurink, S. A., & Fischer, R. (2011). A refocus on foci: A multidimensional and multifoci examination of commitment in work contexts. *New Zealand Journal of Psychology, 40*(3), 160–167.

Viljevac, A., Cooper-Thomas, H., & Saks, A. (2012). An investigation into the validity of two measures of work engagement. *International Journal of Human Resource Management, 23*(17), 3692–3709. http://dx.doi.org/10.1080/09585192.2011.639542

Viljoen, H. G. (1989). The socially-oriented psycho-analytic theories. In W. F. Meyer, C. Moore, & H. G. Viljoen (Eds.), *Personality theories: From Freud to Frankl* (pp. 116–144). Johannesburg: Lexicon.

Vincent-Höper, S., Muser, C., & Janneck, M. (2012). Transformational leadership, work engagement, and occupational success. *Career Development International, 17*(7), 663–682. http://dx.doi.org/10.1108/13620431211283805

Vîrgă, D., Maricuţoiu, L. P., & Iancu, A. (2019). The efficacy of work engagement interventions: A meta-analysis of controlled trials. *Current Psychology: A Journal for Diverse Perspectives on Diverse Psychological Issues.* Published online. http://dx.doi.org/10.1007/s12144-019-00438-z

Vogt, K., Hakanen, J. J., Brauchli, R., Jenny, G. J., & Bauer, G. F. (2016). The consequences of job crafting: A three-wave study. *European Journal of Work and Organizational Psychology, 25*(3), 353–362. http://dx.doi.org/10.1080/1359432X.2015.1072170

Vroom, V. H. (1964). *Work and motivation.* Oxford: Wiley.

Waight, C. L., & Edwards, M. T. (2020). Team engagement in an executive human resource development program: A closed cohort model perspective. *Human Resource Development Quarterly.* http://dx.doi.org/10.1002/hrdq.21419

Walker, C. R. (1950). The problem of the repetitive job. *Harvard Business Review, 28,* 54–58.

Walters, K. N., & Diab, D. L. (2016). Humble leadership: Implications for psychological safety and follower engagement. *Journal of Leadership Studies, 10*(2), 7–18. http://dx.doi.org/10.1002/jls.21434

Walumbwa, F. O., Avolio, B. J., & Zhu, W. (2008). How transformational leadership weaves its influence on individual job performance: The role of identification and efficacy beliefs. *Personnel Psychology, 61*(4), 793–825.

Walumbwa, F. O., Christensen, A. L., & Muchiri, M. K. (2013). Transformational leadership and meaningful work. In B. J. Dik, Z. S. Byrne, & M. F. Steger (Eds.), *Purpose and meaning in the workplace* (pp. 197–215). Washington, DC: American Psychological Association. http://dx.doi.org/10.1037/14183-010

Walumbwa, F. O., Morrison, E. W., & Christensen, A. L. (2012). Ethical leadership and group in-role performance: The mediating roles of group conscientiousness and group voice. *The Leadership Quarterly, 23*(5), 953–964. http://dx.doi.org/10.1016/j.leaqua.2012.06.004

Wang, D.-S., & Hsieh, C.-C. (2013). The effect of authentic leadership on employee trust and employee engagement. *Social Behavior & Personality: An International Journal, 41*(4), 613–624. http://dx.doi.org/10.2224/sbp.2013.41.4.613

Wang, L., Law, K. S., Zhang, M. J., Li, Y. N., & Liang, Y. (2019). It's mine! Psychological ownership of one's job explains positive and negative workplace outcomes of job engagement. *Journal of Applied Psychology, 104*(2), 229–246. http://dx.doi.org/10.1037/apl0000337

Wang, X., Shi, Z., Ng, S., Wang, B., & Chan, C. W. (2011). Sustaining engagement through work in postdisaster relief and reconstruction. *Qualitative Health Research, 21*(4), 465–476. http://dx.doi.org/10.1177/1049732310386049

Warr, P., Cook, J., & Wall, T. (1979). Scales for the measurement of some work attitudes and aspects of psychological well-being. *Journal of Occupational Psychology, 52*(2), 129–148. http://dx.doi.org/10.1111/j.2044-8325.1979.tb00448.x

Wefald, A. J., & Downey, R. (2009). Job engagement in organizations: Fad, fashion, or folderol? *Journal of Organizational Behavior, 30*(1), 141–145.

Wefald, A. J., Mills, M. J., Smith, M. R., & Downey, R. G. (2012). A comparison of three job engagement measures: Examining their factorial and criterion-related validity. *Applied Psychology: Health & Well-Being, 4*(1), 67–90. http://dx.doi.org/10.1111/j.1758-0854.2011.01059.x

Weintraub, J., Cassell, D., & DePatie, T. P. (2021). Nudging flow through "smart" goal setting to decrease stress, increase engagement, and increase performance at work. *Journal of Occupational and Organizational Psychology*, 1–29. http://dx.doi.org/10.1111/joop.12347

Weston, J. W. (2016). *Employee engagement: Understanding the construct's stability.* (Publication No. 10149863) Master's thesis, Colorado State University. ProQuest Dissertations & Theses Global.

White, R. W. (1959). Motivation reconsidered: The concept of competence. *Psychological Review, 66*, 297–333. http://dx.doi.org/10.1037/h0040934

Williams, L. J., & Anderson, S. E. (1991). Job satisfaction and organizational commitment as predictors of organizational citizenship and in-role behaviors. *Journal of Management, 17*(3), 601–617. http://dx.doi.org/10.1177/014920639101700305

Wilson, T. D. (2002). *Strangers to ourselves: Discovering the adaptive unconscious.* Cambridge, MA: Belknap Press/Harvard University Press.

Wilson, T. D., & Kraft, D. (1993a). "Why do I love thee? Effects of repeated introspections about a dating relationship on attitudes toward the relationship": Erratum. *Personality and Social Psychology Bulletin, 19*(6), http://dx.doi.org/10.1177/0146167293196012

Wilson, T. D., & Kraft, D. (1993b). Why do I love thee?: Effects of repeated introspections about a dating relationship on attitudes toward the relationship. *Personality and Social Psychology Bulletin, 19*(4), 409–418. http://dx.doi.org/10.1177/0146167293194006

Wilson, T. D., Dunn, D. S., Bybee, J. A., Hyman, D. B., & Rotondo, J. A. (1984). Effects of analyzing reasons on attitude: Behavior consistency. *Journal of Personality and Social Psychology, 47*(1), 5–16. http://dx.doi.org/10.1037/0022-3514.47.1.5

Wilson, T. D., & Schooler, J. W. (1991). Thinking too much: Introspection can reduce the quality of preferences and decisions. *Journal of Personality and Social Psychology, 60*(2), 181–192. http://dx.doi.org/10.1037/0022-3514.60.2.181

Wojdyło, K. (2015). "Workaholism" does not always mean workaholism? About the controversial nomenclature in the research on work addiction. *Polish Psychological Bulletin, 46*(1), 133–136. http://dx.doi.org/10.1515/ppb-2015-0017

Wollard, K. K. (2011). Quiet desperation: Another perspective on employee engagement. *Advances in Developing Human Resources, 13*(4), 526–537. http://dx.doi.org/10.1177/1523422311430942

Wozniak, D. (2013). The road to employee engagement. *Credit Union Magazine, 79*(2), 44.

Wright, T. A. (2012). Getting serious about employee engagement in 2012!. *Power Engineering, 116*(4), C3.

Wright, T. A., & Staw, B. M. (1999). Affect and favorable work outcomes: Two longitudinal tests of the happy-productive worker thesis. *Journal of Organizational Behavior, 20*(1), 1.

Wrzesniewski, A., Berg, J. M., & Dutton, J. E. (2010). Turn the job you have into the job you want. *Harvard Business Review, 88*(6), 114–117.

Wrzesniewski, A., & Dutton, J. E. (2001). Crafting a job: Revisioning employees as active crafters of their work. *Academy of Management Review, 26*(2), 179–201. http://dx.doi.org/10.5465/AMR.2001.4378011

Wrzesniewski, A., Dutton, J. E., & Debebe, G. (2003). Interpersonal sensemaking and the meaning of work. In R. M. Kramer & B. M. Staw (Eds.), *Research in organizational behavior: An annual series of analytical essays and critical reviews* (Vol. 25, pp. 93–135). Oxford: Elsevier Science.

Xanthopoulou, D., Bakker, A. B., Demerouti, E., & Schaufeli, W. B. (2007). The role of personal resources in the job demands-resources model. *International Journal of Stress Management, 14*(2), 121–141. http://dx.doi.org/10.1037/1072-5245.14.2.121

Xanthopoulou, D., Bakker, A. B., Demerouti, E., & Schaufeli, W. B. (2009). Reciprocal relationships between job resources, personal resources, and work engagement. *Journal of Vocational Behavior, 74*(3), 235–244. http://dx.doi.org/10.1016/j.jvb.2008.11.003

Xanthopoulou, D., Bakker, A. B., Heuven, E., Demerouti, E., & Schaufeli, W. B. (2008). Working in the sky: A diary study on work engagement among flight attendants. *Journal of Occupational Health Psychology, 13*(4), 345–356. http://dx.doi.org/10.1037/1076-8998.13.4.345

Xu, J., & Thomas, H. C. (2011). How can leaders achieve high employee engagement? *Leadership and Organization Development Journal, 32*, 399–416. http://dx.doi.org/101437731111134661

Xu, L., Du, J., Lei, X., & Hipel, K. W. (2020). Effect of locus of control on innovative behavior among new generation employees: A moderated mediation model. *Social Behavior and Personality: An International Journal, 48*(10), 1–12.

Yamada, D. C. (2000). The phenomenon of "workplace bullying" and the need for status-blind hostile work environment protection. *Georgetown Law Journal, 88*, 475–537.

Yan, X., & Su, J. (2013). Core self-evaluations mediators of the influence of social support on job involvement in hospital nurses. *Social Indicators Research, 113*(1), 299–306. http://dx.doi.org/10.1007/s11205-012-0093-x

Yan, X., Yang, K., Su, J., Luo, Z., & Wen, Z. (2018). Mediating role of emotional intelligence on the associations between core self-evaluations and job satisfaction, work engagement as indices of work-related well-being. *Current Psychology: A Journal for Diverse Perspectives on Diverse Psychological Issues, 37*(3), 552–558. http://dx.doi.org/10.1007/s12144-016-9531-2

Yang, F., Liu, J., Huang, X., Qian, J., Wang, T., Wang, Z., & Yu, H. (2018). How supervisory support for career development relates to subordinate work engagement and career outcomes: The moderating role of task proficiency. *Human Resource Management Journal, 28*(3), 496–509. http://dx.doi.org/10.1111/1748-8583.12194

Yang, R., Ming, Y., Ma, J., & Huo, R. (2017). How do servant leaders promote engagement? A bottom-up perspective of job crafting. *Social Behavior and Personality: An International Journal, 45*(11), 1815–1827. http://dx.doi.org/10.2224/sbp.6704

Ybema, J. F., Koopman, A., & Peeters, M. (2020). Working in sheltered employment: A weekly diary study. *International Journal of Stress Management, 27*(2), 160–171. http://dx.doi.org/10.1037/str0000141

Young, H. R., Glerum, D. R., Wang, W., & Joseph, D. L. (2018). Who are the most engaged at work? A meta-analysis of personality and employee engagement. *Journal of Organizational Behavior, 39*(10), 1330–1346. http://dx.doi.org/10.1002/job.2303

Youssef, C. M., & Luthans, F. (2007). Positive organizational behavior in the workplace: The impact of hope, optimism, and resilience. *Journal of Management, 33*(5), 774–800. http://dx.doi.org/10.1177/0149206307305562

Yuan, Z., Ye, Z., & Zhong, M. (2021). Plug back into work, safely: Job reattachment, leader safety commitment, and job engagement in the COVID-19 pandemic. *Journal of Applied Psychology, 106*(1), 62–70. http://dx.doi.org/10.1037/apl0000860

Yukl, G. A. (2010). *Leadership in organizations.* Upper Saddle River, NJ: Pearson Prentice Hall.

Zajonc, R. B. (2008). Feeling and thinking: Preferences need no inferences. In R. H. Fazio & R. E. Petty (Eds.), *Attitudes: Their structure, function, and consequences* (pp. 143–168). New York, NY: Psychology Press.

Zajonc, R. B., & Adelmann, P. K. (1987). Cognition and communication: A story of missed opportunities. *Social Science Information/Sur Les Sciences Sociales, 26*(1), 3–30. http://dx.doi.org/10.1177/053901887026001001

Zaniboni, S., Truxillo, D. M., Fraccaroli, F., McCune, E. A., & Bertolino, M. (2014). Who benefits from more tasks? Older versus younger workers. *Journal of Managerial Psychology, 29*(5), 508–523. http://dx.doi.org/10.1108/JMP-12-2012-0381

Zhu, W., Avolio, B. J., & Walumbwa, F. O. (2009). Moderating role of follower characteristics with transformational leadership and follower work engagement. *Group Organization Management, 34*, 590–619.

Zhu, Y., Liu, C., Guo, B., Zhao, L., & Lou, F. (2015). The impact of emotional intelligence on work engagement of registered nurses: The mediating role of organisational justice. *Journal of Clinical Nursing, 24*(15–16), 2115–2124. http://dx.doi.org/10.1111/jocn.12807

INDEX

Note: Page locators in **bold** indicate a table. Page locators in *italics* indicate a figure.

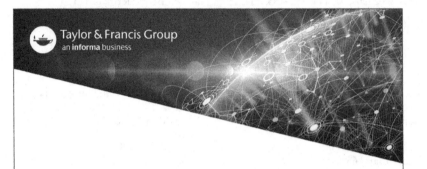

Taylor & Francis Group
an **informa** business

Taylor & Francis eBooks

www.taylorfrancis.com

A single destination for eBooks from Taylor & Francis
with increased functionality and an improved user
experience to meet the needs of our customers.

90,000+ eBooks of award-winning academic content in
Humanities, Social Science, Science, Technology, Engineering,
and Medical written by a global network of editors and authors.

TAYLOR & FRANCIS EBOOKS OFFERS:

A streamlined
experience for
our library
customers

A single point
of discovery
for all of our
eBook content

Improved
search and
discovery of
content at both
book and
chapter level

REQUEST A FREE TRIAL
support@taylorfrancis.com

Routledge
Taylor & Francis Group

CRC Press
Taylor & Francis Group

Printed in the United States
by Baker & Taylor Publisher Services